sendmail Cookbook™

Other networking resources from O'Reilly

Related titles
sendmail
sendmail Desktop Reference
Programming Internet Email
DNS and BIND
DNS and BIND Cookbook
Essential System
   Administration

Essential System Administration Pocket Reference
Kerberos: The Definitive Guide
TCP/IP Network Administration
LDAP System Administration
System Performance Tuning

networking.oreilly.com

networking.oreilly.com is a complete catalog of O'Reilly books on networking and related technologies, including sample chapters and code examples.

oreillynet.com is the essential portal for developers interested in open and emerging technologies, including new platforms, programming languages, and operating systems.

Conferences

O'Reilly & Associates brings diverse innovators together to nurture the ideas that spark revolutionary industries. We specialize in documenting the latest tools and systems, translating the innovator's knowledge into useful skills for those in the trenches. Visit *conferences.oreilly.com* for our upcoming events.

Safari Bookshelf (*safari.oreilly.com*) is the premier online reference library for programmers and IT professionals. Conduct searches across more than 1,000 books. Subscribers can zero in on answers to time-critical questions in a matter of seconds. Read the books on your Bookshelf from cover to cover or simply flip to the page you need. Try it today with a free trial.

sendmail Cookbook™

Craig Hunt

O'REILLY®

Beijing · Cambridge · Farnham · Köln · Paris · Sebastopol · Taipei · Tokyo

sendmail Cookbook™
by Craig Hunt

Copyright © 2004 O'Reilly & Associates, Inc. All rights reserved.
Printed in the United States of America.

Published by O'Reilly & Associates, Inc., 1005 Gravenstein Highway North, Sebastopol, CA
95472.

O'Reilly & Associates books may be purchased for educational, business, or sales promotional
use. Online editions are also available for most titles (*safari.oreilly.com*). For more information,
contact our corporate/institutional sales department: (800) 998-9938 or *corporate@oreilly.com*.

Editor:	Simon St.Laurent
Production Editor:	Marlowe Shaeffer
Cover Designer:	Ellie Volckhausen
Interior Designer:	David Futato

Printing History:

December 2003:   First Edition.

ISBN: 0-596-00471-0
[M]

*To Amanda, Pat, Kathy, Sara, and all mothers
everywhere who continue to renew life and our
love of life.*

Table of Contents

Preface

Introduction

sendmail is the most powerful and widely used Unix email software in the world today. Millions of Unix systems are currently running sendmail. Yet this common tool is a source of confusion for many system administrators, most of whom dread sendmail configuration. This dread has a very rational basis: complexity and lack of familiarity. sendmail configuration languages are as complex as any other programming languages, and, unlike many other languages, sendmail configuration languages are used infrequently. sendmail is configured when it is installed or upgraded; otherwise, an administrator has little interaction with the sendmail configuration. The average system administrator simply does not get enough practice to truly master the sendmail configuration languages.

For me, and a great many other techies, cooking a decent meal also falls into the category of something that I do not often practice. On my own, a Coke and a Snickers constitutes dinner, while beer and pretzels is a party. When it is my turn to cook for others, particularly to cook an elaborate meal, I need help. I don't have time to learn how to cook on my own; I need someone to tell me exactly how it is done. Luckily, cookbooks are created for exactly this situation.

A cookbook provides recipes for a wide variety of situations. The recipes are step-by-step solutions to specific problems. In the kitchen, the problems are how to properly prepare specific dishes. On a sendmail server, the problems are how to configure the system to handle specific situations; for example, how to configure sendmail to relay mail for your clients without creating an open relay that will be abused by spammers.

As the name *sendmail Cookbook* implies, this is a cookbook full of recipes for proper sendmail configuration. A sendmail recipe outlines a configuration problem, presents the configuration code that solves that problem, and then explains the code in detail. The discussions of the code are critical because they provide the insight you need to tweak the code enough to make it right for your server.

The key feature of this book is that it saves you time. Time is something that most system administrators have in very short supply. When you have a specific sendmail configuration problem, looking up a step-by-step solution is much quicker than researching the problem and developing your own custom solution. This book provides quick solutions for many common sendmail configuration problems.

The *sendmail Cookbook* uses the same Problem/Solution/Discussion format used in all O'Reilly cookbooks. As an example of this format, the following section, which explains how this book should be used, is laid out using the recipe format.

Using This Cookbook

Problem

You need to use this cookbook in the most effective manner possible.

Solution

Jump directly to the recipe that addresses your sendmail problem.

Follow the steps in your selected recipe. Combine the elements from the selected recipe with your real configuration.

Read the Discussion section of your selected recipe and perform the tests shown there to ensure that the recipe works in your operational environment.

Discussion

Most books are written as a unit and are intended to be read as a whole. One section transitions to another, one chapter transitions to the next, and a flow is developed to draw you through the book. A cookbook isn't like that. Each recipe is complete unto itself. You don't sit down and read a cookbook from cover to cover. If you did, you would find it repetitious and rather boring (unless you're very hungry!). The *sendmail Cookbook* is a real cookbook. Don't attempt to read it cover to cover. Instead, go directly to the recipe you need for your specific sendmail problem.

The recipes in this book are complete. Follow a recipe, and you have a fully functional configuration that can be tested and verified. Because these are complete, standalone recipes, there is repetition. Every recipe that requires you to rebuild the *sendmail.cf* file says, "rebuild the *sendmail.cf* file." It doesn't assume that you have read several other recipes and therefore know when to rebuild the file. However, to reduce the volume of repetition, steps used in many recipes, such as compiling sendmail or building the *sendmail.cf* file, are covered in detail only once. Subsequent recipes can then refer to these earlier recipes without repeating all of the detailed steps.

An effective technique for using these recipes is to first implement the recipe on a small test system. In that way, you can follow the recipe without attempting to merge the features of that recipe with your current configuration until you evaluate the effectiveness of the recipe for your specific problem. After determining that the function used in the recipe is effective for your problem, it can be merged into your operational configuration, retested, and deployed.

Many system administrators reading this will say, "Where will I find the time to implement and test a separate sendmail configuration?" Don't worry. The step-by-step recipes in this book can be implemented and tested in a matter of minutes. And any old PC running FreeBSD or Linux will serve as a test system. In fact, most of the recipes in this book were implemented on a Red Hat Linux system.

As with all cookbooks, this book is full of recipes for individual dishes. It is your responsibility to select the various recipes you need to create a complete meal. Add the new sendmail configuration features one at a time and test each one as you go. Various configuration features can interact in unexpected ways. Testing the combined configuration is essential.

See Also

The See Also section of each recipe points to other recipes that may provide additional help. It also points to those sections in the O'Reilly book *sendmail*, by Bryan Costales with Eric Allman, that provide technical references for the topic covered in the recipe.

Audience

The *sendmail Cookbook* is intended for everyone who configures the sendmail software running on a Unix computer. This obviously includes the sendmail administrator who runs the mail server and the system administrators who are responsible for running Unix computers, but it also includes any user who maintains the sendmail configuration on a desktop Unix system. The Unix workstation on your desk probably involves you in system administration tasks. If those tasks include sendmail configuration, this book is for you.

We assume that you have a good understanding of computers and their operation, and that you're generally familiar with sendmail configuration. If you're completely new to Unix, this book is not for you. Likewise, if you are an expert in sendmail administration, this book might not be suitable. If you fall anywhere between these two extremes, however, you'll find this book has a lot to offer.

A cookbook will help you cook a decent meal, but a cookbook will not turn you into a four-star chef. Likewise, this book provides effective solutions to common sendmail configuration problems, but it won't make you a sendmail guru. Complete mastery of a subject as complex as sendmail requires more than recommended solutions to common problems. The full range of sendmail information takes a reference and a tutorial in addition to a cookbook. The best and most complete sendmail reference is *sendmail* by Bryan Costales with Eric Allman (O'Reilly). Not surprisingly, my favorite sendmail tutorial is *Linux Sendmail Administration*, by Craig Hunt (Sybex). If your job requires you to become a sendmail guru, you probably need all three of these books.

Organization

sendmail configuration is a means to an end. sendmail is configured in order to perform specific functions effectively. This book focuses on the proper configurations for those functions. sendmail configuration language elements are secondary. The configuration code is explained in sufficient detail for you to fully understand it, so that you can tune the code as necessary for your system. But the goal is to provide useable solutions for common problems. This goal dictates a book that is organized around sendmail's functions

The first chapter defines the basic framework upon which all of the other chapters are built. It provides recipes for downloading and installing the sendmail distribution, for recompiling sendmail to support a variety of features, for building the sendmail configuration, and for testing a new configuration. Starting with Chapter 2 and running through Chapter 10, sample solutions for properly configuring important sendmail functions are given. An overview of the functions and commands used in each chapter are provided by the chapter's Introduction.

The recipes in Chapters 2 through 10 standalone. An administrator can jump directly to an individual solution and come away with enough information to solve a specific problem. Most of these solutions address only one problem. Your configuration will probably need to address multiple problems. You can jump around in this book selecting just those items you need. For example, your server might need to accept mail for several clients, and it might need to hide the hostnames of those clients on outbound mail. Such a configuration would need recipes from Chapter 2 and Chapter 4. Select just those things that suit your needs.

A quick synopsis of the chapters in this book follows:

Chapter 1, *Getting Started*, describes the files and directories used to build a sendmail configuration. It provides how-to recipes for downloading, installing, and compiling sendmail and for building and testing a sendmail configuration.

Chapter 2, *Delivery and Forwarding*, focuses on mail delivery. The sendmail configuration controls what mail is accepted for delivery. Accepting the correct mail is essential for creating a server, particularly one that acts as a mail exchanger. Additionally, only mail that is accepted for delivery can be aliased or forwarded. Properly configured aliasing supports clients and creates mailing lists.

Chapter 3, *Relaying*, focuses on mail relaying. When mail is not accepted for delivery by the local server, sendmail must decide if it should be relayed to another server for delivery. Properly configuring relaying is essential to creating a fully functional server, and it is a primary ingredient in controlling spam. A mistake in relay configuration can get your server blacklisted!

Chapter 4, *Masquerading*, describes why and how the true identity of the end system in a mail exchange is hidden. Masquerading hides the source address of outgoing mail. Both basic masquerading and the *genericstable* database are covered. Configurations that hide both the host portion and the user portion of the source address are given.

Chapter 5, *Routing Mail*, describes how the administrator controls mail routing through the use of sendmail databases. The *mailertable* is used to route mail to a specific mailer for special processing. The *mailertable* provides access to the wide variety of mailers provided by sendmail. Virtual mail domains allow a single mail server to process mail for many different domains. Using the *virtusertable* database to handle virtual mail domains is covered. The *ldap_routing* feature, which reads intranet mail routing information from an LDAP server, is also covered.

Chapter 6, *Controlling Spam*, describes how to configure sendmail to reduce the problem of unsolicited commercial email. The chapter discusses how the *access* database is used to control spam; how sendmail is configured to use *procmail* for personal, local, and outbound mail filtering; how blackhole listing services are used; and how to build your own DNS blackhole list. Custom header processing and *sendmail.cf* regular expressions are also covered.

Chapter 7, *Authenticating with AUTH*, provides solutions for configuring sendmail to act as an SMTP AUTH server or client. Sample sendmail configurations are provided, as are the necessary SASL configuration files. How the *access* database is used with AUTH authentication is also covered.

Chapter 8, *Securing the Mail Transport*, covers STARTTLS, the sendmail feature used to encrypt the mail transport. The sendmail configuration of STARTTLS is given along with the required configuration of the SSL tools used by sendmail. Creating a private sendmail CA, client and server certificates, and signing certificates are all covered. Recipes that control when encryption is used are provided, as are examples of using STARTTLS with the *access* database.

Chapter 9, *Managing the Queue*, covers sendmail configurations that are particularly useful for systems with large mail queues. Creating multiple queues, defining queue groups, and using queue groups with the *access* database are all covered.

Chapter 10, *Securing sendmail*, provides recipes that can increase sendmail security. By default, sendmail has tight security settings. Some configurations loosen sendmail security to increase flexibility. The recipes in this chapter take the opposite approach. These recipes are for those willing to sacrifice flexibility for additional security.

Software Versions

Most of the examples in this book are taken from Red Hat Linux 7.3 and 8.0, and from Solaris 8. However, the versions of Unix used to create the examples makes very little difference. There are small variations in command output or command-line options, but these variations should not present a problem. sendmail software works the same way from system to system.

Much more important differences are introduced by the version of sendmail. sendmail is constantly evolving. The examples in this book are based on sendmail 8.12, specifically 8.12.9 and 8.12.10. We do not know if the recipes will work exactly as shown on other versions of sendmail, but they should work with minimal adjustments.

Conventions

This book uses the following typographical conventions:

Italic

> Indicates the names of files, databases, directories, hostnames, domain names, usernames, sendmail feature names, Unix utilities, programs, and it is used to emphasize new terms when they are first introduced.

`Constant width`

> Indicates *sendmail.cf* literals, commands and variables, m4 macros and built-in commands, and Unix command-line options. It is used to show the contents of files and the output from commands. Keywords are also in `constant width`.

`Constant width bold`

> Used in examples to show commands or text that you would type.

`Constant width italic`

> Used in examples and text to show variables for which a context-specific substitution should be made. (The variable *filename*, for example, would be replaced by some actual filename.)

`$, #`

> When we demonstrate commands that you would give interactively, we normally use the default Bourne shell prompt ($). If the command must be executed as *root*, then we use the default superuser prompt (#).

`[ option ]`

> When showing command syntax, we place optional parts of the command within brackets. For example, `ls [ -l ]` means that the -l option is not required.

 This icon signifies a tip, suggestion, or general note.

This icon indicates a warning or caution.

We'd Like to Hear from You

We have tested and verified all of the information in this book to the best of our ability, but you may find that features have changed (or even that we have made mistakes!). Please let us know about any errors you find, as well as your suggestions for future editions, by writing:

O'Reilly & Associates, Inc.
1005 Gravenstein Highway North
Sebastopol, CA 95472
(800) 998-9938 (in the United States or Canada)
(707) 829-0515 (international or local)
(707) 829-0104 (fax)

There is a web page for this book, which lists errata, examples, or any additional information. You can access this page at:

http://www.oreilly.com/catalog/sendmailckbk/

To comment or ask technical questions about this book, send email to:

bookquestions@oreilly.com

For more information about books, conferences, Resource Centers, and the O'Reilly Network, see the O'Reilly web site at:

http://www.oreilly.com

To find out what else Craig is doing, visit his web site: *http://www.wrotethebook.com.*

Acknowledgments

No book is the product of one person. This one certainly is not! I have many people to thank for their help in producing the book.

The idea for this book came originally from Tim O'Reilly. Mike Loukides explained the idea of the book to me, and I knew I wanted to write it. Tim and Mike deserve thanks for getting the ball rolling.

Two editors have supported me through the long and difficult process of producing this book. Jim Sumser worked with me during the first phase of writing and Simon St.Laurent brought me through to the finish line. Both of these guys have been a great help.

I particularly want to thank my technical reviewers, Greg Shapiro, Claus Assmann, and Nick Christenson. You could not ask for a better technical team. Look at the list of authors for the *Sendmail Installation and Operations Guide* and you'll see Greg and Claus listed there. You'll also see Greg's name on most of the sample configurations provided with the sendmail distribution—no one knows more about sendmail configuration than Greg. As for Nick, he is the author of the book *sendmail Performance Tuning* (Addison Wesley) that Eric Allman simply calls "great." These guys know sendmail and they took the time to meticulously review every page of this book. Their help and insight were invaluable. This is a much better book because of their involvement.

I also want to thank the crew at O'Reilly. Thanks to Marlowe Shaeffer, production editor and proofreader, for getting this book through; Derek Di Matteo for copyediting; Ellie Volckhausen for her work on the cover; and Tom Dinse for the indexing.

Finally, I want to thank my family for having the patience to put up with me when I have no patience left.

## CHAPTER 1

Getting Started

1.0   Introduction

To follow a recipe successfully, you must clearly understand the instructions it contains. You must understand the difference between folding and stirring and be able to find the spices when the recipe calls for a pinch of cumin. Just as you must be able to find your way around the kitchen to become a cook, you must know your way around the sendmail distribution in order to build or customize a sendmail configuration.

The directory structure—created by the sendmail source code distribution tarball—contains the tools and ingredients used to build and configure sendmail. The top-level directory created by the tarball is assigned a name that identifies the *sendmail* version number. At the time of this writing, the current version is *sendmail* 8.12.9; therefore, the top-level directory is named *sendmail-8.12.9*. By the time you read this, there will be a newer version of sendmail, and the directory name will reflect that new version number. An *ls* of the top-level directory shows the following:*

```
$ ls sendmail-8.12.9
Build     doc      INSTALL    libsmdb     mailstats  praliases      sendmail
cf        editmap  KNOWNBUGS  libsmutil   Makefile   README         smrsh
contrib   FAQ      libmilter  LICENSE     makemap    RELEASE_NOTES  test
devtools  include  libsm      mail.local  PGPKEYS    rmail          vacation
```

Most of these files and directories are used to compile sendmail. The *Build* script uses the *Makefile* to compile sendmail and its utilities. The *devtools* directory is used to set compiler options, as discussed in Recipes 1.2 to 1.7. The source code is located in aptly named subdirectories. For example, the sendmail source code is in the *sendmail* directory, the libraries are in directories such as *libsm* and *libsmutil*, and the source code of utilities such as *makemap* and *smrsh* is located in easily identified directories.

---

* Most of the *ls* command output in this book is generated on a Red Hat Linux system. Other versions of Unix and Linux may sort *ls* output in a different way. The listing order may be different, but the files and directories will be the same.

There are also several important sources of information in the distribution:

- The *INSTALL* and *README* files provide the latest information on compiling and installing sendmail.
- The *RELEASE_NOTES* file lists the important features of the new release.
- The *KNOWNBUGS* and *FAQ* files explain solutions to chronic and common problems.
- The *doc* subdirectory contains the *Sendmail Installation and Operations Guide*, which is an excellent source of information for the sendmail administrator.

Of all of these important directories and files, the most important (from the perspective of this book) is the *cf* directory, because the *cf* directory contains the configuration files (and this is a book about sendmail configuration).

The cf directory structure

The *m4* source files and libraries used to build the sendmail configuration are located in the *cf* directory, which contains the following items:

```
$ ls sendmail-8.12.9/cf
cf      feature  m4       ostype  sendmail.schema  siteconfig
domain  hack     mailer   README  sh
```

The *cf* directory contains two files, *README* and *sendmail.schema*, and nine subdirectories. The *sendmail.schema* file is an experimental LDAP schema that predefines attribute types and object classes that can be used with LDAP. The sendmail schema is used in most LDAP examples in this book. The *README* file is a comprehensive reference to the syntax and usage of all of the *m4* macros and variables used to configure sendmail. The *README* file is an invaluable reference, particularly when used with this book.

The directories *hack*, *sh*, and *siteconfig* have very little use for most configurations.

hack directory
> The *hack* directory is intended to hold *m4* source files built by the local system administrator to solve temporary sendmail configuration problems. There is only one file in the *hack* directory, built years ago, which serves as an example of a sendmail hack. The *hack* directory and the HACK macro are still there, but, with all of the power and flexibility available to configure sendmail, there is simply no good reason to use them.

siteconfig directory
> The *siteconfig* directory is intended to hold files that use sendmail *m4* SITE macros to list the locally connected UUCP sites. The *siteconfig* directory, the SITECONFIG macro, and the SITE macro are maintained for backward compatibility. However, the directory and the macros are obsolete and should no longer be used to define the UUCP connectivity for a UUCP mail server.

sh directory

The *sh* directory contains only the *makeinfo.sh* file. Most of the files in the *cf* subdirectories are *m4* macro source files that end with the *.m4* extension. This file, however, ends with the *.sh* extension, indicating that it is a shell script. The script produces three lines of comments for the *sendmail.cf* file that identify who built the configuration, when they built it, and in what directory.

The remaining six directories are the real heart of sendmail configuration. Four of these directories, *domain*, *feature*, *ostype*, and *mailer*, have the same names as sendmail *m4* macros, and provide the source code used by those macros. The purposes of these four directories are:

domain directory

The *domain* directory holds *m4* source files that define configuration values that are specific to your domain or network. If you need to define such values, create your own file; the six files contained in the *domain* directory are just examples. The configuration file you create for your environment is then used in the master configuration file via the DOMAIN macro.

ostype directory

The files in the *ostype* directory define operating system-specific characteristics for the sendmail configuration. Every master configuration file must contain an OSTYPE macro to process the correct macro source file for the sendmail server's operating system.* The *sendmail-8.12.9/ostype* directory contains configuration files for more than 40 different operating systems, each one easily identified by name. Select the file that matches your server's operating system.

mailer directory

In addition to an OSTYPE macro, most master configuration files have at least one MAILER macro. MAILER macros process source files from the *mailer* directory. Each file in the *mailer* directory contains the definition of a set of mailers. The current *mailer* directory contains 12 different files. Many configurations use only the two most basic sets of mailers: *local.m4* for local mail delivery and *smtp.m4* for SMTP mail delivery.

feature directory

The *feature* directory contains the *m4* source code files that implement various sendmail features. There are more than 40 feature files available in the directory. Features are used to address specific configuration problems.

The other two remaining directories, *cf* and *m4*, contain the master configuration files and macro source libraries used by *m4*. The four directories described above contain files that are invoked inside the sendmail configuration by *m4* macros. The *cf/cf* directory and the *cf/m4* directory contain *m4* source files that are normally invoked on the *m4* command line.

---

* Recipe 10.10 shows a trick that is used to create a configuration without using an OSTYPE macro, but the trick is not recommended for general use.

The cf/m4 directory

The *cf/m4* directory contains the *m4* macro definitions and the *sendmail.cf* skeleton code needed to build a *sendmail.cf* configuration file. Remember that *m4* is a general purpose macro language; it is not a language specifically designed to build sendmail configurations. sendmail configurations are built using macros defined by the sendmail developers. The *cf/m4* directory contains the four files that define those macro commands.

version.m4

> The *version.m4* file defines the *sendmail.cf* Z variable, which is assigned the sendmail version number. Because this value changes with each sendmail release, it is defined in a separate file for easy maintenance.*

cf.m4

> The *cf.m4* file is specified on the *m4* command line to incorporate the library of sendmail *m4* macro commands into the *m4* process. The *cf.m4* file includes, by reference, the *cfhead.m4* file that contains the macro definitions.

cfhead.m4

> The *cfhead.m4* file defines the *m4* macros used to configure sendmail. This file includes lots of stuff, most importantly the definition of many of the commands used to build a configuration.

proto.m4

> The *proto.m4* file is the source of most of the content found in the *sendmail.cf* file.

The cf subdirectory

The *cf/cf* directory is the working directory of sendmail configuration. It contains all of the master configuration files, and it is where you will put your own master configuration file when you build a custom configuration. The directory contains more than 40 files.

```
$ ls sendmail-8.12.9/cf/cf
Build               generic-hpux10.cf   generic-solaris.cf  python.cs.mc
chez.cs.mc          generic-hpux10.mc   generic-solaris.mc  README
clientproto.mc      generic-hpux9.cf    generic-sunos4.1.cf s2k-osf1.mc
cs-hpux10.mc        generic-hpux9.mc    generic-sunos4.1.mc s2k-ultrix4.mc
cs-hpux9.mc         generic-linux.cf    generic-ultrix4.cf  submit.cf
cs-osf1.mc          generic-linux.mc    generic-ultrix4.mc  submit.mc
cs-solaris2.mc      generic-mpeix.cf    huginn.cs.mc        tcpproto.mc
cs-sunos4.1.mc      generic-mpeix.mc    knecht.mc          ucbarpa.mc
cs-ultrix4.mc       generic-nextstep3.3.cf mail.cs.mc      ucbvax.mc
```

---

*The sendmail version number is not the same as the *sendmail.cf* version level. In our examples, the sendmail version number is 8.12.9, but the *sendmail.cf* version level is 10. Furthermore, neither one of these has anything to do with the *m4* VERSIONID macro, which is used to place version control information in the master configuration file.

```
cyrusproto.mc        generic-nextstep3.3.mc  mail.eecs.mc         uucpproto.mc
generic-bsd4.4.cf    generic-osf1.cf         mailspool.cs.mc      vangogh.cs.mc
generic-bsd4.4.mc    generic-osf1.mc         Makefile
```

Most of these files—more than 30 of them—are sample master configuration files.
You can identify a master configuration file by the *.mc* extension. Some are examples meant as educational tools, but most are prototypes or generic files meant to be
used as the basis of your own configuration. The generic files designed for specific
operating systems are particularly interesting, such as Solaris, HPUX, BSD, Linux,
and several others. We use the *generic-linux.mc* file in Recipe 1.8.

Several of the files are identified by the *.cf* extension. These files are the result of processing master configuration files through *m4*; they are already in the proper format
to be used as the *sendmail.cf* file. It is unlikely, however, that you will use one of
these files directly. Unless the generic master configuration file is exactly to your lik-
ing, the sendmail configuration file produced from that *.mc* file will not be what you
want. We start with a generic configuration in Recipe 1.8, but the subsequent recipes
in this book modify that generic configuration to create the custom configurations
we need.

1.1   Downloading the Latest Release

Problem

You must keep your sendmail software up-to-date.

Solution

Sticking with the standard software management method used on your system is the
easiest way to upgrade sendmail. If you use a package manager, go to your Unix vendor's web site, download the appropriately packaged sendmail update, and install it
using the package manager. If the vendor cannot provide a critical sendmail update
or does not provide the compiled-in features you need, and you decide to use the
sendmail source code distribution, gracefully transition from the package manager to
the source code distribution by following the Unix vendor's advice on how to
remove a package that was installed by the package manager. The Discussion section shows an example of using the Red Hat Package Manager to remove the sendmail RPM before the sendmail source code distribution is installed.

If you need to use the sendmail source code distribution, download the latest version of sendmail from *ftp://ftp.sendmail.org/*, from *http://www.sendmail.org/current-
release.html*, or from one of a large number of mirror sites. A link to the mirror sites
is found on the *http://www.sendmail.org/* home page. The Discussion section provides an example of downloading the sendmail source code distribution via *ftp*.

Get the signature file associated with the version of sendmail you downloaded. For example, the signature file for the *sendmail.8.12.9.tar.gz* tarball downloaded in the Discussion section is *sendmail.8.12.9.tar.gz.sig*.

Download the PGP keys needed to verify the signature, and add them to your key ring (you only need to do this approximately once a year). After the PGP keys are added to your key ring, they can be used to verify the signature file of any further downloads made during that calendar year.

Use the *pgp* or *gpg* programs to verify the signature of the downloaded file (the Discussion section shows an example using *gpg*). If you accept the signature, restore the sendmail distribution tarball file.

Discussion

sendmail changes frequently. When the first draft of this chapter was written, the latest release of sendmail was about 3 weeks old, and the previous release was only 11 weeks old! Does this mean you must upgrade sendmail every few months? Not at all. Yet you should keep track of new sendmail releases in order to determine when upgrading is important to you. Three reasons that system administrators choose to upgrade are:

Security

> sendmail is a popular target for network intruders. They attack sendmail because it is a large, complex program that runs on many systems; sendmail is even run on desktop workstations that sometimes have less than adequate system administration. The weaknesses exposed by these attacks are quickly fixed in new sendmail releases. Stay informed by subscribing to the *sendmail-announce* mailing list to receive notices of new sendmail releases and by monitoring the *http://www.sendmail.org/* site. It is important to upgrade to a new sendmail release when the release fixes a security problem.

Spammers

> Security attacks usually involve unauthorized access or denial of service. A related problem is the unauthorized use and theft of service that occurs when a spammer misuses your email system. Current sendmail releases do a much better job of preventing mail abuse than old releases did. Watch for new releases that add anti-spam features. If you can reduce spam, the world will thank you.

New features

> Anti-spam features are not the only new features added to sendmail releases. Sometimes you may find a feature that is important enough to warrant an upgrade. For example, sendmail 8.11 added support for Transport Layer Security (TLS), which might be important to your organization.

Of these three reasons for upgrading, security is the most important. If you know of a security problem, you can bet that the bad guys also know and are doing their best to exploit it. Close security holes as quickly as possible. Chapter 10 shows how sendmail can be patched to close security holes.

Once you have decided to upgrade the sendmail software, you need to decide how you will do it. The easiest way to upgrade software is to use the software management tool provided with your version of Unix. A classic example of such a tool is the RPM Package Manager (RPM) that was developed by Red Hat and is used in many different Linux distributions. Tools like RPM install software packages that have already been customized for a particular Unix variant, placing the files in the proper directories and relieving the administrator of the burden of compiling the software. These tools also provide security features, such as the --verify option of the rpm command, that check the software and files for tampering during and after the installation. When you want to upgrade to a new version of sendmail, check your Unix vendor's web site to see if it is available in their package format.*

Despite the benefits of software management tools, sometimes you need to compile your own software to enable special features, and sometimes the latest version of software is not available in a package format. If you must switch to the sendmail tarball on a system where the previous sendmail installation was done by a package manager, backup the current configuration and then uninstall the current version of sendmail using the package manager before you upgrade. The example shows how to uninstall sendmail using RPM:

```
# service sendmail stop
Shutting down sendmail:                                    [  OK  ]
# rpm -qa | grep sendmail
sendmail-8.11.6-15
sendmail-cf-8.11.6-15
sendmail-devel-8.11.6-15
# rpm --erase sendmail-devel-8.11.6-15
# rpm --erase sendmail-cf-8.11.6-15
# rpm --erase --nodeps sendmail-8.11.6-15
warning: /etc/mail/statistics saved as /etc/mail/statistics.rpmsave
```

This example is from a Red Hat 7.3 system. Start by shutting down the current sendmail daemon. Then use rpm -qa to find out which sendmail RPM packages are installed, and rpm --erase to remove each of the packages. Notice that the --nodeps option is used with the final rpm command. The --nodeps option forces rpm to erase the package, even if doing so breaks the dependencies of other packages. Removing the sendmail daemon, which is what the final rpm command does, breaks other packages that depend on the sendmail daemon. Once you install the new sendmail daemon, those packages should function again. However, the negative impact on

---

* If you use RPM, the *rpmfind.net* web site can help you search for RPM compatible packages.

dependencies, caused by switching from an RPM based installation to a tarball installation, is one reason why you should always try to upgrade an RPM installation with another RPM, if possible.

Perform these steps to remove the currently installed sendmail after successfully compiling the new version of sendmail and before installing the newly created sendmail binaries. This uninstall step is necessary to prevent the package manager from falsely reporting errors when the package manager is used to scan the software for possible tampering.

Caution should also be exercised when installing a vendor's sendmail package on a system that already has a custom sendmail configuration. As Recipes 1.2 to 1.7 show, sendmail can be compiled with special options; however, the vendor might not provide the options you need, and the vendor package might overwrite the specially compiled sendmail binary. Bottom line: take care whenever you transition from one installation technique to another. If you're not changing installation techniques, and you don't use a package manager, you don't need to be concerned with any of this before you proceed with installing the sendmail source code distribution—you can just follow the steps that are discussed below.

Begin by downloading the sendmail source code distribution from *http://www.sendmail. org/current-release.html*, from any of the mirror sites, or from *ftp://ftp.sendmail.org/pub/ sendmail/*. Here is an example using *ftp*:

```
$ ftp ftp.sendmail.org
Connected to ftp.sendmail.org (209.246.26.22).
220 services.sendmail.org FTP server (Version 6.00LS) ready.
Name (ftp.sendmail.org:alana): anonymous
331 Guest login ok, send your email address as password.
Password: alana@rodent.wrotethebook.com
230 Guest login ok, access restrictions apply.
Remote system type is UNIX.
Using binary mode to transfer files.
ftp> cd pub/sendmail
250 CWD command successful.
ftp> get sendmail.8.12.9.tar.gz
local: sendmail.8.12.9.tar.gz remote: sendmail.8.12.9.tar.gz
227 Entering Passive Mode (209,246,26,22,207,236)
150 Opening BINARY mode data connection for 'sendmail.8.12.9.tar.gz' (1886008 bytes).
226 Transfer complete.
1886008 bytes received in 10.1 secs (1.8e+02 Kbytes/sec)
```

The new release is stored in the *pub/sendmail* directory as a compressed tarball under the name *sendmail.release.tar.gz* for those who use *gzip* and *sendmail.release.tar.Z* for those who use *compress*. In either case, *release* is the current numeric release number. For example, the release number at this writing is 8.12.9, so the gzipped tarball is named *sendmail.8.12.9.tar.gz* and the compressed tarball is named *sendmail.8.12.9.tar.Z*.

Next, get the signature file associated with the version of sendmail you downloaded. For example, the signature file for *sendmail.8.12.9.tar.gz* is *sendmail.8.12.9.tar.gz.sig*. Here we download it during the same *ftp* session:

```
ftp> get sendmail.8.12.9.tar.gz.sig
local: sendmail.8.12.9.tar.gz.sig remote: sendmail.8.12.9.tar.gz.sig
227 Entering Passive Mode (209,246,26,22,207,238)
150 Opening BINARY mode data connection for 'sendmail.8.12.9.tar.gz.sig' (152 bytes).
226 Transfer complete.
152 bytes received in 0.00221 secs (67 Kbytes/sec)
```

If you do not have the current sendmail PGP keys on your key ring, download the PGP keys needed to verify the signature. Here we add the following step to the *ftp* session to download the keys for the current year:

```
ftp> get PGPKEYS
local: PGPKEYS remote: PGPKEYS
227 Entering Passive Mode (209,246,26,22,207,239)
150 Opening BINARY mode data connection for 'PGPKEYS' (57704 bytes).
226 Transfer complete.
57704 bytes received in 0.491 secs (1.1e+02 Kbytes/sec)
ftp> quit
221 Goodbye.
```

Add the PGP keys to your key ring. In the following example, *gpg* (Gnu Privacy Guard) is used:

```
$ gpg --import PGPKEYS
gpg: key 16F4CCE9: not changed
gpg: key 396F0789: public key imported
gpg: key 678C0A03: not changed
gpg: key CC374F2D: not changed
gpg: key E35C5635: not changed
gpg: key A39BA655: not changed
gpg: key D432E19D: not changed
gpg: key 12D3461D: not changed
gpg: key BF7BA421: not changed
gpg: key A00E1563: non exportable signature (class 10) - skipped
gpg: key A00E1563: not changed
gpg: key 22327A01: not changed
gpg: Total number processed: 11
gpg:               imported: 1  (RSA: 1)
gpg:               unchanged: 10
```

gpg is used in this example because it is included as part of the Red Hat Linux distribution used on our sample sendmail system. Of the 11 exportable keys in the *PGPKEYS* file, only one is imported to our key ring. The *not changed* comment for the other 10 keys shows that they were already installed on the key ring. The first time you import *PGPKEYS*, all 11 keys will be added to the key ring.

Before using the new key, verify its fingerprint, as shown here:

```
$ gpg --fingerprint 396F0789
pub  1024R/396F0789 2003-01-15 Sendmail Signing Key/2003 <sendmail@Sendmail.ORG>
     Key fingerprint = C4 73 DF 4A 97 9C 27 A9  EE 4F B2 BD 55 B5 E0 0F
```

Compare the displayed fingerprint against Table 1-1 that shows sendmail's signing key fingerprints.

Table 1-1. sendmail signing key fingerprints

Year	Fingerprint
1997	CA AE F2 94 3B 1D 41 3C 94 7B 72 5F AE 0B 6A 11
1998	F9 32 40 A1 3B 3A B6 DE B2 98 6A 70 AF 54 9D 26
1999	25 73 4C 8E 94 B1 E8 EA EA 9B A4 D6 00 51 C3 71
2000	81 8C 58 EA 7A 9D 7C 1B 09 78 AC 5E EB 99 08 5D
2001	59 AF DC 3E A2 7D 29 56 89 FA 25 70 90 0D 7E C1
2002	7B 02 F4 AA FC C0 22 DA 47 3E 2A 9A 9B 35 22 45
2003	C4 73 DF 4A 97 9C 27 A9 EE 4F B2 BD 55 B5 E0 0F

If the fingerprint is correct, you can sign, and thus validate, the key. In this *gpg* example, we sign the newly imported sendmail key:

```
$ gpg --edit-key 396F0789
gpg (GnuPG) 1.0.7; Copyright (C) 2002 Free Software Foundation, Inc.
This program comes with ABSOLUTELY NO WARRANTY.
This is free software, and you are welcome to redistribute it
under certain conditions. See the file COPYING for details.

gpg: checking the trustdb
gpg: checking at depth 0 signed=0 ot(-/q/n/m/f/u)=0/0/0/0/0/1
pub  1024R/396F0789  created: 2003-01-15 expires: never    trust: -/-
(1). Sendmail Signing Key/2003 <sendmail@Sendmail.ORG>

Command> sign

pub  1024R/396F0789  created: 2003-01-15 expires: never    trust: -/-
         Fingerprint: C4 73 DF 4A 97 9C 27 A9  EE 4F B2 BD 55 B5 E0 0F
     Sendmail Signing Key/2003 <sendmail@Sendmail.ORG>

How carefully have you verified the key you are about to sign actually belongs to the
person named above?  If you don't know what to answer, enter "0".

   (0) I will not answer. (default)
   (1) I have not checked at all.
   (2) I have done casual checking.
   (3) I have done very careful checking.

Your selection? 3
Are you really sure that you want to sign this key
with your key: "Craig Hunt <craig.hunt@wrotethebook.com>"

I have checked this key very carefully.

Really sign? y
```

```
You need a passphrase to unlock the secret key for
user: "Craig Hunt <craig.hunt@wrotethebook.com>"
1024-bit DSA key, ID 34C9B515, created 2003-07-23


Command> quit
Save changes? y
```

Remember, it is not necessary to download and import the *PGPKEYS* file every time you download a new sendmail release. New keys are only added to the *PGPKEYS* file about once a year.

After the sendmail keys have been added to the key ring and signed, you can verify the sendmail distribution tarball. Here we use the *sendmail.8.12.9.tar.gz.sig* signature file to verify the *sendmail.8.12.9.tar.gz* compressed tarball:[*]

```
$ gpg --verify sendmail.8.12.9.tar.gz.sig sendmail.8.12.9.tar.gz
gpg: Signature made Sat 29 Mar 2003 09:12:38 AM EST using RSA key ID 396F0789
gpg: Good signature from "Sendmail Signing Key/2003 <sendmail@Sendmail.ORG>"
gpg: checking the trustdb
gpg: checking at depth 0 signed=1 ot(-/q/n/m/f/u)=0/0/0/0/0/1
gpg: checking at depth 1 signed=0 ot(-/q/n/m/f/u)=1/0/0/0/0/0
```

Based on this, the distribution can be safely restored, compiled, and installed. Use *tar* to restore the tarball. The tarball creates a directory with a name derived from the sendmail release number. Therefore the following commands create a directory named *sendmail-8.12.9* in */usr/local/src*:

```
# cd /usr/local/src
# tar -zxvf /home/craig/sendmail.8.12.9.tar.gz
```

The path */usr/local/src/sendmail-8.12.9* is used throughout this book. When implementing the recipes, adjust this path as appropriate for your system.

See Also

Recipe 10.4 provides a detailed example of downloading and installing sendmail patches, which are sometimes used as an alternative to downloading a full distribution. *sendmail*, Third Edition, by Bryan Costales with Eric Allman (O'Reilly), covers downloading the sendmail source distribution in section 2.2. *PGP: Pretty Good Privacy*, by Simson Garfinkel (O'Reilly), is a full book about PGP. The *GNU Privacy Handbook (GPH)*, which is available at *http://www.gnupg.org/gph/*, provides detailed information about GPG.

---

[*] In this example, the signature is used to verify the gzipped *tar* file. Signing the compressed files started with Version 8.12.7. Earlier versions of sendmail signed the uncompressed *tar* file. In those cases, the *tar* file is first decompressed and then verified.

1.2   Installing sendmail

Problem

The sendmail tarball is a source code distribution that must be compiled. Additionally, adding a special user ID and group ID may be necessary before the new sendmail software can be installed and used.

Solution

Compile sendmail using the *Build* utility provided by the sendmail developers. For most systems, only a few commands are needed to compile sendmail:

```
# cd sendmail-8.12.9
# ./Build
```

The next installation step is to create the *smmsp* user and group for sendmail to use when it runs as a mail submission program. Do this by using the tools appropriate to your system. Here are the */etc/passwd* and */etc/group* entries added to the example Red Hat system used throughout this book:

```
# grep smmsp /etc/passwd
smmsp:x:25:25:Mail Submission:/var/spool/clientmqueue:/sbin/nologin
# grep smmsp /etc/group
smmsp:x:25:
```

Next, backup the current sendmail binary, the sendmail utilities, and the current sendmail configuration files. After the system is backed up, install the new sendmail and utilities as follows:

```
# ./Build install
```

Discussion

Build detects the architecture of the system and builds a *Makefile* customized to that system. It then uses *make* to compile sendmail. *Build* does an excellent job of correctly detecting the system architecture.

A basic *Build* command should work for most situations. If it doesn't work for you, either because of your unique hardware and software, or because you have unique requirements, create a custom configuration for *Build* to use. sendmail calls these custom configurations *site configurations* and looks for them in the *devtools/Site* directory, where it expects to find the local custom configuration stored under the name *site.config.m4*. By default, *Build* looks for files named site.*OS*.m4, where *OS* is the name of the computer's operating system, *site.config.m4*, and *site.post.m4*. If you use another filename, use the -f argument on the *Build* command line to identify the file.* For example:

```
$ ./Build -f ourconfig.m4
```

As the file extension *.m4* file implies, the *Build* configuration is created with *m4* commands. Three commands are used to set the variables used by *Build*. These commands are:

define

> The define command is a built-in *m4* command. When it is used, any current value stored in the variable is replaced by the new value.

APPENDDEF

> The APPENDDEF macro is an *m4* macro used to append a value to an existing list of values stored in a variable. It does not replace the current value in the variable; it adds values to the end of a list of values.

PREPENDDEF

> The PREPENDDEF macro is an *m4* macro used to prepend a value to an existing list of values stored in a variable. It does not replace the current value in the variable; it adds values to the beginning of a list of values.

Here is an example of when a *site.config.m4* file might be needed. While the sendmail software compiles without error on our sample Red Hat system, we encounter a problem when installing the manpages. The *devtools/OS/Linux* file that comes with sendmail 8.12.9 contains the following command, which puts the manpages in */usr/man*:

```
define(`confMANROOT', `/usr/man/man')
```

Our sample Red Hat Linux system stores manpages in */usr/share/man*. Therefore, we create the following *devtools/Site/site.config.m4* file to set the manpage path to */usr/share/man*:

```
$ cat devtools/Site/site.config.m4
define(`confMANROOT', `/usr/share/man/man')
```

m4 quoted strings are enclosed in unbalanced single quotes. The same unbalanced single quotes used with any *m4* command are used in the *site.config.m4* file.

Most custom *Build* configurations are no more complicated than this example. The next few recipes show additional examples of *Build* configurations. Those examples were chosen because the options they compile into sendmail are required by recipes later in this book. However, there are more than 100 variables that can be set for the *Build* configuration—far too many to cover with individual recipes. See the *devtools/README* file for a complete list.

---

* If you make changes to the *siteconfig.m4* file and rerun *Build*, use the -c command-line argument to alert *Build* of the changes.

It has always been necessary to compile sendmail before installing it. Starting with sendmail 8.12, a new step has been added to the installation procedure. sendmail 8.12 expects to find a user ID and a group ID named *smmsp*. If this user ID and group ID do not exist on your system, create them before installing sendmail because the sendmail binary is no longer installed as set-user-ID root. Traditionally, the sendmail binary was set-user-ID root so that any user could submit mail via the command line and have it written to the queue directory. However, this does not really require a set-user-ID root binary. With the proper directory permissions, a set-group-ID binary will work fine.

Before installing the freshly compiled sendmail, back up the current sendmail binary, the sendmail utilities, and your current sendmail configuration files. (You never know; you might need to drop back to the old sendmail configuration if the new one doesn't work as anticipated.) Remember: if the previous version of sendmail was installed with a package manager, it should be removed using that package manager before the new sendmail software is installed.

Running `Build install` on the sample Red Hat system installs sendmail and the utilities, and it produces more than 100 lines of output. It should run without error. On our sample system, the `install` commands that place the manpages clearly show the path defined earlier in the *devtools/Site/site.config.m4* file. Also notice that *Build* uses the *smmsp* user and group when it creates the *clientmqueue* directory and when it installs the sendmail binary. A quick check of the ownership and permissions for the queue directory and the sendmail binary shows this:

```
drwxrwx---   2 smmsp    smmsp      4096 Aug  7 16:22 clientmqueue
-r-xr-sr-x   1 root     smmsp    568701 Aug  7 16:51 /usr/sbin/sendmail
```

After sendmail is installed, it must be configured. Most of this book discusses how to configure sendmail to do what you want it to do.

See Also

The *sendmail* book covers compiling and installing sendmail in Chapter 2.

1.3   Compiling sendmail to Use LDAP

Problem

sendmail must be compiled with the correct options in order to read data from an LDAP server. The LDAP server must also be properly configured to understand queries from sendmail.

Solution

Use the command `sendmail -bt -d0.1` to check the sendmail compiler options. If the string `LDAPMAP` appears in the "Compiled with:" list, there is no need to recompile sendmail. If `LDAPMAP` does not appear in the "Compiled with:" list, recompile sendmail to add LDAP support.

To add LDAP support, set LDAP values in the *site.config.m4* file and recompile sendmail as shown below:

```
# cd /usr/local/src/sendmail-8.12.9/devtools/Site
# cat >> site.config.m4
APPENDDEF(`confMAPDEF', `-DLDAPMAP')
APPENDDEF(`confLIBS', `-lldap -llber')
Ctrl-D
# cd /usr/local/src/sendmail-8.12.9
# ./Build -c
```

After recompiling sendmail, reinstall it:

```
# ./Build install
```

The LDAP server must also be configured to work with sendmail. Give the LDAP administrator a copy of the *sendmail.schema* file, which is found in the *cf* directory of the sendmail distribution. The LDAP administrator must store the *sendmail.schema* file in the appropriate directory on the LDAP server. For example, an LDAP server running OpenLDAP often stores schema files in the */etc/openldap/schema* directory.

Next, the LDAP administrator must add the *sendmail.schema* file to the LDAP configuration. On a system running OpenLDAP, add the following include to the */etc/openldap/slapd.conf* file:

```
include         /etc/openldap/schema/sendmail.schema
```

Restart LDAP on the LDAP server to ensure that the sendmail schema are included in the LDAP configuration. Here is an example from an LDAP server running OpenLDAP:

```
# ps -ax | grep slapd
 1426 ?        S      0:00 /usr/sbin/slapd -u ldap
# kill -TERM 1426
# /usr/sbin/slapd -u ldap
```

Discussion

In this recipe, two `APPENDDEF` commands are added to the *site.config.m4* file. The first `APPENDDEF` command adds `-DLDAPMAP` to the list of supported map types stored in the `confMAPDEF` define. The second `APPENDDEF` command adds `-lldap` and `-llber` to the list of libraries stored in the `confLIBS` define. `-llber` is required because this sample system uses OpenLDAP.

Build is then used to recompile sendmail. The `-c` option on the *Build* command line is needed to make sure that *Build* detects the changes made to the *site.config.m4* file. After recompiling, sendmail is reinstalled.

Now, rerunning sendmail with the `-d0.1` option would show `LDAPMAP` included in the "Compiled with:" list. sendmail is now ready to be configured to use LDAP. Of course, this doesn't mean that LDAP is ready to work with sendmail.

The sendmail distribution comes with schema designed to work with LDAP. The LDAP server must be configured to include these schema in order to understand and properly process queries from sendmail. For OpenLDAP, this is done by adding an `include` command to the *slapd.conf* file that points to the sendmail schema, as shown in the Solution section. Once this is done, LDAP is ready to work with sendmail's standard schema.

See Also

Recipes 1.2 and 1.4 through 1.7 provide other examples of compiling sendmail. Refer to other recipes in this book for specific examples of reading sendmail data from an LDAP server. For information on LDAP, see *Understanding and Deploying LDAP Directory Services* by Howes, Smith, and Good (Macmillan) and *LDAP System Administration* by Gerald Carter (O'Reilly). The *cf/README* file covers this topic in the *Using LDAP for Aliases, Maps, and Classes* section. The *sendmail* book covers compiling sendmail in section 2.2.

1.4   Adding the regex Map Type to sendmail

Problem

Support for the `regex` map type must be compiled into sendmail if the error message "class regex not available" is displayed when sendmail is run.

Solution

To add support for the regular expression map type, add `MAP_REGEX` to the `confMAPDEF` compiler variable in the *site.config.m4* file and then recompile sendmail. Here is an example:

```
# cd /usr/local/src/sendmail-8.12.9/devtools/Site
# cat >> site.config.m4
APPENDDEF(`confMAPDEF', `-DMAP_REGEX')
Ctrl-D
# cd /usr/local/src/sendmail-8.12.9
# ./Build -c
```

After recompiling sendmail, reinstall it:

```
# ./Build install
```

Discussion

Attempting to run a configuration that specifies a regex map type on a sendmail system without regex support compiled in produces an error, as this test shows:

```
# sendmail -bt
sendmail.cf: line 115: readcf: map dottedquad: class regex not available
ADDRESS TEST MODE (ruleset 3 NOT automatically invoked)
Enter <ruleset> <address>
> /quit
```

The first line after the sendmail -bt command is an error message. It tells us that line 115 in the *sendmail.cf* file contains a K command that defines a map using the regex map type, which results in an error because regex is not supported on this system.

The fix for this requires defining a local compiler variable in the *site.config.m4* file in the *devtools/Site* directory. The APPENDDEF command used in the Solution section appends the -DMAP_REGEX command-line argument to any values that already exist in the confMAPDEF variable. The Build command that is used to recompile sendmail uses the -c flag to ensure that Build incorporates the new data from the *site.config.m4* file.

After compiling sendmail, run it with the -bt and the -d0.1 command-line arguments to check the compiler options:

```
# sendmail -bt -d0.1
Version 8.12.9
 Compiled with: DNSMAP LOG MAP_REGEX MATCHGECOS MIME7TO8 MIME8TO7 NEWDB
                NAMED_BIND NETINET NETUNIX PIPELINING SCANF USERDB XDEBUG

============ SYSTEM IDENTITY (after readcf) ============
      (short domain name) $w = chef
  (canonical domain name) $j = chef.wrotethebook.com
        (subdomain name) $m = wrotethebook.com
              (node name) $k = chef
=======================================================

ADDRESS TEST MODE (ruleset 3 NOT automatically invoked)
Enter <ruleset> <address>
> /quit
```

The "Compiled with:" line output by the -d0.1 argument displays the compiler options. This line should contain MAP_REGEX. If it does, configurations using the regex map type should now run successfully.

See Also

Recipes 1.2, 1.3, 1.5, 1.6, and 1.7 provide other examples of compiling sendmail. Recipe 6.10 uses the regex map type. The *sendmail* book covers compiling sendmail in section 2.2.

1.5 Compiling sendmail with SASL Support

Problem

sendmail must be compiled with SASL support before it can be configured to offer the AUTH protocol extension.

Solution

Check the sendmail compiler options. If sendmail was compiled with the SASL flag, it does not need to be recompiled. If sendmail was not compiled with SASL support, add SASL to the -D flags used to specify compiler environment information, add sasl to the -1 flags used to select libraries for linking, and recompile sendmail. After recompiling sendmail, reinstall and restart it.

Discussion

Use the -d0.1 flag to check the compiler options of the sendmail binary. The SASL flag should be clearly shown in the "Complied with:" list, as in this example:

```
# sendmail -bt -d0.1
Version 8.12.9
 Compiled with: DNSMAP LOG MAP_REGEX MATCHGECOS MIME7TO8 MIME8TO7
                NAMED_BIND NETINET NETUNIX NEWDB PIPELINING SASL
                SCANF USERDB XDEBUG

============ SYSTEM IDENTITY (after readcf) ============
      (short domain name) $w = chef
  (canonical domain name) $j = chef.wrotethebook.com
         (subdomain name) $m = wrotethebook.com
             (node name) $k = chef
========================================================

ADDRESS TEST MODE (ruleset 3 NOT automatically invoked)
Enter <ruleset> <address>
> /quit
```

If the flag is not displayed, create a *site.config.m4* file in the *devtools/Site* directory that contains the following commands:

```
APPENDDEF(`conf_sendmail_ENVDEF', `-DSASL')
APPENDDEF(`conf_sendmail_LIBS', `-lsasl')
```

Recompile, reinstall, and restart sendmail, as in this example:

```
# cd /usr/local/src/sendmail-8.12.9
# ./Build -c
...many lines of output deleted...
# cd /usr/local/src/sendmail-8.12.9/sendmail
# ./Build install
...many lines of output deleted...
# kill -HUP `head -1 /var/run/sendmail.pid`
```

See Also

Recipes 1.2, 1.3, 1.4, 1.6, and 1.7 provide additional examples of compiling send-mail. Chapter 7 covers SASL and AUTH configuration. The *sendmail* book covers AUTH configuration in section 10.9 and compiling sendmail in section 2.2. See the *sysadmin.html* file in the SASL documentation directory for additional information about SASL configuration.

1.6 Compiling sendmail with STARTTLS Support

Problem

sendmail must be specially compiled to support the STARTTLS extension.

Solution

Use the command sendmail -bt -d0.1 to check the sendmail compiler options. If the string STARTTLS appears in the "Compiled with:" list, there is no need to recompile sendmail. If sendmail was not compiled with STARTTLS support, edit the *devtools/Site/site.config.m4* file to add STARTTLS to the compiler's -D flags and to add ssl and crypto to the -l flags used to select libraries for linking. See the following example:

```
# cd /usr/local/src/sendmail-8.12.9/devtools/Site
# cat >> site.config.m4
APPENDDEF(`conf_sendmail_ENVDEF', `-DSTARTTLS')
APPENDDEF(`conf_sendmail_LIBS', `-lssl -lcrypto')
Ctrl-D
```

Recompile, reinstall, and restart sendmail:

```
# cd /usr/local/src/sendmail-8.12.9
# ./Build -c
...many lines of output deleted...
# ./Build install
...many lines of output deleted...
# kill -HUP `head -1 /var/run/sendmail.pid`
```

Discussion

In the sample *site.config.m4* file, the first APPENDDEF command adds -DSTARTTLS to the list of compiler options stored in the conf_sendmail_ENVDEF define. The second APPENDDEF command adds -lssl and -lcrypto to the list of libraries stored in the conf_sendmail_LIBS define.

Build is then used to recompile sendmail. The -c option on the *Build* command line ensures that *Build* detects the changes made to the *site.config.m4* file. Build install is run to install the freshly compiled sendmail binary. The HUP signal is used to restart sendmail with the new binary.

After recompiling sendmail, rerunning *sendmail* with the -d0.1 option shows that STARTTLS is included in the "Compiled with:" list. sendmail can now be configured to offer STARTTLS as described in Chapter 8.

See Also

Recipes 1.2 to 1.5 provide further information on compiling sendmail. Additionally, Recipe 1.7 provides information on fixing a problem that may appear when recompiling sendmail to support STARTTLS. Chapter 8 covers STARTTLS configuration. The *sendmail* book covers compiling sendmail in section 2.2 and STARTTLS in section 10.10.

1.7   Compiling in STARTTLS File Paths

Problem

When compiling sendmail to support the STARTTLS extension, "No such file or directory" errors are displayed in regard to OpenSSL files.

Solution

Set the correct path values in conf_sendmail_INCDIRS and conf_sendmail_LIBDIRS to tell sendmail where the OpenSSL files are located. Add the defines to the *site.config.m4* configuration file, as in this example:

```
# cd /usr/local/src/sendmail-8.12.9/devtools/Site
# cat >> site.config.m4
APPENDDEF(`conf_sendmail_INCDIRS', `-I/usr/share/ssl/include')
APPENDDEF(`conf_sendmail_LIBDIRS', `-L/usr/share/ssl/lib')
Ctrl-D
```

Recompile, reinstall, and restart sendmail:

```
# cd /usr/local/src/sendmail-8.12.9
# ./Build -c
...many lines of output deleted...
# ./Build install
...many lines of output deleted...
# kill -HUP `head -1 /var/run/sendmail.pid`
```

Discussion

The sendmail configuration assumes that OpenSSL is installed in the standard location. If it is not, "No such file or directory" errors are displayed during the sendmail build when the system attempts to use the OpenSSL files. Use APPENDDEF commands to add the correct location of the OpenSSL include file to the `conf_sendmail_INCDIRS` variable and the correct location of the OpenSSL library to the `conf_sendmail_LIBDIRS` variable. The `APPENDDEF` commands are added to the *site.config.m4* file.

After defining the correct values in *site.config.m4*, recompile sendmail with the `Build -c` command. If the path values are correctly defined, the build should run without errors.

See Also

Recipes 1.2 to 1.6 provide additional information on compiling sendmail. In particular, Recipe 1.6 provides an example of compiling sendmail with STARTTLS support. Chapter 8 covers STARTTLS configuration. The *sendmail* book covers compiling sendmail in section 2.2 and STARTTLS in section 10.10.

1.8   Building a sendmail Configuration

Problem

sendmail configurations are written using *m4* macros. The configuration must be processed by *m4* to produce the *sendmail.cf* configuration file that is read by sendmail.

Solution

Change to the configuration directory.

Create the *m4* master configuration file. For this example, we name the master configuration file *sendmail.mc*.

Build the *sendmail.cf* file, copy it to the standard directory, and restart the sendmail daemon:

```
# ./Build sendmail.cf
Using M4=/usr/bin/m4
rm  f sendmail.cf
/usr/bin/m4 ../m4/cf.m4 sendmail.mc > sendmail.cf || ( rm -f sendmail.cf && exit 1 )
chmod 444 sendmail.cf
# cp /etc/mail/sendmail.cf /etc/mail/sendmail.cf.bak
# cp sendmail.cf /etc/mail/sendmail.cf
# kill -HUP `head -1 /var/run/sendmail.pid`
```

Notice, in this example, that sendmail is restarted with a HUP signal. This assumes that sendmail is already running with some current configuration, which is a good assumption for the majority of recipes in this book. If, however, sendmail has just been installed, is not running, and has not been previously configured, use `Build install-cf` to properly install both the *sendmail.cf* file and the *submit.cf* file. See the "Building and installing sendmail.cf" section of the following discussion for an example of the `Build install-cf` command.

Discussion

New sendmail configurations are generally built inside the *cf/cf* directory. Of course, *cf/cf* is a relative path, so where this directory is located can vary from system to system. For example, the Red Hat RPM places the configuration files in */usr/share/sendmail-cf/cf*. If you're using the sendmail distribution, the *cf/cf* directory is relative to where you installed the distribution. All of the examples in this book assume you're using the sendmail 8.12.9 distribution and that you installed it in */usr/local/src*. Given these assumptions, the following *cd* command would put you in the correct directory:

```
# cd /usr/local/src/sendmail-8.12.4/cf/cf
```

Next, create a master configuration file and make any necessary edits to that file. You can create a configuration file from scratch, start with a generic configuration provided by the sendmail developers, or start with a configuration provided by your vendor. Typing in your own configuration file from scratch is easy because sendmail master configuration files are very short. However, the sendmail developers provide a full set of generic and prototype files that are generally a good place to start.

The examples in this book are modifications to the *generic-linux.mc* configuration file that comes with the sendmail distribution. Therefore, we copy the *generic-linux.mc* file, which is the best match for our sample Linux system, to *sendmail.mc*, which we use as a working file. The *generic-linux.mc* file contains the following lines:

```
divert(-1)
#
# Copyright (c) 1998, 1999 Sendmail, Inc. and its suppliers.
#       All rights reserved.
# Copyright (c) 1983 Eric P. Allman.  All rights reserved.
# Copyright (c) 1988, 1993
#       The Regents of the University of California.  All rights reserved.
#
# By using this file, you agree to the terms and conditions set
# forth in the LICENSE file which can be found at the top level of
# the sendmail distribution.
#
#


#
# This is a generic configuration file for Linux.
# It has support for local and SMTP mail only.  If you want to
# customize it, copy it to a name appropriate for your environment
# and do the modifications there.
#

divert(0)dnl
VERSIONID(`$Id: ch01,v 1.21 2003/12/03 15:08:14 marlowe Exp jhawks $')
OSTYPE(linux)dnl
DOMAIN(generic)dnl
MAILER(local)dnl
MAILER(smtp)dnl
```

The divert(-1) command starts a section of comments that ends with a divert(0) command. Therefore, only the last five lines of the generic file are active lines—the rest of the file consists of comments.

The VERSIONID macro specifies version information that is formatted in any way you choose. If you use a version control system, you should probably format the information to be compatible with that system. In any case, you should change this information when you edit the file to indicate when the file was changed and by whom.

The OSTYPE macro loads the configuration required for the operating system. In this case, the file being loaded is *ostype/linux.m4* as you would expect with the generic Linux configuration. We will return to the *linux.m4* file shortly to look at its contents.

The DOMAIN macro loads a configuration file designed specifically for your domain. The *generic-linux.mc* file is a sample file, and the *domain/generic.m4* file that it loads with the DOMAIN macro is also a sample file. Although it is not specifically designed for your domain, the *generic.m4* file is designed to be harmless. The contents of the *domain/generic.m4* file are covered later.

If you do create a custom domain file, note that there is an interesting side effect when all of the configuration changes happen in the domain file and the master configuration file is unchanged. Rebuilding the *sendmail.cf* file with the *Build* script may generate the following error:

```
# ./Build sendmail.cf
Using M4=/usr/bin/m4
make: `sendmail.cf' is up to date.
```

Build does not check for changes in the domain file. It sees that *sendmail.mc* is unchanged since the last build and it refuses to create a new *sendmail.cf* file. Bypass this problem by removing the old *sendmail.cf* file, by running touch sendmail.mc before running *Build*, or by using *m4* instead of *Build* to rebuild the *sendmail.cf* file.

The last two macros in the *generic-linux.mc* file are MAILER macros. The first MAILER macro loads *mailer/local.m4*, which defines the following mailers:

local

> The local mailer delivers mail to user accounts located on this system.

prog

> The prog mailer is used by sendmail to route mail to other processes running on the local system.

Both the local and prog mailers are used in most sendmail configurations.

The second MAILER macro loads *mailer/smtp.m4*, which defines these mailers:

esmtp

> The Extended SMTP (ESMTP) mailer handles the standard TCP/IP mail protocol, including complex message bodies and MIME content types. This is the default mailer used by sendmail for SMTP mail.

relay

> The relay mailer is used to relay SMTP mail through another mail host. Relaying and mail relay hosts are used in Chapter 3.

smtp

> The smtp mailer handles only old-fashioned, 7-bit ASCII SMTP mail. sendmail only uses this mailer when specially configured to do so; for example, if directed to do so by an entry in the *mailertable* database. The *mailertable* is used in recipes in Chapter 5.

smtp8

> The smtp8 mailer is designed to work with remote systems that can handle 8-bit mail but do not understand the standard ESMTP protocol. sendmail only uses this mailer when specially configured to do so; for example, if it is directed to do so by an entry in the *mailertable* database.

dsmtp

> The dsmtp mailer allows the destination host to retrieve mail queued on the mail server. Normally, mail is "pushed" from the source to the destination; the source initiates the connection. This mailer allows the destination host to "pull" mail from the source when it is ready to receive mail by using the optional ETRN SMTP command. sendmail only uses this mailer when specially configured to do so.

The two MAILER macros add the essential mailers to the configuration. The DOMAIN macro, which loads the *domain/generic.m4* file, and the OSTYPE macro, which loads the *ostype/linux.m4* file, also add settings to the configuration. Examine the *generic.m4* and *linux.m4* files to see exactly what those settings are.

The linux.m4 file

Every master configuration file contains an OSTYPE macro.* To fully understand a configuration, you must know exactly what parameters are set by this file. This book uses Linux as a sample operating system and *linux.m4* as a sample *ostype* file. You, however, should examine the *ostype* file specific to your operating systems before using the recipes that follow in later chapters.

After an opening block of comments, the *linux.m4* file contains the following active lines:

```
VERSIONID(`$Id: ch01,v 1.21 2003/12/03 15:08:14 marlowe Exp jhawks $')
define(`confEBINDIR', `/usr/sbin')
ifdef(`PROCMAIL_MAILER_PATH',,
        define(`PROCMAIL_MAILER_PATH', `/usr/bin/procmail'))
FEATURE(local_procmail)
```

We have already discussed VERSIONID, so there is no need to go over it again.

---

* Recipe 10.1 shows a trick to get around this requirement.

The define command defines the path to the directory where certain executables, particularly the sendmail Restricted Shell (*smrsh*), are stored. The default for confEBINDIR is */usr/libexec*. This define sets it to */usr/sbin*, which is correct for Linux systems.

Notice that different single quote marks are used to open and close a quoted string in an *m4* command. The open quote mark is ` and the close quote mark is '. These quote marks are only required when the string contains a blank, a special character, or a keyword. However, the quote marks are frequently used, and when they are used, the quotes must appear exactly as shown.

The ifdef command is a built-in *m4* command. It contains three comma-separated fields:

- First, the name of the variable being tested, which is PROCMAIL_MAILER_PATH in this example.
- Second, the action taken if the variable has been set. In this case, no action is taken because the second field is empty, as indicated by the two commas in a row.
- Third, the action taken if the variable has not been set. In the *linux.m4* file, the define command that sets PROCMAIL_MAILER_PATH to */usr/bin/procmail* is executed only if the variable has not been set previously. PROCMAIL_MAILER_PATH is not set anywhere else in this configuration, so this define executes and sets the variable.

The last line in the *linux.m4* file is a FEATURE macro that adds the *local_procmail* feature to the configuration. The *local_procmail* feature causes sendmail to use *procmail* as the local mailer. *procmail* is a program with very powerful mail filtering features. *procmail* is used in Chapter 6.

The generic.m4 file

After the OSTYPE macro adds the *linux.m4* file to the configuration, the DOMAIN macro adds the *domain/generic.m4* file. It contains the following active lines:

```
VERSIONID(`$Id: ch01,v 1.21 2003/12/03 15:08:14 marlowe Exp jhawks $')
define(`confFORWARD_PATH', `$z/.forward.$w+$h:$z/.forward+$h:$z/.forward.$w:$z/.
forward')dnl
define(`confMAX_HEADERS_LENGTH', `32768')dnl
FEATURE(`redirect')dnl
FEATURE(`use_cw_file')dnl
EXPOSED_USER(`root')
```

We know what the VERSIONID macro does, so there is no need to cover it again.

The first define command sets a value for the confFORWARD_PATH variable, which tells sendmail where to search for *.forward* files. The confFORWARD_PATH variable is discussed in more detail in the Introduction to Chapter 2 and in Recipe 10.8.

The second define command sets the value of the confMAX_HEADERS_LENGTH variable. In turn, this *m4* variable sets the value for the *sendmail.cf* MaxHeadersLength option.

This value is the maximum number of header bytes sendmail will allow for a message. The define sets this value to 32,768, which is the default used when no value is defined.

The first FEATURE macro enables the *redirect* feature. This is a useful feature that can be used to return a message to the sender telling him the correct address of a recipient whose address has changed. The *redirect* feature is used in Recipe 2.8, where it is explained in detail.

The second FEATURE macro enables the *use_cw_file* feature. This feature causes sendmail to load class $=w from the file *local-host-names*. When and how to use this feature are covered in Recipe 2.1

Finally, the EXPOSED_USER macro is used to add the username *root* to class $=E. Values in class $=E are exempted from masquerading when masquerading is used to hide hostnames or usernames. The EXPOSED_USER macro is used repeatedly in Chapter 4.

The *generic-linux.mc* file, the *linux.m4* file, and the *generic.m4* domain file are combined to create a configuration that:

- Sets the confBINDIR directory path to */usr/sbin*
- Sets the path of *procmail* to */usr/bin/procmail*
- Uses *procmail* as the local mailer
- Defines a search path for *.forward* files
- Sets the maximum length of the headers on a message to 32,768 bytes
- Enables the *redirect* feature
- Loads class $=w from the *local-host-names* file
- Exempts the *root* user from masquerading
- Defines the complete set of local and SMTP mailers

Because the *generic-linux.mc* file incorporates both the *linux.m4* file and the *generic.m4* file, all of the configuration settings just listed have been made part of the *sendmail.mc* file simply by copying the *generic-linux.m4* file. It is this *sendmail.mc* file that is the basic configuration modified in subsequent recipes to create custom configurations.

Building and installing sendmail.cf

Run *Build* to create the *sendmail.cf* file from the *sendmail.mc* file. The *Build* script is easy to use. Provide the name of the output file you want to create as an argument on the *Build* command line. The script replaces the *.cf* extension of the output file with the extension *.mc* and uses the macro configuration file with that name to create the output file. Thus, putting *sendmail.cf* on the *Build* command line means that *sendmail.mc* is used to create *sendmail.cf*.

Despite the simplicity of *Build*, many administrators never use it to build a sendmail configuration because the *m4* command line used to build a sendmail configuration is also very simple:

```
$ m4 ../m4/cf.m4 sendmail.mc > sendmail.cf
```

For the average sendmail administrator, the *Build* script doesn't offer any critical advantages. For most of us, deciding to use *Build* or *m4* is primarily a matter of personal preference. It is even possible to invoke the *Makefile* directly with a basic make command. In this book, we use both *Build* and *m4* to build the sendmail configuration file. Use whichever method you prefer.

The *Build* script makes it simple for the people who maintain the sendmail distribution to build a *.cf* file for each *.mc* file in the *cf/cf* directory with a single *Build all* command. If you need to build multiple configurations, it is possible to edit the *Makefile*, changing the $OTHER variable so that it contains the names of all of the configurations you wish to build, and to then use Build other to create all of those configurations at one time. However, most administrators do not have enough different configurations to bother with this.

After building the new *sendmail.cf* file, copy that file to the location where sendmail expects to find its configuration file. On our sample Red Hat system, that location is */etc/mail/sendmail.cf*. In most cases, this is simply done with a *cp* command. However, it can also be done with *Build*, as follows:

```
# cd cf/cf
# ./Build install-cf
Using M4=/usr/bin/m4
../../devtools/bin/install.sh -c -o root -g bin -m 0444 sendmail.cf /etc/mail/
sendmail.cf
../../devtools/bin/install.sh -c -o root -g bin -m 0444 submit.cf /etc/mail/submit.cf
```

The Build install-cf command used above installs two configuration files: the *sendmail.cf* file that is the primary focus of this book and a second file named *submit. cf*. This file doesn't exist unless you create it, but a full *submit.cf* is delivered with the sendmail distribution. The *submit.cf* file is a special configuration used when sendmail is invoked by a user from the command line to submit a piece of mail. *sendmail. cf* is the configuration file used by the sendmail daemon. The Build install-cf command is generally used when a new sendmail distribution is first installed to ensure that both the *sendmail.cf* and *submit.cf* files are installed. Other than the initial installation, however, there is generally no need to copy both files at the same time because it is not usually necessary to create a new *submit.cf* file when you create a new *sendmail.cf* file.

Once the configuration is installed, start sendmail to force it to read the new configuration. In this recipe's Solution section, sendmail is restarted by sending it the HUP signal with a *kill* command. This method of restarting sendmail uses standard sendmail signal processing that is available on any system, which makes the *kill* command technique vendor neutral. Many readers will be familiar with embedding a *cat* command inside a *kill* command to retrieve the process ID stored in a PID file. An interesting aspect of the *kill* command used to restart sendmail is the manner in which the sendmail process ID is retrieved from the *sendmail.pid* file. Here is the example again:

```
# kill -HUP `head -1 /var/run/sendmail.pid`
```

Using *cat* instead of *head* in this command would not work because sendmail writes a multiline PID file. A *cat* of */var/run/sendmail.pid* on our sample system shows this:

```
# cat /var/run/sendmail.pid
1076
/usr/sbin/sendmail -bd -q15m
```

The content of this file is of more than just passing interest to someone planning to restart sendmail with a HUP signal. The first line is the process ID you expect to find in a PID file. The second line of this file is the command that was used to start sendmail. The command must contain the full pathname of the sendmail program in order for the HUP signal to successfully restart sendmail. If the second line of this file shows a partial (or relative) pathname, HUP terminates the currently running sendmail, but it does not start a new copy of sendmail. In effect, sending a HUP signal to sendmail, when the current version of sendmail was not executed using its full pathname, kills sendmail, which, of course, is not what you intended. To be safe, always start sendmail using the full pathname.

Of course, the HUP signal is only used to restart sendmail, which implies that sendmail is already running. The first time sendmail is installed on a system, it is started from the command line using a sendmail command. Here is an example:

```
# /usr/sbin/sendmail -bd -q15m
# /usr/sbin/sendmail -L sm-msp -Ac -q15m
```

The -bd option used on the first command line causes sendmail to run as a daemon and listen for incoming mail on ports 25 and 587. This first command creates the sendmail daemon that reads the *sendmail.cf* configuration file and runs in the traditional role of a mail transfer agent (MTA). The second command starts sendmail as a mail submission program. The -Ac option on this command line directs sendmail to read the *submit.cf* configuration file. The -L option tells this copy of sendmail to use the name *sm-msp* when it logs messages. Without the -L option, both copies of sendmail would log messages using the name *sendmail* making it difficult to determine which copy of sendmail logged the message. The -q15m option on both command lines direct each copy of sendmail to process its mail queue every 15 minutes. See Chapter 9 for more information on mail queues.

Some systems provide their own tools for starting daemons. For example, a Red Hat system using an RPM version of sendmail can start sendmail with the service command:

```
# service sendmail start
Starting sendmail: [ OK ]
```

Regardless of how sendmail is started or restarted, when the daemon starts, it reads in the configuration file */etc/mail/sendmail.cf*, which now contains the new configuration.

This recipe is the basic configuration recipe upon which most of the recipes in this book are built. Subsequent chapters describe solutions to specific problems. These solutions are often shown in the context of this basic recipe. You will need to take those solutions and place them in the basic configuration that you build for your server. We use a basic foundation recipe for subsequent solutions for two reasons:

- First, covering the basic configuration here eliminates the need to repeat this long description over and over again for every recipe, which, in turn, allows us to focus on the unique aspects of those recipes. We explain the basic recipe once and then assume you understand the basic configuration statements as we move forward. Recipes naturally have lots of repetition; this reduces some of it.

- Second, the basic recipe provides a consistent reference point for subsequent recipes. By creating a baseline configuration that you can use as a starting point for most recipes in this book, we ensure that you can duplicate our test results on your system.

See Also

The *sendmail* book covers the VERSIONID macro in section 4.2.3.1, the OSTYPE macro in section 4.2.2.1, the DOMAIN macro in 4.2.2.3, and the MAILER macro in section 4.2.2.2. All of the *m4* macros and configuration commands are covered in the *cf/README* file delivered with the sendmail distribution.

1.9   Testing a New Configuration

Problem

You need to test the sendmail configuration before it is deployed.

Solution

Use the sendmail command-line options -bt, -bv, and -v.

Discussion

At the end of Recipe 1.8, the newly created *sendmail.cf* is copied over the old configuration. Do not copy a customized configuration into the */etc/mail* directory until it is thoroughly tested. sendmail provides excellent test tools that are used extensively in this book.

The single most important tool for testing sendmail is sendmail itself. When started with the -bt command-line option, sendmail enters *test mode*. While in test mode, sendmail accepts a variety of commands that examine the configuration, check settings, and observe how email addresses are processed by sendmail. Table 1-2 lists the commands that are available in test mode.

Table 1-2. sendmail test mode commands

Command	Usage
rulesets address	Process the address through the comma-separated list of rulesets.
=Sruleset	Display the contents of the ruleset.
=M	Display all of the mailer definitions.
$v	Display the value of macro v.
$=c	Display the values in class c.
.Dvvalue	Set the macro v to value.
.Ccvalue	Add value to class c.
-dvalue	Set the debug level to value.
/tryflags flags	Set the flags used for address processing by /try.
/try mailer address	Process the address for the mailer.
/parse address	Return the mailer/host/user delivery triple for the address.
/canon hostname	Canonify hostname.
/mx hostname	Lookup the MX records for hostname.
/map mapname key	Look up key in the database identified by mapname.
/quit	Exit address test mode.

Several commands (=S, =M, $v, and $=c) display current sendmail configuration values defined in the *sendmail.cf* file, and the /map command displays values set in the sendmail database files. The -d command can be used to change the amount of information displayed. A great many debug levels can be set by -d, but only a few are useful to the sendmail administrator. All of the debug values are covered in the *sendmail* book, and a few of the most useful values are discussed in this book.

Two commands, .D and .C, are used to set macro and class values in real time. Use these commands to try alternate configuration settings before rebuilding the entire configuration.

Two commands display the interaction between sendmail and DNS. /canon displays the canonical name returned by DNS for a given hostname. /mx shows the list of mail exchangers returned by DNS for a given host.

Most of the remaining commands process an email address through sendmail's rewrite rules. /parse displays the processing of a delivery address and shows which mailer is used to deliver mail sent to the address. /try displays the processing of addresses for a specific mailer. (The /tryflags command specifies whether the sender or the recipient address should be processed by the /try command.) Use the *ruleset address* command to display the processing of an address through any arbitrary list of rulesets that you wish to test.

The following example uses sendmail test mode to check the configuration created in Recipe 1.8. Invoke the sendmail command with the -bt option to enter test mode and the -C option to specify the configuration file to be tested. If the -C option is not used, the current configuration file *(/etc/mail/sendmail.cf)* is the configuration that is tested.

The following test displays the mailer configuration in the form of a list of *sendmail.cf* M commands:

```
# sendmail -bt -C/usr/local/src/sendmail-8.12.9/cf/cf/sendmail.cf
ADDRESS TEST MODE (ruleset 3 NOT automatically invoked)
Enter <ruleset> <address>
> =M
mailer 0 (prog): P=/bin/sh S=EnvFromL/HdrFromL R=EnvToL/HdrToL M=0 U=0:0
                 F=9DFMeloqsu L=0 E=\n T=X-Unix/X-Unix/X-Unix r=100
                 A=sh -c $u
mailer 1 (*file*): P=[FILE] S=parse/parse R=parse/parse M=0 U=0:0
                   F=9DEFMPloqsu L=0 E=\n T=X-Unix/X-Unix/X-Unix r=100
                   A=FILE $u
mailer 2 (*include*): P=/dev/null S=parse/parse R=parse/parse M=0 U=0:0
                      F=su L=0 E=\n T=<undefined>/<undefined>/<undefined>
                      r=100 A=INCLUDE $u
mailer 3 (local): P=/usr/bin/procmail S=EnvFromL/HdrFromL R=EnvToL/HdrToL
                  M=0 U=0:0 F=/59:@ADFMPSfhlnqsw| L=0 E=\n
                  T=DNS/RFC822/X-Unix r=100 A=procmail -Y -a $h -d $u
mailer 4 (smtp): P=[IPC] S=EnvFromSMTP/HdrFromSMTP R=EnvToSMTP/EnvToSMTP
                 M=0 U=0:0 F=DFMXmu L=990 E=\r\n T=DNS/RFC822/SMTP r=100
                 A=TCP $h
mailer 5 (esmtp): P=[IPC] S=EnvFromSMTP/HdrFromSMTP R=EnvToSMTP/EnvToSMTP
                  M=0 U=0:0 F=DFMXamu L=990 E=\r\n T=DNS/RFC822/SMTP r=100
                  A=TCP $h
mailer 6 (smtp8): P=[IPC] S=EnvFromSMTP/HdrFromSMTP R=EnvToSMTP/EnvToSMTP
                  M=0 U=0:0 F=8DFMXmu L=990 E=\r\n T=DNS/RFC822/SMTP r=100
                  A=TCP $h
mailer 7 (dsmtp): P=[IPC] S=EnvFromSMTP/HdrFromSMTP R=EnvToSMTP/EnvToSMTP
                  M=0 U=0:0 F=%DFMXamu L=990 E=\r\n T=DNS/RFC822/SMTP
                  r=100 A=TCP $h
mailer 8 (relay): P=[IPC] S=EnvFromSMTP/HdrFromSMTP R=MasqSMTP/MasqSMTP
                  M=0 U=0:0 F=8DFMXamu L=2040 E=\r\n T=DNS/RFC822/SMTP
                  r=100 A=TCP $h
> /quit
```

The output shows that all of the SMTP mailers are configured, and so are the prog and local mailers. An examination of the P parameter in the Mlocal line also shows that *procmail* is being used as the local mailer, which verifies the effect of the *local_procmail* feature. Additionally, the P parameter shows that the path to this program matches the one configured by the PROCMAIL_MAILER_PATH define.

sendmail can also be tested by using the -bv command-line option. The -bv option processes an address through sendmail and displays the mail delivery triple for that address. For example:

```
# sendmail -bv tyler@example.com
tyler@example.com... deliverable: mailer esmtp, host example.com, user
tyler@example.com
```

This example clearly shows the mailer, host, and user address of the mail delivery triple. In this case, the mail will be addressed to *tyler@example.com*, sent to the host *example.com* for delivery, and sent to that host using the esmtp mailer.

When a -bv test is run with an address that is directly delivered by the local host, it has the added benefit of applying aliasing to that address and of verifying if the address is deliverable. Here are some examples:

```
# sendmail -bv craig
craig... deliverable: mailer local, user craig
# sendmail bv fred
fred... User unknown
# sendmail -bv admin
anna@crab.wrotethebook.com... deliverable: mailer esmtp, host crab.wrotethebook.com.,
user anna@crab.wrotethebook.com
andy@rodent.wrotethebook.com... deliverable: mailer esmtp, host rodent.wrotethebook.
com., user andy@rodent.wrotethebook.com
jane@rodent.wrotethebook.com... deliverable: mailer esmtp, host rodent.wrotethebook.
com., user jane@rodent.wrotethebook.com
```

The first test shows that *craig* is a local username deliverable through the local mailer. The second test shows that *fred* is not a valid local username. The final test shows that *admin* is expanded by aliasing into three addresses that are forwarded via the esmtp mailer to remote systems for delivery. There are other commands, such as praliases, which allow you to examine the *aliases* file, but sendmail -bv is the best for seeing exactly how aliasing affects a local delivery address.

Both the -bt and -bv arguments show how the local copy of sendmail handles mail. To examine the interaction with a remote system, sendmail can be used to deliver mail with the verbose (-v) option set. For example:

```
$ sendmail -v craig@wrotethebook.com < test.msg
craig@wrotethebook.com... Connecting to chef.wrotethebook.com. via esmtp...
220 chef.wrotethebook.com ESMTP Sendmail 8.12.4/8.12.4; Sat, 2 Aug 2003 16:57:35 -
0400
>>> EHLO rodent.wrotethebook.com
250-chef.wrotethebook.com Hello rodent.wrotethebook.com [192.168.0.3], pleased to
meet you
250-ENHANCEDSTATUSCODES
250-PIPELINING
250-EXPN
250-VERB
250-8BITMIME
```

```
250-SIZE
250-DSN
250-ETRN
250-DELIVERBY
250 HELP
>>> MAIL From:<craig@rodent.wrotethebook.com> SIZE=26
250 2.1.0 <craig@rodent.wrotethebook.com>... Sender ok
>>> RCPT To:<craig@wrotethebook.com>
550 5.7.1 <craig@wrotethebook.com>... Relaying denied
>>> RSET
250 2.0.0 Reset state
/home/craig/dead.letter... Saved message in /home/craig/dead.letter
Closing connection to chef.wrotethebook.com.
>>> QUIT
221 2.0.0 chef.wrotethebook.com closing connection
```

Testing sendmail with the -v argument is useful when you want to see the entire protocol interaction. Notice, however, that in the test above there is a "Relaying denied" error message in the line that begins with the code 550. If the real point of this test was to check the recipient address against the remote host, you might not want to see the entire protocol interaction. In that case, using *telnet* to connect to the SMTP port of the remote system might be a better test tool. For example:

```
$ telnet chef.wrotethebook.com smtp
Trying 192.168.0.8...
Connected to chef.wrotethebook.com.
Escape character is '^]'.
220 chef.wrotethebook.com ESMTP Sendmail 8.12.9/8.12.9; Sat, 2 Aug 2003 16:57:35 -
0400
HELO rodent.wrotethebook.com
250-chef.wrotethebook.com Hello rodent.wrotethebook.com [192.168.0.3], pleased to
meet you
MAIL From:<craig@rodent.wrotethebook.com>
250 2.1.0 <craig@rodent.wrotethebook.com>... Sender ok
RCPT To:<craig@wrotethebook.com>
550 5.7.1 <craig@wrotethebook.com>... Relaying denied
QUIT
221 2.0.0 chef.wrotethebook.com closing connection
Connection closed by foreign host.
```

Using *telnet*, you can go directly to the specific protocol interaction that you wish to test.

It is important to test sendmail thoroughly before deploying a new configuration. In this book, we use all of the test methods described here.

See Also

The *sendmail* book covers the -bt option in Chapter 8, the -bv option in section 15.7.15, and the -v option in section 15.7.45.

1.10 Logging sendmail

Problem

Debugging a problem in the sendmail configuration may require more detailed information than sendmail logs by default.

Solution

Use the LogLevel option, either on the sendmail command line using the -O flag or in the sendmail configuration using the confLOG_LEVEL define, to increase the LogLevel above the default level of 9.

If the confLOG_LEVEL define is used, rebuild and reinstall *sendmail.cf*, and restart sendmail, as described in Recipe 1.8.

Discussion

sendmail logs messages through *syslog* using the *mail* facility. Where the messages are logged is determined by the *syslog.conf* file. A grep of *syslog.conf* shows where the sendmail messages are logged on our sample Linux system:

```
$ grep mail /etc/syslog.conf
# Log anything (except mail) of level info or higher.
*.info;mail.none;authpriv.none;cron.none          /var/log/messages
# Log all the mail messages in one place.
mail.*                                            /var/log/maillog
```

Disregarding the comments, there are two lines in this particular *syslog.conf* file that mention the *mail* facility. The first line has a wildcard character in the facility field, meaning that it applies to every *syslog* facility. At first glance, you might think this applies to sendmail messages until you notice mail.none, which means that no messages from the *mail* facility will be logged in */var/log/messages*. */var/log/maillog* is the place to look for sendmail log entries on this sample Linux system. The mail.* entry means that, no matter what the level, all messages from the *mail* facility are logged in */var/log/maillog*. Of course, this *syslog.conf* file is specific to our sample system. Your file might look different and, even if it looks exactly like this one, you can change it in anyway that you wish. You completely control where sendmail logs messages.

The *syslog.conf* file controls where sendmail messages are logged. The sendmail LogLevel option controls what is logged. The default sendmail LogLevel is 9, which is roughly equivalent to the *syslog* level *info*. Increasing the value of LogLevel increases the amount of data that sendmail logs. The meaningful LogLevel values are:

0

    Log a limited number of severe problems, such as failing to find the system's hostname or qualified domain name.

1

Log serious system failures using *syslog crit* and *alert* levels.

2

Log networking failures at *crit* level.

3

Log connection timeouts, malformed addresses, and forward and include errors using *notice* and *error syslog* levels.

4

Log connection rejections, bad *qf* filenames, and outdated *aliases* databases using *info* and *notice* levels.

5

Log envelope cloning, and log an entry for each message received. These log entries are made at the *syslog info* level.

6

Log a record of each message returned to the original sender, and log incoming SMTP VRFY, EXPN, and ETRN commands using the *info* level.

7

Log delivery failures at the *info* level.

8

Log successful deliveries and alias database rebuilds at the *syslog notice* level.

9

Log mail deferred because of lack of system resources at the *info* level.

10

Log inbound SMTP connections and MILTER connects and replies. Log each database lookup. Log AUTH and STARTTLS errors. All of these messages are logged at *info* level. Also log TLS errors at *syslog warning* level.

11

Log end of processing, and log NIS errors. Log both types of messages at *info* level.

12

Log outbound SMTP connections at *info* level.

13

Log questionable file security, such as world-writable files and bad user shells.

14

Log connection refusals. Log additional STARTTLS information. Log both types of messages at *info* level.

15

Log all incoming SMTP commands at *info* level.

16–98

Log debugging information at *debug* level. This data is mostly suitable for code developers.

Setting LogLevel causes all levels below the specified number to also be logged. Thus the default LogLevel of 9 also logs all of the messages described for levels 1 through 8. Each LogLevel adds more detail while continuing to log the messages of the lower LogLevel settings.

LogLevel can be set inside the sendmail configuration using the confLOG_LEVEL define. For example:

```
define(`confLOG_Level', `14')
```

However, it is often only necessary to increase LogLevel for a short time or for a single test run. This can be done by defining LogLevel on the sendmail command line using the -O argument. Here is an example:

```
# sendmail -O LogLevel=14 -bs -Am
```

This example runs sendmail from the command line. The -Am argument, which does not apply to sendmail versions before 8.12, ensures that sendmail runs as an MTA—this argument is the opposite of the -Ac option discussed earlier in this chapter. The -bs argument allows you to manually input the SMTP commands in a manner similar to the telnet tests used in the previous recipe. The -O argument allows you to set the LogLevel from the command line. A command such as this might be used to log the effect of specific SMTP interactions.

Both techniques for setting LogLevel work well. The technique you use depends on the circumstances and your preference.

See Also

The *sendmail* book covers logging in section 14.3 and LogLevel in section 24.9.56.

## CHAPTER 2

Delivery and Forwarding

2.0 Introduction

Inbound mail is either delivered directly to the addressee or relayed to another mail host for delivery. Mail is directly delivered only if it is destined for the local host; mail destined for any other host is relayed. In this chapter, we look at ways to properly configure sendmail to deliver mail locally and forward it to other systems.

Delivery is a multistep process. First, sendmail must process the host portion of the delivery address and recognize that the mail is, in fact, addressed to the local host. If it isn't addressed to the local host, it is relayed as described in Chapter 3. If it is addressed to the local host, the user portion of the address is processed against the *aliases* file to determine the proper delivery address. If the *aliases* file returns an external address, the mail is forwarded to the external host for delivery. If it returns the address of a local mailbox, sendmail checks for a *.forward* file. If the *.forward* file exists, the mail is delivered as specified by that file. Otherwise, the mail is delivered to the local mailbox. Figure 2-1 illustrates this delivery flow.[*]

sendmail processes each delivery address through the canonify ruleset and through the parse ruleset—rulesets 3 and 0. Aliasing starts when the result of that process tells sendmail to deliver the mail through a mailer that has the A flag set.[†] If ruleset 0 returns the name of a mailer that does not have the A flag set, aliasing is not done. While the A flag can be set for any mailer, only the cyrus mailers and the local mailer set the A flag by default. For our discussion of aliasing, we'll use the local mailer as an example.

Aliasing first looks up the delivery address in the *aliases* database. If the lookup returns a different email address, the new address is processed. If the mailer used for the new address has the A flag set, that address is looked up in the *aliases* database.

---

[*] This is a simplified description based on the default configuration. sendmail flags and options can change the way mail delivery is handled.

[†] Flags are set through the F parameter in each *sendmail.cf* mailer definition.

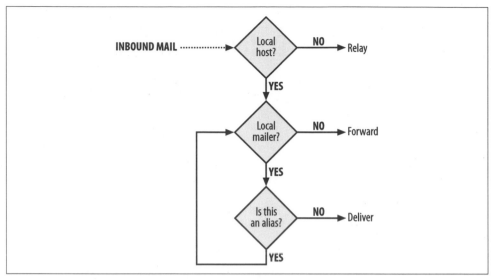

Figure 2-1. The multistep delivery process

This process continues until no new address is returned by the alias lookup. If the mailer used for the final address returned by the *aliases* database has the w flag set, sendmail looks for a delivery address in the user's *.forward* file. By default, only the local mailer has the w flag set. If a *.forward* file is found, delivery is made based on the delivery address that it contains.

Although Figure 2-1 portrays a simplified version of the actual delivery process, it does highlight areas of the configuration that relate to local delivery and forwarding. Class $=w must be properly configured. The *aliases* file must be created and made into a database, and, if used, the *.forward* files must be properly configured.

sendmail only accepts mail for local delivery that is addressed to the local host. All other mail is relayed. Class $=w contains all of the valid hostnames for the local host. If the hostname from the delivery address is found in class $=w, the mail is accepted for local delivery. In fact, ruleset 0 uses class $=w when selecting the local mailer.

Mail delivered by the local mailer must be addressed to a user account that exists on the local host or to an alias that resolves to a valid delivery address. The *aliases* database frees the local mailer from the limitation of having all local mail addressed to actual usernames. It makes sendmail a more flexible system by allowing mail addressed to a single alias to be sent to multiple recipients or mail addressed to several different names to be routed to a single recipient. The *aliases* database is also used to forward mail to other computers, programs, and files.

The *aliases* database is so essential to the functioning of a sendmail system that sendmail complains if the database does not exist. Some users and programs that send out email alerts may also complain because they assume that certain aliases exist.

Additionally, if neither the *aliases* database nor the *aliases* text file is found, send-mail will not apply the user's *.forward* file.

When sendmail looks up a local address in the *aliases* database and no new recipient address is returned by the lookup, sendmail checks to see if the user identified by the local address has a *.forward* file. The possible locations of the user's *.forward* file are defined in the *sendmail.cf* file by the ForwardPath option:

```
$ grep ForwardPath sendmail.cf
O ForwardPath=$z/.forward.$w+$h:$z/.forward+$h:$z/.forward.$w:$z/.forward
```

The path shown above was configured by the confFORWARD_PATH define in the *domain/generic.m4* file used in the sample configuration described in Recipe 1.8. The ForwardPath in this example includes three *sendmail.cf* macros. The $z macro holds the path of the recipient's home directory, as specified in */etc/passwd*. The $w macro holds the primary name of the local host. The $h macro normally holds the name of the recipient host when ruleset 0 constructs the mailer/host/user delivery triple. In this case, however, the mailer is the local mailer so the host is always the local host. This makes the $h macro available for other uses. *procmail* provides one example of how the $h macro can be used in other ways. For example, when the *user+detail* addressing syntax is used and *procmail* is used as the local mailer, the $h macro contains the *detail* value.[*]

Given this specific ForwardPath, if the local mailer is *procmail*, the hostname is *chef*, and the mail is addressed to *kathy+cookbook*, the following *.forward* files are searched: */home/kathy/.forward.chef+cookbook*, */home/kathy/.forward+cookbook*, */home/kathy/.forward.chef*, and */home/kathy/.forward*. Each file is looked for in order, and the search stops as soon as a file with the specified name is found.

Both the *aliases* database and *.forward* files are capable of forwarding mail. Forwarding and relaying are often confused, particularly when mail is forwarded to an external host. When it is, the effect is essentially the same as relaying to that host—mail is passed to an external system for delivery. The difference is this: mail is forwarded only after it has been accepted for local delivery; mail is relayed when it is not accepted for local delivery. Relaying is covered in Chapter 3.

2.1 Accepting Mail for Other Hosts

Problem

You must configure sendmail to accept mail for local delivery that is addressed to other hosts. A common reason for doing this is to configure a mail exchanger to accept mail for a domain or for individual hosts.

---

[*] In the configuration created in Recipe 1.8, *procmail* is used as the local mailer because the *linux.m4* file used in that configuration contains the *local_procmail* feature.

Solution

Create an */etc/mail/local-host-names* file. Put into that file the hostnames and domain names for which sendmail should accept mail for local delivery. Enter the names with one hostname or domain name per line.

Add the *use_cw_file* feature to the sendmail configuration to make use of the newly created *local-host-names* file. Here are sample lines that could be added to the configuration, if it does not already contain the *use_cw_file* feature:

```
dnl Load class $=w with other names for the local host
FEATURE(`use_cw_file')
```

Finally, rebuild the *sendmail.cf* file, copy the new *sendmail.cf* file to */etc/mail*, and restart sendmail, as shown in Recipe 1.8.

Discussion

Mail addressed to one host can be routed to another host for a variety of reasons: forwarding, relaying, *mailertable* entries, and so on. One common reason for routing mail in this manner is because DNS says to do so. A system sending mail routes the mail based on information obtained from DNS. Mail is addressed to some hostname. The remote system takes that hostname and asks DNS if it has mail exchange (MX) records for that host. If no MX record is found for a given host, the address record of the host is obtained from DNS, and the mail is sent directly to the host. If DNS returns MX records, the remote system sends the mail to the system with the lowest preference number listed on the MX record.

Regardless of why the mail is routed to your mail host, the sendmail system must be configured to accept the mail or it will generate a *Relaying denied* error. This is an interesting error because the remote system is not necessarily trying to relay mail; it may be attempting to deliver the mail to the mail exchanger as directed by DNS. However, sendmail only accepts inbound mail for delivery that is addressed to the local system. All other mail is relayed. For local delivery, sendmail accepts mail that is addressed to another host only if it finds the name of that host in class $=w. Class $=w is an array that contains all of the names that sendmail considers valid for local mail delivery.

There are three ways to load names into class $=w. The recommended method for solving this problem is to use the *use_cw_file* feature. Two alternatives are also discussed: placing local hostnames directly in *sendmail.cf* itself or using the *bestmx_is_local* feature.

Using the use_cw_file feature

The *use_cw_file* feature directs sendmail to load the */etc/mail/local-host-names* file into class $=w. It does this by placing the following F command in the *sendmail.cf* file:[*]

```
Fw/etc/mail/local-host-names
```

Once the *use_cw_file* feature is added to the configuration, sendmail expects to find the *local-host-names* file and displays a nonfatal error message when it doesn't. It is possible to configure sendmail to treat *local-host-names* as an optional file by placing the following define in the configuration *before* the *use_cw_file* feature:

```
define(`confCW_FILE', `-o /etc/mail/local-host-names')
```

The -o flag makes the file optional, which stops sendmail from complaining if the file is not found. The confCW_FILE define can also be used to set a different pathname for the *local-host-names* file, if you decide to place the file in another directory or give it another name. Don't change the pathname unless you absolutely must. Use default pathnames for files whenever possible; it makes it easier for others to find these files when maintaining your system.

Frankly, there is little reason to make the *local-host-names* file optional; in fact, making it optional can hide real errors, such as an error opening the file. If you're not ready to add hostnames to the file, simply create an empty file. But, in all likelihood, if you add the *use_cw_file* feature to your configuration, it is because you have hostnames that you want to add to the *local-host-names* file. As an example, let's create a *local-host-names* file for our sample system that contains the following lines:

```
wrotethebook.com
horseshoe.wrotethebook.com
```

After creating the *local-host-names* file and building the new *sendmail.cf* file, use the -bt option to test the new configuration. First, run sendmail -bt to examine the contents of the class $=w array:

```
# sendmail -bt -C./sendmail.cf
ADDRESS TEST MODE (ruleset 3 NOT automatically invoked)
Enter <ruleset> <address>
> $=w
chef
localhost.localdomain
localhost
[192.168.0.8]
[127.0.0.1]
[chef.wrotethebook.com]
horseshoe.wrotethebook.com
wrotethebook.com
chef.wrotethebook.com
> /quit
```

---

[*] The generic Linux configuration created in Recipe 1.8 specifies the *use_cw_file* feature in the *domain/generic.m4* file. If the feature is already defined, it does not need to be added.

This test shows that the *horseshoe.wrotethebook.com* and the *wrotethebook.com* values stored in the *local-host-names* file are added to class $=w. It also shows that several other values are stored in this array. These values are all of the hostnames, hostname aliases, and IP addresses assigned to this host that sendmail discovered by probing the various network interfaces. The hostnames associated with the interface addresses are obtained from both the */etc/hosts* file and from DNS.*

 Limit the interface probing done by sendmail by adding the following define to the sendmail configuration:

```
define(`confDONT_PROBE_INTERFACES', `true')
```

When this define is used, only the hostnames assigned to the system in the */etc/hosts* file and in DNS, and the system's primary IP address are used as starting values for class $=w. This define is not used when you want to accept mail addressed to any of your server's interfaces as local mail. However, the confDONT_PROBE_INTERFACES define is very useful when probing the interfaces gives sendmail erroneous information or when a large number of virtual interfaces are used.

Mail addressed to any hostname defined in class $=w is delivered by the local mailer. The $=w output shown above tells us that this system will deliver mail addressed to *chef*, *localhost*, *horseshoe*, or *wrotethebook.com* using the local mailer. A second test, this time using sendmail -bv, verifies this:

```
# hostname
chef
# sendmail -bv alana@crab.wrotethebook.com
alana@crab.wrotethebook.com... deliverable: mailer esmtp, host crab.wrotethebook.com.
, user alana@crab.wrotethebook.com
# sendmail -bv payton@horseshoe.wrotethebook.com
payton@horseshoe.wrotethebook.com... deliverable: mailer local, user payton
```

The hostname command shows that the local host is *chef* to illustrate that none of this mail is actually addressed to the local host. The sendmail -bv command verifies a delivery address and shows the mailer that will be used to deliver the mail. The first -bv test shows that mail addresses to *crab* will be delivered over the network using the esmtp mailer. This is just what you would expect because *crab* is an external system. Yet the second -bv test shows that mail addressed to *horseshoe*, another external system, will be delivered using the local mailer. Mail addressed to *horseshoe* is treated as if it were addressed to *chef*. This is because *horseshoe* is defined in the *local-host-names* file, and the configuration uses the *use_cw_file* feature to add hostnames from that file to class $=w. This test shows that the system is properly configured to handle mail addressed to *horseshoe* as if it were local mail.

---

* The hostname *localhost.localdomain* is a value that Red Hat puts in the */etc/hosts* file for the loopback address (127.0.0.1).

Using sendmail.cf directly

The *use_cw_file* feature works well, and it is the recommended solution for this problem, but there are alternative solutions. For example, placing local hostnames in *sendmail.cf* itself or using the *bestmx_is_local* feature. The sample *local-host-names* file created earlier in this section contained only two lines. Such a small number of names could be placed directly inside of *sendmail.cf* by using the following two lines instead of the *use_cw_file* feature:

```
LOCAL_DOMAIN('wrotethebook.com')
LOCAL_DOMAIN('horseshoe.wrotethebook.com')
```

This alternative solution, however, is more difficult to maintain as the list of clients grows. Every time a LOCAL_DOMAIN macro is added to the configuration, the *sendmail.cf* file must be rebuilt, tested, and moved to the */etc/mail* directory. When the *local-host-names* file is used, there is no need to rebuild *sendmail.cf* just because the *local-host-names* file has been edited.

Using the bestmx_is_local feature

The *bestmx_is_local* feature works well if the only reason that hostnames are being added to the *local-host-names* file is because the local host is a mail exchanger. Mail addressed to any system that lists the local host as its preferred mail exchanger is accepted as local mail when the *bestmx_is_local* feature is used. To use this approach, put the following line in the configuration:

```
FEATURE(`bestmx_is_local', `wrotethebook.com')
```

The great advantage of the *bestmx_is_local* feature is that it is easy—there is no *local-host-names* file to maintain. However, that simplicity is also a disadvantage because control over what mail is accepted as local by your system is given to someone else—the domain administrator. The potential problems caused by this lack of control are limited by using an optional domain list in the sample command. Adding the `wrotethebook.com' argument to the *bestmx_is_local* feature means that only MX records from that domain are accepted as proof that a host is a valid client. If the optional domain list is not specified for the *bestmx_is_local* feature, any domain in the world can control the mail your system accepts as local simply by putting in an MX record that points to your host, which creates an opportunity for abuse.

Another potential problem with the *bestmx_is_local* solution is that it increases the processing overhead for each piece of mail. This would not be a problem for our small sample system, but it could be a problem for any system that deals with a high volume of mail.

One other limitation of the *bestmx_is_local* solution is that it depends completely on MX records. *bestmx_is_local* works for a mail exchanger because all of the hostnames it handles have MX records; however, it is possible to have other reasons to accept mail as local mail. The *local-host-names* file can store any hostnames that you wish; it is not limited to hosts that define your system as their mail exchanger. *local-host-names* is fast, flexible, and completely under your control. For those reasons, we chose the *use_cw_file* feature as the preferred solution for this problem.

See Also

The *sendmail* book covers *use_cw_file*, `confCW_FILE`, and `LOCAL_DOMAIN` in 4.8.48; *bestmx_is_local* in 4.8.7; and `confDONT_PROBE_INTERFACES` in 24.9.39.

2.2   Fixing the Alias0 Missing Map Error and Creating Simple Aliases

Problem

sendmail displays the following error message:

```
hash map "Alias0": missing map file /etc/mail/aliases.db: No such file or directory
```

Solution

Create a text file named */etc/mail/aliases* and populate that file with entries in the form of:

```
alias: recipient
```

where `alias` is an alias username and `recipient` is the address to which mail addressed to the alias is delivered.

Run *newaliases* to process the text file and build the *aliases* database file required by sendmail:

```
# newaliases
```

Discussion

No *m4* configuration commands are needed to access the *aliases* database. Any basic sendmail configuration should work.

Most systems come with an *aliases* database. All you need to do is add the aliases that you desire to the existing *aliases* text file and run the *newaliases* command. However, if your system displays the "missing map file" error shown in the problem description, you either do not have an *aliases* database or the one you have is placed in the wrong directory. In either case, you need to put a valid *aliases* database in the proper path. If your system does not have an *aliases* file, use one from a similar system or the sample *aliases* file from the *sendmail* directory of the sendmail distribution as a starting point. If the file you have is in the wrong path, move it or change the sendmail configuration to point to the place where you keep the *aliases* database.

Some older systems store the *aliases* database in the */etc* directory. To keep it in that directory, add the following `ALIAS_FILE` define to the *sendmail.mc* file:

```
define(`ALIAS_FILE', `/etc/aliases')
```

The `ALIAS_FILE` define can accept various flags. You can make the *aliases* database optional using the -o flag exactly as it was used in Recipe 2.1 with the `confCW_FILE` define. However, this is not a good idea. The -o flag prevents sendmail from displaying the "missing map file" error, but it does not stop sendmail from turning off aliasing when it cannot find an *aliases* file (i.e., it hides the error but does not fix the problem).

Instead of changing the default path or hiding the error with an `ALIAS_FILE` define, place the *aliases* text file in the */etc/mail* directory. This is probably the best solution for most versions of Unix because */etc/mail* is the default directory where most administrators expect to find this file. The following example moves the *aliases* text file and runs *newaliases* to solve the "missing map file" problem:

```
# sendmail -bv ftp
hash map "Alias0": missing map file /etc/mail/aliases.db: No such file or directory
ftp... deliverable: mailer local, user ftp
# mv aliases /etc/mail/aliases
# sendmail -bv ftp
hash map "Alias0": missing map file /etc/mail/aliases.db: No such file or directory
root... deliverable: mailer local, user root
# newaliases
/etc/mail/aliases: 40 aliases, longest 10 bytes, 395 bytes total
# sendmail -bv ftp
root... deliverable: mailer local, user root
```

The *mv* command and the *newaliases* command solve the problem. The three sendmail -bv ftp lines are used to show the effect of the *mv* and *newaliases* commands. The first -bv command shows the error message that we expect, and it shows that mail addressed to *ftp* will be sent to username *ftp* via the local mailer. After the *mv* command is executed, the second -bv command again shows the error message because we have not yet built the *aliases* database from the *aliases* text file. However, this time the -bv command shows that mail addressed to *ftp* will be delivered to the *root* user account via the local mailer. Clearly something has happened, and that something is aliasing. sendmail used the *aliases* text file to find that the correct delivery address for the *ftp* alias is *root*. Finally, *newaliases* is executed to build the database, and the last -bv test is run. This time there is no error, and we are again told the mail will be delivered to *root* via the local mailer. The output of the *newaliases* command says that *newaliases* processed 40 aliases.

The three sendmail -bv tests show exactly how sendmail handles the *aliases* files. If sendmail can find the *aliases* database, it uses it. If no *aliases* database is found, sendmail displays an error and checks for the *aliases* text file. If it finds the text file, sendmail uses it. If neither the database nor the text file can be found, sendmail turns off aliasing.

Entries from the sample Red Hat *aliases* file are shown below:

```
# Basic system aliases -- these MUST be present.
mailer-daemon:  postmaster
postmaster:     root

# General redirections for pseudo accounts.
bin:            root
daemon:         root
adm:            root
lp:             root
sync:           root
shutdown:       root
halt:           root
mail:           root
news:           root
ftp:            root

# trap decode to catch security attacks
decode:         root

# Person who should get root's mail
#root:          marc
```

Lines that begin with a hash mark (#) are comments and can be ignored. The active entries begin with an alias and a colon that is followed by the recipient address. Notice that the recipient can be another alias. For example, *mailer-daemon* points to *postmaster*, which is really an alias for *root*. A -bv test shows the effect of this double alias:

```
$ sendmail -bv mailer-daemon
root... deliverable: mailer local, user root
```

Most of the entries in the sample Red Hat *aliases* file route mail addressed to non-login system accounts to the *root* user. No one actually logs in as *root*, yet all of the mail addressed to system accounts is routed to the *root* account. Notice the last comment in the sample *aliases* file is a commented-out alias for *root*. Remove the hash mark from the beginning of this line and change the recipient field to the user ID of the administrator's login account to route mail addressed to *root* to someplace where it will be read. Here is an example:

```
# Person who should get root's mail
root:           logan
```

In this example, the administrator logs in to the *logan* account to read *root*'s mail. A sendmail –bv command shows the effect of this alias:

```
# sendmail -bv bin
logan... deliverable: mailer local, user logan
```

sendmail first looks up *bin* and finds that it points to *root*. It then looks up *root* and finds that it points to *logan*. *logan* is not an alias, so delivery is made to the *logan* account. In this case, the aliases were nested two levels deep. By default, sendmail will search up to 10 levels of nested aliases and then display the following error if the alias does not resolve to a delivery address:

```
aliasing/forwarding loop broken (11 aliases deep; 10 max)
aliasing/forwarding loop broken
```

Add the confMAX_ALIAS_RECURSION define to the sendmail configuration to change the depth to which sendmail will search nested aliases; for example:

```
define(confMAX_ALIAS_RECURSION, 5)
```

The line shown above reduces recursion to a maximum of five nested aliases. However, there is usually no good reason to change the default provided by sendmail. Reducing the amount of recursion doesn't enhance performance because the only time the maximum amount of recursion is reached is on those rare occasions that you have created an alias loop. You never want more recursion because if you need more than 10 levels of nesting you have designed your aliases incorrectly, which impacts sendmail's performance. As with most sendmail defines, the default value is the best.

You can control alias recursion for individual aliases without using an *m4* macro or changing the *sendmail.cf* file. Force aliasing to stop at a specific alias by placing a backslash in front of the recipient address for that alias. For example:

```
bin:            \root
```

This is a contrived example. Of course, you don't really want to deliver mail to the *root* account. However, this contrived example works well to illustrate the impact of the backslash because the specific recursion of *bin* to *root* to *logan* is described just a few paragraphs back. Rerunning the sendmail -bv test after this alias is inserted in the *aliases* database shows the following result:

```
# sendmail -bv bin
\root... deliverable: mailer local, user \root
```

Here the *bin* alias resolves to *root* and aliasing terminates—sendmail does not go on to resolve *root* to *logan*. Usually, this type of recipient address is used in combination with the mail being copied to a file or forwarded to a program, and it is most commonly found in the *.forward* file instead of the *aliases* file. It is used in a *.forward* file in Recipe 2.9.

After creating the *aliases* text file, run *newaliases* to build the *aliases* database. The *aliases* database is actually built by sendmail; *newaliases* is really a symbolic link to the sendmail program and is equivalent to the sendmail command with the -bi flag.

See Also

Recipe 2.3 is a related recipe that shows how aliases can be read from an LDAP server. The *sendmail* book covers the *aliases* database in Chapter 12.

2.3   Reading Aliases via LDAP

Problem

When your organization stores aliases on an LDAP server, you need to configure sendmail to read aliases from the LDAP server.

Solution

Use `sendmail -bt -d0.1` to check the sendmail compiler options. If sendmail was not compiled with LDAP support, recompile and reinstall sendmail as described in Recipe 1.3.

If the LDAP server has not yet been configured to support sendmail queries, copy the *sendmail.schema* file to the appropriate location on the LDAP server and update the server configuration to use the schema file. Recipe 1.3 covers the necessary LDAP server configuration.

Once the LDAP server is configured to support the sendmail schema, add sendmail aliases to the LDAP database using the format defined by that schema. When OpenLDAP is used, this is done by first creating an LDIF file containing the LDAP records and then running *ldapadd* to add these records to the LDAP database. The Discussion section shows an example of doing this for alias records.

On the sendmail system, add an `ALIAS_FILE` define, containing the string `ldap:`, to the sendmail configuration. Also add a `confLDAP_CLUSTER` define containing the same value as the `sendmailMTACluster` attribute used in the entries added to the LDAP server. Here is an example of these configuration commands:

```
# Set the LDAP cluster value
define(`confLDAP_CLUSTER', `wrotethebook.com')
# Tell sendmail that aliases are available via LDAP
define(`ALIAS_FILE', `ldap:')
```

Build the sendmail configuration file, copy it to */etc/mail/sendmail.cf*, and restart sendmail with the new configuration, as described in Recipe 1.8.

Discussion

This recipe provides instructions for both the sendmail administrator and the LDAP administrator because the LDAP server must be properly installed, configured, and running, and it must include the sendmail schema in order to understand and properly process queries from sendmail. Nothing in this recipe will work without the close cooperation of the LDAP administrator. In fact, the bulk of the configuration takes place on the LDAP server. You should have some experience with LDAP before attempting to use it with sendmail.

To add sendmail aliases to the LDAP database, start by building an LDIF file formatted according to the sendmail schema. Here is an example that adds the *mailer-daemon*, *postmaster*, and *root* aliases from Recipe 2.2 to the LDAP database:

```
# cat > ldap-aliases
dn: sendmailMTAKey=mailer-daemon, dc=wrotethebook, dc=com
objectClass: sendmailMTA
objectClass: sendmailMTAAlias
objectClass: sendmailMTAAliasObject
sendmailMTAAliasGrouping: aliases
sendmailMTACluster: wrotethebook.com
sendmailMTAKey: mailer-daemon
sendmailMTAAliasValue: postmaster

dn: sendmailMTAKey=postmaster, dc=wrotethebook, dc=com
objectClass: sendmailMTA
objectClass: sendmailMTAAlias
objectClass: sendmailMTAAliasObject
sendmailMTAAliasGrouping: aliases
sendmailMTACluster: wrotethebook.com
sendmailMTAKey: postmaster
sendmailMTAAliasValue: root

dn: sendmailMTAKey=root, dc=wrotethebook, dc=com
objectClass: sendmailMTA
objectClass: sendmailMTAAlias
objectClass: sendmailMTAAliasObject
sendmailMTAAliasGrouping: aliases
sendmailMTACluster: wrotethebook.com
sendmailMTAKey: root
sendmailMTAAliasValue: logan
Ctrl-D
# ldapadd -x -D "cn=Manager,dc=wrotethebook,dc=com" \
> -W -f ldap-aliases
Enter LDAP Password: SecretLDAPpassword
adding new entry "sendmailMTAKey=mailer-daemon, dc=wrotethebook, dc=com"
adding new entry "sendmailMTAKey=postmaster, dc=wrotethebook, dc=com"
adding new entry "sendmailMTAKey=root, dc=wrotethebook, dc=com"
```

The example just shown names the LDIF file *ldap-aliases*. Running the *ldapadd* command adds these entries to the LDAP database. A quick check with the *ldapsearch* command shows the newly added records:

```
# ldapsearch -x '(objectclass=sendmailMTAAlias)' \
> sendmailMTAKey sendmailMTAAliasValue
version: 2
#
# filter: (objectclass=sendmailMTAAlias)
# requesting: sendmailMTAKey sendmailMTAAliasValue
#
# mailer-daemon, wrotethebook, com
dn: sendmailMTAKey=mailer-daemon, dc=wrotethebook, dc=com
sendmailMTAKey: mailer-daemon
sendmailMTAAliasValue: postmaster
```

```
# postmaster, wrotethebook, com
dn: sendmailMTAKey=postmaster, dc=wrotethebook, dc=com
sendmailMTAKey: postmaster
sendmailMTAAliasValue: root

# root, wrotethebook, com
dn: sendmailMTAKey=root, dc=wrotethebook, dc=com
sendmailMTAKey: root
sendmailMTAAliasValue: logan

# search result
search: 2
result: 0 Success

# numResponses: 4
# numEntries: 3
```

Notice that this *ldapsearch* command works without either an -h or a -b argument. (-h defines the LDAP server name and -b defines the LDAP default base distinguished name.) This test works without these arguments because the correct LDAP server hostname and base distinguished name are defined in the *ldap.conf* file. If those *ldap.conf* values are not correct for the sendmail query, provide the correct -h and -b values on the *ldapsearch* command line. If you must provide -h and -b values to *ldapsearch* to successfully run this test, the sendmail administrator must provide the same values to sendmail. Use the confLDAP_DEFAULT_SPEC define to set -h and -b values for sendmail. See Recipe 5.9 for an example of how confLDAP_DEFAULT_SPEC is used.

The *ldapsearch* test shows that the LDAP server is now ready to answer sendmail's queries for aliases. sendmail must also be properly prepared to work with LDAP. sendmail must be compiled with LDAP support, as described in Recipe 1.3, and it must have the correct configuration. In most cases, adding two defines to a basic sendmail configuration is all that is required to configure sendmail to read aliases via LDAP. The two defines are:

```
define(`confLDAP_CLUSTER', `wrotethebook.com')
define(`ALIAS_FILE', `ldap:')
```

ALIAS_FILE defines the location of the *aliases* database. Instead of providing a file path as the argument for the ALIAS_FILE define, the example provides the string ldap:, which tells sendmail to read aliases from the LDAP server using the standard sendmail schema. The ALIAS_FILE define just shown is equivalent to:

```
define(`ALIAS_FILE', `ldap: -k (&(objectClass=sendmailMTAAliasObject)
(sendmailMTAAliasGrouping=aliases) (|(sendmailMTACluster=${sendmailMTACluster})
(sendmailMTAHost=$j)) (sendmailMTAKey=%0)) -v sendmailMTAAliasValue')
```

The expanded command shows the search key, which is defined by the -k argument, and the return value, which is defined by the -v argument. The return value is easy to understand, it is the value stored in the sendmailMTAAliasValue attribute. The search key is more complex; however, it is the same search criteria syntax used with the *ldapsearch* command, which is something all LDAP administrators are familiar with.

The tricky part is that the key combines basic LDAP search criteria with sendmail macros. ${sendmailMTACluster} holds the value defined by confLDAP_CLUSTER in the master configuration file. $j returns the fully qualified name of the local host. In this case, %0 is the alias for which sendmail is searching. Put all together, this key searches for a record with:

- An objectClass of sendmailMTAAliasObject
- A sendmailMTAAliasGrouping of aliases
- Either a sendmailMTACluster matching the value defined by confLDAP_CLUSTER or a sendmailMTAHost attribute containing the name of the local host
- A sendmailMTAKey matching the desired alias

The effect of the search key can be easily simulated using the *ldapsearch* command:

```
# ldapsearch -LLL -x '(&(objectClass=sendmailMTAAliasObject) \
> (sendmailMTAAliasGrouping=aliases) \
> (|(sendmailMTACluster=wrotethebook.com) \
> (sendmailMTAHost=rodent.wrotethebook.com)) \
> (sendmailMTAKey=postmaster))' \
> sendmailMTAAliasValue
dn: sendmailMTAKey=postmaster, dc=wrotethebook, dc=com
sendmailMTAAliasValue: root
```

This *ldapsearch* command shows the key that sendmail would use to look up the *postmaster* alias when running on a host named *rodent.wrotethebook.com* with confLDAP_CLUSTER defined as *wrotethebook.com*. The value returned is *root*.

This recipe uses the confLDAP_CLUSTER define to set a value for ${sendmailMTACluster} because all of the entries added to the LDAP database in this recipe contain a sendmailMTACluster attribute. In order to match those LDAP records, sendmail queries must containing the correct ${sendmailMTACluster} value.

The alternative to using a cluster value is to have LDAP database entries defined for individual hosts. In that case, the LDAP entry does not use the sendmailMTACluster attribute. Instead, it uses the sendmailMTAHost attribute, and the value assigned to the attribute is the fully qualified hostname of a specific host. If you decide to create LDAP entries for individual hosts, the sendmailMTAHost attribute must be specified in each LDAP entry. But no special host value needs to be configured for sendmail because sendmail uses the value in $j. When the sendmailMTACluster attribute is not used on the LDAP records, the confLDAP_CLUSTER define is not required for the sendmail configuration. However, when the confLDAP_CLUSTER define is not used, sendmail can retrieve only those LDAP records that contain a sendmailMTAHost attribute that matches the value returned by $j.

The cluster value provides a way for a group of hosts to share common LDAP data. It is similar to a NIS domain. The sample confLDAP_CLUSTER define uses the DNS domain name as the cluster value. However, the cluster value is arbitrary and does not need to be a NIS or DNS domain name.

After configuring the LDAP server and the sendmail system, a test shows that aliases are successfully retrieved from the LDAP server. The effect of the aliases can be seen using the sendmail –bv command:

```
# sendmail -bv -Cgeneric-linux.cf mailer-daemon
root... deliverable: mailer local, user root
# sendmail -bv mailer-daemon
logan... deliverable: mailer local, user logan
```

This test shows the LDAP server in action. When the first test is run using the generic configuration, the *mailer-daemon* alias is resolved using the local *aliases* database because the generic configuration does not override the default ALIAS_FILE path. The second test uses the sendmail configuration created in this recipe, which points to the LDAP server. The *mailer-daemon* alias is resolved using the three records added to the LDAP database earlier in this section.

See Also

Refer to the other recipes in this chapter for descriptions of the various alias formats—all of which can be read from an LDAP server. For information on LDAP, see *Understanding and Deploying LDAP Directory Services* by Howes, Smith, and Good (Macmillan) and *LDAP System Administration* by Gerald Carter (O'Reilly). The *cf/ README* file covers this topic in the *Using LDAP for Aliases, Maps, and Classes* section. The *sendmail* book covers the ALIAS_FILE define in section 24.9.1 and the confLDAP_CLUSTER define in section 21.9.82.

2.4   Configuring Red Hat 7.3 to Read Aliases from a NIS Server

Problem

You want to use NIS to access the *aliases* database on a Red Hat 7.3 system.

Solution

Change to the */etc/mail* directory and create a *service.switch* file. Here is an example:

```
# cd /etc/mail
# cat - > service.switch
aliases nis files
hosts   dns files
passwd  files nis
```

Discussion

No *m4* configuration commands are needed to enable support for the *service.switch* file—it is available by default. The basic sendmail configuration already installed on your system will probably work with this file; the generic configuration discussed in Recipe 1.8 certainly will.

Network Information Service (NIS), developed by Sun Microsystems, makes many system administration databases available over the network. NIS allows an organization to centrally control and maintain important configuration files for all Unix clients. The *aliases* database is one of the files that can be centrally maintained and accessed through NIS.

A service switch file defines the sources for various system administration files and the order in which those sources should be queried. *service.switch* is the default filename that sendmail uses for a service switch file if the system does not have a service switch file that sendmail can use.* When running on a Red Hat Linux system, current versions of sendmail look for *service.switch* in the */etc/mail* directory; earlier versions looked for the file in the */etc* directory. The path to the sendmail service switch file can be changed using the confSERVICE_SWITCH_FILE define. However, it is generally easier to place the *service.switch* file in the */etc/mail* directory where sendmail, and most administrators, expect to find it.

The sendmail *service.switch* file is much shorter than the system's service switch file because sendmail is only interested in three types of system administration information: mail aliases, host information, and user information.

The *service.switch* file contains an entry for each type of information identified by the name of the file that traditionally provides the information: *aliases*, *hosts*, or *passwd*. The name is followed by the list of sources for that type of information. The aliases entry in the example is:

```
aliases nis files
```

NIS is listed first, meaning that sendmail will first attempt to resolve an alias via NIS and will only look the alias up in the local *aliases* file if NIS cannot resolve the alias. Thus, aliases that only exist in the local file will still be resolved, but aliases in the NIS map file will take precedence.

Several sources of information can be specified in the *service.switch* file:

files
> The local */etc/mail/aliases*, */etc/hosts*, and */etc/passwd* files.

nis
> NIS Version 2, which can be used for *aliases*, *hosts*, and *passwd* information.

---

* Red Hat 7.3 has a service switch file named */etc/nsswitch.conf*. However, as the manpage makes clear, the aliases entry in the *nsswitch.conf* file is ignored.

nisplus

> NIS Version 3, which can be used for *aliases*, *hosts*, and *passwd* information.

ldap

> LDAP can be used for *aliases*, *hosts*, and *passwd* information. Recipe 2.3 shows the correct way to read aliases from an LDAP server.

hesiod

> The Hesiod service can be used for *aliases*, *hosts*, and *passwd* information, but it is primarily used for *passwd* information.

dns

> DNS can be used for *hosts* information.

To use any of these services, your system must be able to act as a client for the service and must be properly configured. Configuring these services is beyond the scope of this book.

Wrapping some tests around our recipe shows the immediate impact of our solution:

```
# praliases bin
bin:craig
# ypmatch bin aliases
root
# sendmail -bv bin
craig... deliverable: mailer local, user craig
# cd /etc/mail
# cat - > service.switch
aliases nis files
hosts   dns files
passwd  files nis
Ctrl-D
# sendmail -bv bin
root... deliverable: mailer local, user root
# praliases kathy
kathy:kathy@chef.wrotethebook.com
# ypmatch kathy aliases
Can't match key kathy in map mail.aliases. Reason: No such key in map
# sendmail -bv kathy
kathy@chef.wrotethebook.com... deliverable: mailer esmtp, host chef.wrotethebook.com.
, user kathy@chef.wrotethebook.com
```

The first praliases command shows the value stored for the *bin* alias in the local *aliases* database, and the first ypmatch command shows the value stored for that alias in the NIS database. The local file maps *bin* to *craig* and the NIS database maps *bin* to *root*—a more reasonable value. The first sendmail -bv test shows that the delivery address from the local file is being used. Then we prepare our simple recipe. As soon as the *service.switch* file is built, the sendmail -bv test is rerun. This time, the delivery address used for *bin* is the one defined on the NIS server. Clearly, our simple recipe causes the local system to use NIS to resolve aliases.

The last three lines in the test illustrate the fact that the local file is still used when NIS cannot resolve an alias. In this case, an alias exists for *kathy* in the local file but not in the NIS map. Still, mail will be delivered to *kathy* using the value from the local file.

Alternatives

An alternative to creating a *service.switch* file is to define the sources of information, and the order in which they are searched, using the `ALIAS_FILE` define in *sendmail.cf*. For example, the following define would do the same thing as the aliases entry from the *service.switch* file in our recipe:

```
define(ALIAS_FILE, `nis:mail.aliases,/etc/mail/aliases')
```

This define tells sendmail that the first source of alias information is the NIS *mail.aliases* map, and the second source of information is the local */etc/mail/aliases* file. To implement this alternative solution, add this line to the *sendmail.mc* file, rebuild the *sendmail.cf* file, copy the *sendmail.cf* file to */etc/mail*, and restart sendmail.

This alternative solution is harder to implement and more difficult to maintain than the *service.switch* file. Changing the search order requires modifying *sendmail.mc*, rebuilding *sendmail.cf*, copying the *sendmail.cf* file to the correct directory, and restarting sendmail. To modify the search order using the *service.switch* file, simply change the aliases line in that file. The change is immediately effective. Time and again, the best sendmail configuration solutions do not involve any changes to the *sendmail.cf* file.

One final note about this alternative. Don't use both solutions at the same time. If we used both the *service.switch* file created in our recipe and the `ALIAS_FILE` define just shown, sendmail would first follow the instructions in the *service.switch* file and lookup the alias via NIS and in the local *aliases* file. Then sendmail would perform any optional processing requested by the `ALIAS_FILE` define, meaning it would lookup the same alias with NIS again. This is not a major problem, but it does add unnecessary overhead.

See Also

Recipe 2.5 provides a solution to a similar configuration problem for Solaris. The *sendmail* book covers the *service.switch* file in 12.1.1, the `confSERVICE_SWITCH_FILE` define in 24.9.100, and the `ALIAS_FILE` define in 24.9.1. *Managing NFS and NIS*, Second Edition, by Stern, Eisler, and Labiaga (O'Reilly), covers NIS in detail.

2.5   Configuring Solaris 8 to Read Aliases from a NIS Server

Problem

You must configure a Solaris 8 system to read aliases from a NIS server.

Solution

Edit the aliases entry in the */etc/nsswitch.conf* file, changing it to the following:

```
aliases:    nis files
```

Discussion

No *m4* configuration commands are needed to use the *nsswitch.conf* file on a Solaris system. The basic sendmail configuration already installed on your system should work. If your system is not yet configured to run sendmail, use the *generic-solaris.mc* file as a starting point to get your Solaris server running.

Both the Linux system and the Solaris system have a system-wide service switch file named */etc/nsswitch.conf*. The difference is that the Red Hat Linux 7.3 system does not use the aliases entry in that file, and the Solaris system does. When the system has an active system service switch file, sendmail uses that file and ignores the file identified by the confSERVICE_SWITCH_FILE define. The correct solution for the Solaris system is to identify the sources of alias information in the *nsswitch.conf* file. Any source that is compatible with the *nsswitch.conf* syntax and with sendmail can be specified. See the *nsswitch.conf* manpage for information about the syntax supported on your computer.

Recipes 2.3 and 2.4 also show aliases being read from an external server. But Recipe 2.2 and most examples in this book assume the *aliases* database is a local file located directly on the sendmail system. This is a common design, and there are some good reasons why.

Aliases are only searched for mailers that have the A flag set. On most systems, only the local mailer has this flag set, which means that aliases only apply to inbound mail that has been accepted for delivery through the local mailer. A centralized database that includes aliases for all of the users in the organization is needed only by a server that will accept mail for all of the users in the organization. For most Unix workstations, the bulk of the entries in a centralized database are unused—only those users who actually receive their mail at the workstation are looked up.

Placing the *aliases* file directly on the system that needs it improves performance and reduces network overhead. It also enhances security—data that passes over the network is subject to corruption and spoofing, and adding another protocol to the mix, in this case NIS, makes the system vulnerable to any bugs that might appear in that protocol.

Security, performance, and applicability limit the demand for a centralized *aliases* database accessible through the network. Think hard about why you want to put the *aliases* database on an external NIS or LDAP server before you proceed. However, if you decide to read aliases from an external server, sendmail can be configured to do so.

See Also

Recipe 2.4 provides a solution to the same problem for different operating systems. The *nsswitch.conf* file is covered in the books *TCP/IP Network Administration*, Third Edition, by Craig Hunt (O'Reilly), and *Managing NFS and NIS*, Second Edition, by Stern, Eisler, and Labiaga (O'Reilly).

2.6   Forwarding to an External Address

Problem

Mail addressed to the local host needs to be forwarded to another host for final delivery.

Solution

Add an alias to the *aliases* file for each user whose mail must be forwarded to another system. The recipient field of the alias entry must be a full email address that includes the host part.

After adding the desired aliases, rebuild the *aliases* database file with the *newaliases* command.

Discussion

There are many reason why mail delivered to your system must then be forwarded to another host. For example, a user may have changed addresses, a user may have several addresses but only read mail at one of them, or your host might be a mail hub that collects mail for several different systems. A mail exchanger is a good example of a system that receives mail that might need to be forwarded to another host for delivery.

A mail exchanger receives mail addressed to other hosts and accepts that mail as local mail. (This is discussed in Recipe 2.1.) It is possible, however, that not every user on every host that routes mail to the mail exchanger has a local account on the mail exchanger. Two sendmail -bv tests illustrate this:

```
# sendmail -bv pat@wrotethebook.com
pat@wrotethebook.com... deliverable: mailer local, user pat
```

```
# sendmail -bv andy@wrotethebook.com
andy@wrotethebook.com... User unknown
```

In the first case, *pat* is a user account on the mail exchanger, so the mail can be delivered directly to Pat's local mailbox. In the second case, *andy* is not a local user account, so the mail is bounced with a "User unknown" error. Assume, however, that this mail should not be returned with an error because Andy is a current employee who is allowed to receive mail at the address *andy@wrotethebook.com*. Andy doesn't have an account on the mail exchanger, but he does have a valid account on another system in the *wrotethebook.com* domain, and it is on that system that Andy reads his mail.

The "User unknown" error is solved by creating the correct aliases. For example, on our sample mail exchanger, we might add the following alias for *andy*:

```
andy:           andy@rodent.wrotethebook.com
```

The alias is available as soon as *newaliases* is run. Rerunning the sendmail -bv test that previously produced the "User unknown" error shows the following result:

```
# sendmail -bv andy@wrotethebook.com
andy@rodent.wrotethebook.com... deliverable: mailer esmtp, host rodent.wrotethebook.
com., user andy@rodent.wrotethebook.com
```

The error is gone. Now, mail addressed to *andy@wrotethebook.com* is forwarded through the esmtp mailer to *andy@rodent.wrotethebook.com*. Remote users do not even need to know that a host named *rodent* exists. They send mail to *user@wrotethebook.com*, and the mail exchanger forwards it to the correct host for delivery.

See Also

Recipe 2.2 provides instructions on building a basic *aliases* file. The *sendmail* book covers the *aliases* database in Chapter 12.

2.7   Creating Mailing Lists

Problem

You have been asked to create mailing lists.

Solution

Add an entry to the *aliases* text file for each mailing list, where the alias field contains the name of the mailing list, and the recipient field contains a comma-separated list of all of the recipients of the mailing list.

Add the special alias that sendmail uses to deliver error messages concerning the mailing list. This special alias must have a name in the format of owner-*list*, where owner- is a required string and *list* is the name of the list for which this owner alias is being declared. For example, if the list is named *admin*, this alias must be named *owner-admin*. The recipient field of the special alias should contain the address where the errors are to be sent.

For the convenience of users, add an alias that can be used to reach the person who maintains the mailing list. The format of the alias field should be *list*-request, where *list* is the name of the list for which this request alias is being declared, and -request is a required string. For example, if the list is named *admin*, this alias should be named *admin-request*.

Run *newaliases* to rebuild the *aliases* database file:

```
# newaliases
/etc/mail/aliases: 43 aliases, longest 30 bytes, 592 bytes total
```

Discussion

To illustrate how to create mailing lists, let's assume we have been asked to create three different mailing lists:

- Mail addressed to *root* is to be sent to the normal login accounts of the three people who administer the mail server.

- The boss wants to have a mailing list for the management council, which is composed of the four department chiefs and their scientific advisor, and he wants an archive kept of all the mail sent to that mailing list.

- The boss wants a mailing list for all mail users.

To do this, create an *admin* mailing list for the system administrators, a *chiefs* list for the department heads, and an *employees* mailing list for all mail users, similar to the following:

```
# Mailing lists

admin:           alana, logan, pat
owner-admin:     admin-request
admin-request:   alana

chiefs:          reba, sara, tyler@example.com,
                 jane@rodent.wrotethebook.com, kathy,
                 /home/payton/chiefs-archive
owner-chiefs:    chiefs-request
chiefs-request:  alana

employees:           :include:/etc/mail/allusers
owner-employees:     employees-request
employees-request:   alana
```

Next, edit any aliases in the file that need to reference the newly created aliases. In this example, we want mail addressed to *root* to be sent to the newly created *admin* alias so we make the following change:

```
# Person who should get root's mail
root:          admin
```

The first mailing list is the simplest. It defines three local recipients (*alana*, *logan*, and *pat*) who will receive copies of mail addressed to *admin*. The address *admin* can be used directly to reach these three users, as the following sendmail -bv command shows:

```
# sendmail -bv admin
pat... deliverable: mailer local, user pat
logan... deliverable: mailer local, user logan
alana... deliverable: mailer local, user alana
```

We also want mail addressed to *root* to be sent to the three administrators. To that end, we edited the *aliases* text file to point the *root* alias to the *admin* mailing list. Another sendmail -bv command illustrates the impact of that edit:

```
# sendmail -bv bin
pat... deliverable: mailer local, user pat
logan... deliverable: mailer local, user logan
alana... deliverable: mailer local, user alana
```

In this case, sendmail looks up the *bin* alias and finds that it points to *root*. It then looks up the *root* alias and finds that it points to *admin*. When it looks up *admin*, it finds that it points to *alana*, *logan*, and *pat*. Each of these are looked up and discovered to be delivery addresses that are deliverable through the local mailer.

Immediately following the *admin* alias is an alias with the name *owner-admin*. This is a special alias that sendmail expects to find. sendmail uses it to deliver error messages if it encounters any errors delivering mail to the *admin* mailing list.

The next alias, *admin-request*, is required only because it is referenced by the *owner-admin* alias; however, using aliases in this format is common with mailing lists because they provide two benefits. First, many users expect to be able to reach the person who maintains the list at an alias in the format of *list*-request—providing this alias meets these user expectations. A second benefit comes from the recipient field of the owner-*list* alias, which is used to construct the Unix From line and the Return-Path: header. Refer back to our example. If the *owner-admin* alias pointed directly to *alana*, the Return-Path: and the Unix From line for mail from the *admin* mailing list would appear to come from *alana*. End users who poke around in the headers and see the Unix From information may assume the mail was sent to them directly by *alana* instead of coming from the mailing list. Pointing the *owner-admin* alias to *admin-request* means that those users see *admin-request* as the source of the mail, which most users find less confusing. Since *admin-request* resolves to *alana* before final delivery is made, errors still get back to *alana* for analysis. Users are happy, and the purpose of the *owner-admin* alias is fulfilled.

Like most formal mailing lists, the *chiefs* mailing list also has the owner-*list* and *list*-request aliases described above. The *chiefs* mailing list delivers mail to the four department heads and their advisor. Three of the recipients (*reba*, *sara*, and *kathy*) are local email accounts. Two (*tyler* and *jane*) are aliases that point to user accounts on other hosts.

The sixth recipient on the *chiefs* mailing list is not a person—it's a file. Defining the full pathname of a file on the right hand side of an alias causes sendmail to append a copy of the mail to that file.* This is a simple way of creating an archive for a mailing list, and it is adequate for the small *chiefs* mailing list. However, the overhead associated with having sendmail copy mail to a file makes this a less than ideal solution for large, busy mailing lists. A better solution for high-volume mailing lists is to have sendmail pipe the mail to an external program that writes the archive. Recipe 2.9 shows how sendmail pipes mail to a program.

Notice that the six recipients of the *chiefs* mailing list are defined on three different lines. When a line in the *aliases* file begins with whitespace (space or tab characters), the line is treated as a continuation of the previous line. Thus, the recipient list for an alias can span multiple lines.

The *employees* mailing list sends mail to all users. It has the same supporting owner-*list* and *list*-request aliases as the other mailing lists. The most interesting thing about this mailing list is the :include: syntax used on the recipient side of the alias. The :include: syntax causes sendmail to read a list of recipients from an external file. In the example, sendmail reads a file named */etc/mail/allusers*, which contains the delivery address of everyone served by our sample mail server.

On our small sample system, the *alluser* file contains ten local users and three external users. sendmail includes that file into the *aliases* database as the recipients of the *employees* mailing list. Again, a sendmail -bv command demonstrates this:

```
# sendmail -bv employees
craig... deliverable: mailer local, user craig
kathy... deliverable: mailer local, user kathy
pat... deliverable: mailer local, user pat
logan... deliverable: mailer local, user logan
alana... deliverable: mailer local, user alana
payton... deliverable: mailer local, user payton
david... deliverable: mailer local, user david
reba... deliverable: mailer local, user reba
sara... deliverable: mailer local, user sara
jay... deliverable: mailer local, user jay
anna@crab.wrotethebook.com... deliverable: mailer esmtp, host crab.wrotethebook.com.,
user anna@crab.wrotethebook.com
andy@rodent.wrotethebook.com... deliverable: mailer esmtp, host rodent.wrotethebook.
com., user andy@rodent.wrotethebook.com
jane@rodent.wrotethebook.com... deliverable: mailer esmtp, host rodent.wrotethebook.
com., user jane@rodent.wrotethebook.com
```

* The file *must* be identified by a full pathname that starts with the root (/).

Ten of the recipients are local users who get mail delivered through the local mailer. Three are external users whose mail is forwarded through the esmtp mailer to other hosts in the local domain.

In each of our sample mailing lists, there were no duplicate recipients. For example, the *admin* list resolved to *alana*, *logan*, and *pat*—three unique user addresses. However, as we saw earlier, multiple aliases can point to the same recipient. In particular, all of the nonlogin system user accounts on our sample system point to *root*. What would happen if we had a mailing list that included several of these accounts? For example:

```
sysusers:         daemon, bin, ftp, root, alana
owner-sysusers:   sysusers-request
sysusers-request: alana
```

In this sample mailing list, *daemon*, *bin*, *ftp*, and *root* all resolve to *root*. sendmail recognizes this problem and deletes the duplicate recipients. When mail is addressed to this sample mailing list, *root* receives only one copy of the mail. If sendmail did not delete duplicates, *root* would recieve four copies of exactly the same message.

See Also

The *sendmail* book covers the *aliases* database in Chapter 12 and provides information on mailing lists in Chapter 13.

2.8   Migrating Ex-Users to New Addresses

Problem

You have been told to gracefully migrate ex-users to their new delivery addresses.

Solution

Add the *redirect* feature to the sendmail configuration using the following FEATURE command:

```
dnl Notify senders about discontinued addresses
FEATURE(`redirect')
```

Rebuild the *sendmail.cf* file, copy the new *sendmail.cf* file to */etc/mail*, and restart sendmail, as described in Recipe 1.8.

Add an entry to the *aliases* text file for each ex-user. The alias field of the entry is the local username where the ex-user previously received mail. The recipient field is the user's new email address with the string .REDIRECT appended to the end of the address.

As always, when the *aliases* file is updated, run the *newaliases* script:

```
# newaliases
/etc/mail/aliases: 45 aliases, longest 30 bytes, 670 bytes total
```

Discussion

The first two steps in the Solution section create a sendmail configuration containing the *redirect* feature. Of course, if your configuration already contains that feature, as does the generic Linux configuration described in Recipe 1.8, you can skip those first two steps and go right to creating the aliases.

As an example, let's assume we want to gracefully handle mail for an ex-employee for six months. Michael recently left the company. Proper customer relations is the first and most important step in transitioning Michael's mail. Jay has taken over all of his customers, and we now want those customers to send their business communications to Jay. During Michael's last week in the office, he took Jay to visit all of his local customers, and used conference calls to introduce Jay to all of his remote customers. The customers have been notified, and the business mail should flow to the right destination. If management drops the ball on customer relations, there is very little that a sendmail administrator can do about it. However, you can make sure that Michael gets his personal mail by adding an alias to forward the mail to his new address:

```
michael:                michael@new.job.ora.com
```

Michael is sent monthly reminders that his mail forwarding account will be closed in six months. Six month after his departure, the *michael* alias is edited as follows:

```
michael:                michael@new.job.ora.com.REDIRECT
```

At first, Michael's mail is forwarded to his new address, as this -bv test shows:

```
# sendmail -bv michael@wrotethebook.com
michael@new.job.ora.com... deliverable: mailer esmtp,
    host new.job.ora.com, user michael@new.job.ora.com
```

Forwarding, however, should not go on indefinitely. As long as the mail gets through, there are a certain number of senders who will not update their address books. At some point you must cut them off and stop forwarding the mail. In the example, we have a small site and are willing to forward mail for six months. A larger site might not want to do any forwarding at all.

At the end of six months, the .REDIRECT pseudodomain is added to the alias to terminate forwarding. The effect of the .REDIRECT pseudodomain can be seen in a sendmail -bv test:

```
# sendmail -bv michael@wrotethebook.com
User has moved; please try <michael@new.job.ora.com>
```

Mail addressed to *michael* is now returned to the original sender with an error message that tells the sender to try Michael's new address. The mail is not forwarded, but the sender is told how to deliver the mail directly.

.REDIRECT is clearly not a valid domain name. In sendmail parlance it is a *pseudodomain*. Pseudodomains are listed in class $=P, and sendmail does not attempt a DNS lookup for any domain listed in class $=P. Pseudodomains are used to signal special processing. However, simply adding REDIRECT to class $=P is not enough. The *redirect* feature must be included in the sendmail configuration for the .REDIRECT pseudo-domain to be handled in the manner described in this recipe.

Alternatives

Simply removing an ex-employee's account is a popular and viable alternative for migrating ex-employees off of your mail system. This alternative was rejected for the example problem because Michael is a sales person. We depend on sales for the survival of our business and did not want to alienate and confuse customers with a "User unknown" error when they attempted to reach their sales representative. For this reason, the solution emphasizes customer relations. However, if Michael had been a programmer working on internal projects, removing his account without any gentle migration may have been acceptable.

Another tempting alternative solution is to place the following alias in the *aliases* database:

```
michael:        jay
```

Jay has replaced Michael. This alias would forward all of Michael's mail to Jay. However, we rejected this alternative. If this alias is used, Jay receives unwanted mail from all of the remote mailing lists that Michael joined as well as Michael's personal mail, such as the invitation to Michael's high school reunion. We want to maintain a friendly relationship with Michael, so we can't just discard his mail. At the same time, Jay should not be obligated to forward Michael's mail. We chose to use the *redirect* feature. But these choices are a matter of policy that should be reviewed with management.

See Also

The *sendmail* book covers the *redirect* feature in section 4.8.39.

2.9 Delivering Mail to a Program

Problem

You want sendmail to pass mail messages to another program.

Solution

Address the mail to the program using the pathname of the program preceded by a pipe character.

Discussion

A recipient email address can contain a pipe character and the name of a program. For example:

```
|/usr/local/bin/rtmproc
```

sendmail uses the prog mailer to deliver mail to a recipient address that begins with the pipe character. The P parameter of the prog mailer definition defines the path to the prog mailer program and the A parameter defines the command used to run the mailer. With the generic sendmail configuration described in Recipe 1.8, the P parameter is P=/bin/sh and the A parameter is A=sh -c $u. $u is a sendmail macro that contains the email address of the user to which the mail is being delivered. Using the sample email address shown above, the command executed for the prog mailer would be:

```
/bin/sh -c "/usr/local/bin/rtmproc"
```

When the -c option is used with */bin/sh*, shell commands are read from the string that follows -c. In this case, sendmail causes the shell to execute a program named *rtmproc*. sendmail attaches its output to the standard input of the shell and prints out the mail message, which, in the example, sends the mail message to the *rtmproc* program. sendmail also attaches the standard output and standard error of the shell to its input.

The shell executes any command passed to it. The potential security risks of executing any command that follows the pipe character in a recipient address are obvious, and the fact that users are in control of defining such addresses in their *.forward* files adds to the risk. To reduce these risks, use the Sendmail Restricted Shell (*smrsh*) for the prog mailer instead of */bin/sh*. *smrsh* enhances security by limiting the commands that can be executed, and it is discussed in Chapter 10.

Email addresses that begin with pipe characters can be used in the *aliases* database or in *.forward* files. For example, the system administrator might create the following alias if *rtmproc* is some program created to process mail addressed to *root*:

```
root:      "/usr/local/bin/rtmproc"
```

In another example, Rebecca might create the following *.forward* file to filter her mail through the *slocal* program:

```
"|/usr/lib/nmh/slocal -user reba"
```

Aliases that forward to a program are more commonly used in the *.forward* file than in any other manner. System administrators create the *aliases* database, but users create their own *.forward* files. The structure of the *.forward* file is similar to that of an :include: file. Each entry in a *.forward* file defines one or more recipient addresses to which mail addressed to the user is delivered. Anything that can appear in the recipient field of an entry in the *aliases* database can also appear in a *.forward* entry. For example, Jill can forward her mail to an external host:

```
jill@ms.foo.edu.
```

Julie can deliver the mail to her local mailbox and make a backup copy in an archive file:

```
\julie
/mnt/nsf1/sara/mail.archive
```

Kathy can define the following *.forward* file when she goes on vacation:

```
\kathy, "|/usr/local/bin/vacation kathy"
```

Notice Kathy's entry. Kathy wants to put a copy of the mail in her mailbox before running the *vacation* program. Her *.forward* file starts with \kathy. The \ causes sendmail to deliver mail to the *kathy* account without further aliasing. The \ is necessary; without it, placing the address *kathy* in Kathy's *.forward* file would cause a loop.

See Also

The *sendmail* book covers the *aliases* database in Chapter 12.

2.10 Using Program Names in Mailing Lists

Problem

sendmail eliminates duplicates in mailing lists; however, you must ensure that all users listed in a mailing list receive their mail, even when multiple users receive their mail through a pipe to the same program.

Solution

If recipient addresses in the *aliases* file are not unique because they identify the same program, make them unique by inserting a harmless shell comment after the program's pathname.

Discussion

Duplicate recipients are deleted during mailing list processing to prevent delivery of multiple copies of the same piece of mail to the same user. This can cause problems when the duplicate recipients are really separate instantiations of the same program. The following *aliases* file illustrates this:

```
sales:          frank, clark, amanda, jill, jeff
owner-sales:    sales-request
sales-request:  alana
clark:          "|/usr/bin/procmail"
jeff:           "|/usr/bin/procmail"
jill:           "|/usr/bin/procmail"
```

In this case, mail to *clark*, *jeff*, and *jill* all appears to go to the same recipient—|/usr/bin/procmail. When duplicates are eliminated, only one of the three users gets a copy of the mail.

Most programs that are designed to work with sendmail are written to require a username as a command-line argument. It is not that the program necessarily needs this value, it is done to avoid duplicates when the program is used as a recipient in the *aliases* file. *procmail*, however, does not require the username as a command-line argument; in fact, it runs very nicely without any command-line arguments.

Make each recipient value unique by adding the username as a shell comment after the *procmail* command. The comment is ignored, so it has no impact on the execution of *procmail*, but it makes each recipient line unique, so there are no problems with duplicate recipients. Here is the corrected mailing list for the *aliases* file.

```
sales:          frank, clark, amanda, jill, jeff
owner-sales:    sales-request
sales-request:  alana
clark:          "|/usr/bin/procmail #clark"
jeff:           "|/usr/bin/procmail #jeff"
jill:           "|/usr/bin/procmail #jill"
```

Users do not need to add a username when they pipe to the *procmail* program from their *.forward* files. When multiple references to *procmail* come from a single file (e.g., the *aliases* file), sendmail needs help to resolve the duplication. sendmail does not need help resolving the duplication when the entries are retrieved from different *.forward* files.

See Also

Recipe 2.7 also discusses the elimination of duplicates in mailing lists.

2.11   Allowing Nonlogin Users to Forward to Programs

Problem

You want to allow users who have not been given a valid login shell to forward mail to programs.

Solution

Add /SENDMAIL/ANY/SHELL/ to the */etc/shell* file. For example:

```
# echo /SENDMAIL/ANY/SHELL/ >> /etc/shells
```

Discussion

Users' home directories can be located on an NFS file server that is configured to allow the user to mount the home directory but is not configured to allow the user to log in. Therefore, the user is not given a valid login shell. A user needs a valid login shell in order to forward mail to a program. Even when *smrsh* is used, as described in Chapter 10, adding programs to the *smrsh* program directory is not enough to make those programs available to the user if the user does not have a valid login shell.

sendmail considers a valid shell to be any shell listed in the */etc/shells* file. If the system does not have an */etc/shells* file, a default list of shells, defined by the `DefaultUserShells` variable in the sendmail source code, is used. If the shell in the user's */etc/passwd* entry is not a valid shell, sendmail refuses to run a program from the user's *.forward* file.

Some NFS servers are configured to allow mounting of home directories while denying login access. A user's */etc/passwd* entry on such a server contains something like */sbin/nologin* or */bin/false* as the user's login shell. These "nonlogin" shells should never be listed in */etc/shells*. Thus, sendmail does not find the user's shell in */etc/shells* and refuses to run the program the user has placed in the *.forward* file.

Place the string `/SENDMAIL/ANY/SHELL/` in the */etc/shells* file to tell sendmail that it should run the program from the user's *.forward* file, even if the user does not have a valid login shell. This recipe adds the entry to the end of an existing */etc/shells* file. If your system does not have an */etc/shells* file, the *echo* command shown in the Solution section creates one that contains the required string.

When *smrsh* is used, putting `/SENDMAIL/ANY/SHELL/` in */etc/shells* doesn't change the fact that only programs found in the *smrsh* program directory will execute. The valid login shell requirement is in addition to the *smrsh* requirement. The `/SENDMAIL/ANY/SHELL/` string bypasses the valid login shell requirement; it does not bypass the *smrsh* configuration requirement. Because `/SENDMAIL/ANY/SHELL/` bypasses a security check, it should be used only when it is absolutely necessary.

See Also

The *cf/README* file covers the use of `/SENDMAIL/ANY/SHELL/` in the */etc/shells* file.

2.12   Fixing a .forward Loop

Problem

Mail addressed to a user is being bounced with the error "too many hops."

Solution

First, check the *aliases* database to make sure that it is not the cause of the problem. If the *aliases* database is not the source of the loop, create an alias for the looping username to bypass the user's *.forward* file and force local delivery. The alias field of the new database entry should be the looping username and the recipient field should be the looping username preceded by a \ character.

Second, check out the contents of the user's *.forward* file. If the user forwards to a remote system, and you have root access to that system, print out the user's *.forward* file on that system. If you don't have root access, *telnet* to the SMTP port of the remote system and use the SMTP EXPN command to see how that system delivers mail addressed to the looping account.

If these tests show you the loop, tell the user exactly what is wrong and what needs to be fixed. If you cannot get the necessary information quickly from the remote system, tell the user that he probably has a loop in his *.forward* files, that he needs to fix it, and that his *.forward* file on your system will be ignored until he does.

Discussion

Users create and maintain their own *.forward* files. Sometimes, of course, a user makes a mistake when configuring the *.forward* file, and it is up to you to help him correct that mistake. One of the most common configuration errors is a forwarding loop in which the user configures the *.forward* file to forward mail to another system and then configures the *.forward* file on that system to forward mail back to the original system. Sometimes, more than two systems are involved because users often have login accounts on several systems. Let's look at an example.

Assume the username for which mail is bounced is *norman*. Examine how your system handles the *norman* email address by adding the verbose option (-v) to the sendmail -bv command, as follows:

```
# sendmail -v -bv norman
/home/norman/.forward: line 1: forwarding to norman@crab.wrotethebook.com
norman@crab.wrotethebook.com... deliverable: mailer esmtp, host crab.wrotethebook.
com., user norman@crab.wrotethebook.com
```

Adding -v to the sendmail -bv command provides additional information on how an address is rewritten on the local system. In this case, there is no alias for *norman*, so the *aliases* database cannot be part of the forwarding loop. (It is always best to make sure that you are not the cause of a problem before you get a user involved.) In fact, the sendmail -v -bv command makes clear that the information used to rewrite the *norman* address comes from the */home/norman/.forward* file.

Add an alias to the *aliases* database to break the loop:

```
norman:         \norman
```

The \ syntax terminates aliasing before Norman's *.forward* file is read. Mail addressed to *norman* that arrives at this host is no longer forwarded off of this host, which breaks the loop.

If you want to investigate further, you can examine the user's *.forward* file on the remote system or use the SMTP EXPN command to check how the remote system handles the user's mail. The sendmail -bv command just shown tells us that Norman forwards his mail to *crab.wrotethebook.com*. The following test shows how *crab* handles Norman's mail:

```
# telnet crab.wrotethebook.com smtp
Trying 192.168.0.15...
Connected to crab.wrotethebook.com.
Escape character is '^]'.
220 crab.wrotethebook.com ESMTP Sendmail 8.12.9/8.12.9; Mon, 11 Aug 2003 10:31:49 -
0400
HELO rodent.wrotethebook.com
250 crab.wrotethebook.com Hello rodent.wrotethebook.com [192.168.0.3], pleased to
meet you
EXPN norman
250 2.1.5 Norman Edwards <norman@wrotethebook.com>
QUIT
221 2.0.0 crab.wrotethebook.com closing connection
Connection closed by foreign host.
```

The local system forwards Norman's mail to *crab.wrotethebook.com,* and *crab* forwards the mail to *wrotethebook.com*. If the local system is the mail exchanger for *wrotethebook.com*, the cause of the loop is obvious. This example uses the SMTP EXPN command to examine forwarding on the remote system. However, many mail hosts do not implement the EXPN command. In that case, an error message similar to the following is displayed in response to the EXPN command:

```
502 5.7.0 Sorry, we do not allow this operation
```

It is not absolutely necessary that you gather information from the local and remote *.forward* files. If it is simple to do, your insights about what is wrong with the configuration of these files may speed a permanent solution. However, the *.forward* file is the user's responsibility. If the *norman* alias you added to the *aliases* database breaks the loop and the information about the *.forward* files cannot be gathered easily, you probably have more productive ways to spend your time than trying to gather forwarding information. Norman can easily print out his *.forward* files and bring the information to you later if he needs help.

See Also

The SMTP commands, including EXPN, are covered in the "Simple Mail Transfer Protocol" section of *TCP/IP Network Administration*, Third Edition, by Craig Hunt (O'Reilly). The *sendmail* book covers EXPN in section 10.3.2.

2.13 Enabling the User Database

Problem

Despite the fact that the sendmail developers discourage its use, you have decided to configure the user database.

Solution

Use the sendmail debug option -d0.1 to check that sendmail was compiled with the USERDB flag. If necessary, recompile sendmail to include user database support.

Create the user database source file and place a balanced pair of maildrop and mailname entries in the file for each username that will be mapped by the user database.

Use the *makemap* script to convert the completed source file into the required btree map type.

Assuming that the database file is created in the */etc/mail* directory and is named *userdb*, add the following define to the sendmail configuration:

```
define(`confUSERDB_SPEC', `/etc/mail/userdb')
```

Rebuild the *sendmail.cf* file, copy the new file to */etc/mail*, and restart sendmail as described in Recipe 1.8.

Discussion

Three things are required before sendmail will check for a user database: sendmail must be compiled with the USERDB compiler flag, the mailer must have @ flag set, and the path to the user database must be defined inside the sendmail configuration using the confUSERDB_SPEC define. The Solution section assumes the file is named *userdb* and is placed in the */etc/mail* directory.

The sendmail -d0.1 debug option displays the compiler flags used to create the sendmail binary. Examine the compiler flags listed after "Compiled with:". If USERDB is not listed, recompile the sendmail source code using either the NEWDB or HESIOD compiler flag and reinstall sendmail. (When either NEWDB or HESIOD are used, the USERDB flag is automatically set.) Select NEWDB or HESIOD based on whether the user database information will be stored on a Hesiod server or locally in a database file. Chapter 1 provides several examples of recompiling sendmail and, in particular, Recipe 1.4 shows how to add an optional map type to sendmail.

The user database file must be converted to a true database before it can be used by sendmail. Use the *makemap* command to build the database. For example, to create a database file named *userdb* from a user database source file named */etc/mail/userdb*, use the following *makemap* command:

```
# cd /etc/mail
# makemap btree userdb < userdb
```

The *makemap* program reads the standard input and writes out the specified database of the type selected. The command generally has two arguments: the database type and the name of the database to be written. The user database must be of the btree type, and the name of the user database must be the one defined inside the sendmail configuration. The *makemap* command is used extensively in this book with a variety of command-line options.

The user database is applied to inbound mail after the *aliases* database and before the *.forward* file when the mailer has the @ flag set.

 The user database is not recommended. The sendmail developers tell me that it will probably be removed from the distribution sometime in the future. This recipe is shown only because you might have a great idea of how to use it. Just remember that the user database is not recommended for simply mapping outbound sender addresses. If you use it, you should have a special reason for doing so.

The entries in the user database look something like the entries in the *aliases* database except for the addition of a keyword, either maildrop or mailname. Generally, user database entries are balanced pairs, where each user has both a maildrop and a mailname entry. A pair of entries for the *andy* user account might be:

```
andy.wright:maildrop andy
andy:mailname andy.wright@wrotethebook.com
```

The entries that use the keyword maildrop are almost exactly like entries in the *aliases* database. The value before the colon (:) is the user alias and the value after the keyword maildrop is the recipient address. The sample maildrop entry shown above performs exactly the same function as the following line placed in the *aliases* database:

```
andy.wright: andy
```

Both of these entries take mail addressed to *andy.wright* and deliver it to the *andy* user account. Of course maildrop lines are not needed if they replicate lines in the *aliases* file. The *aliases* file has already mapped inbound addresses before the user database is called. Real maildrop entries don't duplicate entries already found in the *aliases* database.

The similarity between entries in the *aliases* database and maildrop entries in the user database is very strong. The only difference in these entries, other than the addition of the keyword maildrop, is that maildrop entries cannot point to aliases. The recipient address in a maildrop entry must be a real address.

The added feature of the user database is that, unlike the *aliases* and *.forward* files, the user database also applies to outbound mail. `mailname` entries in the user database transform the sender address to create a *reverse alias*. In a `mailname` entry, the value before the colon (:) is the local username, and the value following the keyword `mailname` is the sender address that should be used for mail originating from the user. The `mailname` entry shown above converts the sender address on all mail from the user *andy* to *andy.wright@wrotethebook.com*.

However, the user database is not the only way, or even the recommended way, to rewrite outbound addresses. The sendmail FAQ, in question 3.3, states "the user database is no longer the recommended solution" for rewriting sender addresses. The *genericstable* database is the recommended tool for this task. Chapter 4 covers the *genericstable*.

The *aliases* database and the *genericstable* are preferred alternatives to the user database because:

- The user database is more difficult to use than the alternatives. The *aliases* database is available in all sendmail configurations, but the user database requires *m4* changes to the configuration. The *genericstable* also requires *m4* changes, but in addition to *m4* changes, the user database requires that the sendmail source code be compiled with a special compiler flag.

- The user database replicates, but does not replace, the *aliases* database. For example, the user database cannot point an alias to an alias. Even if you create a user database, you still need an *aliases* database, meaning you now have two files to maintain.

- The user database interacts with other features in ways you might not anticipate, as the sendmail FAQ makes clear in questions 3.3 and 3.4.

The sendmail developers make it clear in the response to FAQ question 3.4 that the user database was developed for a specific configuration requirement at UC Berkeley, and that it may not be applicable to a wide range of configurations. If you still insist on using it for something, this recipe points out the steps necessary to enable the user database.

See Also

Chapter 4 covers the *genericstable*, which is the preferred alternative for writing outbound addresses. The sendmail FAQ provides advice on the user database in questions 3.3 and 3.4. The *sendmail* book covers the user database in 23.7.26.

## CHAPTER 3

Relaying

3.0 Introduction

A mail relay is a system that resends mail that it receives. When mail that should be delivered by some other host arrives at the mail relay host, the system decides whether it should relay the mail. If relaying is allowed, the relay host sends the mail on to the destination address. If relaying is denied, a "Relaying denied" error message is returned to the sender. This chapter contains recipes that control when relaying is allowed or denied and recipes to configure a system to make use of a mail relay.

Relaying is different from forwarding. Mail that is forwarded arrives at the system addressed to the local host; it is forwarded only if the host is instructed to do so by the *aliases* database or the *.forward* file. Mail that is relayed arrives at the system addressed to some other host; it is only relayed if sendmail is configured to allow relaying.

In the same way that sendmail must be configured to act as a mail relay, a system must be configured to use a mail relay. Any system running sendmail can directly deliver its own mail; sendmail does not depend on relays by default. However, there are a variety of different sendmail configurations that use relay servers:

Relaying all mail

> A system can be configured to send all of its mail to a relay. This type of configuration is called a *null client*, not because the *sendmail.cf* file is empty, but because the system depends on an external host for all email service.

Relaying local mail

> A system can be configured to use a relay for mail that is normally delivered by the local mailer, while delivering all other mail itself. Thus, mail from one user to another, even when those users are both logged into the same client, is sent through a relay server.

Relaying mail to external hosts

    sendmail can be configured to send all mail bound for external hosts through a mail relay. Only mail delivered by the local mailer is not sent to the relay.

Relaying mail for pseudodomains

    sendmail can be configured to send "non-SMTP" mail to a mail relay host for delivery. Pseudodomains are internal tags used by sendmail to identify mail that is not standard SMTP mail. Special configuration commands exist for sending UUCP, BITNET, DECnet, and FAX mail to a mail relay host when that mail is identified by a pseudodomain.

Mail is sent to the mail relay host via the SMTP relay mailer. The configuration of the relay mailer can be changed with the *m4* macros RELAY_MAILER_ARGS, RELAY_MAILER_FLAGS, RELAY_MAILER_QGRP, and RELAY_MAILER_MAXMSG. sendmail can even be configured to use a different mailer for relaying by specifying a different mailer name with the confRELAY_MAILER define. However, changing the mailer name or fiddling with the relay mailer configuration is generally a bad idea because it creates an unnecessarily complex configuration that must be maintained. It is better to configure a mail relay host that is capable of handling standard SMTP mail than it is to create a custom mailer for every system that uses the relay host for the simple reason that there are fewer systems to maintain.

By default, sendmail does not relay mail—thus, a default sendmail system does not consider itself a mail relay. There is a good reason for this: relaying opens a system to the possibility of being abused by spammers. Spammers love to find a system that they can relay through in order to hide the true source of the spam mail. Everything you do to create a relay weakens this security. Therefore, care must be taken to use only those configuration tools that you really need to get the job done.

Several features are available that turn a sendmail system into a mail relay:

promiscuous_relay

    This feature tells sendmail to relay mail from any source to any destination. It should not be used on a system that is accessible from the Internet because it creates an open relay that will quickly be found and exploited by spammers.

relay_local_from

    This causes sendmail to relay any mail in which the envelope sender address contains the name of a host in the local domain. Because the envelope sender address in mail is easily forged, spammers can exploit a relay that uses this feature. For this reason, the *relay_local_from* feature should be avoided.

relay_mail_from

    This feature tells sendmail to relay mail if the envelope sender address of that mail contains the name of a host in any domain listed in the *relay-domains* file or listed as RELAY in the *access* database. Because the envelope sender address in mail is easily forged, spammers can exploit a relay that uses this feature if they can figure out the entries in the *relay-domains* file or the *access* database. For this reason, the *relay_mail_from* feature should be avoided.

relay_based_on_MX

This feature enables relaying for any host or domain that lists the local host as its mail exchanger. The disadvantage of this feature is that you lose direct control over which systems can use your system as a relay, and you place that control into the hands of others—the domain administrators. Domain administrators can simply place MX records in their domains to enable relaying through your system.

relay_entire_domain

When this feature is specified, sendmail relays mail for any host in a domain identified in class $=m. Class $=m contains the name of the local host's domain, as determined by sendmail during startup. Thus, this feature enables relaying for hosts in the local domain.

relay_hosts_only

By default, values in the *relay-domains* file or the *access* database are interpreted as domain names, and relaying is granted to any of the hosts in those domains. This feature changes that. When *relay_hosts_only* is specified, the values in the *relay-domains* file and in the *access* database are interpreted as hostnames, and mail is only relayed for the specific hosts listed in those files.

Other than the *relay_hosts_only* feature, which works with the *relay-domains* file and the *access* database, the features listed above tend to reduce the amount of control the sendmail administrator has over relaying. Generally, a better way to enable relaying is by using the *relay-domains* file. Using the *relay-domains* file requires no special *m4* configuration because sendmail reads this file by default. To use it, all you need to do is create a text file named *relay-domains* that contains a list of the domains for which relaying is allowed.

Entries in the *relay-domains* file enable relaying to or from the domains listed in the file. To have more control over the condition in which relaying is approved, use the *access* database. The *access* database is not designed specifically for relaying—it has broader security applications. However, it can be used to control relaying as demonstrated in Recipe 3.10.

For maximum security, use SMTP AUTH or STARTTLS to authenticate the hosts granted relay privileges. Chapters 7 and 8 cover these security protocols.

Because spammers may abuse a mail relay, special care should be taken to thoroughly test the relay configuration. If your server fails any of the tests, adjust the configuration to close the security hole. No tests are infallible, but they do provide clear indications of possible configuration problems.

3.1 Passing All Mail to a Relay

Problem

You have been asked to create a sendmail configuration that sends all mail through a relay. The identity of the local host is to be hidden so that all mail appears to come from the mail relay host.

Solution

Create a minimal sendmail configuration containing only an OSTYPE statement to specify the correct operating system and a FEATURE command to select the *nullclient* feature:

```
# cd /usr/local/src/sendmail-8.12.9/cf/cf
# cat > sendmail.mc
VERSIONID(`Recipe 3.1 nullclient master configuration file.')
dnl Select the correct operating system
OSTYPE(`linux')
dnl Select the nullclient feature and specify the relay server
FEATURE(`nullclient', `smtp.wrotethebook.com')
Ctrl-D
```

Build the new *sendmail.cf* file, copy it to the correct path, and restart sendmail. An example of building and installing a *sendmail.cf* file is shown in the last step of Recipe 1.8.

Discussion

Any Unix system running sendmail, even when the system is used as a single-user workstation, is fully capable of handling its own mail. Some workstations configure sendmail to handle both inbound and outbound mail—just like a mail server. Many Unix workstations, even those that depend on a mail server to collect their inbound mail, have a full sendmail configuration for handling outbound mail. Yet, it is also possible to create a very simple sendmail configuration on a workstation that relies on a mail server for both inbound and outbound mail service. When the *nullclient* feature is used, a system sends all of its mail through a mail relay host.

Most of the recipes in this book show configuration lines that are added to a pre-existing sendmail configuration. This recipe does not; the Solution section shows the complete configuration file. The *nullclient* configuration contains only two essential lines: the OSTYPE macro that identifies the client's operating system and the FEATURE macro that configures the *nullclient* feature. The *nullclient* feature has two fields. The first is the feature name: *nullclient*. The second is the name of the relay host to which outbound mail is sent. The format of the second field is *mailer:host.*, where *mailer* is the name of a mailer defined in the configuration and *host* is the domain name of the relay host. The basic *nullclient* configuration contains only the local and prog mailers, and the five SMTP mailers: smtp, esmtp, smtp8, dsmtp, and relay. *mailer* defaults to relay if no other mailer name is provided. This default is correct and should only be changed if you add other mailers to the configuration and have a specific reason for using another mailer. We allow *mailer* to default to relay in the sample configuration, and we recommend that you do the same.

The server value is assigned to the $S, $H, and $M macros in the *sendmail.cf* configuration file. These macros are, respectively, the smart host, mail hub, and masquerade macros. sendmail:

- Sends all outbound mail to the server identified by the $S macro; sends all mail that would normally be delivered by the local mailer to the server identified by the $H macro.

- Changes the hostname in the sender address of outbound mail to the hostname defined in macro $M.

A few sendmail -bv tests show the impact of the *nullclient* configuration on mail delivery:

```
# sendmail -bv tyler@example.com
tyler@example.com... deliverable: mailer relay, host smtp.wrotethebook.com, user
tyler@example.com
# sendmail -bv sara@crab
sara@crab... deliverable: mailer relay, host smtp.wrotethebook.com, user
sara@crab.wrotethebook.com
# sendmail -bv craig
craig... deliverable: mailer relay, host smtp.wrotethebook.com, user
craig@smtp.wrotethebook.com
```

The host value displayed by the first test shows that mail addressed to a user on an external host is sent through the mail relay host. In the generic configuration, mail addressed to an external system is sent directly to that system or to its MX server, using the esmtp mailer. On the *nullclient* system, the mail is sent to the relay host using the relay mailer. In this example, the client then relies on *smtp.wrotethebook.com* to relay the mail to *tyler@example.com*.

The second test is very similar to the first. In the second test, mail is addressed to another host within the local *wrotethebook.com* domain. Again, the mail is sent to the relay server instead of directly to the external host.

Probably the most interesting is the third test, which shows how mail is delivered to the local username *craig*. Normally, mail addressed in this manner would be handled by the local mailer and delivered directly to the local user's mailbox. Under the *nullclient* configuration, this mail is sent to the relay host for delivery, even though the mail is addressed to a user who has an account directly on the local system.

Note that the -bv test is often the best way to view delivery information. In this particular case, a test using -bt could have given a confusing result. For example, assume you decided to run sendmail -bt and use the /parse command to examine the mail delivery triple. You would see something like the following:

```
# cat > special-test
/parse tyler@science.foo.edu
/parse sara@crab
/parse craig
CTRL-D
# sendmail -bt < special-test | grep '^mailer'
mailer relay, host smtp.wrotethebook.com, user tyler@science.foo.edu
mailer relay, host smtp.wrotethebook.com, user sara@crab.wrotethebook.com
mailer local, user craig
```

The first two results obtained by /parse provide the correct information. The third result, however, is potentially misleading. You might look at this and think that, even with the *nullclient* configuration in place, mail addressed to local users is handled by the local mailer instead of being forwarded to the relay server. The problem comes from assuming that parsing the delivery address is the end of the story. In this case, it isn't. Because the mailer is the local mailer, the delivery address is processed through the *aliases* database. When sendmail finishes aliasing, it processes the localaddr ruleset (ruleset 5) if the local mailer has the Γ-5 flag set, which it does by default. It is the localaddr ruleset that then decides this mail needs to be sent to the mail relay, as the following -bt test shows:

```
# sendmail -bt
ADDRESS TEST MODE (ruleset 3 NOT automatically invoked)
Enter <ruleset> <address>
> localaddr craig
localaddr          input: craig
MailerToTriple     input: < server . wrotethebook . com > craig < @ smtp .
wrotethebook . com >
MailerToTriple   returns: $# relay $@ smtp . wrotethebook . com $: craig < @ smtp .
wrotethebook . com >
localaddr        returns: $# relay $@ smtp . wrotethebook . com $: craig < @ smtp .
wrotethebook . com >
> /quit
```

It can be confusing trying to remember when to call each ruleset. In general, it is easier to use -bv when all you want is information about the mail delivery.

In addition to sending all mail through the relay server, the *nullclient* configuration replaces the hostname of the client with the name of the server in the email sender address. A sendmail -bt test demonstrates this function of the *nullclient* configuration:

```
# sendmail -bt
ADDRESS TEST MODE (ruleset 3 NOT automatically invoked)
Enter <ruleset> <address>
> /tryflags HS
> /try relay kathy@giant.wrotethebook.com
```

```
Trying header sender address kathy@giant.wrotethebook.com for mailer relay
canonify          input: kathy @ giant . wrotethebook . com
Canonify2         input: kathy < @ giant . wrotethebook . com >
Canonify2       returns: kathy < @ giant . wrotethebook . com . >
canonify        returns: kathy < @ giant . wrotethebook . com . >
1                 input: kathy < @ giant . wrotethebook . com . >
1               returns: kathy < @ giant . wrotethebook . com . >
HdrFromSMTP       input: kathy < @ giant . wrotethebook . com . >
PseudoToReal      input: kathy < @ giant . wrotethebook . com . >
PseudoToReal    returns: kathy < @ giant . wrotethebook . com . >
MasqSMTP          input: kathy < @ giant . wrotethebook . com . >
MasqSMTP        returns: kathy < @ giant . wrotethebook . com . >
MasqHdr           input: kathy < @ giant . wrotethebook . com . >
MasqHdr         returns: kathy < @ smtp . wrotethebook . com . >
HdrFromSMTP     returns: kathy < @ smtp . wrotethebook . com . >
final             input: kathy < @ smtp . wrotethebook . com . >
final           returns: kathy @ smtp . wrotethebook . com
Rcode = 0, addr = kathy@smtp.wrotethebook.com
> /quit
```

The /tryflags command specifies the particular address we wish to process. In this case, we ask to see the processing of the header/sender (HS) address.* The /try command specifies the mailer for which the address should be processed (relay) and the email address that is to be processed (*kathy@giant.wrotethebook.com*). The result shows that the sender's hostname (*giant.wrotethebook.com*) is replaced by the mail relay host's name (*smtp.wrotethebook.com*). This example uses the sender's fully qualified domain name, but it could have used any hostname alias found in class $=w. Any of them would be replaced by *smtp.wrotethebook.com* in this test.

The two line configuration shown in this recipe sends all mail that originates on the local host to the relay for processing. It also masquerades that mail so that it appears to originate from the mail relay host. The *nullclient* configuration is intended for systems that depend on the mail server for all email needs. The classic examples of systems that might use such a configuration are diskless clients that depend completely on a server. But the benefits of the *nullclient* configuration have far wider utility. Centralizing mail services can simplify queue management, mail policy control, security, and logging. Many sites use the *nullclient* configuration on desktop workstations.

See Also

Replacing the hostname in the sender address is called masquerading, and it is covered extensively in Chapter 4. The third edition of *sendmail* covers the *nullclient* configuration in 4.8.33. Recipes 3.2, 3.3, and 3.4 all provide configurations that use a mail relay host; evaluate those recipes if the *nullclient* feature does not match your needs.

---

* Set /tryflags to ES and rerun this test to verify that the envelope/sender address is also rewritten.

3.2 Passing Outbound Mail to a Relay

Problem

You have been asked to configure sendmail to send all mail bound for external systems through a mail relay host.

Solution

Create a sendmail configuration that uses the SMART_HOST define to identify the mail relay host:

```
dnl Define a relay for all outbound mail
define(`SMART_HOST', `smtp.wrotethebook.com')
```

Build the new *sendmail.cf* file, copy it to the correct path, and restart sendmail, as described in Recipe 1.8.

Discussion

The SMART_HOST define sets a value for the *sendmail.cf* $S macro. The $S macro identifies the *smart host*. sendmail uses the smart host to relay mail to external systems. A few -bv tests show the impact of the SMART_HOST define:

```
# sendmail -bv sara@crab
sara@crab... deliverable: mailer relay, host smtp.wrotethebook.com, user sara@crab.
wrotethebook.com
# sendmail -bv tyler@example.com
tyler@example.com... deliverable: mailer relay, host smtp.wrotethebook.com, user
tyler@example.com
# sendmail -bv craig
craig... deliverable: mailer local, user craig
```

The first two tests show that all mail addressed to an external host, whether the host is part of the local *wrotethebook.com* domain or part of some other domain, is sent to the smart host for delivery to the external host. The third test shows that all mail that can be delivered by the local mailer is kept on the local system and delivered by the local mailer.

This configuration differs from the *nullclient* configuration in two ways:

1. Local mail remains on the local host.
2. Mail that originates from the local host has the local host's hostname in the sender address.

This creates a sendmail configuration that can handle its own local mail but must depend on a mail relay host for access to external systems. The concept of a smart host originally developed because many organizations had limited Internet connectivity. In those days, mail was relayed through the smart host because the smart host was the only host that could deliver the mail. These conditions still exist in some locations, but a more common reason that this configuration is popular is because network managers want to route all outbound mail through a single server for increased security, simplified queue management, and centralized logging.

See Also

Section 4.3.3.6 in the *sendmail* book discusses the SMART_HOST define.

3.3   Passing Local Mail to a Mail Hub

Problem

You have been asked to create a sendmail configuration that sends all local mail to a mail hub, while directly delivering mail addressed to external systems.

Solution

Create a sendmail configuration containing the MAIL_HUB define to identify the mail relay host for local mail. Use the LOCAL_USER command to exempt the *root* user's mail from relaying. Here are sample commands:

```
dnl Define a relay server for local mail
define(`MAIL_HUB', `smtp.wrotethebook.com')
dnl Users whose mail is not passed to the mail hub
LOCAL_USER(root)
```

Rebuild and reinstall *sendmail.cf*, and then restart sendmail. Examples of these steps can be found in Recipe 1.8.

Discussion

The MAIL_HUB define sets a value for the *sendmail.cf* $H macro. The $H macro identifies a mail hub that sendmail uses to deliver local mail. A few -bv tests show the impact of the MAIL_HUB define:

```
# sendmail -bv tyler@example.com
tyler@example.com... deliverable: mailer esmtp, host example.com, user
tyler@example.com
# sendmail -bv sara@crab
sara@crab... deliverable: mailer esmtp, host crab.wrotethebook.com., user sara@crab.
wrotethebook.com
# sendmail -bv craig
craig... deliverable: mailer relay, host smtp.wrotethebook.com, user craig@smtp.
wrotethebook.com
```

The tests demonstrate that sendmail uses the esmtp mailer to directly deliver mail bound for systems in external domains and external systems in the local domain. Mail that is normally delivered by the local mailer, however, is sent to the mail hub (*smtp.wrotethebook.com*) via the relay mailer.

Notice the user address field of the mail delivery triple displayed by the third test. The address *craig* has been rewritten to *craig@smtp.wrotethebook.com*. The address is rewritten even if the delivery address contains the fully qualified name of the local host, for example:

```
# sendmail -bv craig@jamis.wrotethebook.com
craig@jamis.wrotethebook.com... deliverable: mailer relay, host smtp.wrotethebook.
com, user craig@smtp.wrotethebook.com
```

Thus, all mail that would be delivered by the local mailer, even mail arriving from an external source, is forwarded to the mail hub. When configuring the mail hub, be careful not to forward mail back to a system that relays mail to the hub as this will cause a mail loop.

In this example, the mail hub must be configured with either a *craig* account or an alias for *craig*. Often, the mail hub maintains a central mail spool directory and holds the mail for all of its clients. The clients themselves do not have local mail spool directories. They either mount the server's spool directory via NFS, download the mail to a mail reader using POP or IMAP, or read the mail directly on the server.

Because the mail hub has an account or alias for every user on every client, it is important that the usernames on the clients are unique. If Craig Hunt has an account named *craig* on *crab*, and Craig Rider has an account named *craig* on *jamis*, and both systems use *smtp.wrotethebook.com* as a mail hub, then both systems will send mail to the hub using the same delivery address *craig@smtp.wrotethebook.com*, even though the mail is intended for two different users. Using a mail hub requires coordination among all of the clients.

One username that is obviously duplicated on all clients is *root*. Use the LOCAL_USER macro to ensure that sendmail does not relay mail to the mail hub when the mail is addressed to *root*. The LOCAL_USER macro adds users to *sendmail.cf* class $=L. Class $-L is a list of local users whose mail is not relayed to the mail hub.

The following test shows that without the LOCAL_USER macro, mail addressed to the *root* user is sent to the mail hub:

```
# sendmail -bv root
root... deliverable: mailer relay, host smtp.wrotethebook.com, user root@smtp.
wrotethebook.com
```

Clearly, sendmail is attempting to forward mail addressed to *root* to the mail hub. To prevent this, the following line was added to this recipe's configuration:

```
LOCAL_USER(root)
```

With this command in the configuration, the sendmail -bv test shows the following results:

```
# sendmail -bv root
root... deliverable: mailer local, user root
```

The test shows the effect of the LOCAL_USER macro. It keeps *root* mail local, which is just what we intended. However, before you use the LOCAL_USER macro, make sure that keeping *root* mail local is correct for your configuration. Often, mail to the *root* account is routed via an alias to the administrator's real login account. For example, you might route *root* to *alana* if Alana is the administrator of this system and *alana* is the account she uses to login. In that case, you would use an alias and you would not need the LOCAL_USER macro—although adding the macro would do no harm.

Alternatives

An alternative to MAIL_HUB is the LOCAL_RELAY define. LOCAL_RELAY provides another way to define a mail relay host for mail that is normally delivered by the local mailer. This alternative was rejected because the LOCAL_RELAY define has been deprecated by the sendmail developers for a number of years. When both MAIL_HUB and LOCAL_RELAY are included in the same configuration, they interact in a number of ways. We recommend that you avoid LOCAL_RELAY and use only MAIL_HUB in your configurations.

See Also

Chapter 2 provides extensive examples of using aliases; in particular, Recipe 2.2 provides an example of routing root's mail to another username. Recipe 3.1 also sets a value for the mail hub in the $H macro. The *sendmail* book covers MAIL_HUB in 4.5.7, LOCAL_USER in 4.5.5, and LOCAL_RELAY in 4.5.5.

3.4   Passing Apparently Local Mail to a Relay

Problem

Apparently local mail is mail that appears to be addressed to local users (i.e., the delivery address does not contain a hostname portion, yet the mail is not really addressed to a local username). Configure sendmail to send this mail to a mail relay server that is configured to properly handle it.

Solution

Create a sendmail configuration containing a LUSER_RELAY define that identifies the host that can handle apparently local mail. Here is a sample LUSER_RELAY command:

```
dnl Define a relay server for apparently local mail
define(`LUSER_RELAY', `smtp.wrotethebook.com')
```

Rebuild and reinstall *sendmail.cf*. Restart sendmail to read the new configuration. Recipe 1.8 covers these steps.

Discussion

A delivery address without a hostname is passed to the local mailer for delivery to a local user. If the user portion of the address does not specify a valid local username or alias, the "User unknown" error is returned. The following tests show how this works with a generic configuration:

```
# sendmail -bv fred -Cgeneric-linux.cf
fred... User unknown
# sendmail -bv craig -Cgeneric-linux.cf
craig... deliverable: mailer local, user craig
```

craig is a valid username on this host, so the mail is delivered by the local mailer. *fred* is not a valid local username, so an error is returned. After adding the LUSER_ RELAY define to the configuration, mail to *craig* is delivered as before, but mail to *fred* is now sent to the mail relay host for delivery:

```
# sendmail -bv fred
fred... deliverable: mailer relay, host smtp.wrotethebook.com, user fred@smtp.
wrotethebook.com
# sendmail -bv craig
craig... deliverable: mailer local, user craig
```

The LUSER_RELAY define sets the value of the *sendmail.cf* $L macro and adds two rules to the localaddr ruleset (ruleset 5). Ruleset 5 is invoked after a local address is processed through the *aliases* database.* The two rewrite rules added by the LUSER_RELAY define are only executed if the recipient address has not already been resolved to a valid delivery address. The first LUSER_RELAY rewrite rule checks to see if the username from the email address is a key in the user database. If the username is found in the user database, the mail is delivered according to that database's instructions. If the username is not found in the database, the mail is sent to the relay server identified by the $L macro. Thus, if a local delivery address does not resolve to a local username or is not covered by the *aliases* database or the user database, the mail is sent to the LUSER_RELAY server for delivery.

In the last test above, mail addressed to *fred* is forwarded to the LUSER_RELAY server. The LUSER_RELAY configuration assumes that the server knows how to deliver the mail to *fred*. Often, this means that the server has a large *aliases* file that defines how mail is routed to the users. Unlike the MAIL_HUB configuration described in Recipe 3.3, the LUSER_RELAY configuration does not assume that the server maintains a central mail spool directory. The LUSER_RELAY configuration allows the client to deliver some pieces of local mail and sends others to the server for delivery.

---

* Ruleset 5 is invoked only when the F=5 flag is set for the selected mailer. By default, this flag is set for the local mailer, which is the mailer used in our examples.

An alternative to LUSER_RELAY is to have a large *aliases* file on the client. This could be a local file or a centrally maintained file accessible via NIS or some other database service. An even more popular alternative is to require users to add the hostname to the email address when the hostname is required for delivery—in other words, let the users see the "User unknown" error until they understand that they need to address email properly. All of these are viable alternatives.

See Also

Chapter 2 provides examples of both the *aliases* database and the user database. The *sendmail* book covers LUSER_RELAY in 4.5.6.

3.5 Passing UUCP Mail to a Relay

Problem

You have been asked to configure sendmail to send UUCP mail to a mail relay host that has a direct UUCP connection.

Solution

Create a sendmail configuration containing a UUCP_RELAY define that identifies the mail relay capable of handling UUCP mail. Here is an example:

```
dnl Define a relay server for UUCP mail
define(`UUCP_RELAY', `uucp.wrotethebook.com')
```

Build and reinstall *sendmail.cf*, and restart sendmail, as described in Recipe 1.8.

Discussion

The UUCP_RELAY define sets the value of the *sendmail.cf* $Y macro, adds UUCP to class $=P, and adds a rule to the Parse1 ruleset. The new Parse1 rewrite rule sends UUCP mail that cannot be delivered by the local host to the mail relay identified by the $Y macro. If $Y is not defined, sendmail assumes that the local host can deliver all UUCP mail. Class $=P contains a list of pseudodomains (domain names used internally by sendmail), that sendmail does not attempt to look up in DNS. The .UUCP pseudodomain is used by sendmail to mark mail that should be handled as UUCP mail. When mail addressed to the .UUCP pseudodomain hits the new rule in the Parse1 ruleset, the address is rewritten as a mail delivery triple that sends the mail to the UUCP mail relay host defined in macro $Y. A sendmail -bt test shows all of this:

```
# sendmail -bt
ADDRESS TEST MODE (ruleset 3 NOT automatically invoked)
Enter <ruleset> <address>
> /parse crab!craig
```

```
Cracked address = $g
Parsing envelope recipient address
canonify           input: crab ! craig
Canonify2          input: craig < @ crab . UUCP >
Canonify2          returns: craig < @ crab . UUCP . >
canonify           returns: craig < @ crab . UUCP . >
parse              input: craig < @ crab . UUCP . >
Parse0             input: craig < @ crab . UUCP . >
Parse0             returns: craig < @ crab . UUCP . >
Parse1             input: craig < @ crab . UUCP . >
MailerToTriple     input: < uucp . wrotethebook . com > craig < @ crab . UUCP . >
MailerToTriple     returns: $# relay $@ uucp . wrotethebook . com $: craig < @ crab .
UUCP . >
Parse1             returns: $# relay $@ uucp . wrotethebook . com $: craig < @ crab .
UUCP . >
parse              returns: $# relay $@ uucp . wrotethebook . com $: craig < @ crab .
UUCP . >
2                  input: craig < @ crab . UUCP . >
2                  returns: craig < @ crab . UUCP . >
MasqSMTP           input: craig < @ crab . UUCP . >
MasqSMTP           returns: craig < @ crab . UUCP . >
final              input: craig < @ crab . UUCP . >
final              returns: crab ! craig
mailer relay, host uucp.wrotethebook.com, user crab!craig
> /quit
```

This test asks sendmail to parse a delivery address written in the traditional UUCP
bang format, *host!user*. The canonify ruleset rewrites the address into the standard
Internet address format and adds the .UUCP pseudodomain. The address continues
unchanged until the Parse1 ruleset, which rewrites the address into a mail delivery
triple. relay is the mailer used in the triple, and the value retrieved from the $Y macro
is the host used in the triple. However, the user address remains in the .UUCP pseudodomain format until the final ruleset, which returns the user address to the UUCP
bang format. The effect of all of this is to send bang formatted delivery addresses to
the UUCP relay host and to count on that host to deliver the mail.

The UUCP_RELAY is not the only pseudodomain mail relay that can be configured in
sendmail. The following defines are also available:

BITNET_RELAY

Identifies a mail relay connected to the BITNET network (an outdated network
that you probably will not use).

DECNET_RELAY

Identifies a mail relay host connected to a DECnet network. DECnet is an outdated network technology that was once a product of the Digital Equipment
Corporation. You probably will not use this network.

FAX_RELAY

Identifies an email to FAX server.

All of these relays are defined in the same way as the UUCP_RELAY in this recipe. Simply replace the keyword and the name of the relay host in the recipe with the values you require and rebuild the *sendmail.cf* file. However, none of these defines—UUCP_RELAY, BITNET_RELAY, DECNET_RELAY, or FAX_RELAY—are in widespread use. BITNET and DECnet are grossly out of date technologies and should not be used. UUCP carries only a small fraction of global email, and most of that passes transparently through Internet/UUCP gateways using the standard Internet address format. FAX_RELAY is not flexible enough to easily handle the variety of email to FAX servers. FAX server vendors cannot limit their market to those sites that have administrators knowledge-able enough to customize sendmail. For this reason, the vendors usually provide a technique that allows a user to send a FAX without any modifications to sendmail. Of the four defines, UUCP_RELAY is the only one that gets any real use, and thus it is the one covered in this book.

See Also

See the *sendmail* book for coverage of UUCP_RELAY in 4.5.8, the FAX_RELAY in 4.5.3, the BITNET_RELAY in 21.9.11, and the DECNET_RELAY in 4.5.2.

3.6 Relaying Mail for All Hosts in a Domain

Problem

You have been asked to setup a mail relay host to relay mail for every host within the local domain.

Solution

On the mail relay host, create a *relay-domains* file containing the name of your local domain. For example:

```
# cat >> /etc/mail/relay-domains
wrotethebook.com
Ctrl-D
```

Restart sendmail to ensure that it reads the *relay-domains* file:

```
# kill -HUP `head -1 /var/run/sendmail.pid`
```

Discussion

No *m4* configuration commands are needed to create this mail relay host. sendmail checks for a file named */etc/mail/relay-domains* and adds the names it finds there to class $=R by default. There are two ways to change the default pathname of the */etc/mail/relay-domains* file:

confCR_FILE

This define sets the path of the file loaded into class $=R. The confCR_FILE define is only used when it is necessary to change the default filename. For example, to load class $=R from a file named */etc/sendmail.cr*, add the following line to the master configuration file:

```
define(`confCR_FILE', `/etc/sendmail.cr')
```

RELAY_DOMAIN_FILE

This macro specifies the path to an additional file that provides data for class $=R. If the default file, which is usually named */etc/mail/relay-domains*, also exists, it is added to class $=R. For example, the following command adds data from the */etc/sendmail.cr* file to class $=R:

```
RELAY_DOMAIN_FILE(`/etc/sendmail.cr')
```

Neither of these commands appears in this recipe because it is generally a bad idea to change the default pathname of any file used in the sendmail configuration. Other administrators may need to find information on your system. It is easier for them to do so if the information is stored in the standard location.

Before we created the *relay-domains* file, sendmail blocked all mail relaying—even relaying from other hosts within the local domain. By default, sendmail does not permit relaying. A test conducted before the *relay-domains* file is created shows this. Below, *telnet* is used on *rodent.wrotethebook.com* to connect directly to the SMTP port on the sendmail server *smtp.wrotethebook.com*:

```
$ telnet 192.168.0.8 smtp
Trying 192.168.0.8...
Connected to 192.168.0.8.
Escape character is '^]'.
220 smtp.wrotethebook.com ESMTP Sendmail 8.12.9/8.12.9; Fri, 15 Aug 2003 14:25:01 -
0400
HELO rodent.wrotethebook.com
250 smtp.wrotethebook.com Hello rodent.wrotethebook.com [192.168.0.3], pleased to
meet you
MAIL From:<craig@rodent.wrotethebook.com>
250 2.1.0 craig@rodent.wrotethebook.com... Sender ok
RCPT To:<sara@crab.wrotethebook.com>
550 5.7.1 sara@crab.wrotethebook.com... Relaying denied
QUIT
221 2.0.0 smtp.wrotethebook.com closing connection
Connection closed by foreign host.
```

This test shows that the "Relaying denied" error is returned to the sender, indicating that the default sendmail configuration does not allow hosts in the local domain to relay mail to any third host.

After the domain name *wrotethebook.com* is written into the */etc/mail/relay-domains* file and sendmail is restarted, rerunning the test produces a different result:

```
$ telnet 192.168.0.8 smtp
Trying 192.168.0.8...
```

```
Connected to 192.168.0.8.
Escape character is '^]'.
220 smtp.wrotethebook.com ESMTP Sendmail 8.12.9/8.12.9; Fri, 15 Aug 2003 15:12:21 -
0400
HELO rodent.wrotethebook.com
250 smtp.wrotethebook.com Hello rodent.wrotethebook.com [192.168.0.3], pleased to
meet you
MAIL From:<craig@rodent.wrotethebook.com>
250 2.1.0 craig@rodent.wrotethebook.com... Sender ok
RCPT To:<sara@crab.wrotethebook.com>
250 2.1.5 sara@crab.wrotethebook.com... Recipient ok
DATA
354 Enter mail, end with "." on a line by itself
Subject: Test

This is a test of wrotethebook.com entry in the relay-domains file.
.
250 2.0.0 g8RJCLXf001550 Message accepted for delivery
QUIT
221 2.0.0 smtp.wrotethebook.com closing connection
Connection closed by foreign host.
```

Now, hosts within the local domain are allowed to relay through *smtp.wrotethebook. com*—all without any changes to the *m4* configuration or any need to rebuild the *sendmail.cf* file. Mail from or to hosts in the *wrotethebook.com* domain is relayed. Mail that is neither from nor to a host in the *wrotethebook.com* domain is still blocked from relaying mail.

Alternatives

There are four alternative solutions: the RELAY_DOMAIN macro, the *relay_entire_ domain* feature, the *promiscuous_relay* feature, and the *relay_local_from* feature.

The example in the Solution section adds only one domain name to class $=R. It is possible to add individual domains to class $=R from inside the *m4* configuration by using the RELAY_DOMAIN macro. The following lines added to the sendmail configuration would have the same effect as the *relay-domains* file defined above:

```
dnl RELAY_DOMAIN adds a domain name to class R
RELAY_DOMAIN(`wrotethebook.com')
```

However, the RELAY_DOMAIN command requires modifying the *m4* configuration and rebuilding and reinstalling the *sendmail.cf* file. Using the *relay-domains* file does not have these requirements, which makes the *relay-domains* file simpler to use.

There are a few other alternative solutions to this problem. We could have used the *relay_entire_domain* feature to enable relaying for hosts in the local domain. The following command added to a basic configuration would produce the same result as this recipe:

```
dnl A feature that relays mail for the local domain
FEATURE(`relay_entire_domain')dnl
```

The *relay_entire_domain* feature adds a few rewrite rules that relay mail from any host in a domain listed in class $=m. By default, class $=m contains the domain name of the server system. Thus, class $=m contains *wrotethebook.com* on a server named *smtp.wrotethebook.com*.

This alternative solution works well, but was rejected for a few reasons. First, this solution is slightly more complex that the one used in this recipe. Using the *relay_entire_domain* feature requires modifications to the *m4* configuration, which means that the *sendmail.cf* file must be rebuilt and reinstalled before sendmail is restarted. Using the *relay-domains* file only requires sendmail to be restarted.

Second, the value in class $=m is determined internally by sendmail. It is usually correct, so this might be a minor point, but setting the value in *relay-domains* gives the administrator more control. Third, *relay-domains* is self-documenting. Looking in the file quickly tells you which domains the server is configured to relay mail.

Fourth, the *relay-domains* file is very flexible. The problem section describes creating a mail relay for other hosts in the local domain, which is the most common relaying example. However, any domain can be listed in the *relay-domains* file, and mail originating from any host in that domain will be relayed. For example, imagine we wanted to create a mail relay that would relay mail for the *wrotethebook.com* domain, the *ora.com* domain, the *oreilly.com* domain and the *sybex.com* domain. To do that we would just need the following *relay-domains* file:

```
# cat /etc/mail/relay-domains
wrotethebook.com
ora.com
oreilly.com
sybex.com
```

This recipe is used to permit relaying from any host in a specified domain. These reasons give the *relay-domains* file a slight advantage over the *relay_entire_domain* feature for this specific application, which is why *relay-domains* was chosen for this recipe.

Two other alternative solutions were rejected for security reasons:

promiscuous_relay

This feature turns on relaying for all hosts, which includes the local domain, so it would solve our problem. However, this feature would cause many more problems than it would solve because spammers would quickly find and abuse the relay. Never use the *promiscuous_relay* feature. Even if your host is protected by a firewall, you need to secure your own system from attack—this is a basic tenet of "defense in depth security." Creating an open relay is always a bad idea.

relay_local_from

This feature sounds like a great solution for the problem. It turns on relaying for mail if the email address in the envelope sender address of the mail contains the name of a host in the local domain. The problem is that this feature depends solely on the email address in the envelope sender address. Unfortunately, spammers can easily rewrite the envelope sender address on the spam to make it appear that it originates from your local domain. For this reason, it was rejected as a possible solution for our problem.

See Also

The *sendmail* book covers the RELAY_DOMAIN_FILE macro in 7.4.1.2, the *relay_entire_domain* feature in 7.4.5, the *relay_local_from* feature in 7.4.7, and the *promiscuous_relay* feature in 7.4.3. The *cf/README* contains current information about all of these relay features.

3.7   Relaying Mail for Individual Hosts

Problem

You have been asked to configure a mail relay host to relay mail for specific hosts but not for every host within a domain.

Solution

On the mail relay host, create a *relay-domains* file that contains the name of each host for which mail should be relayed.

Add the *relay_hosts_only* feature to the sendmail configuration on the mail relay host. Here is the required FEATURE command:

```
dnl Configure the server to relay mail for specific hosts
FEATURE(`relay_hosts_only')
```

Then build *sendmail.cf*, copy it to */etc/mail,* and restart sendmail, as described in Recipe 1.8.

Discussion

On our sample mail relay host, we create the following *relay-domains* file:

```
# cat > /etc/mail/relay-domains
rodent.wrotethebook.com
horseshoe.wrotethebook.com
jamis.wrotethebook.com
tcp.ora.com
chill.sybex.com
wrotethebook.com
Ctrl-D
```

A sendmail -bt test shows the values stored in class $=R:

```
# sendmail -bt
ADDRESS TEST MODE (ruleset 3 NOT automatically invoked)
Enter <ruleset> <address>
> $=R
tcp.ora.com
rodent.wrotethebook.com
chill.sybex.com
jamis.wrotethebook.com
horseshoe.wrotethebook.com
wrotethebook.com
> /quit
```

Normally, values in class $=R are interpreted as domain names, and any host within a domain listed in class $=R is allowed to relay mail through the server. Recipe 3.6 uses this fact to relay mail for entire domains. In this case, however, we want *wrotethebook.com* interpreted as a hostname, not a domain name, and we want mail routed for that host.

The *relay_hosts_only* feature changes how the entries in class $=R are used. In the default configuration, pattern matches against class $=R contain the string $*$=R, which matches zero or more tokens and any value stored in $=R. Thus *wrotethebook. com*, *crab.wrotethebook.com*, and *fun.rodent.wrotethebook.com* would all pattern match the *wrotethebook.com* value found in the class $=R array shown above. The *relay_hosts_only* feature changes the string in the pattern match to $=R, meaning that only exact matches of values found in class $=R are valid matches. When *relay_hosts_only* is used with our sample class $=R values, *rodent.wrotethebook.com* matches the pattern because *rodent.wrotethebook.com* is included in $=R; however, *crab. wrotethebook.com* does not match—even though the value *wrotethebook.com* appears in the array. Only a host named *wrotethebook.com* would match that specific value when *relay_hosts_only* is used.

A couple of tests demonstrate the impact of the *relay_hosts_only* feature. A *telnet* test from *rodent* shows that *smtp* is configured to allow relaying for *rodent*:

```
$ telnet smtp.wrotethebook.com smtp
Trying 192.168.0.8...
Connected to 192.168.0.8.
Escape character is '^]'.
220 smtp.wrotethebook.com ESMTP Sendmail 8.12.9/8.12.9; Fri, 15 Aug 2003 15:36:52 -
0400
HELO rodent.wrotethebook.com
250 smtp.wrotethebook.com Hello rodent.wrotethebook.com [192.168.0.3], pleased to
meet you
MAIL From:<craig@rodent.wrotethebook.com>
250 2.1.0 craig@rodent.wrotethebook.com... Sender ok
RCPT To:<tyler@example.com>
250 2.1.5 tyler@example.com... Recipient ok
QUIT
221 2.0.0 smtp.wrotethebook.com closing connection
Connection closed by foreign host.
```

The same test run from *crab* shows that *crab* is not allowed to relay through *smtp*:

```
# telnet smtp.wrotethebook.com smtp
Trying 192.168.0.8...
Connected to 192.168.0.8.
Escape character is '^]'.
220 smtp.wrotethebook.com ESMTP Sendmail 8.12.9/8.12.9; Fri, 15 Aug 2003 20:43:11 -
0400
HELO crab.wrotethebook.com
250 smtp.wrotethebook.com Hello crab.wrotethebook.com [192.168.0.15], pleased to meet
you
MAIL From:<craig@crab.wrotethebook.com>
250 2.1.0 craig@crab.wrotethebook.com... Sender ok
RCPT To:<tyler@example.com>
550 5.7.1 tyler@example.com... Relaying denied
QUIT
221 2.0.0 smtp.wrotethebook.com closing connection
Connection closed by foreign host.
```

One final test from *crab* shows the full impact of class $=R on relaying:

```
$ telnet smtp.wrotethebook.com smtp
Trying 192.168.0.8...
Connected to smtp.
Escape character is '^]'.
220 smtp.wrotethebook.com ESMTP Sendmail 8.12.9/8.12.9; Fri, 15 Aug 2003 14:20:16 -
0400
HELO crab.wrotethebook.com
250 smtp.wrotethebook.com Hello crab.wrotethebook.com [192.168.0.3], pleased to meet
you
MAIL From:<craig@crab.wrotethebook.com>
250 2.1.0 craig@crab.wrotethebook.com... Sender ok
RCPT To:<kathy@rodent.wrotethebook.com>
250 2.1.5 kathy@rodent.wrotethebook.com... Recipient ok
QUIT
221 2.0.0 smtp.wrotethebook.com closing connection
Connection closed by foreign host.
```

In this case, *crab* successfully relays mail through *smtp*. If either the sending host or the recipient host is listed in class $=R, the mail is accepted for relaying. Therefore, mail sent from *crab* to *rodent* is accepted for relaying, even though *crab* is not granted relaying privileges, because *rodent* is allowed to relay and *rodent* is the destination of this piece of mail.

See Also

Section 7.4.6 in the *sendmail* book covers the *relay_hosts_only* feature. Recipes 3.6 and 3.8 provide solutions to similar problems that may also need to be evaluated.

3.8   Configuring Relaying on a Mail Exchanger

Problem

You are asked to configure sendmail on a mail exchanger to permit relaying for all systems that legitimately use it as their mail exchanger.

Solution

Obtain from the domain administrator a listing of the hostnames whose MX records point to the local system as their mail exchanger. Add the list of hostnames to the *local-host-names* file to handle inbound mail that should be delivered to a mailbox on the mail exchanger or forwarded as directed by the *aliases* or *.forward* files. Add the hostnames from the list to the *relay-domains* file to handle mail that should be relayed.

Discussion

If you have access to a system that can list the entire domain, you can use the following bit of Unix magic to create a listing of every host in the domain that uses your mail system as its MX server:*

```
# cd /etc/mail
# host -l wrotethebook.com | \
> grep 'mail.*mail\.wrotethebook\.com' | \
> awk '{ print $1 }' > temp-relay-domains
```

This example writes the list to a file named *temp-relay-domains* file. Verify the file contents before storing the data in either the *relay-domains* file or the *local-host-names* file. Additionally, this example requires the sendmail administrator to have direct access to a system that is entitled to list the entire domain file. Unless you pull double duty as both DNS administrator and sendmail administrator, you might have to rely on the domain administrator for the list of hostnames.

The *local-host-names* file configures the mail exchanger to accept mail for local delivery or forwarding, as discussed in Chapter 2. The *relay-domains* file configures the mail exchanger for relaying.

Mail to or from hosts in the *relay-domains* file will be relayed. Note that the names in the *relay-domains* file in this example are treated as hostnames, not domain names, because we are using the *relay_hosts_only* feature.

---

* In the example, we list a domain named *wrotethebook.com* and grep for *mail.wrotethebook.com*. Replace these values with the correct values for your domain and mail system hostname.

Alternatives

The *relay_based_on_MX* feature is an alternative solution to the problem described in the Problem section. When the *relay_based_on_MX* feature is used, sendmail relays mail for any system that lists the local host on its MX record. The *relay_based_on_MX* solution is simpler than this recipe, and just as effective, but it was rejected for two reasons:

- First, the creation of MX records is not under your control. Any domain administrator, anywhere in the world, could define your mail relay host as a mail exchanger for his domain. After that, any host in that remote domain can use your host as a mail relay. Thus, you are not in control of which hosts use your relay.

- Second, the sendmail developers state that it "is usually better to maintain a list of hosts/domains for which the server acts as a relay" than it is to use the *relay_based_on_MX* feature. In addition to the lack of control mentioned above, they cite the possibility of delivery problems when the remote DNS server is slow, and that some address formats (specifically the %hack) are not treated as you might suppose.

Loss of control and the recommendation of the sendmail developers were enough to make us choose the solution in Recipe 3.8. If simplicity is more important to you, the *relay_based_on_MX* feature also works.

See Also

The discussion of the *relay_based_on_MX* feature in the *cf/README* file explains the developers' recommendations. The *sendmail* book covers *relay_based_on_MX* in 7.4.4. Recipes 2.1 and 3.7 provide important material for this recipe.

3.9   Loading Class $=R via LDAP

Problem

You have been asked to configure sendmail to read the names of hosts and domains that are granted relaying privileges from an LDAP server.

Solution

On the LDAP server, add support for the sendmail schema as described in Recipe 1.3. Note that this only needs to be done once.

On the LDAP server, add to the LDAP database the names of the hosts and domains that are allowed to relay. Use the sendmailMTAClass object class format defined in the *sendmail.schema* file. The Discussion section shows an example doing this on a server that runs OpenLDAP.

On the mail relay host, use the command `sendmail -bt -d0.1` to check if sendmail was compiled with LDAP support. The string `LDAPMAP` must appear in the "Compiled with:" list. If sendmail was not compiled with LDAP support, recompile and reinstall sendmail as shown in Recipe 1.3. Once sendmail supports LDAP, continue with the next steps.

On the mail relay host, add a `RELAY_DOMAIN_FILE` macro to the sendmail configuration specifing `@LDAP` as the relay domain file path, which tells sendmail to read class $=R values from the LDAP server using the standard sendmail schema. Use the `confLDAP_CLUSTER` define to set the `${sendmailMTACluster}` macro to the same value used in the `sendmailMTACluster` attribute of the LDAP entry. Here are sample sendmail configuration commands:

```
dnl Set the LDAP cluster value
define(`confLDAP_CLUSTER', `wrotethebook.com')
dnl Tell sendmail to load $=R via LDAP
RELAY_DOMAIN_FILE(`@LDAP')
```

Build the configuration file, copy it to */etc/mail/sendmail.cf*, and restart sendmail with the new configuration, as described in Recipe 1.8.

Discussion

This recipes assumes that LDAP is properly installed and running. This is not the place to start experimenting with LDAP. Both LDAP and sendmail are large, complex systems. You should have some experience with LDAP before attempting to use it with sendmail.

The *sendmail.schema* file that comes with the sendmail distribution must be included in the LDAP configuration in order for LDAP to understand and properly process queries from sendmail.[*] The LDAP administrator must ensure that LDAP is ready to work with sendmail's standard schema before adding sendmail data to the LDAP database.

The LDAP administrator builds an LDIF file using the sendmail schema to define the list of hosts granted relay privileges and then runs *ldapadd* to add the contents of the LDIF file to the LDAP database. Here is an example that adds all of the hostnames from the *relay-domains* file used in Recipe 3.7:

```
# cat > ldap-relay-domains
dn: sendmailMTAClassName=R, dc=wrotethebook, dc=com
objectClass: sendmailMTA
objectClass: sendmailMTAClass
sendmailMTACluster: wrotethebook.com
sendmailMTAClassName: R
sendmailMTAClassValue: rodent.wrotethebook.com
sendmailMTAClassValue: horseshoe.wrotethebook.com
sendmailMTAClassValue: jamis.wrotethebook.com
```

---

[*] You can, of course, design your own schema. But that is not a topic for a sendmail book.

```
sendmailMTAClassValue: tcp.ora.com
sendmailMTAClassValue: chill.sybex.com
sendmailMTAClassValue: wrotethebook.com
Ctrl-D
# ldapadd -x -D "cn=Manager,dc=wrotethebook,dc=com" \
> -W -f ldap-relay-domains
Enter LDAP Password: SecretLDAPpassword
adding new entry "sendmailMTAClassName=R, dc=wrotethebook, dc=com"
```

An *ldapsearch* test shows the data in the LDAP database:[*]

```
# ldapsearch -LLL -x '(sendmailMTAClassName=R)' sendmailMTAClassValue
dn: sendmailMTAClassName=R, dc=wrotethebook, dc=com
sendmailMTAClassValue: rodent.wrotethebook.com
sendmailMTAClassValue: horseshoe.wrotethebook.com
sendmailMTAClassValue: jamis.wrotethebook.com
sendmailMTAClassValue: tcp.ora.com
sendmailMTAClassValue: chill.sybex.com
sendmailMTAClassValue: wrotethebook.com
```

Once the data is added to the LDAP server, the sendmail system can be configured to read it.

The list of hosts granted relaying privileges are added to the LDAP database as values in a single sendmailMTAClass object class record. As the sendmailMTAClassName attribute makes clear, these values will be stored in class $=R. Normally, class $=R is loaded from the file */etc/mail/relay-domains*. Use the RELAY_DOMAIN_FILE macro to add another source of data for class $=R. The string @LDAP in the path field of the macro tells sendmail to load class $=R with values obtained from the LDAP server. The effect of the @LDAP string on the RELAY_DOMAINS_FILE macro can be easily seen using the sendmail -bt command:

```
# rm -f /etc/mail/relay-domains
# sendmail -bt -Cgeneric-linux.cf
ADDRESS TEST MODE (ruleset 3 NOT automatically invoked)
Enter <ruleset> <address>
> $=R
> /quit
# sendmail -bt
ADDRESS TEST MODE (ruleset 3 NOT automatically invoked)
Enter <ruleset> <address>
> $=R
rodent.wrotethebook.com
chill.sybex.com
jamis.wrotethebook.com
horseshoe.wrotethebook.com
wrotethebook.com
tcp.ora.com
> /quit
```

---

[*] If *ldapsearch* requires -h and -b arguments, matching values will also be required by sendmail. See Recipe 5.9 for an example of setting -h and -b for sendmail.

The *rm* command in this test is just to show the reader that no values are being loaded into class $=R from the *relay-domains* file. On a real system, you might want to use both the *relay-domains* file and LDAP.

The first sendmail -bt test loads the *generic-linux.cf* configuration provided with the sendmail distribution. The $=R command displays the contents of the class $=R, which, in this case, is empty. The sendmail -bt test is rerun using the *sendmail.cf* configuration file created in this recipe. This time the $-R command displays the values retrieved from the LDAP server.

Class $=R is not the only class that can be loaded via LDAP. Any class loaded from a file can be loaded via LDAP by replacing the file pathname on the F command with the string @LDAP, using this syntax:

    F{*name*}@LDAP

where *name* is the class' name. The same name is then used as the value for the sendmailMTAClassName attribute in the LDAP record that defines the values loaded into the class. Note that this is the class name without the curly braces.

This recipe uses the confLDAP_CLUSTER define because the LDAP record created for this recipe contains the sendmailMTACluster attribute. sendmail LDAP records apply to either a single host or a group of hosts, which sendmail calls a *cluster*. A record that applies to a single host uses the sendmailMTAHost attribute; a record that applies to a group of hosts uses the sendmailMTACluster attribute. If confLDAP_CLUSTER is not specified, a cluster name is not used, and only records with a sendmailMTAHost attribute that matches the hostname of the sendmail host are retrieved. The record added to the LDAP database in the example above used the sendmailMTACluster attribute, and sets that attribute to *wrotethebook.com*. Therefore, it is necessary to define a matching cluster value in the sendmail configuration. The confLDAP_CLUSTER define shown in the Solution section sets the *sendmail.cf* macro ${sendmailMTACluster}, which holds the cluster name, to *wrotethebook.com*. If that define was not used, queries from the local host would not successfully retrieve the sample class $=R values from the LDAP server.

See Also

Recipes 3.6 and 3.7 provide information about class $=R and how it is used for relaying. Information about LDAP is available in *Understanding and Deploying LDAP Directory Services* by Howes, Smith, and Good (Macmillan) and in *LDAP System Administration* by Gerald Carter (O'Reilly). The *cf/README* file covers this topic in the *Using LDAP for Aliases, Maps, and Classes* section. The *sendmail* book covers the RELAY_DOMAIN_FILE macro in section 7.4.1.2 and the confLDAP_CLUSTER define in section 21.9.82.

3.10   Relaying Only Outbound Mail

Problem

You have been asked to configure a mail relay host to handle only outbound mail. The host is to relay mail sent from selected hosts without relaying mail addressed to those hosts.

Solution

Add support for the *access* database to the sendmail configuration by using the *access_db* feature. Here is the required FEATURE macro:

```
dnl Add support for the access database
FEATURE(`access_db')
```

Build an *access* database that defines all of the clients from which this server should accept mail for relaying. The *access* database entries should be in the form of Connect:*address* RELAY, where *address* is the IP address or DNS name of the source from which mail will be accepted.

Rebuild and reinstall *sendmail.cf*, then restart sendmail. These steps are covered in Recipe 1.8.

Discussion

Mail from, or addressed to, any domain defined in the *relay-domains* file is relayed. Thus, the *relay-domains* file creates a relay that handles both inbound and outbound mail, which is generally the configuration used. Occasionally, however, network designers decide to use separate systems for inbound and outbound mail. For example, a mail exchanger for all inbound mail and a mail relay host for all outbound mail might be placed on two physically separate systems. The *access* database provides the fine-grained control necessary to implement these design decisions. The *access_db* feature adds support for the *access* database to the sendmail configuration.

Entries in the *access* file, from which the *access* database is built, contain two basic fields:

- The conditional test that determines whether an action is taken
- The action taken when the condition is met

The conditional test can contain various types of data depending on what the *access* database entry is being used for. For relaying, the conditional test usually includes an address, which can be a full or partial domain name, hostname, or IP address. It can also be a full email address or just the user portion of an email address. Here is an example of creating an *access* database entry that relays mail received via a connection from any host in the local *wrotethebook.com* domain:

```
# cd /etc/mail
# cat > access
Connect:wrotethebook.com          RELAY
Ctrl-D
# makemap hash access < access
```

The example uses the domain name *wrotethebook.com* as the data in the conditional test because we want to relay mail for every host in that domain. An alternative would be to use the network address to relay mail for every host on the local network, for example:

```
Connect:192.168.0     RELAY
```

The keyword Connect: that is placed before the data in the conditional test is called a *tag*. A tag is used to limit the scope of the test. Tags are optional. Normally, the data in the conditional test field of an entry in the *access* database are tested against three different values—the sender and recipient addresses from the message envelope, and the IP address of the remote system that connected to the server to transfer the mail. If any one of these three addresses matches the conditional data in the *access* database, the condition is met, and the action defined in the database is taken. Use a tag to change this default behavior and limit the conditional test to one of the three possible addresses. The basic tag values are:

To:
>   Only the recipient address in the message envelope is matched against the conditional test data.

From:
>   Only the sender address in the message envelope is matched against the conditional test data.

Connect:
>   Only the IP address of the remote system that initiated the connection over which the mail was received is matched against the conditional test data.

The example above uses the Connect: tag to limit relaying to only those hosts that connect to the relay server from the *wrotethebook.com* domain. Mail from any other source is not relayed.

The action field in the sample *access* file entry contains the keyword RELAY, which simply means that the server should relay mail that matches the specified conditional test. RELAY is the only keyword that directly relates to relaying. Several other action keywords are covered in Chapter 7.

The *access* file must be converted to a hash database before sendmail can use it. The *makemap* program does the required conversion. It reads ASCII text from *stdin* and writes out a database of the specified type to the specified file. In our example, note that the input and output names appear the same. They're not. The input file is named *access* and the output file is named *access.db*. However, you do not need to add the *.db* extension to the output filename. *makemap* automatically adds the correct extension based on the type of database specified. *makemap* is provided as part of the sendmail distribution.

After building the *access* database, building *sendmail.cf*, and restarting sendmail, the system relays mail from clients in the local domain but will not relay mail to those clients if the mail originates in some other domain.[*] Two tests show this. The first test is mail sent from a host in the local domain to a remote host:

```
$ telnet smtp.wrotethebook.com smtp
Trying 192.168.0.8...
Connected to smtp.
Escape character is '^]'.
220 smtp.wrotethebook.com ESMTP Sendmail 8.12.9/8.12.9; Fri, 15 Aug 2003 16:47:57 -
0400
HELO rodent.wrotethebook.com
250 smtp.wrotethebook.com Hello rodent.wrotethebook.com [192.168.0.3], pleased to
meet you
MAIL From:<craig@rodent.wrotethebook.com>
250 2.1.0 craig@rodent.wrotethebook.com... Sender ok
RCPT To:<tyler@example.com>
250 2.1.5 tyler@example.com... Recipient ok
QUIT
221 2.0.0 smtp.wrotethebook.com closing connection
Connection closed by foreign host.
```

The second test is mail sent from a remote host to a host in the local domain. If the local domain was specified in the *relay-domain* file, this mail would be accepted. This test shows that with the *access* database from this recipe, the mail is rejected:

```
$ telnet smtp.wrotethebopok.com smtp
Trying 192.168.0.8...
Connected to smtp.
Escape character is '^]'.
220 smtp.wrotethebook.com ESMTP Sendmail 8.12.9/8.12.9; Fri, 15 Aug 2003 16:52:07 -
0400
HELO example.com
250 smtp.wrotethebook.com Hello example.com {10.20.3.3], pleased to meet you
MAIL From:<tyler@example.com>
250 2.1.0 tyler@example.com... Sender ok
RCPT To:<craig@rodent.wrotethebook.com>
550 5.7.1 craig@rodent.wrotethebook.com... Relaying denied
QUIT
221 2.0.0 smtp.wrotethebook.com closing connection
Connection closed by foreign host.
```

See Also

Chapter 6 provides more information about the *access* database. The *Finer control by using tags for the LHS of the access map* section of the *cf/README* file provides additional information about tags. The *sendmail* book covers the *access* database in section 7.5.

---

[*] sendmail does not need to be restarted when a database changes. The only reason a restart was needed for this recipe was because the *sendmail.cf* file changed.

## CHAPTER 4

Masquerading

4.0 Introduction

Masquerading is sendmail-speak for rewriting the hostname in the address of outbound mail. The reasons for masquerading fall into two general categories:

Mail routing

Many networks are designed to route all inbound mail through a central mail hub. When a host sends out mail using its own hostname in the sender address, replies to that mail may well come back to the host. Replacing the sending system's hostname with the mail hub's hostname in the sender address guarantees that replies come back to the hub. Masquerading is not the only way to do this. An MX record can also route mail to the hub. However, maintenance of the DNS zone file is under the control of the domain administrator. The sendmail administrator maintains masquerading, and most sendmail administrators prefer to be in charge of their own fate. Also, hostnames change over time. Masquerading can provide more consistent email addresses and can simplify maintenance.

Organizational requirements

Some organizations simply have a policy of hiding hostnames. Management may think that "busy" hostnames project an image of disorganization. Marketing may think that "frivolous" hostnames project the wrong image to customers. Naive security people may even believe that hiding hostnames increases security. For whatever reason, management requires masquerading, which, in turn, creates the need for systems configured to receive replies to the masqueraded mail.

The MASQUERADE_AS macro enables masquerading. This macro stores a value in the *sendmail.cf* $M macro and adds code to the MasqHdr ruleset to rewrite the header sender address using the value returned by $M.* By default, masquerading applies to

---

* Even configurations that don't use MASQUERADE_AS have a MasqHdr ruleset that adds the fully qualified name of the local host returned by $j to the sender address when the address lacks a hostname.

all of the mail that originates on the local host. All of the valid hostnames for the local host are stored in class $=w. When MASQUERADE_AS is used, sendmail replaces the hostname of the sender with the value of $M—if the original address lacks a hostname or the hostname matches a value in class $=w.

sendmail checks both class $=w and class $=M when masquerading.* Class $=M, however, starts out empty. Use the MASQUERADE_DOMAIN macro to add individual hostnames to class $=M. To add multiple hosts, create a file containing a list of hosts and use the MASQUERADE_DOMAIN_FILE macro to load the file into class $=M.

Normally, masquerading interprets the values in class $=M as hostnames and only exact matches are masqueraded. Use the *masquerade_entire_domain* feature to interpret the values in class $=M as domain names. When *masquerade_entire_domain* is used, every host in a domain listed in class $=M is masqueraded. *masquerade_entire_domain* is used in Recipe 4.8.

By default, masquerading is applied to the header sender address. The *masquerade_envelope* feature causes sendmail to also apply masquerading to the envelope sender address. Recipe 4.10 shows an example of how the *masquerade_envelope* feature is used. Using the *allmasquerade* feature applies masquerading to both sender and recipient addresses. Recipe 4.5 discusses the *allmasquerade* feature.

Masquerading is widely used and highly configurable, yet it is not the only way, or even the most powerful way, to rewrite the sender address in the From: header. Masquerading rewrites the hostname in the sender address; the *genericstable* rewrites the entire address—both the username and the hostname. The *genericstable* is related to masquerading in that they both modify the sender address, however, there are distinct differences:

- Masquerading rewrites the hostname based on the input hostname. The *genericstable* is applied to addresses based on the input hostname but can rewrite the entire address based on all or part of the input address.

- Masquerading replaces each masqueraded hostname with the same value, whereas the *genericstable* can replace each input address with a different value.

The *genericstable* feature defines the generics database in the *sendmail.cf* file and adds code to the MasqHdr ruleset to use that database to rewrite the sender address in the From: header. The key to the *genericstable* database is a username or a full email address, and the value returned for the key is a complete email address. To use the *genericstable*, first construct a text file in which each line of the file is a key/value pair using the format: username, whitespace, email address. A sample input entry in the text file is:

```
pat        patstover@butler.wrotethebook.com
```

---

* To force sendmail to ignore class $=w and use only class $=M for masquerading, use the *limited_masquerade* feature.

In this example, *pat* is the key against which the input username is matched, and *patstover@butler.wrotethebook.com* is the email address returned for that key. Before the *genericstable* can be used, the text file containing the key/value pairs must be converted to a hash type database using the sendmail *makemap* command.[*]

Both the username and the hostname from the input sender address are used by the *genericstable* process. The key to the *genericstable* database always contains a username, either by itself or as part of a full email address. However, sendmail only searches for that key if the hostname in the input sender address matches a value in class $=G or if the input sender address contains no hostname.

By default, class $=G is empty. Use the GENERICS_DOMAIN macro to add individual hostnames to class $=G, or the GENERICS_DOMAIN_FILE macro to load class $=G from a file. Normally, the values in class $=G are interpreted as hostnames. Use the *generics_entire_domain* feature to make sendmail interpret the values in class $=G as domain names. When the *generics_entire_domain* feature is used, the *genericstable* is applied to mail sent from every host in every domain listed in class $=G.

Both masquerading and the *genericstable* are used in the recipes in this chapter. But first we start with a recipe that uses the *always_add_domain* feature. *always_add_domain* has nothing to do with the *genericstable*, and, strictly speaking, it is not a masquerading command. However, it does rewrite the sender address, which is the common thread running through this chapter.

4.1 Adding Domains to All Sender Addresses

Problem

You have been asked to configure sendmail to add a hostname to every header sender address, even when the input address has no hostname part and the mail is being delivered by the local mailer.

Solution

Add the *always_add_domain* feature to the sendmail configuration. The command that you add is:

```
dnl Add the domain to all sender addresses
FEATURE(`always_add_domain')
```

Using Recipe 1.8 as a guide, build and install the sendmail configuration and then restart sendmail.

---

[*] Recipe 4.11 provides an example of building a *genericstable* database.

Discussion

The *always_add_domain* feature causes sendmail to make sure that every sender address includes a hostname part. By default, sendmail does not add a hostname part to the sender address when the address has no hostname part and the local mailer is delivering the mail. Thus, mail from the address *alana* goes through the local mailer's header sender process unchanged when the default configuration is used, as this test shows:

```
# sendmail -bt -Cgeneric-linux.cf
ADDRESS TEST MODE (ruleset 3 NOT automatically invoked)
Enter <ruleset> <address>
> /tryflags HS
> /try local alana
Trying header sender address alana for mailer local
canonify          input: alana
Canonify2         input: alana
Canonify2         returns: alana
canonify          returns: alana
1                 input: alana
1                 returns: alana
HdrFromL          input: alana
MasqHdr           input: alana
MasqHdr           returns: alana
HdrFromL          returns: alana
final             input: alana
final             returns: alana
Rcode = 0, addr = alana
> /quit
```

Rerunning the test after adding the *always_add_domain* feature to the configuration shows a different result:

```
# sendmail -bt
ADDRESS TEST MODE (ruleset 3 NOT automatically invoked)
Enter <ruleset> <address>
> /tryflags HS
> /try local alana
Trying header sender address alana for mailer local
canonify          input: alana
Canonify2         input: alana
Canonify2         returns: alana
canonify          returns: alana
1                 input: alana
1                 returns: alana
HdrFromL          input: alana
AddDomain         input: alana
AddDomain         returns: alana < @ *LOCAL* >
MasqHdr           input: alana < @ *LOCAL* >
MasqHdr           returns: alana < @ chef . wrotethebook . com . >
HdrFromL          returns: alana < @ chef . wrotethebook . com . >
final             input: alana < @ chef . wrotethebook . com . >
final             returns: alana @ chef . wrotethebook . com
Rcode = 0, addr = alana@chef.wrotethebook.com
> /quit
```

Here, the address goes in as *alana* and comes out with the hostname added as *alana@chef.wrotethebook.com*.

See Also

Recipe 4.4 shows how the *always_add_domain* feature can be used with masquerading. The *sendmail* book covers *always_add_domain* in section 4.8.4.

4.2   Masquerading the Sender Hostname

Problem

You have been asked to configure sendmail to replace the local hostname in the header sender address with a different hostname.

Solution

Add the MASQUERADE_AS macro to the sendmail configuration to rewrite the hostname in the From: address to the hostname specified by the MASQUERADE_AS macro. Add the EXPOSED_USER macro to the sendmail configuration to exclude non-unique user names from the address rewrite. Here are examples of these two macros:

```
dnl Masquerade the From address as wrotethebook.com
MASQUERADE AS(`wrotethebook.com')
dnl Users whose mail is not masqueraded
EXPOSED_USER(root)
```

Build the new *sendmail.cf* file, copy it to */etc/mail,* and restart sendmail as described in Recipe 1.8.

Discussion

Use the MASQUERADE_AS macro to configure sendmail to rewrite the host portion of the sender address on outbound mail. The value provided on the MASQUERADE_AS command line is stored in the *sendmail.cf* $M macro. sendmail uses the value from the $M macro to rewrite the hostname portion of the header sender address when the hostname matches any value found in *sendmail.cf* class $=w or class $=M. sendmail also uses the value from $M (instead of the value from the *sendmail.cf* $j macro) as the hostname portion of the header sender address, when the address lacks a hostname part. $j holds the fully qualified name of the local host. Normally, $j is added to the username to create a full email address. A test using the generic Linux configuration, which does not contain the MASQUERADE_AS macro, shows this:

```
# sendmail -bt –Cgeneric-linux.cf
ADDRESS TEST MODE (ruleset 3 NOT automatically invoked)
Enter <ruleset> <address>
```

```
> $M
Undefined
> $j
chef.wrotethebook.com
> /tryflags HS
> /try esmtp alana
Trying header sender address alana for mailer esmtp
canonify          input: alana
Canonify2         input: alana
Canonify2         returns: alana
canonify          returns: alana
1                 input: alana
1                 returns: alana
HdrFromSMTP       input: alana
PseudoToReal      input: alana
PseudoToReal      returns: alana
MasqSMTP          input: alana
MasqSMTP          returns: alana < @ *LOCAL* >
MasqHdr           input: alana < @ *LOCAL* >
MasqHdr           returns: alana < @ chef . wrotethebook . com . >
HdrFromSMTP       returns: alana < @ chef . wrotethebook . com . >
final             input: alana < @ chef . wrotethebook . com . >
final             returns: alana @ chef . wrotethebook . com
Rcode = 0, addr = alana@chef.wrotethebook.com
> /quit
```

The -C option on the sendmail command line loads the *generic-linux.cf* configuration, which does not contain the MASQUERADE_AS macro. The $M command shows that the $M macro is not defined. The $j command shows the fully qualified name of this host. In the example, the name is *chef.wrotethebook.com*. The /tryflags command tells sendmail to process the header sender (HS) address. The /try command tells sendmail to process *alana* as the header sender address for the esmtp mailer. Notice that *alana* is an email address that does not contain a host part. sendmail adds a hostname to the unqualified username, and, by default, it adds the hostname found in $j. The value returned by the MasqHdr ruleset shows this.

A second test, this time using the generic configuration with the addition of the sample lines shown in the Solution section, yields a different result. This time, a value is returned by the $M command, in addition to the value returned for $j. When *alana* is processed as the header sender address for the esmtp mailer, the MasqHdr ruleset rewrites the address using the value from $M instead of the value from $j:

```
# sendmail -bt
ADDRESS TEST MODE (ruleset 3 NOT automatically invoked)
Enter <ruleset> <address>
> $M
wrotethebook.com
> $j
chef.wrotethebook.com
> /tryflags HS
> /try esmtp alana
```

```
Trying header sender address alana for mailer esmtp
canonify          input: alana
Canonify2         input: alana
Canonify2        returns: alana
canonify         returns: alana
1                 input: alana
1                returns: alana
HdrFromSMTP       input: alana
PseudoToReal      input: alana
PseudoToReal     returns: alana
MasqSMTP          input: alana
MasqSMTP         returns: alana < @ *LOCAL* >
MasqHdr           input: alana < @ *LOCAL* >
MasqHdr          returns: alana < @ wrotethebook . com . >
HdrFromSMTP      returns: alana < @ wrotethebook . com . >
final             input: alana < @ wrotethebook . com . >
final            returns: alana @ wrotethebook . com
Rcode = 0, addr = alana@wrotethebook.com
> /quit
```

The *nullclient* configuration covered in Recipe 3.1 also masquerades mail so that it appears to come from the mail hub instead of the local host. This configuration, however, differs substantially from the *nullclient* configuration. The *nullclient* did not deliver its own mail. All of its mail was relayed through the hub. In that sense, the *nullclient*'s mail really did originate from the mail hub. This recipe creates a configuration that delivers its own mail and changes the hostname in the header sender address even though the mail originates from the local host.

In this example, the host masquerades using the domain name. Because all hosts in this sample domain masquerade using the same value, the possibility exists for conflicts caused by non-unique usernames. The classic example of a non-unique username is *root*—every Unix system has a *root* account. If mail from *root@crab.wrotethebook.com* and mail from *root@jamis.wrotethebook.com* was sent out as mail from *root@wrotethebook.com*, it would be difficult to sort out where the mail really came from and who should receive replies to the mail. For that reason, the EXPOSED_USER macro is used to ensure that mail from the root user is not masqueraded. A test shows this:

```
# sendmail -bt
ADDRESS TEST MODE (ruleset 3 NOT automatically invoked)
Enter <ruleset> <address>
> /tryflags HS
> /try esmtp root
Trying header sender address root for mailer esmtp
canonify          input: root
Canonify2         input: root
Canonify2        returns: root
canonify         returns: root
1                 input: root
1                returns: root
```

```
HdrFromSMTP       input: root
PseudoToReal      input: root
PseudoToReal    returns: root
MasqSMTP          input: root
MasqSMTP        returns: root < @ *LOCAL* >
MasqHdr           input: root < @ *LOCAL* >
MasqHdr         returns: root < @ chef . wrotethebook . com . >
HdrFromSMTP     returns: root < @ chef . wrotethebook . com . >
final             input: root < @ chef . wrotethebook . com . >
final           returns: root @ chef . wrotethebook . com
Rcode = 0, addr = root@chef.wrotethebook.com
> /quit
```

The example in this recipe has only one username specified in an EXPOSED_USER macro. To specify multiple usernames, add additional EXPOSED_USER macros—one for each username. For more than a few usernames, use the EXPOSED_USER_FILE macro as in this example:

```
EXPOSED_USER_FILE(`/etc/mail/exposed.users')
```

The file, */etc/mail/exposed.users* in our example, contains a list of usernames, with one username on each line. The sample file might look something like the following:

```
$ cat /etc/mail/exposed.users
root
postmaster
bin
daemon
adm
mail
news
operator
smmsp
nobody
```

This is just an example. Only non-unique usernames from which mail is actually sent would be placed in this file.

See Also

The *nullclient* configuration in Recipe 2.1 is a related configuration. Recipes 4.3 to 4.11 show masquerading with added features. The *sendmail* book covers MASQUERADE_AS in 4.4.2, and EXPOSED_USER and EXPOSED_USER_FILE are explained in 4.4.1. The "Address Masquerading" section of *Linux Sendmail Administration*, by Craig Hunt (Sybex), is a tutorial on masquerading. The *cf/README* file covers masquerading in the section *Masquerading and Relaying*.

4.3   Eliminating Masquerading for the Local Mailer

Problem

You have been asked to configure sendmail to masquerade the header sender address on all mail sent to external hosts, without adding the masquerade hostname to mail delivered by the local mailer.

Solution

Add the *local_no_masquerade* feature, the MASQUERADE_AS macro, and the EXPOSED_USER macro to the sendmail configuration. Here are examples of these configuration commands:

```
dnl Masquerade the From address as wrotethebook.com
MASQUERADE_AS(`wrotethebook.com')
dnl Users whose mail is not masqueraded
EXPOSED_USER(root)
dnl Don't masquerade addresses for the local mailer
FEATURE(`local_no_masquerade')
```

Build and install the new *sendmail.cf* file, and then restart sendmail. These steps are shown in Recipe 1.8.

Discussion

The hostname defined on the MASQUERADE_AS command line is stored in the *sendmail.cf* $M macro. sendmail rewrites the hostname in the From:' address to the value found in the $M macro if the original hostname is listed in class $=w or class $=M. By default, class $=w contains all of the names and addresses of the local host. Thus, mail sent from the local host is masqueraded using the value from $M. This is exactly what you want when mail is sent to an external host, but it might not be exactly what you want when the local mailer delivers the mail locally. Some tests show how local mail is handled by the MASQUERADE_AS macro.

First, we run two tests using the configuration defined in Recipe 4.2 (i.e., masquerading without the *local_no_masquerade* feature):

```
# sendmail -bt -Crecipe4.2.cf
ADDRESS TEST MODE (ruleset 3 NOT automatically invoked)
Enter <ruleset> <address>
> /tryflags HS
> /try local alana
Trying header sender address alana for mailer local
canonify           input: alana
Canonify2          input: alana
Canonify2        returns: alana
```

```
canonify          returns: alana
1                   input: alana
1                 returns: alana
HdrFromL            input: alana
MasqHdr             input: alana
MasqHdr           returns: alana
HdrFromL          returns: alana
final               input: alana
final             returns: alana
Rcode = 0, addr = alana
> /try local alana@chef.wrotethebook.com
Trying header sender address alana@chef.wrotethebook.com for mailer local
canonify            input: alana @ chef . wrotethebook . com
Canonify2           input: alana < @ chef . wrotethebook . com >
Canonify2         returns: alana < @ chef . wrotethebook . com . >
canonify          returns: alana < @ chef . wrotethebook . com . >
1                   input: alana < @ chef . wrotethebook . com . >
1                 returns: alana < @ chef . wrotethebook . com . >
HdrFromL            input: alana < @ chef . wrotethebook . com . >
MasqHdr             input: alana < @ chef . wrotethebook . com . >
MasqHdr           returns: alana < @ wrotethebook . com . >
HdrFromL          returns: alana < @ wrotethebook . com . >
final               input: alana < @ wrotethebook . com . >
final             returns: alana @ wrotethebook . com
Rcode = 0, addr = alana@wrotethebook.com
> /quit
```

Two valid local addresses are processed as header sender addresses for the local mailer. The first address is the local address for the username *alana* without any host part. In this case, the address goes in as *alana,* is processed, and comes out as *alana.* This is fine. Local addresses do not need a hostname part for delivery. Any local user receiving mail from *alana* can reply to that address and the mail will be successfully delivered by the local mailer. The second address, *alana@chef.wrotethebook.com*, is also a valid local address for *alana* because *chef.wrotethebook.com* is the name of the local host. This time, however, the address is changed to *alana@wrotethebook.com* by the header sender process. If a local user replies to *alana@wrotethebook.com*, the local mailer does not deliver the mail locally; instead, it is sent to the mail exchanger for *wrotethebook.com* by the esmtp mailer. Final delivery becomes the responsibility of the mail exchanger.

After adding the configuration lines shown in the Solution section, and building and installing the *sendmail.cf* file, the test results are different:

```
# sendmail -bt
ADDRESS TEST MODE (ruleset 3 NOT automatically invoked)
Enter <ruleset> <address>
> =SHdrFromL
R< @ >            MAILER-DAEMON
R@ < @ $* >            MAILER-DAEMON
R$+              $: $> AddDomain $1
> /tryflags HS
> /try local alana
```

```
Trying header sender address alana for mailer local
canonify          input: alana
Canonify2         input: alana
Canonify2         returns: alana
canonify          returns: alana
1                 input: alana
1                 returns: alana
HdrFromL          input: alana
HdrFromL          returns: alana
final             input: alana
final             returns: alana
Rcode = 0, addr = alana
> /try local alana@chef.wrotethebook.com
Trying header sender address alana@chef.wrotethebook.com for mailer local
canonify          input: alana @ chef . wrotethebook . com
Canonify2         input: alana < @ chef . wrotethebook . com >
Canonify2         returns: alana < @ chef . wrotethebook . com . >
canonify          returns: alana < @ chef . wrotethebook . com . >
1                 input: alana < @ chef . wrotethebook . com . >
1                 returns: alana < @ chef . wrotethebook . com . >
HdrFromL          input: alana < @ chef . wrotethebook . com . >
HdrFromL          returns: alana < @ chef . wrotethebook . com . >
final             input: alana < @ chef . wrotethebook . com . >
final             returns: alana @ chef . wrotethebook . com
Rcode = 0, addr = alana@chef.wrotethebook.com
> /quit
```

Processing *alana* as a header sender address yields the same result as before. The address goes in as *alana* and comes out as *alana*. However, this time the process is different—the MasqHdr ruleset is not called by the HdrFromL ruleset. The difference is more clearly seen in the processing of the *alana@chef.wrotethebook.com* address, which also goes through the process unchanged. A reply to the header sender address for either *alana* or *alana@chef.wrotethebook.com* is handled as local mail and delivered by the local mailer.

Using *local_no_masquerade* reduces overhead by keeping local mail local, but the impact of having some local mail go through an external host is probably not too large. The *local_no_masquerade* feature also ensures that all mail from local users addressed to local users is handled in the same way. Consistency is an advantage of this feature. Recipe 4.4 shows the opposite approach to obtaining consistency, which is to force masquerading of all sender addresses.

See Also

Recipes 4.2 and 4.4 describe similar recipes. The *sendmail* book covers MASQUERADE_AS in 4.4.2, EXPOSED_USER in 4.4.1, and *local_no_masquerade* in 4.8.20. The "Address Masquerading" section of *Linux Sendmail Administration*, by Craig Hunt (Sybex), is a tutorial on masquerading. The *cf/README* file covers masquerading in the section *Masquerading and Relaying*.

4.4 Forcing Masquerading of Local Mail

Problem

You have been asked to configure sendmail to masquerade all header sender addresses, even those processed by the local mailer that lack a hostname part.

Solution

Create a sendmail configuration that combines the *always_add_domain* feature used in Recipe 4.1 with the MASQUERADE_AS and EXPOSED_USER macros used in Recipe 4.2. Examples of these commands are:

```
dnl Masquerade the From address as wrotethebook.com
MASQUERADE_AS(`wrotethebook.com')
dnl Users whose mail is not masqueraded
EXPOSED_USER(`root')
dnl Add the domain name to all addresses
FEATURE(`always_add_domain')
```

Build and install the new *sendmail.cf* file, and restart sendmail as described in Recipe 1.8.

Discussion

The *always_add_domain* feature is not specific to masquerading. When *always_add_domain* is used without the MASQUERADE_AS macro, sendmail uses the fully qualified name of the local host found in the $j macro to create the hostname part of the sender address.* However, for this recipe we want to masquerade the hostname portion of the address; so the MASQUERADE_AS macro is used together with the *always_add_domain* feature in the recipe. After completing this recipe, running a sendmail -bt test produces the following result:

```
# sendmail -bt
ADDRESS TEST MODE (ruleset 3 NOT automatically invoked)
Enter <ruleset> <address>
> /tryflags HS
> /try local alana
Trying header sender address alana for mailer local
canonify          input: alana
Canonify2         input: alana
Canonify2       returns: alana
canonify        returns: alana
1                 input: alana
1               returns: alana
HdrFromL          input: alana
```

* Recipe 4.1 shows the effect of *always_add_domain* when used without masquerading.

```
AddDomain              input: alana
AddDomain              returns: alana < @ *LOCAL* >
MasqHdr                input: alana < @ *LOCAL* >
MasqHdr                returns: alana < @ wrotethebook . com . >
HdrFromL               returns: alana < @ wrotethebook . com . >
final                  input: alana < @ wrotethebook . com . >
final                  returns: alana @ wrotethebook . com
Rcode = 0, addr = alana@wrotethebook.com
> /try local alana@chef
Trying header sender address alana@chef for mailer local
canonify               input: alana @ chef
Canonify2              input: alana < @ chef >
Canonify2              returns: alana < @ chef . wrotethebook . com . >
canonify               returns: alana < @ chef . wrotethebook . com . >
1                      input: alana < @ chef . wrotethebook . com . >
1                      returns: alana < @ chef . wrotethebook . com . >
HdrFromL               input: alana < @ chef . wrotethebook . com . >
AddDomain              input: alana < @ chef . wrotethebook . com . >
AddDomain              returns: alana < @ chef . wrotethebook . com . >
MasqHdr                input: alana < @ chef . wrotethebook . com . >
MasqHdr                returns: alana < @ wrotethebook . com . >
HdrFromL               returns: alana < @ wrotethebook . com . >
final                  input: alana < @ wrotethebook . com . >
final                  returns: alana @ wrotethebook . com
Rcode = 0, addr = alana@wrotethebook.com
> /try local alana@chef.wrotethebook.com
Trying header sender address alana@chef.wrotethebook.com for mailer local
canonify               input: alana @ chef . wrotethebook . com
Canonify2              input: alana < @ chef . wrotethebook . com >
Canonify2              returns: alana < @ chef . wrotethebook . com . >
canonify               returns: alana < @ chef . wrotethebook . com . >
1                      input: alana < @ chef . wrotethebook . com . >
1                      returns: alana < @ chef . wrotethebook . com . >
HdrFromL               input: alana < @ chef . wrotethebook . com . >
AddDomain              input: alana < @ chef . wrotethebook . com . >
AddDomain              returns: alana < @ chef . wrotethebook . com . >
MasqHdr                input: alana < @ chef . wrotethebook . com . >
MasqHdr                returns: alana < @ wrotethebook . com . >
HdrFromL               returns: alana < @ wrotethebook . com . >
final                  input: alana < @ wrotethebook . com . >
final                  returns: alana @ wrotethebook . com
Rcode = 0, addr = alana@wrotethebook.com
> /quit
```

This test shows that local user addresses of all possible formats (*user*, *user@host*, and *user@host.domain*) are all rewritten into exactly the same format. The masquerade hostname stored in the $M macro is added to addresses that have no host part, and it is used to replace the hostname on addresses that do have a host part. Thus, the addresses *alana*, *alana@chef*, and *alana@chef.wrotethebook.com* all come out of the local mailer header sender address process rewritten to *alana@wrotethebook.com*. This consistency ensures that a reply to mail from Alana, regardless of how the original sender address was formatted, is handled in exactly the same way. In this case, all replies to mail from Alana will go to the mail exchanger first.

The goal of this recipe is to force sendmail to masquerade all sender addresses. At first glance, the *allmasquerade* feature might appear to be the correct choice for this recipe. However, the *allmasquerade* feature affects recipient addresses, and, in this recipe, we wish to rewrite only sender addresses. Recipe 4.5 covers masquerading the recipient address using the *allmasquerade* feature.

See Also

Recipes 4.1, 4.2, 4.3, and 4.5 provide information on related configurations. Recipe 3.1 covers the *nullclient* configuration. Recipe 3.3 covers the MAIL_HUB macro. The *sendmail* book covers the *always_add_domain* feature in 4.8.5 and the *allmasquerade* feature in 4.8.4.

4.5 Masquerading Recipient Addresses

Problem

By default, masquerading only affects sender addresses. In addition to masquerading sender addresses, you have been asked to configure sendmail to masquerade recipient addresses when those addresses include masqueraded hostnames.

Solution

Add the MASQUERADE_AS and EXPOSED_USER macros and the *allmasquerade* feature to the sendmail configuration. Here is an example of the lines that could be added:

```
dnl Masquerade as wrotethebook.com
MASQUERADE_AS(`wrotethebook.com')
dnl Users whose mail is not masqueraded
EXPOSED_USER(root)
dnl Masquerade recipient and sender addresses
FEATURE(`allmasquerade')
```

Build and install the new *sendmail.cf* file, and restart sendmail as described in Recipe 1.8.

Discussion

Using the basic masquerading configuration from Recipe 4.2, the header recipient address is not rewritten, as this test shows:

```
# sendmail -bt -Crecipe4.2.cf
ADDRESS TEST MODE (ruleset 3 NOT automatically invoked)
Enter <ruleset> <address>
> /tryflags HR
> /try esmtp david@chef
Trying header recipient address david@chef for mailer esmtp
canonify           input: david @ chef
```

```
Canonify2         input: david < @ chef >
Canonify2         returns: david < @ chef . wrotethebook . com . >
canonify          returns: david < @ chef . wrotethebook . com . >
2                 input: david < @ chef . wrotethebook . com . >
2                 returns: david < @ chef . wrotethebook . com . >
EnvToSMTP         input: david < @ chef . wrotethebook . com . >
PseudoToReal      input: david < @ chef . wrotethebook . com . >
PseudoToReal      returns: david < @ chef . wrotethebook . com . >
MasqSMTP          input: david < @ chef . wrotethebook . com . >
MasqSMTP          returns: david < @ chef . wrotethebook . com . >
EnvToSMTP         returns: david < @ chef . wrotethebook . com . >
final             input: david < @ chef . wrotethebook . com . >
final             returns: david @ chef . wrotethebook . com
Rcode = 0, addr = david@chef.wrotethebook.com
> /quit
```

The /tryflags command requests a test of the header recipient (HR) address processing. The /try command tells sendmail to process the address *david@chef* as a header recipient address for the esmtp mailer. The hostname *chef* is converted by DNS to the canonical name *chef.wrotethebook.com*. The hostname, however, is not masqueraded.

A configuration that contains the *allmasquerade* feature, in addition to the MASQUERADE_AS macro, rewrites recipient addresses for the emstp mailer, as this test shows:

```
# sendmail -bt
ADDRESS TEST MODE (ruleset 3 NOT automatically invoked)
Enter <ruleset> <address>
> /tryflags HR
> /try esmtp david@chef
Trying header recipient address david@chef for mailer esmtp
canonify          input: david @ chef
Canonify2         input: david < @ chef >
Canonify2         returns: david < @ chef . wrotethebook . com . >
canonify          returns: david < @ chef . wrotethebook . com . >
2                 input: david < @ chef . wrotethebook . com . >
2                 returns: david < @ chef . wrotethebook . com . >
HdrFromSMTP       input: david < @ chef . wrotethebook . com . >
PseudoToReal      input: david < @ chef . wrotethebook . com . >
PseudoToReal      returns: david < @ chef . wrotethebook . com . >
MasqSMTP          input: david < @ chef . wrotethebook . com . >
MasqSMTP          returns: david < @ chef . wrotethebook . com . >
MasqHdr           input: david < @ chef . wrotethebook . com . >
MasqHdr           returns: david < @ wrotethebook . com . >
HdrFromSMTP       returns: david < @ wrotethebook . com . >
final             input: david < @ wrotethebook . com . >
final             returns: david @ wrotethebook . com
Rcode = 0, addr = david@wrotethebook.com
> /quit
```

When the *allmasquerade* feature is used, masqueraded hostnames are hidden when they appear in the list of recipients. The advantage of this is that it provides a consistent view of the masqueraded addresses. A remote user might notice that people inside the *wrotethebook.com* domain send mail to the *david* account using the address *david@chef.wrotethebook.com*. That remote user might then try to do the same. If the organization really wants to encourage people to use the address *david@wrotethebook.com* to reach the *david* account, masquerading recipient addresses helps to do this by showing users only the preferred address.

See Also

Recipes 4.1 to 4.11 cover other masquerading features. The *sendmail* book covers MASQUERADE_AS in 4.4.2 and EXPOSED_USER in 4.4.1.

4.6 Masquerading at the Relay Host

Problem

You have been asked to configure the mail relay host to masquerade the header sender address of mail that originates on specific hosts as that mail passes through the mail relay.

Solution

Create a file that lists all of the hostnames that you want sendmail to masquerade. The file can be named anything you wish. This example names the file */etc/mail/masquerade-domains*.

Add the MASQUERADE_AS, EXPOSED_USER, and MASQUERADE_DOMAIN_FILE macros to the sendmail configuration on the mail relay host. The MASQUERADE_DOMAIN_FILE macro must specify the *masquerade-domains* file created in the first step. Here are examples of the commands added to the mail relay's configuration:

```
dnl Masquerade the From address as wrotethebook.com
MASQUERADE_AS(`wrotethebook.com')
dnl Users whose mail is not masqueraded
EXPOSED_USER(root)
dnl Load the list of hostnames that will be masqueraded
MASQUERADE_DOMAIN_FILE(`/etc/mail/masquerade-domains')
```

Build the new *sendmail.cf* file, copy it to */etc/mail*, and restart sendmail. Recipe 1.8 provides examples of these steps.

Discussion

The MASQUERADE_DOMAIN_FILE macro specifies a file that is loaded into *sendmail.cf* class $=M. sendmail masquerades hosts listed in class $=M, as well as those listed in class $=w. However, hosts listed in class $=M are not equivalent to those listed in class $=w. Placing a hostname in class $=M enables masquerading. But, unlike mail addressed to hosts listed in class $=w, mail addressed to hosts in class $=M is not accepted for local delivery. Class $=M makes it possible to extend the set of hosts for which masquerading is performed without adding to the list of local hostname aliases. A simple test shows the effect of the MASQUERADE_DOMAIN_FILE macro:

```
# sendmail -bt
ADDRESS TEST MODE (ruleset 3 NOT automatically invoked)
Enter <ruleset> <address>
> $=M
horseshoe.wrotethebook.com
rodent.wrotethebook.com
jamis.wrotethebook.com
> /tryflags HS
> /try esmtp david@jamis.wrotethebook.com
Trying header sender address david@jamis.wrotethebook.com for mailer esmtp
canonify         input: david @ jamis . wrotethebook . com
Canonify2        input: david < @ jamis . wrotethebook . com >
Canonify2        returns: david < @ jamis . wrotethebook . com . >
canonify         returns: david < @ jamis . wrotethebook . com . >
1                input: david < @ jamis . wrotethebook . com . >
1                returns: david < @ jamis . wrotethebook . com . >
HdrFromSMTP      input: david < @ jamis . wrotethebook . com . >
PseudoToReal     input: david < @ jamis . wrotethebook . com . >
PseudoToReal     returns: david < @ jamis . wrotethebook . com . >
MasqSMTP         input: david < @ jamis . wrotethebook . com . >
MasqSMTP         returns: david < @ jamis . wrotethebook . com . >
MasqHdr          input: david < @ jamis . wrotethebook . com . >
MasqHdr          returns: david < @ wrotethebook . com . >
HdrFromSMTP      returns: david < @ wrotethebook . com . >
final            input: david < @ wrotethebook . com . >
final            returns: david @ wrotethebook . com
Rcode = 0, addr = david@wrotethebook.com
> $=w
chef
localhost.localdomain
localhost
[192.168.0.8]
[localhost.localdomain]
[127.0.0.1]
chef.wrotethebook.com
> /quit
```

The $=M command displays the contents of class $=M and shows that class $=M contains the data from the */etc/mail/masquerade-domains* file we created. The email address *david@jamis.wrotethebook.com* is masqueraded as *david@wrotethebook.com* when it is processed as a header sender address for the esmtp mailer, even though *jamis.wrotethebook.com* is not included in class $=w because it is included in class $=M.

Alternatives

The sample *masquerade-domains* file contains only three entries. It is possible to replicate this configuration without creating the *masquerade-domains* file by placing three MASQUERADE_DOMAIN macros in the sendmail configuration file.

```
dnl Host names that will be masqueraded
MASQUERADE_DOMAIN(`rodent.wrotethebook.com')
MASQUERADE_DOMAIN(`horseshoe.wrotethebook.com')
MASQUERADE_DOMAIN(`jamis.wrotethebook.com')
```

This alternative was rejected because it is not as flexible as creating a separate *masquerade-domains* file. This recipe masquerades individual hostnames. Individual hosts come and go. Hostnames change. Each change would necessitate a change to the *m4* configuration with the associated rebuild, reinstall, and restart if the MASQUERADE_DOMAIN solution were used. Changes in the *masquerade-domains* file only require a restart.

If you're positive that you want to masquerade every host granted relay privileges, you might be tempted to use the *relay-domains* file as the MASQUERADE_DOMAIN_FILE:

```
MASQUERADE_DOMAIN_FILE(`/etc/mail/relay-domains')
```

This is generally a bad idea. A standard file should be used only for its standard purpose. The *relay-domains* file should be used only to grant relay privileges, and a separate file should be created to define masqueraded hostnames—even if those files are identical. The reason is that you cannot guarantee that they will remain identical into the future. In the long run, creating a separate file dedicated to a single purpose causes fewer problems than misusing a standard file.

See Also

Recipes 3.8 and 4.2 provide supporting information for this recipe. Recipes 4.4 and 4.7 cover similar configurations that should be evaluated before implementing this recipe. The *sendmail* book covers MASQUERADE_AS in 4.4.2, EXPOSED_USER in 4.4.1, MASQUERADE_DOMAIN in 4.4.3, and MASQUERADE_DOMAIN_FILE in 4.4.4. The "Address Masquerading" section of *Linux Sendmail Administration*, by Craig Hunt (Sybex), is a tutorial on masquerading. The *cf/README* file covers masquerading in the section *Masquerading and Relaying*.

4.7   Limiting Masquerading

Problem

By default, every hostname that is accepted for local delivery (i.e., every hostname that is accepted as an alias for the local host) is masqueraded when masquerading is enabled. You have been asked to create a sendmail configuration that does not masquerade every local hostname alias. Instead you are to masquerade only those hostnames that are specifically identified for masquerading.

Solution

Build a file that contains the names of just those hosts that you wish to masquerade. In this example, we name the file */etc/mail/masquerade-domains*.

Create a sendmail configuration containing the MASQUERADE_AS, EXPOSED_USER, and MASQUERADE_DOMAIN_FILE macros and the *limited_masquerade* feature. Here are sample commands:

```
dnl Masquerade the From address as wrotethebook.com
MASQUERADE_AS(`wrotethebook.com')
dnl Users whose mail is not masqueraded
EXPOSED_USER(root)
dnl Load the list of hostnames that will be masqueraded
MASQUERADE_DOMAIN_FILE(`/etc/mail/masquerade-domains')
dnl Only masquerade names listed in class $=M
FEATURE(`limited_masquerade')
```

Rebuild and reinstall the *sendmail.cf* file, and then restart sendmail, as described in Recipe 1.8.

Discussion

By default, every host listed in class $=w is allowed to relay, and mail addressed to any host in class $=w is accepted for local delivery. In addition, when the MASQUERADE_AS macro is used, mail from any host listed in class $=w is masqueraded. This is usually just what you want. An exception, however, occurs when class $=w defines a larger set of hosts for relaying or local delivery than the set that should be masqueraded. For example, assume that you have a mail exchanger that handles mail for a few domains, and that your *local-host-names* file contains the following entries:

```
horseshoe.wrotethebook.com
wrotethebook.com
ora.com
example.com
stateu.edu
```

Two of these entries (*horseshoe.wrotethebook.com* and *wrotethebook.com*) are in the local domain. The others are not.

Normally, both the hostnames in class $=w and those in class $=M are masqueraded. While this system is the mail exchanger for *ora.com*, *example.com*, and *stateu.edu*, it should not masquerade those domains as *wrotethebook.com*. The *limited_masquerade* feature limits masquerading to just those hosts listed in class $=M. Relaying and local delivery continue to be influenced by class $=w, but class $=w is ignored for masquerading when the *limited_masquerade* feature is used. A few tests illustrate this.

The first test is a sendmail -bt test using the *local-host-names* file just shown and a masquerading configuration that does *not* use the *limited_masquerade* feature.

```
# sendmail -bt -Crecipe4.2.cf
ADDRESS TEST MODE (ruleset 3 NOT automatically invoked)
Enter <ruleset> <address>
> $=w
example.com
chef
ora.com
localhost.localdomain
localhost
[192.168.0.8]
[localhost.localdomain]
stateu.edu
[127.0.0.1]
horseshoe.wrotethebook.com
wrotethebook.com
chef.wrotethebook.com
> /tryflags HS
> /try esmtp amanda@stateu.edu
Trying header sender address amanda@stateu.edu for mailer esmtp
canonify        input: amanda @ stateu . edu
Canonify2       input: amanda < @ stateu . edu >
Canonify2       returns: amanda < @ stateu . edu . >
canonify        returns: amanda < @ stateu . edu . >
1               input: amanda < @ stateu . edu . >
1               returns: amanda < @ stateu . edu . >
HdrFromSMTP     input: amanda < @ stateu . edu . >
PseudoToReal    input: amanda < @ stateu . edu . >
PseudoToReal    returns: amanda < @ stateu . edu . >
MasqSMTP        input: amanda < @ stateu . edu . >
MasqSMTP        returns: amanda < @ stateu . edu . >
MasqHdr         input: amanda < @ stateu . edu . >
MasqHdr         returns: amanda < @ wrotethebook . com . >
HdrFromSMTP     returns: amanda < @ wrotethebook . com . >
final           input: amanda < @ wrotethebook . com . >
final           returns: amanda @ wrotethebook . com
Rcode = 0, addr = amanda@wrotethebook.com
> /quit
```

In this case, the header sender address *amanda@stateu.edu* is rewritten to *amanda@wrotethebook.com*. The people at *stateu.edu* do not want their addresses rewritten in this manner, even though they use the services of the mail exchanger. To fix this, add a MASQUERADE_DOMAIN_FILE macro to the configuration and create a *masquerade-domains* file containing the names of the hosts that should be masqueraded. The file might, for example, contain the following:

```
rodent.wrotethebook.com
crab.wrotethebook.com
jamis.wrotethebook.com
giant.wrotethebook.com
horseshoe.wrotethebook.com
```

The MASQUERADE_DOMAIN_FILE macro loads the file into class $=M. Adding the *limited_masquerade* feature to the configuration causes sendmail to ignore class $=w and use $=M for masquerading, as the following test shows:

```
# sendmail -bt
ADDRESS TEST MODE (ruleset 3 NOT automatically invoked)
Enter <ruleset> <address>
> $=w
example.com
chef
ora.com
localhost.localdomain
localhost
[192.168.0.8]
[localhost.localdomain]
stateu.edu
[127.0.0.1]
horseshoe.wrotethebook.com
wrotethebook.com
chef.wrotethebook.com
> $=M
rodent.wrotethebook.com
crab.wrotethebook.com
jamis.wrotethebook.com
giant.wrotethebook.com
horseshoe.wrotethebook.com
> /tryflags HS
> /try esmtp amanda@stateu.edu
Trying header sender address amanda@stateu.edu for mailer esmtp
canonify          input: amanda @ stateu . edu
Canonify2         input: amanda < @ stateu . edu >
Canonify2         returns: amanda < @ stateu . edu . >
canonify          returns: amanda < @ stateu . edu . >
1                 input: amanda < @ stateu . edu . >
1                 returns: amanda < @ stateu . edu . >
HdrFromSMTP       input: amanda < @ stateu . edu . >
PseudoToReal      input: amanda < @ stateu . edu . >
PseudoToReal      returns: amanda < @ stateu . edu . >
MasqSMTP          input: amanda < @ stateu . edu . >
MasqSMTP          returns: amanda < @ stateu . edu . >
MasqHdr           input: amanda < @ stateu . edu . >
MasqHdr           returns: amanda < @ stateu . edu . >
HdrFromSMTP       returns: amanda < @ stateu . edu . >
final             input: amanda < @ stateu . edu . >
final             returns: amanda @ stateu . edu
Rcode = 0, addr = amanda@stateu.edu
> /quit
```

Now, mail from *amanda@stateu.edu* goes out with her full *stateu.edu* address despite the fact that *stateu.edu* still appears in class $=w. Only the hostnames in class $=M will be masqueraded.

The example used for these tests shows a single mail exchanger hosting multiple mail domains. This can also be done using virtual mail domains, which are covered in Chapter 5.

See Also

Recipes 2.1, 4.2, 4.4, and 4.6 provide supporting information for this recipe. Recipes 4.4 and 4.6 cover similar configurations that should be evaluated before implementing this recipe. The *sendmail* book covers MASQUERADE_AS in 4.4.2, EXPOSED_USER in 4.4.1, MASQUERADE_DOMAIN in 4.4.3, MASQUERADE_DOMAIN_FILE in 4.4.4, and the *limited_masquerade* feature in 4.8.18. The "Address Masquerading" section of *Linux Sendmail Administration*, by Craig Hunt (Sybex), is a tutorial on masquerading. The *cf/README* file covers masquerading in the section *Masquerading and Relaying*.

4.8   Masquerading All Hosts in a Domain

Problem

You want to masquerade every host within a domain without defining every individual hostname in class $=M or class $=w.

Solution

Create a sendmail configuration containing the MASQUERADE_AS and the EXPOSED_USER macros. Add the MASQUERADE_DOMAIN macro to define the domain to which the masqueraded hosts belong. Also add the *masquerade_entire_domain* feature to ensure that every host in the domain is masqueraded. Here is an example of these commands:

```
dnl Masquerade the From address as wrotethebook.com
MASQUERADE_AS(`wrotethebook.com')
dnl Users whose mail is not masqueraded
EXPOSED_USER(root)
dnl Store the domain name that will be masqueraded in class $=M
MASQUERADE_DOMAIN(`wrotethebook.com')
dnl Masquerade every host in the domain
FEATURE(`masquerade_entire_domain')
```

Build the new *sendmail.cf* file, install it, and restart sendmail. Recipe 1.8 provides an example of these steps.

Discussion

By default, every hostname listed in class $=w and class $=M is masqueraded when the MASQUERADE_AS macro is included in the configuration. This works perfectly on most systems because the system is only masquerading mail that originates on that system, and every valid hostname for the local host is defined in class $=w. Therefore, the system will masquerade all mail that is sent with one of its valid hostnames.

Mail exchangers, hubs, and relays are more complicated because they may handle mail for a variety of hosts. It is very common for a mail exchanger to handle mail for every host within a domain and to wish to masquerade mail from every host in that domain. Simply adding the domain name to class $=w or class $=M is not enough because the domain name is interpreted as a hostname, as this test shows:

```
# sendmail -bt -Crecipe4.6.cf
ADDRESS TEST MODE (ruleset 3 NOT automatically invoked)
Enter <ruleset> <address>
> $=m
wrotethebook.com
horseshoe.wrotethebook.com
> /tryflags HS
> /try esmtp michael@crab.wrotethebook.com
Trying header sender address michael@crab.wrotethebook.com for mailer esmtp
canonify          input: michael @ crab . wrotethebook . com
Canonify2         input: michael < @ crab . wrotethebook . com >
Canonify2         returns: michael < @ crab . wrotethebook . com . >
canonify          returns: michael < @ crab . wrotethebook . com . >
1                 input: michael < @ crab . wrotethebook . com . >
1                 returns: michael < @ crab . wrotethebook . com . >
HdrFromSMTP       input: michael < @ crab . wrotethebook . com . >
PseudoToReal      input: michael < @ crab . wrotethebook . com . >
PseudoToReal      returns: michael < @ crab . wrotethebook . com . >
MasqSMTP          input: michael < @ crab . wrotethebook . com . >
MasqSMTP          returns: michael < @ crab . wrotethebook . com . >
MasqHdr           input: michael < @ crab . wrotethebook . com . >
MasqHdr           returns: michael < @ crab . wrotethebook . com . >
HdrFromSMTP       returns: michael < @ crab . wrotethebook . com . >
final             input: michael < @ crab . wrotethebook . com . >
final             returns: michael @ crab . wrotethebook . com
Rcode = 0, addr = michael@crab.wrotethebook.com
> /quit
```

The test above shows that class $=M contains the value *wrotethebook.com*. However, mail from *crab*, which is a host in the *wrotethebook.com* domain, is not masqueraded because the values in $=M are viewed as hostnames, and only exact matches are masqueraded.

Adding the *masquerade_entire_domain* feature to the configuration changes this behavior. With this feature added, values in class $=w are still interpreted as hostnames, but values in class $=M are interpreted as domain names, and every host in a domain listed in class $=M is masqueraded. The *masquerade_entire_domain* feature is always associated with either a MASQUERADE_DOMAIN macro or a MASQUERADE_DOMAIN_FILE macro, both of which load values into class $=M, because the *masquerade_entire_domain* feature only affects values in class $=M. Testing the configuration created by this recipe shows the impact of this feature:

```
# sendmail -bt
ADDRESS TEST MODE (ruleset 3 NOT automatically invoked)
Enter <ruleset> <address>
> $=M
wrotethebook.com
> /tryflags HS
> /try esmtp michael@crab.wrotethebook.com
Trying header sender address michael@crab.wrotethebook.com for mailer esmtp
```

```
canonify          input: michael @ crab . wrotethebook . com
Canonify2         input: michael < @ crab . wrotethebook . com >
Canonify2        returns: michael < @ crab . wrotethebook . com . >
canonify         returns: michael < @ crab . wrotethebook . com . >
1                 input: michael < @ crab . wrotethebook . com . >
1                returns: michael < @ crab . wrotethebook . com . >
HdrFromSMTP       input: michael < @ crab . wrotethebook . com . >
PseudoToReal      input: michael < @ crab . wrotethebook . com . >
PseudoToReal     returns: michael < @ crab . wrotethebook . com . >
MasqSMTP          input: michael < @ crab . wrotethebook . com . >
MasqSMTP         returns: michael < @ crab . wrotethebook . com . >
MasqHdr           input: michael < @ crab . wrotethebook . com . >
MasqHdr          returns: michael < @ wrotethebook . com . >
HdrFromSMTP      returns: michael < @ wrotethebook . com . >
final             input: michael < @ wrotethebook . com . >
final            returns: michael @ wrotethebook . com
Rcode = 0, addr = michael@wrotethebook.com
> /quit
```

The $=M command shows the value stored in class $=M by the MASQUERADE_DOMAIN macro. In this case we have only one value to store in class $=M, and we do not anticipate changing it, so MASQUERADE_DOMAIN works well. If you have several values, you may want to use MASQUERADE_DOMAIN_FILE, which is used in Recipe 4.6. In this test, *crab.wrotethebook.com* is masqueraded because it is a host in a domain listed in class $=M—the impact of the *masquerade_entire_domain* feature. This feature does not impact values in class $=w. Those values are still interpreted as hosts and are still masqueraded. If you want to limit masquerading to just the domains defined in class $=M, add the *limited_masquerade* feature to the configuration, as described in Recipe 4.7.

See Also

Recipes 4.4 and 4.7 cover similar configurations that should be evaluated before implementing this recipe. The *sendmail* book covers the *masquerade_entire_domain* feature in 4.8.25, MASQUERADE_AS in 4.4.2, EXPOSED_USER in 4.4.1, MASQUERADE_DOMAIN in 4.4.3, and MASQUERADE_DOMAIN_FILE in 4.4.4. The "Address Masquerading" section of *Linux Sendmail Administration*, by Craig Hunt (Sybex), is a tutorial on masquerading. The *cf/README* file covers masquerading in the section *Masquerading and Relaying*.

4.9   Masquerading Most of the Hosts in a Domain

Problem

You have been asked to create a sendmail configuration that masquerades all of the hosts in a domain, with the exception of a few special purpose hosts that should be exposed to the outside world.

Solution

Create a file listing all of the hosts in the domain that should be exempted from masquerading. The name of the file is arbitrary. This recipe uses the name */etc/mail/masquerade-exceptions*.

Add the *masquerade_entire_domain* feature and the MASQUERADE_AS, EXPOSED_USER, MASQUERADE_DOMAIN, and MASQUERADE_EXCEPTION_FILE macros to the sendmail configuration. Examples of the relevant commands are shown below:

```
dnl Masquerade the From address as wrotethebook.com
MASQUERADE_AS(`wrotethebook.com')
dnl Users whose mail is not masqueraded
EXPOSED_USER(root)
dnl Store the domain name that will be masqueraded in class $=M
MASQUERADE_DOMAIN(`wrotethebook.com')
dnl Masquerade all hosts in the domain
FEATURE(`masquerade_entire_domain')
dnl Load the list of hosts that should not be masqueraded
MASQUERADE_EXCEPTION_FILE(`/etc/mail/masquerade-exceptions')
```

Using Recipe 1.8 as a guide, rebuild and reinstall *sendmail.cf*, and then restart sendmail.

Discussion

The *masquerade_entire_domain* feature causes sendmail to treat every name in class $=M as a domain, and, when combined with the MASQUERADE_AS macro, to masquerade every host within those domains. Recipe 4.8 shows the effect of the *masquerade_entire_domain* feature. If you want to masquerade most of the hosts in a domain, it is often easier to masquerade the entire domain and then make exceptions than it is to list all of the individual hosts that you want to masquerade. The file identified by the MASQUERADE_EXCEPTION_FILE macro is loaded into *sendmail.cf* class $=N. Class $=N contains a lists of hosts that should not be masqueraded even if they belong to a domain that is being masqueraded. For example, assume the */etc/mail/masquerade-exceptions* file created for this recipe contains the following entries:

```
# cat > /etc/mail/masquerade-exceptions
www.wrotethebook.com
info.wrotethebook.com
sales.wrotethebook.com
Ctrl-D
```

This recipe masquerades all hosts in *wrotethebook.com* except for these three hosts, as this test shows:

```
# sendmail -bt
ADDRESS TEST MODE (ruleset 3 NOT automatically invoked)
Enter <ruleset> <address>
> $=M
wrotethebook.com
> /tryflags HS
> /try esmtp peyton@crab.wrotethebook.com
```

```
Trying header sender address peyton@crab.wrotethebook.com for mailer esmtp
canonify           input: peyton @ crab . wrotethebook . com
Canonify2          input: peyton < @ crab . wrotethebook . com >
Canonify2          returns: peyton < @ crab . wrotethebook . com . >
canonify           returns: peyton < @ crab . wrotethebook . com . >
1                  input: peyton < @ crab . wrotethebook . com . >
1                  returns: peyton < @ crab . wrotethebook . com . >
HdrFromSMTP        input: peyton < @ crab . wrotethebook . com . >
PseudoToReal       input: peyton < @ crab . wrotethebook . com . >
PseudoToReal       returns: peyton < @ crab . wrotethebook . com . >
MasqSMTP           input: peyton < @ crab . wrotethebook . com . >
MasqSMTP           returns: peyton < @ crab . wrotethebook . com . >
MasqHdr            input: peyton < @ crab . wrotethebook . com . >
MasqHdr            returns: peyton < @ wrotethebook . com . >
HdrFromSMTP        returns: peyton < @ wrotethebook . com . >
final              input: peyton < @ wrotethebook . com . >
final              returns: peyton @ wrotethebook . com
Rcode = 0, addr = peyton@wrotethebook.com
> $=N
into.wrotethebook.com
www.wrotethebook.com
sales.wrotethebook.com
> /try esmtp jill@sales.wrotethebook.com
Trying header sender address jill@sales.wrotethebook.com for mailer esmtp
canonify           input: jill @ sales . wrotethebook . com
Canonify2          input: jill < @ sales . wrotethebook . com >
Canonify2          returns: jill < @ sales . wrotethebook . com . >
canonify           returns: jill < @ sales . wrotethebook . com . >
1                  input: jill < @ sales . wrotethebook . com . >
1                  returns: jill < @ sales . wrotethebook . com . >
HdrFromSMTP        input: jill < @ sales . wrotethebook . com . >
PseudoToReal       input: jill < @ sales . wrotethebook . com . >
PseudoToReal       returns: jill < @ sales . wrotethebook . com . >
MasqSMTP           input: jill < @ sales . wrotethebook . com . >
MasqSMTP           returns: jill < @ sales . wrotethebook . com . >
MasqHdr            input: jill < @ sales . wrotethebook . com . >
MasqHdr            returns: jill < @ sales . wrotethebook . com . >
HdrFromSMTP        returns: jill < @ sales . wrotethebook . com . >
final              input: jill < @ sales . wrotethebook . com . >
final              returns: jill @ sales . wrotethebook . com
Rcode = 0, addr = jill@sales.wrotethebook.com
> /quit
```

The $=M command shows that class $=M contains the domain name *wrotethebook.com*.
In this configuration, the *masquerade_entire_domain* feature is used, so processing
peyton@crab.wrotethebook.com as a header sender address for the esmtp mailer yields
the address *peyton@wrotethebook.com* because *crab* is a host in the *wrotethebook.com*
domain. However, processing the address *jill@sales.wrotethebook.com* as a header
sender address for the esmtp mailer returns the original address with no masquerading, even though *sales.wrotethebook.com* is a host in the *wrotethebook.com* domain.
The reason that *sales.wrotethebook.com* is not masqueraded is because it is listed in
class $=N as the $=N command shows.

Alternatives

Given the small number of hostnames in the *masquerade-exceptions* file, using the MASQUERADE_EXCEPTION macro would be a viable alternative to creating a file for the MASQUERADE_EXCEPTION_FILE macro. This recipe could be rewritten by replacing the MASQUERADE_EXCEPTION macro with the following lines:

```
dnl Define hosts that should not be masqueraded
MASQUERADE_EXCEPTION(`www.wrotethebook.com')
MASQUERADE_EXCEPTION(`info.wrotethebook.com')
MASQUERADE_EXCEPTION(`sales.wrotethebook.com')
```

The systems that are listed as exceptions to masquerading are generally special purpose systems. There are usually only a limited number of these systems, and there are few changes to this set of systems. For these reasons, the MASQUERADE_EXCEPTION macro is a viable alternative to creating a file to hold this list of hostnames. When you have a large number of hosts that should be excepted from masquerading, or the list of exempted hosts changes frequently, the MASQUERADE_EXCEPTION_FILE is the best choice. Use the macro that you prefer—they both work well.

See Also

Recipes 4.7 and 4.8 cover similar configurations that should be evaluated before implementing this recipe. The *sendmail* book covers the *masquerade_entire_domain* feature in 4.8.25, MASQUERADE_AS in 4.4.2, EXPOSED_USER in 4.4.1, MASQUERADE_DOMAIN in 4.4.3, MASQUERADE_DOMAIN_FILE in 4.4.4, and MASQUERADE_EXCEPTION and MASQUERADE_EXCEPTION_FILE in 4.4.5. The "Address Masquerading" section of *Linux Sendmail Administration*, by Craig Hunt (Sybex), is a tutorial on masquerading. The *cf/README* file covers masquerading in the section *Masquerading and Relaying*.

4.10   Masquerading the Envelope Address

Problem

In addition to masquerading the header sender address, you have been asked to create a configuration that masquerades the envelope sender address used by the SMTP protocol.

Solution

Add the *masquerade_envelope* feature, the MASQUERADE_AS macro, and the EXPOSED_ USER macro to the sendmail configuration file. Here are examples:

```
dnl Masquerade the From address as wrotethebook.com
MASQUERADE_AS(`wrotethebook.com')
dnl Users whose mail is not masqueraded
```

```
EXPOSED_USER(root)
dnl Masquerade the envelope address as wrotethebook.com
FEATURE(`masquerade_envelope')
```

Build and install the new configuration, and then restart sendmail. Recipe 1.8 provides an example.

Discussion

By default, the MASQUERADE_AS macro replaces the hostname in the From: message header with the masquerade value. The From: header address is referred to as the *header sender address*. From the point of view of the SMTP protocol, the message headers are just part of the message—the data sent after the SMTP DATA command. The addresses exchanged by the SMTP protocol before the SMTP DATA command are called the *envelope addresses*, and the address of the source of the mail is called the *envelope sender address*. The envelope sender address appears in the SMTP protocol exchange as the value in the SMTP MAIL From: command. By default, the MASQUERADE_ AS macro does not masquerade the hostname in the envelope sender address. A test of the basic masquerade configuration shows this:

```
# sendmail -bt -Crecipe4.2.cf
ADDRESS TEST MODE (ruleset 3 NOT automatically invoked)
Enter <ruleset> <address>
> /tryflags HS
> /try esmtp clark@horseshoe.wrotethebook.com
Trying header sender address clark@horseshoe.wrotethebook.com for mailer esmtp
canonify         input: clark @ horseshoe . wrotethebook . com
Canonify2        input: clark < @ horseshoe . wrotethebook . com >
Canonify2       returns: clark < @ horseshoe . wrotethebook . com . >
canonify        returns: clark < @ horseshoe . wrotethebook . com . >
1                input: clark < @ horseshoe . wrotethebook . com . >
1               returns: clark < @ horseshoe . wrotethebook . com . >
HdrFromSMTP      input: clark < @ horseshoe . wrotethebook . com . >
PseudoToReal     input: clark < @ horseshoe . wrotethebook . com . >
PseudoToReal    returns: clark < @ horseshoe . wrotethebook . com . >
MasqSMTP         input: clark < @ horseshoe . wrotethebook . com . >
MasqSMTP        returns: clark < @ horseshoe . wrotethebook . com . >
MasqHdr          input: clark < @ horseshoe . wrotethebook . com . >
MasqHdr         returns: clark < @ wrotethebook . com . >
HdrFromSMTP     returns: clark < @ wrotethebook . com . >
final            input: clark < @ wrotethebook . com . >
final           returns: clark @ wrotethebook . com
Rcode = 0, addr = clark@wrotethebook.com
> /tryflags ES
> /try esmtp clark@horseshoe.wrotethebook.com
Trying envelope sender address clark@horseshoe.wrotethebook.com for mailer esmtp
canonify         input: clark @ horseshoe . wrotethebook . com
Canonify2        input: clark < @ horseshoe . wrotethebook . com >
Canonify2       returns: clark < @ horseshoe . wrotethebook . com . >
canonify        returns: clark < @ horseshoe . wrotethebook . com . >
1                input: clark < @ horseshoe . wrotethebook . com . >
```

```
1                       returns: clark < @ horseshoe . wrotethebook . com . >
EnvFromSMTP     input: clark < @ horseshoe . wrotethebook . com . >
PseudoToReal    input: clark < @ horseshoe . wrotethebook . com . >
PseudoToReal    returns: clark < @ horseshoe . wrotethebook . com . >
MasqSMTP        input: clark < @ horseshoe . wrotethebook . com . >
MasqSMTP        returns: clark < @ horseshoe . wrotethebook . com . >
MasqEnv         input: clark < @ horseshoe . wrotethebook . com . >
MasqEnv         returns: clark < @ horseshoe . wrotethebook . com . >
EnvFromSMTP     returns: clark < @ horseshoe . wrotethebook . com . >
final           input: clark < @ horseshoe . wrotethebook . com . >
final           returns: clark @ horseshoe . wrotethebook . com
Rcode = 0, addr = clark@horseshoe.wrotethebook.com
> /quit
```

The first /tryflags command configures sendmail to test header sender (HS) address processing. The first /try command processes *clark@horseshoe.wrotethebook.com* as the header sender address for the esmtp mailer. The result shows that the address is masqueraded as *clark@wrotethebook.com*. The second /tryflags command configures the system for envelope sender (ES) address processing. This time, the address is not masqueraded. This is the basic masquerade configuration; it masquerades header addresses but not envelope addresses. The *masquerade_envelope* feature changes this, as the following test of this recipe's configuration shows:

```
# sendmail -bt
ADDRESS TEST MODE (ruleset 3 NOT automatically invoked)
Enter <ruleset> <address>
> /tryflags ES
> /try esmtp clark@horseshoe.wrotethebook.com
Trying envelope sender address clark@horseshoe.wrotethebook.com for mailer esmtp
canonify        input: clark @ horseshoe . wrotethebook . com
Canonify2       input: clark < @ horseshoe . wrotethebook . com >
Canonify2       returns: clark < @ horseshoe . wrotethebook . com . >
canonify        returns: clark < @ horseshoe . wrotethebook . com . >
1               input: clark < @ horseshoe . wrotethebook . com . >
1               returns: clark < @ horseshoe . wrotethebook . com . >
EnvFromSMTP     input: clark < @ horseshoe . wrotethebook . com . >
PseudoToReal    input: clark < @ horseshoe . wrotethebook . com . >
PseudoToReal    returns: clark < @ horseshoe . wrotethebook . com . >
MasqSMTP        input: clark < @ horseshoe . wrotethebook . com . >
MasqSMTP        returns: clark < @ horseshoe . wrotethebook . com . >
MasqEnv         input: clark < @ horseshoe . wrotethebook . com . >
MasqHdr         input: clark < @ horseshoe . wrotethebook . com . >
MasqHdr         returns: clark < @ wrotethebook . com . >
MasqEnv         returns: clark < @ wrotethebook . com . >
EnvFromSMTP     returns: clark < @ wrotethebook . com . >
final           input: clark < @ wrotethebook . com . >
final           returns: clark @ wrotethebook . com
Rcode = 0, addr = clark@wrotethebook.com
> /quit
```

This test replicates the second part of the earlier test. With the basic masquerade configuration, the envelope sender address was not masqueraded—now it is.

Users and user mail tools deal with header sender addresses. A reply in a user mail tool will reply to an address found in a message header. Masquerading header sender addresses ensures that remote users receive the correct address for replying to local users. In this way, masquerading benefits users.

Users, however, do not usually deal with envelope addresses. Masquerading envelope addresses simplifies machine interactions, and there are several good reasons to do this:

- To enable relaying. Evaluating the envelope address is one of the standard checks sendmail performs to authorize relaying. The header sender address is not normally used in relaying. Thus, if hosts need to masquerade in order to pass mail through a relay, it is the envelope sender address that is masqueraded.

- To ensure proper delivery of error messages, which are sent to the envelope address.

- To prevent sendmail from rejecting mail from hosts using private hostnames. sendmail checks the envelope sender address to see if it can be resolved via DNS. When private hostnames are used internally, mail from those hosts must be masqueraded to a hostname found in the public DNS and that masquerading must be applied to the envelope address. Otherwise, the mail might be rejected by the sendmail process running on the remote system.

For these and other reasons, many sites that use masquerading apply it to both the header and the envelope addresses.

See Also

Recipe 4.2 provides supporting information for this configuration. Chapter 3 covers configuring a mail relay and discusses the use of the envelope address in relaying. The *sendmail* book covers the MASQUERADE_AS macro in 4.4.2, the EXPOSED_USER macro in 4.4.1, and the *masquerade_envelope* feature in 4.8.26. The "Address Masquerading" section of *Linux Sendmail Administration*, by Craig Hunt (Sybex), is a tutorial on masquerading. The *cf/README* file covers masquerading in the section *Masquerading and Relaying*.

4.11 Rewriting the From Address with the genericstable

Problem

You have been asked to configure sendmail to replace the login name used as the sender address for mail originating from the local host with an address that meets the organization's desired address format.

Solution

Build a *genericstable* database to map the input sender address to the format you desire in the header sender address. Each entry in the *genericstable* contains two fields: the key and the value returned for that key. The key field of a *genericstable* entry can be either a full email address or a username. The value returned is the value that will be used as the rewritten sender address, which is normally a full address containing both a username and a hostname. To create the *genericstable*, first create a text file that contains the database entries and then run that text file through the *makemap* script to build the *genericstable* database.

To use the newly created *genericstable* database, create a sendmail configuration containing the *genericstable* feature and the GENERICS_DOMAIN macro. The domain name argument of the GENERICS_DOMAIN macro tells sendmail when to use the *genericstable*. Here are sample lines that could be added to the sendmail configuration:

```
dnl Process login names through the genericstable
FEATURE(`genericstable')
dnl Identify the host that the genericstable applies to
GENERICS_DOMAIN(`chef.wrotethebook.com')
```

Rebuild, reinstall, and restart sendmail as described in Recipe 1.8.

Discussion

By default, mail originating on the local host uses the user's login name as the username part, so, in this example, the key field of the *genericstable* is a login name and the value returned is a full email address. The mapping can be anything you wish, but, for this example, we map login names to the user's real name and the local domain name formatted as *firstname.lastname@domain*.* To do this, a text file is created and then run through *makemap*:

```
# cd /etc/mail
# cat > genericstable
kathy       kathy.mccafferty@wrotethebook.com
craig       craig.hunt@wrotethebook.com
sara        sara.henson@wrotethebook.com
dave        david.craig@wrotethebook.com
becky       rebecca.fro@wrotethebook.com
alana       alana.smiley@wrotethebook.com
jay         jay.james@wrotethebook.com
Ctrl-D
# makemap hash genericstable < genericstable
```

Of course, if mail arrives at the local host addressed to *firstname.lastname@domain*, aliases are needed to deliver the mail to the users' real address. Aliases based on the

---

* The *firstname.lastname@domain* format is not universally appreciated. See the FAQ for some reasons why you might not want to use this address format.

genericstable entries shown above could be added to the *aliases* database in the following manner:

```
# cd /etc/mail
# cat > aliases
kathy.mccafferty: kathy
craig.hunt:       craig
sara.henson:      sara
david.craig:      dave
rebecca.fro:      becky
alana.smiley:     alana
jay.james:        jay
Ctrl-D
# newaliases
```

After building the *genericstable* database and adding the *genericstable* feature to the configuration, the *genericstable* data is available to sendmail, as this sendmail -bt test shows:

```
# sendmail  bt
ADDRESS TEST MODE (ruleset 3 NOT automatically invoked)
Enter <ruleset> <address>
> /map generics sara
map_lookup: generics (sara) returns sara.henson@wrotethebook.com (0)
> /quit
```

Here sendmail is run with the -bt option and the /map command is used to lookup the entry for the login name *sara*. The value returned is *sara.henson@wrotethebook.com*. Thus, one would expect that any mail originating on this host from *sara* would have the sender address rewritten to *sara.henson@wrotethebook.com*. That would be the case here, but only because this recipe includes the GENERICS_DOMAIN macro. Without the GENERICS_DOMAIN macro, the *genericstable* feature does not act as one might expect. Here is an example using the *genericstable* feature without the GENERICS_DOMAIN macro:

```
# sendmail -bt -Cspecial4-11-test.cf
ADDRESS TEST MODE (ruleset 3 NOT automatically invoked)
Enter <ruleset> <address>
> $j
chef.wrotethebook.com
> /tryflags HS
> /try esmtp sara
Trying header sender address sara for mailer esmtp
canonify         input: sara
Canonify2        input: sara
Canonify2      returns: sara
canonify       returns: sara
1                input: sara
1              returns: sara
HdrFromSMTP      input: sara
PseudoToReal     input: sara
PseudoToReal   returns: sara
MasqSMTP         input: sara
```

```
MasqSMTP          returns: sara < @ *LOCAL* >
MasqHdr            input: sara < @ *LOCAL* >
canonify          input: sara . henson @ wrotethebook . com
Canonify2         input: sara . henson < @ wrotethebook . com >
Canonify2         returns: sara . henson < @ wrotethebook . com . >
canonify          returns: sara . henson < @ wrotethebook . com . >
MasqHdr           returns: sara . henson < @ wrotethebook . com . >
HdrFromSMTP       returns: sara . henson < @ wrotethebook . com . >
final             input: sara . henson < @ wrotethebook . com . >
final             returns: sara . henson @ wrotethebook . com
Rcode = 0, addr = sara.henson@wrotethebook.com
> /try esmtp sara@chef
Trying header sender address sara@chef for mailer esmtp
canonify          input: sara @ chef
Canonify2         input: sara < @ chef >
Canonify2         returns: sara < @ chef . wrotethebook . com . >
canonify          returns: sara < @ chef . wrotethebook . com . >
1                 input: sara < @ chef . wrotethebook . com . >
1                 returns: sara < @ chef . wrotethebook . com . >
HdrFromSMTP       input: sara < @ chef . wrotethebook . com . >
PseudoToReal      input: sara < @ chef . wrotethebook . com . >
PseudoToReal      returns: sara < @ chef . wrotethebook . com . >
MasqSMTP          input: sara < @ chef . wrotethebook . com . >
MasqSMTP          returns: sara < @ chef . wrotethebook . com . >
MasqHdr           input: sara < @ chef . wrotethebook . com . >
MasqHdr           returns: sara < @ chef . wrotethebook . com . >
HdrFromSMTP       returns: sara < @ chef . wrotethebook . com . >
final             input: sara < @ chef . wrotethebook . com . >
final             returns: sara @ chef . wrotethebook . com
Rcode = 0, addr = sara@chef.wrotethebook.com
> /quit
```

The test just shown is run on a host named *chef.wrotethebook.com*, as the $j command shows. This host is using the *genericstable* feature without the GENERICS_DOMAIN macro. Because Unix login names must be unique on a given host, we know that *sara, sara@chef,* and *sara@chef.wrotethebook.com* are all the same person. Yet the test shows that sendmail does not treat these input addresses the same with regard to the *genericstable*. When the input address has no host part, it is rewritten; otherwise, it is not rewritten. The reason is simple: the *genericstable* we created only maps login names; none of the database keys contains a hostname part. However, we want to create a consistent header sender address—not an address that varies depending on the address input by the user.

For this to be accomplished, this recipe uses the GENERICS_DOMAIN macro and sets that macro to the fully qualified name used in the $j macro. This causes sendmail to consistently apply the *genericstable* to rewriting the header sender address for all mail that originates on this host. Here is a test run with this recipe's configuration:

```
# sendmail -bt
ADDRESS TEST MODE (ruleset 3 NOT automatically invoked)
Enter <ruleset> <address>
> $=G
```

```
chef.wrotethebook.com
> /tryflags HS
> /try esmtp sara@[127.0.0.1]
Trying header sender address sara@[127.0.0.1] for mailer esmtp
canonify          input: sara @ [ 127 . 0 . 0 . 1 ]
Canonify2         input: sara < @ [ 127 . 0 . 0 . 1 ] >
Canonify2         returns: sara < @ chef . wrotethebook . com . >
canonify          returns: sara < @ chef . wrotethebook . com . >
1                 input: sara < @ chef . wrotethebook . com . >
1                 returns: sara < @ chef . wrotethebook . com . >
HdrFromSMTP       input: sara < @ chef . wrotethebook . com . >
PseudoToReal      input: sara < @ chef . wrotethebook . com . >
PseudoToReal      returns: sara < @ chef . wrotethebook . com . >
MasqSMTP          input: sara < @ chef . wrotethebook . com . >
MasqSMTP          returns: sara < @ chef . wrotethebook . com . >
MasqHdr           input: sara < @ chef . wrotethebook . com . >
canonify          input: sara . henson @ wrotethebook . com
Canonify2         input: sara . henson < @ wrotethebook . com >
Canonify2         returns: sara . henson < @ wrotethebook . com . >
canonify          returns: sara . henson < @ wrotethebook . com . >
MasqHdr           returns: sara . henson < @ wrotethebook . com . >
HdrFromSMTP       returns: sara . henson < @ wrotethebook . com . >
final             input: sara . henson < @ wrotethebook . com . >
final             returns: sara . henson @ wrotethebook . com
Rcode = 0, addr = sara.henson@wrotethebook.com
> /quit
```

The GENERICS_DOMAIN macro loads the value specified on its command line into
sendmail.cf class $=G. sendmail applies the *genericstable* to any sender address that
has a name listed in class $=G as its hostname part. In this test, the $=G command
shows that class $=G contains only *chef.wrotethebook.com*, which is the fully qualified
name of this host—the same value found in $j. Therefore, any hostname that send-
mail rewrites to $j will match the value in $=G and will also be processed through the
genericstable. In this test, we show an extreme case using the loopback address [127.
0.0.1] as the hostname, which sendmail rewrites to the value returned by $j and
then rewrites through the *genericstable*. We could just as easily have used *chef*,
localhost, [192.168.0.8], or *chef.wrotethebook.com* as the hostname—all valid variations of the local host's name work.[*]

In this recipe, the email processed through the *genericstable* all originates on the local
host. Thus, the input sender address either has no hostname part, or the hostname in
the sender address is a hostname of the local host. Many systems (mail relay hosts
are an example) handle mail from a variety of hosts. The sender address in that case
can contain the hostname of any host granted relaying privileges. Because mail is
only processed through the *genericstable* when the sender's hostname is found in
class $=G, the hostnames of all of the hosts allowed to send mail through the relay

---

[*] This does not necessarily mean that all of the local hostname aliases found in class $=w will be processed
through the *genericstable*. This recipe only processes hostnames that resolve to the value returned by $j.

should be loaded into class $=G. If this is a small number of hostnames, it can be done by placing multiple GENERICS_DOMAIN macros in the configuration. If there are more than a few hostnames, it is simpler to create a file that lists all of the hosts and then to reference that file inside the configuration with a GENERICS_DOMAIN_FILE macro. For example, the following macro used in this recipe, in place of the GENERICS_DOMAIN macro, would load $=G with all of the hostnames listed in a file called */etc/mail/generics-domains*:

```
GENERICS_DOMAIN_FILE(`/etc/mail/generics-domains')
```

The GENERICS_DOMAIN_FILE macro makes it possible to coordinate *genericstable* processing with other sendmail functions simply by extracting hostnames from the files that control those other functions and storing those names in the file loaded by the GENERICS_DOMAIN_FILE macro. For example, copying the hostnames from */etc/mail/local-host-names* to the file loaded by the GENERICS_DOMAIN_FILE macro enables *genericstable* processing for all systems that use a mail exchanger.

See Also

Recipe 4.12 shows another *genericstable* example. Recipe 4.14 shows how the *genericstable* can be read from an LDAP server. The *sendmail* book covers the *genericstable* in 4.8.16, the GENERICS_DOMAIN macro in 4.8.16.1, and the GENERICS_DOMAIN_FILE macro in 4.8.16.2. Chapter 9 of *Linux Sendmail Administration*, by Craig Hunt (Sybex), contains the tutorial section "Masquerading Usernames" that provides additional information.

4.12   Rewriting Sender Addresses for an Entire Domain

Problem

You have been asked to configure sendmail to rewrite the sender address into your organization's standard header sender address format on all mail originating from the local domain.

Solution

Build a *genericstable* database to map the input address to the format desired for the header sender address. Each entry in the *genericstable* contains two fields. The first field matches the input address and the second field rewrites the address. To create the *genericstable*, first create a text file that contains the database entries, then run that text file through the *makemap* command to build the *genericstable* database.

Add the *genericstable* feature, the GENERICS_DOMAIN macro, and the *generics_entire_domain* feature to the sendmail configuration. The added commands would look something like the following:

```
dnl Process login names through the genericstable
FEATURE(`genericstable')
dnl Load wrotethebook.com into G
GENERICS_DOMAIN(`wrotethebook.com')
dnl Interpret the value in G as a domain name
FEATURE(`generics_entire_domain')
```

Build *sendmail.cf*, copy it to */etc/mail*, and then restart sendmail. See Recipe 1.8 if you need an example of this step.

Discussion

The input sender address is rewritten as specified by the *genericstable*. All or part of the input address is used as a key to search the *genericstable*. When a value is returned by the search, that value is used to rewrite the address. For this example, we create the following *genericstable*:

```
# cd /etc/mail
# cat > genericstable
kathy                          kathy.mccafferty@wrotethebook.com
craig                          craig.hunt@wrotethebook.com
sara                           sara.henson@wrotethebook.com
dave                           david.craig@wrotethebook.com
becky                          rebecca.fro@wrotethebook.com
jay                            jay.james@wrotethebook.com
alana@blur.wrotethebook.com    alana.darling@wrotethebook.com
alana@giant.wrotethebook.com   alana.henson@wrotethebook.com
alana                          alana.smiley@wrotethebook.com
Ctrl-D
# makemap hash genericstable < genericstable
```

The *genericstable* feature adds the code sendmail needs to make use of the *genericstable*. The GENERICS_DOMAIN macro adds the value specified on the macro command line to sendmail class $=G.

Normally, the values listed in class $=G are interpreted as hostnames, and only exact matches enable *genericstable* processing. The *generics_entire_domain* feature causes sendmail to interpret the values in class $=G as domain names, and any host within one of those domains is processed through the *genericstable*. Here is a test of a system running this recipe:

```
# sendmail -bt
ADDRESS TEST MODE (ruleset 3 NOT automatically invoked)
Enter <ruleset> <address>
> $=G
wrotethebook.com
> /tryflags HS
> /try esmtp dave@tassajara.wrotethebook.com
```

```
Trying header sender address dave@tassajara.wrotethebook.com for mailer esmtp
canonify          input: dave @ tassajara . wrotethebook . com
Canonify2         input: dave < @ tassajara . wrotethebook . com >
Canonify2         returns: dave < @ tassajara . wrotethebook . com . >
canonify          returns: dave < @ tassajara . wrotethebook . com . >
1                 input: dave < @ tassajara . wrotethebook . com . >
1                 returns: dave < @ tassajara . wrotethebook . com . >
HdrFromSMTP       input: dave < @ tassajara . wrotethebook . com . >
PseudoToReal      input: dave < @ tassajara . wrotethebook . com . >
PseudoToReal      returns: dave < @ tassajara . wrotethebook . com . >
MasqSMTP          input: dave < @ tassajara . wrotethebook . com . >
MasqSMTP          returns: dave < @ tassajara . wrotethebook . com . >
MasqHdr           input: dave < @ tassajara . wrotethebook . com . >
canonify          input: david . craig @ wrotethebook . com
Canonify2         input: david . craig < @ wrotethebook . com >
Canonify2         returns: david . craig < @ wrotethebook . com . >
canonify          returns: david . craig < @ wrotethebook . com . >
MasqHdr           returns: david . craig < @ wrotethebook . com . >
HdrFromSMTP       returns: david . craig < @ wrotethebook . com . >
final             input: david . craig < @ wrotethebook . com . >
final             returns: david . craig @ wrotethebook . com
Rcode = 0, addr = david.craig@wrotethebook.com
> /map generics dave
map_lookup: generics (dave) returns david.craig@wrotethebook.com (0)
> /quit
```

The test shows that the hostname *tassajara.wrotethebook.com* is not in class $=G; in fact, class $=G only contains the domain name *wrotethebook.com*. Yet the header sender address *dave@tassajara.wrotethebook.com* is rewritten to *david.craig@wrotethebook. com*, which is the value returned by the *genericstable* for the key dave.

In this example, every *dave* account in the entire *wrotethebook.com* domain belongs to David Craig. No matter what host in that domain he sends mail from, when the mail passes through this system, it is rewritten to *david.craig@wrotethebook.com*. For replies to the rewritten address to work correctly, the rewritten hostname must resolve to a host that will accept the mail, and that host must have an alias for *david.craig* that delivers the mail to the real *dave* account.

A more interesting case is the mapping of the username *alana*. Three people in the *wrotethebook.com* domain have this username: Alana Darling, Alana Henson, and Alana Smiley. The following test shows how each of these names are mapped:

```
# sendmail -bt
ADDRESS TEST MODE (ruleset 3 NOT automatically invoked)
Enter <ruleset> <address>
> /tryflags HS
> /try esmtp alana@blur.wrotethebook.com
Trying header sender address alana@blur.wrotethebook.com for mailer esmtp
canonify          input: alana @ blur . wrotethebook . com
Canonify2         input: alana < @ blur . wrotethebook . com >
Canonify2         returns: alana < @ blur . wrotethebook . com . >
canonify          returns: alana < @ blur . wrotethebook . com . >
```

```
1                    input: alana < @ blur . wrotethebook . com . >
1                    returns: alana < @ blur . wrotethebook . com . >
HdrFromSMTP          input: alana < @ blur . wrotethebook . com . >
PseudoToReal         input: alana < @ blur . wrotethebook . com . >
PseudoToReal         returns: alana < @ blur . wrotethebook . com . >
MasqSMTP             input: alana < @ blur . wrotethebook . com . >
MasqSMTP             returns: alana < @ blur . wrotethebook . com . >
MasqHdr              input: alana < @ blur . wrotethebook . com . >
canonify             input: alana . darling @ wrotethebook . com
Canonify2            input: alana . darling < @ wrotethebook . com >
Canonify2            returns: alana . darling < @ wrotethebook . com . >
canonify             returns: alana . darling < @ wrotethebook . com . >
MasqHdr              returns: alana . darling < @ wrotethebook . com . >
HdrFromSMTP          returns: alana . darling < @ wrotethebook . com . >
final                input: alana . darling < @ wrotethebook . com . >
final                returns: alana . darling @ wrotethebook . com
Rcode = 0, addr = alana.darling@wrotethebook.com
> /try esmtp alana@giant.wrotethebook.com
Trying header sender address alana@giant.wrotethebook.com for mailer esmtp
canonify             input: alana @ giant . wrotethebook . com
Canonify2            input: alana < @ giant . wrotethebook . com >
Canonify2            returns: alana < @ giant . wrotethebook . com . >
canonify             returns: alana < @ giant . wrotethebook . com . >
1                    input: alana < @ giant . wrotethebook . com . >
1                    returns: alana < @ giant . wrotethebook . com . >
HdrFromSMTP          input: alana < @ giant . wrotethebook . com . >
PseudoToReal         input: alana < @ giant . wrotethebook . com . >
PseudoToReal         returns: alana < @ giant . wrotethebook . com . >
MasqSMTP             input: alana < @ giant . wrotethebook . com . >
MasqSMTP             returns: alana < @ giant . wrotethebook . com . >
MasqHdr              input: alana < @ giant . wrotethebook . com . >
canonify             input: alana . henson @ wrotethebook . com
Canonify2            input: alana . henson < @ wrotethebook . com >
Canonify2            returns: alana . henson < @ wrotethebook . com . >
canonify             returns: alana . henson < @ wrotethebook . com . >
MasqHdr              returns: alana . henson < @ wrotethebook . com . >
HdrFromSMTP          returns: alana . henson < @ wrotethebook . com . >
final                input: alana . henson < @ wrotethebook . com . >
final                returns: alana . henson @ wrotethebook . com
Rcode = 0, addr = alana.henson@wrotethebook.com
> /try esmtp alana@anywhere.wrotethebook.com
Trying header sender address alana@anywhere.wrotethebook.com for mailer esmtp
canonify             input: alana @ anywhere . wrotethebook . com
Canonify2            input: alana < @ anywhere . wrotethebook . com >
Canonify2            returns: alana < @ anywhere . wrotethebook . com . >
canonify             returns: alana < @ anywhere . wrotethebook . com . >
1                    input: alana < @ anywhere . wrotethebook . com . >
1                    returns: alana < @ anywhere . wrotethebook . com . >
HdrFromSMTP          input: alana < @ anywhere . wrotethebook . com . >
PseudoToReal         input: alana < @ anywhere . wrotethebook . com . >
PseudoToReal         returns: alana < @ anywhere . wrotethebook . com . >
MasqSMTP             input: alana < @ anywhere . wrotethebook . com . >
MasqSMTP             returns: alana < @ anywhere . wrotethebook . com . >
MasqHdr              input: alana < @ anywhere . wrotethebook . com . >
```

```
canonify         input: alana . smiley @ wrotethebook . com
Canonify2        input: alana . smiley < @ wrotethebook . com >
Canonify2       returns: alana . smiley < @ wrotethebook . com . >
canonify        returns: alana . smiley < @ wrotethebook . com . >
MasqHdr         returns: alana . smiley < @ wrotethebook . com . >
HdrFromSMTP     returns: alana . smiley < @ wrotethebook . com . >
final            input: alana . smiley < @ wrotethebook . com . >
final           returns: alana . smiley @ wrotethebook . com
Rcode = 0, addr = alana.smiley@wrotethebook.com
> /quit
```

The complete addresses used in the *genericstable* keys for Alana Darling and Alana Henson make it possible for sendmail to do one-to-one mappings for those addresses. The key used for Alana Smiley's entry, however, is just a username. That key matches any input address that contains the username *alana*, except for the input addresses *alana@blur.wrotethebook.com* and *alana@giant.wrotethebook.com*.

When a system handles mail that originates from several hosts, it is possible to have duplicate login names. The fact that the key in the *genericstable* can contain a full email address allows you to map these overlapping usernames.

See Also

Recipe 4.11 provides another *genericstable* example, and Recipe 4.14 shows how the *genericstable* can be read from an LDAP server. The *sendmail* book covers the *genericstable* in 4.8.16, the GENERICS_DOMAIN macro in 4.8.16.1, and the *generics_entire_domain* feature in 4.8.15. Chapter 9 of *Linux Sendmail Administration*, by Craig Hunt (Sybex), contains the tutorial section "Masquerading Usernames" that provides additional information.

4.13   Masquerading with LDAP

Problem

You have been asked to configure sendmail so that it reads data that controls masquerading from an LDAP server.

Solution

On the LDAP server, add the *sendmail.schema* file to the LDAP configuration as described in Recipe 1.3.

On the LDAP server, add the masquerade configuration data to the LDAP database. To do this, create an LDIF file containing the list of masqueraded domains and an LDIF file containing the list of exposed users. The object class of the data in both files must be the sendmailMTAClass defined in the *sendmail.schema* file. Use *ldapadd* to add this data to the LDAP database.

Check the sendmail compiler options on the sendmail host. If sendmail does not list LDAPMAP among the "Compiled with:" flags, recompile and reinstall sendmail as described in Recipe 1.3.

On the sendmail host, create a configuration that reads the MASQUERADE_DOMAIN_FILE and the EXPOSED_USER files from the LDAP server. Set confLDAP_CLUSTER to match the sendmailMTACluster attribute used in the records added to the LDAP database. Here is an example of the lines added to the sendmail configuration:

```
dnl Masquerade the From address as wrotethebook.com
MASQUERADE_AS(`wrotethebook.com')
dnl Define the LDAP cluster to which this host belongs
define(`confLDAP_CLUSTER', `wrotethebook.com')dnl
dnl Use LDAP to read usernames that are not masqueraded
EXPOSED_USER_FILE(`@LDAP')
dnl Get the list of masqueraded hostnames from LDAP
MASQUERADE_DOMAIN_FILE(`@LDAP')
```

Build the new *sendmail.cf* file and copy it to */etc/mail*. Restart sendmail. See Recipe 1.8 for examples.

Discussion

This recipe assumes that you have a fully functional LDAP server to which the sendmail masquerading information can be added. If you need help on LDAP, see *Understanding and Deploying LDAP Directory Services*, by Howes, Smith, and Good (Macmillan), and *LDAP System Administration*, by Gerald Carter (O'Reilly). Get the LDAP server up, running, and debugged before you attempt this recipe.

After ensuring that the LDAP server is ready to support sendmail, add the masquerade data to the LDAP database. This example creates a record for the hostnames that will be loaded into the $=M class:

```
# cat > ldap-masquerade-domains
dn: sendmailMTAClassName=M, dc=wrotethebook, dc=com
objectClass: sendmailMTA
objectClass: sendmailMTAClass
sendmailMTACluster: wrotethebook.com
sendmailMTAClassName: M
sendmailMTAClassValue: rodent.wrotethebook.com
sendmailMTAClassValue: horseshoe.wrotethebook.com
sendmailMTAClassValue: jamis.wrotethebook.com
Ctrl-D
# ldapadd -x -D "cn=Manager,dc=wrotethebook,dc=com" \
> -W -f ldap-masquerade-domains
Enter LDAP Password: SecretLDAPpassword
adding new entry "sendmailMTAClassName=M, dc=wrotethebook, dc=com"
```

This example adds the list of exposed users to the LDAP database:

```
# cat > ldap-exposed-users
dn: sendmailMTAClassName=E, dc=wrotethebook, dc=com
```

```
objectClass: sendmailMTA
objectClass: sendmailMTAClass
sendmailMTACluster: wrotethebook.com
sendmailMTAClassName: E
sendmailMTAClassValue: root
Ctrl-D
# ldapadd -x -D "cn=Manager,dc=wrotethebook,dc=com" \
> -W -f ldap-exposed-users
Enter LDAP Password: SecretLDAPpassword
adding new entry "sendmailMTAClassName=E, dc=wrotethebook, dc=com"
```

The examples above show the LDAP format used for sendmail class data. The class to which the LDAP record applies is defined by the sendmailMTAClassName attribute. The values that should be loaded into the specified class are defined in the LDAP record using one or more sendmailMTAClassValue attributes. In the examples, the record for class $=M contains three values, and the record for class $=E contains one value. Convert the LDIF data to LDAP format and add it to the LDAP database using the *ldapadd* command.* Use the *ldapsearch* command to examine the new data:†

```
# ldapsearch -LLL -x '(sendmailMTAClassName=M)' sendmailMTAClassValue
dn: sendmailMTAClassName=M, dc=wrotethebook, dc=com
sendmailMTAClassValue: rodent.wrotethebook.com
sendmailMTAClassValue: horseshoe.wrotethebook.com
sendmailMTAClassValue: jamis.wrotethebook.com
# ldapsearch -LLL -x '(sendmailMTAClassName=E)' sendmailMTAClassValue
dn: sendmailMTAClassName=E, dc=wrotethebook, dc=com
sendmailMTAClassValue: root
```

LDAP is ready. Now configure sendmail to ask LDAP for the masquerade data by using the string @LDAP in place of the file path in the MASQUERADE_DOMAIN_FILE and the EXPOSED_USER_FILE macros. When @LDAP is specified, sendmail queries LDAP for the required data using the standard sendmail schema.

This recipe also defines a value for confLDAP_CLUSTER. sendmail LDAP records apply either to an individual host or to a group of hosts called a *cluster*. A cluster is analogous to a NIS domain—it is a group of hosts that use the same LDAP data. The cluster name is defined in the sendmail configuration with the confLDAP_CLUSTER variable and in the LDAP records using the sendmailMTACluster attribute. If the LDAP records apply to a single host, the host is identified in the LDAP records by the sendmailMTAHost attribute, but no special sendmail configuration is needed because the hostname value returned by $j is used for the LDAP query. Note that if the confLDAP_CLUSTER variable is configured for a host that also has host-specific LDAP data, both the host data and the cluster data will be returned when that host issues an LDAP query. This recipe defines a cluster name in the sendmail configuration and uses only cluster data in the LDAP database.

---

* All LDAP examples in this book assume that OpenLDAP is being used. Adjust the commands to fit your system.

† If *ldapsearch* requires -h and -b values, use confLDAP_DEFAULT_SPEC to set the same values for sendmail, as described in Recipe 5.9.

A simple test shows the impact of this recipe:

```
# sendmail -bt -Cgeneric-linux.cf
ADDRESS TEST MODE (ruleset 3 NOT automatically invoked)
Enter <ruleset> <address>
> $=M
> $=E
> /quit
# sendmail -bt -Csendmail.cf
ADDRESS TEST MODE (ruleset 3 NOT automatically invoked)
Enter <ruleset> <address>
> $=M
rodent.wrotethebook.com
jamis.wrotethebook.com
horseshoe.wrotethebook.com
> $=E
root
> /quit
```

A sendmail -bt test using the generic configuration shows that, by default, class $=M and class $=E are empty. When the test is rerun using the *sendmail.cf* file created in this recipe, class $=M and class $=E contain the data defined in the LDAP database.

The MASQUERADE_DOMAIN_FILE and the EXPOSE_USER_FILE are not the only files that can be read from LDAP. The MASQUERADE_EXCEPTION_FILE, used in Recipe 4.9, can also be read from an LDAP server by replacing the pathname in the macro command with the string @LDAP. In fact, any file that is loaded into a class can be read from LDAP. Additionally, sendmail databases can be read from LDAP, as the next recipe illustrates with the *genericstable*.

Because classes are loaded during startup, you must restart sendmail whenever you add, change, or delete any LDAP records that affect sendmail classes. The changes only take effect after sendmail is restarted.

See Also

Recipe 4.6 explains the role that class $=M plays in masquerading, and Recipe 4.2 explains why class $=E is needed. Recipe 3.9 is another recipe that uses LDAP to load a class, which provides additional insight on using LDAP. The *sendmail* book covers the MASQUERADE_DOMAIN_FILE macro in section 4.4.4, the EXPOSE_USER_FILE macro in section 4.4.1.1, and the confLDAP_CLUSTER define in section 21.9.82. The *cf/README* file covers LDAP in the *Using LDAP for Aliases, Maps, and Classes* section.

4.14   Reading the genericstable via LDAP

Problem

You have been asked to configure sendmail to read the *genericstable* from an LDAP server.

Solution

On the LDAP server, add support for the *sendmail.schema* file to the LDAP configuration as described in Recipe 1.3.

On the LDAP server, add the *genericstable* data to the LDAP database by first creating an LDIF file and then running *ldapadd*. Use the sendmailMTAMap object class defined in the *sendmail.schema* file to format the *genericstable* data in the LDIF file.

On the LDAP server, you can also create an LDIF file containing the generics domain data for class $=G. The data should be formatted using the sendmailMTAClass object class defined in the *sendmail.schema* file. Use *ldapadd* to add the data from the LDIF file to the LDAP database.

On the sendmail system, check that sendmail includes LDAP support. If the command sendmail -bt -d0.1 does not display the string LDAPMAP in the "Compiled with:" list, recompile and reinstall sendmail as described in Recipe 1.3.

On the sendmail system, add a *genericstable* FEATURE macro that loads the *genericstable* from the LDAP server to the sendmail configuration. Use the GENERICS_ DOMAIN_FILE macro to load class $=G from the LDAP server. Set the confLDAP_CLUSTER define to match the sendmailMTACluster attribute used in the *genericstable* entries added to the LDAP database. Here are sample lines you might add to a sendmail configuration to read the *genericstable* from an LDAP server:

```
dnl Define the sendmailMTACluster value
define(`confLDAP_CLUSTER', `wrotethebook.com')
dnl Load the genericstable from the LDAP server
FEATURE(`genericstable', `LDAP')
dnl Load class $=G from the LDAP server
GENERICS_DOMAIN_FILE(`@LDAP')
```

Follow the example in Recipe 1.8 to build and install the *sendmail.cf* file and then restart sendmail.

Discussion

This recipe uses an LDAP server to duplicate the configuration used in Recipe 4.11. Why and how the *genericstable* is used is covered in Recipe 4.11. This recipe focuses on how the *genericstable* data is stored in and retrieved from an LDAP server.

The data is first entered into an LDIF file. Each data entry is formatted in a manner compatible with the sendmail schema. The LDAP record format used for the *genericstable* can be used for any sendmail database by simply placing the database's map name in the sendmailMTAMapName attribute, the correct key data in the sendmailMTAKey attribute, and the correct return value in the sendmailMTAMapValue attribute. Here is an example using the *dave, becky,* and *alana* entries from the *genericstable* described in Recipe 4.11.

```
# cat > ldap-generics
dn: sendmailMTAMapName=generics, dc=wrotethebook, dc=com
objectClass: sendmailMTA
objectClass: sendmailMTAMap
sendmailMTACluster: wrotethebook.com
sendmailMTAMapName: generics

dn: sendmailMTAKey=dave, sendmailMTAMapName=generics, dc=wrotethebook, dc=com
objectClass: sendmailMTA
objectClass: sendmailMTAMap
objectClass: sendmailMTAMapObject
sendmailMTAMapName: generics
sendmailMTACluster: wrotethebook.com
sendmailMTAKey: dave
sendmailMTAMapValue: david.craig@wrotethebook.com

dn: sendmailMTAKey=becky, sendmailMTAMapName=generics, dc=wrotethebook, dc=com
objectClass: sendmailMTA
objectClass: sendmailMTAMap
objectClass: sendmailMTAMapObject
sendmailMTAMapName: generics
sendmailMTACluster: wrotethebook.com
sendmailMTAKey: becky
sendmailMTAMapValue: rebecca.fro@wrotethebook.com

dn: sendmailMTAKey=alana, sendmailMTAMapName=generics, dc=wrotethebook, dc=com
objectClass: sendmailMTA
objectClass: sendmailMTAMap
objectClass: sendmailMTAMapObject
sendmailMTAMapName: generics
sendmailMTACluster: wrotethebook.com
sendmailMTAKey: alana
sendmailMTAMapValue: alana.smiley@wrotethebook.com
Ctrl-D
# ldapadd -x -D "cn=Manager,dc=wrotethebook,dc=com" \
> -W -f ldap-generics
Enter LDAP Password: SecretLDAPpassword
adding new entry "sendmailMTAMapName=generics, dc=wrotethebook, dc=com"

adding new entry "sendmailMTAKey=dave, sendmailMTAMapName=generics, dc=wrotethebook,
dc=com"

adding new entry "sendmailMTAKey=becky, sendmailMTAMapName=generics, dc=wrotethebook,
dc=com"

adding new entry "sendmailMTAKey=alana, sendmailMTAMapName=generics, dc=wrotethebook,
dc=com"
```

Notice that four entries are used to enter the first three *genericstable* values in the LDAP database. The first entry defines the *genericstable* map name, which is generics. Once the map name is known to LDAP, data can be associated with that map name. The next three entries contain the actual *genericstable* data.

The sendmail configuration in this recipe also uses LDAP to load class $=G. The following example adds a class $=G entry to the LDAP database containing a sendmailMTAClassValue attribute that matches the GENERICS_DOMAIN value used in Recipe 4.11:

```
# cat > ldap-generics-domain
dn: sendmailMTAClassName=G, dc=wrotethebook, dc=com
objectClass: sendmailMTA
objectClass: sendmailMTAClass
sendmailMTAHost: chef.wrotethebook.com
sendmailMTAClassName: G
sendmailMTAClassValue: chef.wrotethebook.com
Ctrl-D
# ldapadd -x -D "cn=Manager,dc=wrotethebook,dc=com" \
> -W -f ldap-generics-domain
Enter LDAP Password: SecretLDAPpassword
adding new entry "sendmailMTAClassName=G, dc=wrotethebook, dc=com"
```

Again, the data is first entered into an LDIF file and then stored in the LDAP database using the *ldapadd* command. The sendmailMTAClassName attribute identifies the class to which the data belongs. The individual values bound for class $=G are defined by the sendmailMTAClassValue attributes in the LDAP record. Only one sendmailMTAClassValue is used in the example, but a single sendmailMTAClassName record can hold multiple values.

The *ldapsearch* command can be used to examine the results:

```
# ldapsearch -LLL -x '(sendmailMTAMapName=generics)' sendmailMTAMapValue
dn: sendmailMTAMapName=generics, dc=wrotethebook, dc=com

dn: sendmailMTAKey=dave, sendmailMTAMapName=generics, dc=wrotethebook, dc=com
sendmailMTAMapValue: david.craig@wrotethebook.com

dn: sendmailMTAKey=becky, sendmailMTAMapName=generics, dc=wrotethebook, dc=com
sendmailMTAMapValue: rebecca.fro@wrotethebook.com

dn: sendmailMTAKey=alana, sendmailMTAMapName=generics, dc=wrotethebook, dc=com
sendmailMTAMapValue: alana.smiley@wrotethebook.com
# ldapsearch -LLL -x '(sendmailMTAClassName=G)' sendmailMTAClassValue
dn: sendmailMTAClassName=G, dc=wrotethebook, dc=com
sendmailMTAClassValue: chef.wrotethebook.com
```

Three modifications were made to the sendmail configuration from Recipe 4.11 to create a configuration that reads *genericstable* data from LDAP:

- The confLDAP_CLUSTER define was added to the configuration to set the *sendmail. cf* ${sendmailMTACluster} macro to the same value as the sendmailMTACluster attribute used in the *genericstable* LDAP records. This ensures that sendmail retrieves the correct values from the LDAP server. If the confLDAP_CLUSTER define is not used, sendmail only retrieves LDAP records with a sendmailMTAHost attribute set to the fully qualified hostname of the sendmail host. In this example, the class $=G LDAP record uses the sendmailMTAHost attribute, so it would be retrieved by a host named *chef.wrotethebook.com* even if confLDAP_CLUSTER was not defined in that host's sendmail configuration.

- The GENERICS_DOMAIN macro used in Recipe 4.11 was changed to a GENERICS_ DOMAIN_FILE macro in this recipe. The @LDAP string in the GENERICS_DOMAIN_FILE macro tells sendmail to load class $=G with data retrieved from the LDAP server. (Traditionally, the value passed to the GENERICS_DOMAIN_FILE macro is the pathname of a local file that contains the data for class $=G.)

- The string LDAP was added to the *genericstable* FEATURE command. The LDAP string tells sendmail to read the *genericstable* data from the LDAP server using the standard sendmail schema.

Adding the LDAP string to the *genericstable* FEATURE command changes the format of the *sendmail.cf* K command that defines the generics database. A *grep* shows the effect of the LDAP string:

```
# grep 'Kgenerics' recipe4-10.cf
Kgenerics hash /etc/mail/genericstable
# grep '^Kgenerics' sendmail.cf
Kgenerics ldap -1 -v sendmailMTAMapValue -k
(&(objectClass=sendmailMTAMapObject)(|(sendmailMTACluster=${sendmailMTACluster})
(sendmailMTAHost=$j))(sendmailMTAMapName=generics)(sendmailMTAKey=%0))
```

The first *grep* shows the default format of the K command used to declare the generics database when no arguments are used with the *genericstable* FEATURE command. By default, sendmail looks for a hash type database in the local file */etc/mail/genericstable*. Adding the LDAP argument to the *genericstable* FEATURE command changes the database type to ldap and adds some LDAP-specific options to the K command. The -v option specifies the LDAP attribute used as the return value. The -k option defines the LDAP search criteria used as a database key.

All of the attribute names used in the K command shown above are attributes defined in the sendmail schema. If you define your own schema, you cannot simply use the LDAP string in the *genericstable* FEATURE command. You must instead manually define -v and -k options that use your custom schema. For example:

```
FEATURE(`genericstable', `ldap: -1 -k (&(objectClass=LocalUserObject)
(LocalUserKey=%0)) -v LocalUserEmailAddress')
```

Of course, the attribute names used in this example are imaginary and would need to be replaced with the attributes you defined when you designed your custom schema. However, the format of the *genericstable* FEATURE command is similar to the command you would use in your sendmail configuration.

Notice that the K command created by adding the LDAP argument to the *genericstable* feature does not include the LDAP server name or the LDAP default base distinguished name. The server and the base can be added to the K command using the same -h and -b arguments that you would use with the *ldapsearch* command. In the sendmail configuration, the -h and -b arguments are defined using confLDAP_ DEFAULT_SPEC; see Recipe 5.9 for an example. However, it is not necessary to use confLDAP_DEFAULT_SPEC if the HOST and BASE values in the *ldap.conf* file are correct for sendmail.

After this recipe is installed, *genericstable* data can be read from LDAP exactly as if it were being read from a local database, as the following test illustrates:

```
# rm -f /etc/mail/genericstable*
# sendmail -bt
ADDRESS TEST MODE (ruleset 3 NOT automatically invoked)
Enter <ruleset> <address>
> /map generics alana
map_lookup: generics (alana) returns alana.smiley@wrotethebook.com (0)
> /quit
```

The *rm* command proves that the test cannot be reading *genericstable* data from a local file. The /map command passes the key *alana* to the generics database and gets the return value *alana.smiley@wrotethebook.com*. The /map command in this example is formatted exactly as it was in Recipe 4.11, when data was read from a local database. The only difference is that, here, data is being read from an LDAP server.

The test that was used in Recipe 4.11 to evaluate the effect of the $=G class can be rerun after this recipe is installed. Again, it works exactly as expected despite the fact that the data comes from an LDAP server:

```
# sendmail -bt
ADDRESS TEST MODE (ruleset 3 NOT automatically invoked)
Enter <ruleset> <address>
> $=G
chef.wrotethebook.com
> /tryflags HS
> /try esmtp alana@[127.0.0.1]
Trying header sender address alana@[127.0.0.1] for mailer esmtp
canonify        input: alana @ [ 127 . 0 . 0 . 1 ]
Canonify2       input: alana < @ [ 127 . 0 . 0 . 1 ] >
Canonify2       returns: alana < @ rodent . wrotethebook . com . >
canonify        returns: alana < @ rodent . wrotethebook . com . >
1               input: alana < @ rodent . wrotethebook . com . >
1               returns: alana < @ rodent . wrotethebook . com . >
HdrFromSMTP     input: alana < @ rodent . wrotethebook . com . >
PseudoToReal    input: alana < @ rodent . wrotethebook . com . >
PseudoToReal    returns: alana < @ rodent . wrotethebook . com . >
MasqSMTP        input: alana < @ rodent . wrotethebook . com . >
MasqSMTP        returns: alana < @ rodent . wrotethebook . com . >
MasqHdr         input: alana < @ rodent . wrotethebook . com . >
canonify        input: alana . smiley @ wrotethebook . com
Canonify2       input: alana . smiley < @ wrotethebook . com >
Canonify2       returns: alana . smiley < @ wrotethebook . com . >
canonify        returns: alana . smiley < @ wrotethebook . com . >
MasqHdr         returns: alana . smiley < @ wrotethebook . com . >
HdrFromSMTP     returns: alana . smiley < @ wrotethebook . com . >
```

```
final            input: alana . smiley < @ wrotethebook . com . >
final          returns: alana . smiley @ wrotethebook . com
Rcode = 0, addr = alana.smiley@wrotethebook.com
> /quit
```

The data for any sendmail database and for any sendmail class can be defined centrally through an LDAP server. sendmail treats the data the same, regardless of the source.

See Also

Recipe 4.11 explains how the *genericstable* is used and it explains the importance of class $=G. Chapter 5 provides additional examples of using LDAP for sendmail databases. The *sendmail* book covers the GENERICS_DOMAIN_FILE macro in section 4.8.16.2, the *genericstable* in section 4.8.16, and the confLDAP_CLUSTER define in section 21.9.82. The *cf/README* file covers LDAP in the section *Using LDAP for Aliases, Maps, and Classes*.

Routing Mail

5.0 Introduction

sendmail is a mail router. Mail from external hosts is routed to local users. Mail from local users is routed to the outside world. Mail from the user's mail tool is routed to the correct mailer for delivery. In fact, all of the functions covered so far in this book—delivery, forwarding, relaying, and masquerading—are part of the work sendmail does as a mail router. The roles that the *aliases* database and the *.forward* file play in routing mail from one user account to another, and that relaying plays in routing mail from one host to another, are obviously components of mail routing. Even masquerading, which ensures that replies to the mail that originates from your site are routed to the correct system, is an aspect of routing.

Given that every recipe discussed so far has something to do with mail routing, why do we have a separate chapter with routing in the title? The reason is that the recipes in this chapter take mail routing and "BAM! Kick it up a notch!"* This chapter focuses on sendmail features that provide increased control over mail routing.

sendmail routes mail to internal mailers based on the mail's delivery address. When sendmail processes a delivery address, it returns a mail delivery triple that identifies the mailer that will be used, the host to which the mail will be sent, and the recipient address of the user to whom the mail is bound. The result of this process can be seen with a sendmail -bv test:

```
# sendmail -bv james@big.wrotethebook.net
james@big.wrotethebook.net... deliverable: mailer esmtp, host big.wrotethebook.net,
user james@big.wrotethebook.net
```

The mailer used to send the mail, the host to which it is sent, and the recipient address used in that mail can all be seen in this simple test. The processing of a delivery address into a mail delivery triple is a fundamental part of what sendmail does, and it determines how mail is routed for delivery.

---

* My apologies to Chef Emeril Lagasse and the Food Network, but, heck, this is a cookbook.

The mailertable

The *mailertable* database gives you direct control over this process by allowing you to specify which mailer is used and what remote host the mail is sent to based on the hostname part of the delivery address. Each *mailertable* entry contains two fields: a key that is matched against the hostname part of the delivery address and a return value that contains the mailer and host values for the mail delivery triple.

The key to a *mailertable* database entry is a full or partial domain name. A partial domain name key starts with a dot (.); e.g., *jamis.wrotethebook.com* is a full domain name key and *.wrotethebook.com* is a partial domain name key. To match a full domain name key, the entire hostname part of the delivery address must match the key. For example, if the key is *crab.wrotethebook.com*, only a delivery address of *user*@crab.wrotethebook.com matches the key. A partial domain name key is matched by any delivery address that ends with the key value. For example, if the key is *.wrotethebook.com*, any delivery address of the form *user@host*.wrotethebook.com matches the key. A special key composed of a standalone dot (.) matches every possible hostname.

The return value in a *mailertable* entry is the internal name of the mailer through which the mail should be routed, and the hostname of the remote mail host to which the mail should be sent, written in the form `mailer:host`. The `mailer` field must always be a valid sendmail internal mailer name (e.g., `esmtp`, `local`, `error`, and so on). The *host* field is more flexible because its content is determined by what the specified mailer expects in the host part of a mail delivery triple. The *host* field often contains the hostname of a remote host. But in the case of the `error` mailer, the *host* field contains the error message; in the case of the `local` mailer, it contains a username. Recipes in this chapter provide examples of the various *host* field formats, but a basic *mailertable* entry looks something like the following:

```
big.wrotethebook.net        smtp:mail.wrotethebook.com
```

The impact of this *mailertable* entry is easy to see:

```
# sendmail -bv james@big.wrotethebook.net
james@big.wrotethebook.net... deliverable: mailer smtp, host mail.wrotethebook.com,
user james@big.wrotethebook.net
```

Here, sendmail no longer uses the default `esmtp` mailer nor does it route mail through that mailer to the remote system *big.wrotethebook.net*. Instead, it uses the routing specified in the *mailertable;* in this case, mail addressed to *big.wrotethebook.net* is routed through the `smtp` mailer to *mail.wrotethebook.com*.

In the test above, only the mailer and host values changed, as specified in the *mailertable*. However, the recipient address in the user field is sometimes also rewritten. Specifying the mailer is one way the *mailertable* affects how the recipient address is processed. The R parameter in each mailer definition specifies the rulesets applied to the recipient address. All *mailertable* entries affect the recipient address indirectly through the mailer's R parameter. The *mailertable* can also directly control the recipient address in the user value of the mail delivery triple as described below.

The *host* field of a *mailertable* entry can contain a username. This is common when the entry routes mail through the local mailer:

```
info.wrotethebook.com      local:pat
```

With this entry, mail with a recipient address of *user*@info.wrotethebook.com is delivered to *pat* on the local host. In this case, *user* can be any username—it does not need to really exist on any system.

Another database, the *virtusertable*, can route mail for hosts that do not exist as separate physical computers. The *cf/README* file calls these *virtual domains*, and the support for them in sendmail is called *virtual hosting*.

The virtusertable

sendmail provides support for virtual hosting through the *virtusertable* feature. The *virtusertable* allows multiple virtual mail domains to be hosted on one machine, which are similar to the virtual hosts used on Apache web servers. In the same way that a single web server can serve web pages for many virtual hosts, sendmail can provide mail service for many virtual mail domains.

Entries in the *virtusertable* have two fields: a key and an email address. The key contains the value that is matched against the input delivery address. The key can be a complete address in the form of *user*@*domain*, or it can be a partial address in the form @*domain*. When the @*domain* format is used, mail to any user in the specified domain is routed to the mail address contained in the second field. The second field contains the address to which the mail is really delivered. There are only two exceptions to the use of a basic email address in the second field:

- The second field may contain an error message. The error messages starts with the keyword error, which is separated by a colon from an error code keyword, and followed by the text of the message. Table 5-1 contains a list of the sendmail error code keywords.

- An email address in the second field can contain variables. These variables are replaced by values from the input address that are passed to the outbound address. The username part of the input address is passed in the %1 variable, and the *detail* value in the +*detail* syntax is passed in the %2 variable. When the %2 variable is used in the second field, place +* before the @ in the first field of the *virtusertable* entry to indicate that the +*detail* syntax is used. For an example of how +* is used with %2, see the last line of the sample *virtusertable* entries shown in the following example.

These sample *virtusertable* entries show the possible formats of the two fields:

```
sales@example.com          jill
info@wrotethebook.org      sara@crab.wrotethebook.com
@wrotethebook.net          david@new-business.ora.com
sales@chll.ora.com         error:nouser User address is not valid
@other.wrotethebook.org    %1@blur.wrotethebook.com
+*@thatplace.ora.com       %2@newplace.ora.com
```

The first three sample entries show basic virtual domains and delivery addresses. Mail addressed to *sales@example.com* is delivered to the *jill* account on the local host. Requests emailed to *info@wrotethebook.org* are forwarded to *sara@crab. wrotethebook.com*. Mail sent to any username in the *wrotethebook.net* domain is routed to *david@new-business.ora.com*. Mail is accepted with a virtual domain address and routed to a real email address

The fourth sample entry illustrates the formatting of error messages. Mail addressed to *sales@chll.ora.com* is not delivered. Instead an error message that says "User address is not valid" is returned to the sender. The error code is indicated by the keyword *nouser* in the example shown above. The keyword must be one of the valid keywords shown in Table 5-1.

Table 5-1. Error code keywords

Keyword	Meaning
config	A configuration error or routing loop was detected.
nohost	The host portion of the sender or recipient address is invalid.
nouser	The user portion of the sender or recipient address is invalid.
protocol	Network delivery failed.
tempfail	A temporary failure was detected.
unavailable	A delivery resource is not available.
usage	The syntax of the delivery address is bad.

The last two sample entries are examples of how values from the input address are used in the outbound address. In the *@other.wrotethebook.org* entry, the username part of the input address is passed in the %1 variable and used in the outbound address. Therefore, mail addressed to *pat@other.wrotethebook.org* is routed to *pat@blur.wrotethebook.com*, and mail addressed to *doris@other.wrotethebook.org* is sent on to *doris@blur.wrotethebook.com*.

The last entry passes the *detail* value from the +*detail* syntax used in the input address to the outbound address as %2. Given the sample *virtusertable* entry just shown, mail sent to *sales+info@thatplace.ora.com* would be delivered to *info@newplace.ora.com* and mail to *sales+orders@thatplace.ora.com* would be delivered to *orders@newplace.ora.com*.

sendmail must be configured to accept mail addressed to virtual domains listed in the *virtusertable* database. Given the *virtusertable* just shown, sendmail must either accept *example.com*, *wrotethebook.org*, *wrotethebook.net*, *chll.ora.com*, *other. wrotethebook.org*, and *thatplace.ora.com* as aliases for the local host or recognize them as virtual domains. One solution is to create hostname aliases for each virtual domain. sendmail accepts any name contained in class $=w as an alias for the local host, and Recipe 2.1 shows how class $=w is loaded via the *local-host-names* file. When the *use_cw_file* feature is included in the configuration, listing the virtual domains in the *local-host-names* file loads them into class $=w and tells sendmail to accept mail for these domains.

However, it is not necessary to turn a virtual domain into a hostname alias to get the *virtusertable* working. An alternative is to store the virtual domain name in the ${VirtHost} class. Add virtual domain names to the ${VirtHost} class one at a time using the VIRTUSER_DOMAIN macro, or load the ${VirtHost} class from a file using the VIRTUSER_DOMAIN_FILE macro. Whenever virtual domains are added to the file, restart sendmail with a SIGHUP signal to make sure it loads the new values into class ${VirtHost}.

Before either the *mailertable* or the *virtusertable* can be used by sendmail, the text file that contains the database entries must be turned into a database using *makemap*. Specify the database type and the name of the database on the *makemap* command line:

```
# makemap hash /etc/mail/mailertable < /etc/mail/mailertable
```

By default, the *sendmail.cf* K commands for these databases define both *mailertable* and *virtusertable* as hash databases. The default filename for the *mailertable* is */etc/ mail/mailertable*, and the default name for the *virtusertable* database is */etc/mail/ virtusertable*. The default filenames and database types can be overridden in the sendmail configuration using the optional fields in the FEATURE macro. For example, a sendmail configuration that used the defaults for the *mailertable*, and overrode the defaults for the *virtusertable*, might contain the following FEATURE macros:

```
FEATURE(`mailertable')
FEATURE(`virtusertable', `dbm /etc/virtual-mail-domains')
```

Changing the default database filename is not recommended. All of the documentation that comes with the sendmail distribution points to */etc/mail/mailertable* and */etc/mail/virtusertable* as the location of these files. Changing the filename provides no real advantages, and it makes it harder for other system administrators to locate the file when maintenance is required. Also, if you override the default database type, make sure that your sendmail program has the necessary database support compiled in.

LDAP Routing

sendmail can obtain mail routing information from an LDAP server. It can do this by reading the *mailertable* and the *virtusertable* from an LDAP server—all sendmail databases can be read via LDAP. Recipe 5.5 shows how the *mailertable* is read from an LDAP server, and Recipe 5.8 shows how to read the *virtusertable* via LDAP. In addition to this, sendmail supports the *IETF Internet Draft LDAP Schema for Intranet Mail Routing*. The IETF draft schema defines the inetLocalMailRecipient object class. The attributes of this object class are:

mailLocalAddress

This attribute contains an email address, which is the key to the LDAP database. sendmail looks for records in which the mailLocalAddress attribute matches the recipient address that sendmail is processing. Every inetLocalMailRecipient object class record contains a mailLocalAddress attribute.

mailHost

This attribute contains the hostname of the mail host that handles mail address to the recipient identified by the mailLocalAddress attribute. Mail addressed to that recipient should be routed to this host for delivery. The mailHost attribute is a possible return value provided to sendmail in response to a query.

mailRoutingAddress

This attribute contains an email address. Mail addressed to the recipient identified by the mailLocalAddress attribute is delivered to the address specified by the mailRoutingAddress attribute. The mailRoutingAddress attribute is a possible return value provided to sendmail in response to a query.

Adding the *ldap_routing* feature to a sendmail configuration causes sendmail to query LDAP for routing information when sendmail processes a piece of mail addressed to a host listed in the $={LDAPRoute} class. If the query returns a mailHost value, sendmail uses that as the $h host value in the mail delivery triple. If the query returns a mailRoutingAddress value, sendmail uses that as the $u user address value in the mail delivery triple. Recipes 5.9 and 5.10 show how to use *ldap_routing* and the effect that the feature has on the mail delivery triple.

The mail routing information defined by the IETF draft schema does not provide any information that cannot already be provided by traditional sendmail databases, which is no surprise given the wide scope of sendmail configuration. Sites use the *ldap_routing* feature because they are already running an LDAP server, and they find the IETF schema more compatible with their database architecture. However, this is a draft schema, which may change in the future; hence, anything implemented using a draft schema may be affected by future changes. Consider your options carefully before using LDAP mail routing.

5.1 Routing Mail to Special Purpose Mailers

Problem

You have been asked to configure sendmail to deal with specific remote systems that cannot handle standard Extended SMTP mail.

Solution

Build a *mailertable* database that routes mail bound for specific remote systems through the appropriate special-purpose mailers. Do this by first creating a text file and then processing that file with the *makemap* script to create a hash type map. The key for these *mailertable* entries is a full or partial domain name that must match the hostname part of the recipient address on mail that needs to be handled by a special-purpose mailer. The return value is the internal name of the special-purpose mailer separated by a colon from the name of the remote system that will accept the mail.

Add the *mailertable* feature to the sendmail configuration. Here is the required *mailertable* FEATURE macro:

```
dnl Add support for the mailertable
FEATURE(`mailertable')
```

Build the *sendmail.cf* file. Copy it to */etc/mail*, and restart sendmail. See Recipe 1.8 for an example.

Discussion

A basic sendmail configuration contains MAILER macros that load *local.m4* and *smtp.m4*. The local MAILER macro adds the prog and local mailers to the *sendmail.cf* configuration. The SMTP MAILER macro defines five mailers. Two, esmtp and relay, are essential for basic SMTP mail delivery. The three other mailers defined by the SMTP MAILER macro (smtp8, dsmtp, and smtp) are not referenced by any mail delivery triple in the *sendmail.cf* file. The best way to make use of these unused mailers is through the *mailertable*.

For this example, assume that you must send mail to one remote system that cannot handle binary mail or the standard Extended SMTP syntax, and to other systems that can handle binary mail but cannot process the standard Extended SMTP syntax. Here is a sample *mailertable* with entries for these systems:

```
# cd /etc/mail
# cat > mailertable
fakeu.edu          smtp8:mail.fakeu.edu
.falseu.edu        smtp8:ms.falseu.edu
.stateu.edu        smtp:mail.stateu.edu
```

```
new.stateu.edu      esmtp:new.stateu.edu
Ctrl-D
# makemap hash mailertable < mailertable
```

The first two sample *mailertable* entries use the smtp8 mailer—a special SMTP mailer for use with a remote server that can handle binary mail but cannot handle the Extended SMTP protocol that is normally associated with binary mail. A simple test shows the impact of these *mailertable* entries:

```
# sendmail -bv -Cgeneric-linux.cf jeff@fakeu.edu
jeff@fakeu.edu... deliverable: mailer esmtp, host fakeu.edu., user jeff@fakeu.edu
# sendmail -bv –Cgeneric-linux.cf reba@foo.falseu.edu
reba@foo.falseu.edu... deliverable: mailer esmtp, host foo.falseu.edu, user reba@foo.
falseu.edu
# sendmail -bv jeff@fakeu.edu
jeff@fakeu.edu... deliverable: mailer smtp8, host mail.fakeu.edu, user jeff@fakeu.edu
# sendmail -bv reba@foo.falseu.edu
reba@foo.falseu.edu... deliverable: mailer smtp8, host ms.falseu.edu, user reba@foo.
falseu.edu
# sendmail -bv becky@falseu.edu
becky@falseu.edu... deliverable: mailer esmtp, host falseu.edu, user becky@falseu.edu
```

The first two sendmail -bv tests show how a basic sendmail configuration routes mail to *fakeu.edu* and *foo.falseu.edu*. Rerunning these tests after this recipe is completed shows the impact of the *mailertable*. Notice the last two tests. Addresses in the form of *user@host*.falseu.edu match the *.falseu.edu mailertable* entry and are processed as directed by that *mailertable* entry. However, mail addressed to *user@*falseu.edu does not match and thus is not processed by the *mailertable* in this example. The *.falseu. edu mailertable* entry defines a partial domain name. To control routing for both *foo. falseu.edu* and *falseu.edu*, put two entries in the *mailertable*—one for the full domain name *falseu.edu* and one for the partial domain name *.falseu.edu*.

The last two entries in the sample *mailertable* use the smtp mailer and the esmtp mailer. The esmtp mailer is the default mailer used for most Internet mail. The smtp mailer implements the old version of the SMTP protocol that existed before Extended SMTP was created. The smtp mailer is only needed if the remote site cannot run Extended SMTP. The interesting thing about these two entries is that they contain overlapping references to the *stateu.edu* domain:

```
.stateu.edu      smtp:mail.stateu.edu
new.stateu.edu   esmtp:new.stateu.edu
```

The first entry defines a partial domain name that will match any input hostname that ends in *.stateu.edu*. This appears to be in conflict with the second entry. The second entry exactly matches the hostname *new.stateu.edu*. However, *new.stateu.edu* also matches the first entry because it ends in *.stateu.edu*. Which entry will sendmail use to route mail addressed to *new.stateu.edu*? In this case, it will use the second entry because that entry provides the most complete match, and the longest match takes precedence. This precedence is independent of the order in which the entries appear in the *mailertable*—the longest match always takes precedence. These two lines, taken together, cause sendmail to use *mail.stateu.edu* as the host value for the mail delivery triple for all mail addressed to the *stateu.edu* domain with the exception of mail addressed to *new.stateu.edu*, which uses *new.stateu.edu* as the host value. *new.stateu.edu* is a modern system that handles standard Extended SMTP mail. Unfortunately, *mail.stateu.edu* is an outdated system that can only handle the obsolete SMTP protocol.

Alternatives

Updating the hardware and software of the target systems to fully support esmtp is a better alternative than using the *mailertable* to route mail through special mailers. If you have control of a destination system that must use a mailer like smtp or smtp8 to communicate with the outside world, replace it. Using outdated technology is a bad idea. Of course, you're not always in control of the remote system. For those times, the *mailertable* is an effective workaround.

See Also

Recipes 5.2 and 5.3 further describe *mailertable* features that you may wish to include in your *mailertable*. Recipe 5.4 provides additional information on rewriting the user address via the *mailertable*. The *sendmail* book covers the *mailertable* in section 4.8.24. The *cf/README* file contains a *Using Mailertables* section.

5.2   Sending Error Messages from the mailertable

Problem

You have been asked to configure sendmail to reject mail bound for certain hosts and domains with an error.

Solution

Create *mailertable* entries using the domain names as the key to which mail will not be delivered and using the error messages as the return value that should be returned when the mail is rejected. Process that file with *makemap* to build a hash database.

Create a sendmail configuration that includes the *mailertable* feature. The following lines add the *mailertable* to a sendmail configuration:

```
dnl Add support for the mailertable
FEATURE(`mailertable')
```

Build and install *sendmail.cf*, and then restart sendmail, as described in Recipe 1.8.

Discussion

The error mailer is built into the sendmail binary. The error mailer returns an error message to the sender of the mail message. Like other mailers, the error mailer can be specified in the mailer field of a *mailertable* entry. When it is, the host field of the entry contains the error message, the SMTP response code, and the Delivery Status Notification (DSN) code. The syntax of a *mailertable* entry for the error mailer is:

```
key  error:D.S.N:code message
```

where *key* is a full or partial domain name, error is the name of the mailer, *D.S.N* is an enhanced status code defined as three dot separated numeric fields or an SMTP error code keyword,* *code* is a numeric SMTP response code, and *message* is the text message returned to the sender. *D.S.N* values must comply with the specifications of RFC 1893, *Enhanced Mail System Status Codes*. *D* specifies success or failure; *S* identifies the error category; and *N* provides additional detail. The RFC calls these three values *class*, *subject*, and *detail* and defines them as follows:

class

Provides a broad classification of the status. Three values are defined for class in the RFC: 2 means success, 4 means temporary failure, and 5 means permanent failure.

subject

Classifies the error messages as relating to one of eight categories:

0 (Undefined)

The specific category cannot be determined.

1 (Addressing)

A problem was encountered with the address.

2 (Mailbox)

A problem was encountered with the delivery mailbox.

3 (Mail system)

The destination mail delivery system is having a problem.

4 (Network)

The network infrastructure is having a problem.

5 (Protocol)

A protocol problem was encountered.

6 (Content)

The message content caused a translation error.

7 (Security)

A security problem was reported.

---

* See Table 5-1 for a list of SMTP error code keywords.

detail

Provides the details of the specific error. The detail value is only meaningful in the context of the subject code. For example, x.1.1 means a bad destination user address, and x.1.2 means a bad destination host address, while x.2.1 means the mailbox is disabled, and x.2.2 means the mailbox is full. See RFC 1893 for the list of detail codes.

Let's examine a sample *mailertable* entry:

```
oldname.ora.com    error:5.7.1:550 oldname.ora.com is out of service
```

Testing this entry with sendmail -bv shows that the *mailertable* is operational and that the entry works, but it does not make clear the role of the SMTP code or the DSN code:

```
# sendmail -bv richard@oldname.ora.com
richard@oldname.ora.com... oldname.ora.com is out of service
```

In fact, the -bv test in this case does not show all of the values in the mail delivery triple. Instead, you see the same messages that anyone sending mail to *oldname.ora.com* would see. To see the full mail delivery triple for the error mailer, run *sendmail* with the -bt option and use the /parse command:

```
# sendmail -bt
ADDRESS TEST MODE (ruleset 3 NOT automatically invoked)
Enter <ruleset> <address>
> /parse richard@oldname.ora.com
Cracked address = $g
Parsing envelope recipient address
canonify         input: richard @ oldname . ora . com
Canonify2        input: richard < @ oldname . ora . com >
Canonify2        returns: richard < @ oldname . ora . com >
canonify         returns: richard < @ oldname . ora . com >
parse            input: richard < @ oldname . ora . com >
Parse0           input: richard < @ oldname . ora . com >
Parse0           returns: richard < @ oldname . ora . com >
Parse1           input: richard < @ oldname . ora . com >
MailerToTriple   input: < error : 5 . 7 . 1 : 550 oldname . ora . com is out of
service > richard < @ oldname . ora . com >
MailerToTriple   returns: $# error $@ 5 . 7 . 1 $: 550 oldname . ora . com is out of
service
Parse1           returns: $# error $@ 5 . 7 . 1 $: 550 oldname . ora . com is out of
service
parse            returns: $# error $@ 5 . 7 . 1 $: 550 oldname . ora . com is out of
service
richard@oldname.ora.com... oldname.ora.com is out of service
mailer *error*, host 5.7.1, user 550 oldname.ora.com is out of service
> /quit
```

The /parse command shows that the SMTP code or the DSN code is used as the host value in the mail delivery triple, and the error message appears as the user value. When the DSN code is used as the host value, the SMTP code appears as the first string of the user value. The effect of all of this is best seen in the SMTP protocol interactions. A simple *telnet* test shows the real impact of this mailer table entry:

```
# telnet localhost smtp
Trying 127.0.0.1...
Connected to localhost.
Escape character is '^]'.
220 chef ESMTP Sendmail 8.12.9; Mon, 4 Nov 2002 18:32:51 -0500
HELO chef.wrotethebook.com
250 chef.wrotethebook.com Hello localhost.localdomain [127.0.0.1], pleased to meet
you
MAIL From:<craig@chef.wrotethebook.com>
250 2.1.0 craig@chef.wrotethebook.com... Sender ok
RCPT To:<richard@oldname.ora.com>
550 5.7.1 richard@oldname.ora.com... oldname.ora.com is out of service
QUIT
221 2.0.0 chef.wrotethebook.com closing connection
Connection closed by foreign host.
```

The RCPT To: command contains a recipient address that matches the key in the *oldname.ora.com mailertable* entry. Notice the SMTP response to this recipient address. Like all SMTP responses, it starts with a response code. The code is 550, which is the value we defined in the *mailertable* entry. The next field in the SMTP response is the DSN code—again, it is the value we defined in the *mailertable*. This is followed by the recipient address and the error message we defined in the mailer table. Clearly, the *mailertable* entry for *oldname.ora.com* controlled all aspects of this response.

I recommend using the DSN value on all *mailertable* entries for the error mailer because doing so places you in control of all aspects of the error response.

See Also

Recipes 5.1, 5.3, and 5.4 describe additional *mailertable* features. The *sendmail* book covers the *mailertable* in section 4.8.24 and the error mailer in section 20.4.4.

5.3   Disabling MX Processing to Avoid Loops

Problem

When a host's *mailertable* routes mail to a destination whose MX records point back to the host, a mail loop is possible.

Solution

Disabling MX processing for the *mailertable* entry avoids this type of mail loop. Enclose the host field of the *mailertable* entry in square brackets when the system identified in the host field uses the sendmail system as its mail exchanger. The *mailertable* [*host*] syntax bypasses MX record processing. After creating the *mailertable*, process the *mailertable* text file with the *makemap* script to build a hash database.

Include the *mailertable* feature in the sendmail configuration using lines such as the following:

```
dnl Add support for the mailertable
FEATURE(`mailertable')
```

Build the *sendmail.cf* file, copy it to */etc/mail*, and restart sendmail following the example in Recipe 1.8.

Discussion

Usually a mail exchanger handles the mail routed to it by MX records through sendmail's basic relaying and forwarding functions, as discussed in Chapter 2 and Chapter 3. On those occasions when a mail exchanger handles this mail through the *mailertable*, special care is needed to avoid mail loops. To understand this, let's look at a couple of sample *mailertable* entries:

```
.wrotethebook.net      smtp:[mail.wrotethebook.net]
wrotethebook.net       smtp:[mail.wrotethebook.net]
```

The *wrotethebook.net* domain is handled through the *mailertable*. This domain cannot be handled through standard forwarding or relaying because those methods use the esmtp mailer and the host *mail.wrotethebook.net* does not understand Extended SMTP. For that same reason, MX records for the *wrotethebook.net* domain do not point directly to *mail.wrotethebook.net*. If the MX records did point directly, remote systems would attempt to send mail directly to *mail.wrotethebook. net* using the Internet's standard Extended SMTP protocol, which that system does not support. Our local system is a mail gateway configured to handle this problem. Mail is directed to our local host by MX records. The *mailertable* on the local host is configured to route mail to *mail.wrotethebook.net* using the mailer that *mail.wrotethebook.net* supports.

The two sample *mailertable* entries for *wrotethebook.net* look almost identical to the *mailertable* entries used in other recipes in this chapter. The primary difference is the use of the [*host*] syntax. This syntax prevents sendmail from doing an MX record lookup when delivering mail, as directed by the *mailertable*. Without this syntax, sendmail checks the MX record and follows its direction when making a final delivery. In this case, following the MX record would cause a loop because the MX record points right back to the local host. Using the [*host*] syntax bypasses the MX record and avoids the loop.

The sample *mailertable* entries refer to the same domain: one entry is a partial domain name and the other is a full domain name. The entry for the full domain name is used to catch mail addressed to *user@domain*, in case there is an MX record for the entire domain. The entry for the partial domain name catches mail addressed to *user@host.domain* for those hosts that have individual MX records. The recipient address *pat@wrotethebook.net* matches this *mailertable* entry:

```
wrotethebook.net      smtp:[mail.wrotethebook.net]
```

and the address *pat@sales.wrotethebook.net* matches this entry:

```
.wrotethebook.net     smtp:[mail.wrotethebook.net]
```

Neither entry by itself is sufficient to catch both address formats. Both *mailertable* entries are needed if both types of MX records exist. Because the sendmail administrator may not have control over the exact format of the MX records placed in the DNS zone file, it is safest to put both entries in the *mailertable*.

See Also

Recipes 5.1, 5.2, and 5.4 describe additional *mailertable* features. The *sendmail* book covers the *mailertable* in section 4.8.24.

5.4   Routing Mail for Local Delivery

Problem

You have been asked to configure sendmail to route mail addressed to selected hostnames to specific local user accounts.

Solution

Create *mailertable* entries that route mail through the local mailer to local user accounts. Process the *mailertable* text file with *makemap* to build a hash database.

Create a sendmail configuration that includes the *mailertable* feature. Here is a sample FEATURE macro:

```
dnl Add support for the mailertable
FEATURE(`mailertable')
```

Rebuild and reinstall *sendmail.cf*, and then restart sendmail using Recipe 1.8 as a guide.

Discussion

The local mailer delivers mail to users on the local host. For this reason, it does not require the name of a remote host for the host value of the mail delivery triple. Likewise, the host field of a *mailertable* entry for the local mailer does not contain the name of a remote host. Instead, that field is either blank or it contains a local username. If the host field is blank, the username from the input address is used, and mail is delivered to the local user account of that name. If the host field contains a username, the mail is delivered to that local user. Here are three local mailer *mailertable* entries—two with a username and one without:

```
support.wrotethebook.com        local:admin
sales.wrotethebook.com          local:
info.wrotethebook.com           local:pat
```

There is no need for physical computers named *sales*, *support*, or *info*, and there probably are no computers with those names. Instead, those names are associated with MX records in the DNS zone file that point to the mail exchanger, and the *mailertable* entries on the mail exchanger deliver the mail to local user accounts.

A few tests show how these entries affect mail routing. First, a test of the *info. wrotethebook.com* entry:

```
# sendmail -bv logan@info.wrotethebook.com
logan@info.wrotethebook.com... deliverable: mailer local, host logan@info.
wrotethebook.com, user pat
```

This test shows how mail addressed to *logan@info.wrotethebook.com* is handled. The hostname part of this input address matches the key of one of the *mailertable* entries. The impact of the *mailertable* process can be seen in the mailer and user values displayed by the sendmail -bv test.* The mail is delivered via the local mailer to the local user account *pat* because *pat* is specified in the host field of the *info. wrotethebook.com mailertable* entry. Mail to any user at *info.wrotethebook.com* is delivered to the local *pat* account. A second test shows how far the local mailer process can take you:

```
# sendmail -bv alana@support.wrotethebook.com
anna@crab.wrotethebook.com... deliverable: mailer esmtp, host crab.wrotethebook.com.,
user anna@crab.wrotethebook.com
andy@rodent.wrotethebook.com... deliverable: mailer esmtp, host rodent.wrotethebook.
com., user andy@rodent.wrotethebook.com
jane@rodent.wrotethebook.com... deliverable: mailer esmtp, host rodent.wrotethebook.
com., user jane@rodent.wrotethebook.com
```

In this test, mail is addressed to *alana@support.wrotethebook.com*. Looking at the *mailertable* entry for *support.wrotethebook.com* you might expect the -bv test to display local as the mailer value and *admin* as the user value. Instead, mail addressed to *alana@support.wrotethebook.com* is delivered via the esmtp mailer to three different users who are located on external systems. The reason for this is that *admin* is a mailing list defined in the *aliases* database. (Mailing lists and the *aliases* database are discussed in Chapter 2.) The *mailertable* is not necessarily the end of the delivery process. Aliasing also applies to most *mailertable* entries that point to the local mailer because the local mailer is usually configured with the F=A mailer flag.

---

* sendmail passes the local mailer the original delivery address as the host value of the mail delivery triple.

Finally, we test the *sales.wrotethebook.com* entry, which provides no local username in the return field:

```
# sendmail -bv logan@sales.wrotethebook.com
logan@sales.wrotethebook.com... deliverable: mailer local, host logan@sales.
wrotethebook.com, user logan
```

In this test, mail is addressed to *logan@sales.wrotethebook.com*. The *mailertable* entry tells sendmail to use the local mailer to deliver the mail but does not provide a local username for that delivery. sendmail uses the username from the input address, which, in this case, is *logan*. The net result is that mail addressed to any user at *sales.wrotethebook.com* is delivered to a like-named user account on the local host.

Alternatives

Use the *virtusertable* as an alternative to local mailer *mailertable* entries that include a username. When no username is defined in the *mailertable* entry, use the *local-host-names* file as an alternative to the *mailertable* to route mail to the local mailer. Placing the hostname *sales.wrotethebook.com* in the *local-host-names* file gives the same result as the *mailertable* entry shown above. This test using configuration Recipe 2.1 illustrates that the *local-host-names* file is a good alternative solution:

```
# cat >> /etc/mail/local-host-names
sales.wrotethebook.com
# sendmail -bv -Crecipe2-1.cf logan@sales.wrotethebook.com
logan@sales.wrotethebook.com... deliverable: mailer local, user logan
```

See Also

Recipes 5.1 to 5.3 describe additional *mailertable* features. Recipes 5.6 and 5.7 describe the *virtusertable*, which should be evaluated as an alternative to this recipe before it is implemented. Recipe 2.7 covers the *aliases* database and mailing lists. The *sendmail* book covers the *mailertable* in section 4.8.24. The *cf/README* file describes the syntax of local mailer *mailertable* entries.

5.5   Reading the mailertable via LDAP

Problem

You have been asked to configure sendmail to read the *mailertable* from an LDAP server.

Solution

On the LDAP server, add support for the *sendmail.schema* file to the LDAP configuration. Recipe 1.3 shows an example of how this is done on a server running OpenLDAP.

On the LDAP server, create an LDIF file containing *mailertable* data formatted according to the sendmail schema sendmailMTAMap object class. Add the *mailertable* data to the LDAP database using *ldapadd*.

On the sendmail host, run the sendmail -bt -d0.1 command to check for the string LDAPMAP in the "Compiled with:" list. If it is there, sendmail includes LDAP support and is ready to run. If it is not listed there, recompile and reinstall sendmail as described in Recipe 1.3.

Create a sendmail configuration that includes the *mailertable* feature. Add the string LDAP to the *mailertable* FEATURE command to direct sendmail to read the *mailertable* from an LDAP server. Set the confLDAP_CLUSTER define to the same value used for the sendmailMTACluster attribute in the *mailertable* records. Here are sample configuration lines:

```
dnl Set the LDAP cluster value
define(`confLDAP_CLUSTER', `wrotethebook.com')
dnl Read the mailertable via LDAP
FEATURE(`mailertable', `LDAP')
```

Build the *sendmail.cf* file, copy it to */etc/mail*, and restart sendmail. Recipe 1.8 provides an example.

Discussion

The *mailertable* data is first entered into an LDIF file. This example adds one *mailertable* record from each of the databases used in Recipes 5.1 and 5.2 for a total of two data records:

```
# cat > ldap-mailer
dn: sendmailMTAMapName=mailer, dc=wrotethebook, dc=com
objectClass: sendmailMTA
objectClass: sendmailMTAMap
sendmailMTACluster: wrotethebook.com
sendmailMTAMapName: mailer

dn: sendmailMTAKey=fakeu.edu, sendmailMTAMapName=mailer, dc=wrotethebook, dc=com
objectClass: sendmailMTA
objectClass: sendmailMTAMap
objectClass: sendmailMTAMapObject
sendmailMTAMapName: mailer
sendmailMTACluster: wrotethebook.com
sendmailMTAKey: fakeu.edu
sendmailMTAMapValue: smtp8:mail.fakeu.edu
```

```
dn: sendmailMTAKey=oldname.ora.com, sendmailMTAMapName=mailer, dc=wrotethebook,
dc=com
objectClass: sendmailMTA
objectClass: sendmailMTAMap
objectClass: sendmailMTAMapObject
sendmailMTAMapName: mailer
sendmailMTACluster: wrotethebook.com
sendmailMTAKey: oldname.ora.com
sendmailMTAMapValue: error:5.7.1:550 oldname.ora.com is out of service
Ctrl-D
# ldapadd -x -D "cn=Manager,dc=wrotethebook,dc=com" \
> -W -f ldap-mailer
Enter LDAP Password: SecretLDAPpassword
adding new entry "sendmailMTAMapName=mailer, dc=wrotethebook, dc=com"

adding new entry "sendmailMTAKey=fakeu.edu, sendmailMTAMapName=mailer,
dc=wrotethebook, dc=com"

adding new entry "sendmailMTAKey=oldname.ora.com, sendmailMTAMapName=mailer,
dc=wrotethebook, dc=com"
```

Each LDAP *mailertable* record is formatted according to the sendmail schema. The internal *sendmail.cf* map name for the *mailertable*, which is mailer, is assigned to the sendmailMTAMapName attribute by the first LDAP record. After the map name is defined, data can be associated with that map name. The next two LDAP records contain the actual *mailertable* data. Both of those records define a *mailertable* key using the sendmailMTAKey attribute and the return value associated with that key using the sendmailMTAMapValue attribute. Thus, the:

```
fakeu.edu          smtp8:mail.fakeu.edu
```

mailertable entry from Recipe 5.1 becomes the following LDAP record:

```
dn: sendmailMTAKey=fakeu.edu, sendmailMTAMapName=mailer, dc=wrotethebook, dc=com
objectClass: sendmailMTA
objectClass: sendmailMTAMap
objectClass: sendmailMTAMapObject
sendmailMTAMapName: mailer
sendmailMTACluster: wrotethebook.com
sendmailMTAKey: fakeu.edu
sendmailMTAMapValue: smtp8:mail.fakeu.edu
```

After running the *ldapadd* command to add the LDIF data to the LDAP database, use *ldapsearch* to examine the results:[*]

```
# ldapsearch -LLL -x '(sendmailMTAMapName=mailer)' sendmailMTAMapValue
dn: sendmailMTAMapName=mailer, dc=wrotethebook, dc=com

dn: sendmailMTAKey=fakeu.edu, sendmailMTAMapName=mailer, dc=wrotethebook, dc=com
sendmailMTAMapValue: smtp8:mail.fakeu.edu
```

---

[*] If *ldapsearch* requires -h and -b values, those same values must be defined for sendmail using confLDAP_DEFAULT_SPEC, as shown in Recipe 5.9.

```
dn: sendmailMTAKey=oldname.ora.com, sendmailMTAMapName=mailer, dc=wrotethebook,
dc=com
sendmailMTAMapValue: error:5.7.1:550 oldname.ora.com is out of service
```

The LDAP database is ready. Now sendmail must be configured to use it.

The sendmail schema defines two attributes that specify the scope of an LDAP record. The scope of a record can be either a single host, as indicated by the presence of a sendmailMTAHost attribute, or a group of hosts called a *cluster*, as indicated by the use of a sendmailMTACluster attribute. The records in this recipe all use the sendmailMTACluster attribute. Use the confLDAP_CLUSTER define to tell sendmail the cluster name. If the confLDAP_CLUSTER define is not used, sendmail only retrieves LDAP records with a sendmailMTAHost attribute set to the fully qualified hostname of the sendmail host, which, in this case, would not match any of the LDAP records and thus would return no *mailertable* values. If the sendmailMTACluster attribute is used in the LDAP records that you need, you *must* use the confLDAP_CLUSTER define. If you don't intend to use the confLDAP_CLUSTER define, the LDAP records *must* use the sendmailMTAHost attribute.

The string LDAP in the *mailertable* FEATURE command tells sendmail to read the *mailertable* data from the LDAP server using the standard sendmail schema. Rerunning tests from earlier recipes show that the *mailertable* works the same whether it is read from a local database or an LDAP server. After completing this recipe, rerunning the test from Recipe 5.1 shows the same result as the original test:

```
# sendmail -bv -Cgeneric-linux.cf jeff@fakeu.edu
jeff@fakeu.edu... deliverable: mailer esmtp, host fakeu.edu., user jeff@fakeu.edu
# sendmail -bv jeff@fakeu.edu
jeff@fakeu.edu... deliverable: mailer smtp8, host mail.fakeu.edu, user jeff@fakeu.edu
```

Rerunning the test from Recipe 5.2 also shows the correct result:

```
# sendmail -bv richard@oldname.ora.com
richard@oldname.ora.com... oldname.ora.com is out of service
```

In fact, any record that can be entered into a local *mailertable* database can be entered into LDAP and retrieved from the LDAP server, and it will work exactly as expected.

See Also

Recipes 5.1 and 5.2 explain the *mailertable* records used in this recipe. Recipe 4.14 and Recipe 5.8 provide additional examples of using LDAP for sendmail databases. The *cf/README* file covers this topic in the section *Using LDAP for Aliases, Maps, and Classes*. The *sendmail* book covers the *mailertable* in section 4.8.24 and the confLDAP_CLUSTER define in section 21.9.82.

5.6 Routing Mail for Individual Virtual Hosts

Problem

You have been asked to configure sendmail to route mail for virtual hosts.

Solution

On the DNS server, the domain administrator adds MX records that route mail for each virtual domain to the sendmail system that is acting as the mail exchanger. These records must be added to the zone file for every domain that contains virtual hostnames.

On the mail exchanger, create an */etc/mail/virtuser-domains* file that lists each virtual hostname, one hostname per line.

Next, create an */etc/mail/virtusertable* text file that defines the routing for the virtual hosts. The structure of a *virtusertable* entry is described in the Introduction to this chapter. Use *makemap* to build a hash database from the text file.

Create a sendmail configuration containing a VIRTUSER_DOMAIN_FILE macro that loads the *virtuser-domains* file into class $={VirtHost} and a FEATURE macro that enables the *virtusertable* feature. Here are sample lines that could be added to the sendmail configuration:

```
dnl Load $={VirtHost} from a file
VIRTUSER_DOMAIN_FILE(`/etc/mail/virtuser-domains')
dnl Use the virtusertable for mail routing
FEATURE(`virtusertable')
```

Finally, rebuild the *sendmail.cf* file, copy the new *sendmail.cf* file to */etc/mail*, and restart sendmail, as shown in Recipe 1.8.

Discussion

The *virtusertable* routes mail for virtual hosts; however, the sendmail system that contains the *virtusertable* is not involved in the mail routing unless the mail is first routed to that sendmail system. The initial routing is accomplished via DNS MX records. For example, assume the DNS administrator adds the following MX records to the *wrotethebook.com* zone file:

```
support.wrotethebook.com.       MX    5 mail.wrotethebook.com.
sales.wrotethebook.com.         MX    5 mail.wrotethebook.com.
```

The DNS administrator of *techbooksrus.ora.com* adds:

```
techbooksRus.ora.com.           MX    5 mail.wrotethebook.com.
```

and the administrator of the *wrotethebook.org* zone file adds:

```
phd.wrotethebook.org.           MX    5 mail.wrotethebook.com.
```

Given these MX records, the *virtuser-domains* file, the *virtusertable* database, and the sendmail configuration described in the Solution section all must be created on *mail.wrotethebook.com*. Here is a sample *virtuser-domain* file that might be created on *mail.wrotethebook.com*:

```
# cat > /etc/mail/virtuser-domains
support.wrotethebook.com
sales.wrotethebook.com
techbooksRus.ora.com
phd.wrotethebook.org
Ctrl-D
```

And the following *virtusertable* is built on *mail.wrotethebook.com* to route mail for the virtual hosts listed in the *virtuser-domains* file:

```
# cd /etc/mail
# cat > virtusertable
@support.wrotethebook.com        admin
@sales.wrotethebook.com          %1@orders.example.com
sales@techbooksRus.ora.com       jay@orders.example.com
@phd.wrotethebook.org            error:nohost:553 Invalid address
Ctrl-D
# makemap hash virtusertable < virtusertable
```

The *virtuser-domains* file is essential. Without it, mail addressed to the four hosts listed above is rejected with a "Relaying denied" error. With it, mail addressed to those hosts is accepted by *mail.wrotethebook.com* where it can then be processed against the *virtusertable*.

Mail must pass four hurdles before it is modified by the *virtusertable*:

1. Mail must be routed to the local host for processing.

   The DNS MX records handle this job. It is also possible for mail to be routed based on a DNS address (A) record. However, MX records take precedence over other DNS records when it comes to mail routing.

2. Mail must be accepted by the local host for processing.

   To meet this condition, the mail must be addressed to a host listed in class $=w or class $=R. When class $=w is used to identify virtual hosts, the mail is accepted because the values in class $=w are the hostnames aliases of the local host—mail addressed to any host in class $=w is accepted as mail addressed to the local host. When class $={VirtHost} is used to identify virtual hosts, the mail is accepted because the values in $={VirtHost} are replicated in class $=R by the *sendmail.cf* command CR{VirtHost}. Relaying is allowed for any domain listed in class $=R. Therefore, mail to or from any host in a domain listed in class $={VirtHost} is accepted by the local host as mail for a valid relay client.

3. The hostname in the recipient address must be accepted for processing by the *virtusertable*.

A recipient address is only processed against the *virtusertable* if the hostname in that address matches a value in class $=w or class $={VirtHost}. This check is similar to Step 2, except that hostnames listed in class $=R pass Step 2 but do not pass Step 3.

4. The recipient address must match a key in the *virtusertable* database.

   Matching a value in class $=w or class $={VirtHost} is no guarantee that there is a key for that value in the *virtusertable*. Only mail with a recipient address that matches a key is routed by the *virtusertable*.

The sendmail configuration in this recipe uses the VIRTUSER_DOMAIN_FILE macro to load class $={VirtHost} from an external file. Alternatively, individual values can be added to $={VirtHost} using the VIRTUSER_DOMAIN macro. The following macros would add the same values to $={VirtHost} as the sample *virtuser-domains* file shown above:

```
VIRTUSER_DOMAIN_FILE(`support.wrotethebook.com')
VIRTUSER_DOMAIN_FILE(`sales.wrotethebook.com')
VIRTUSER_DOMAIN_FILE(`techbooksRus.ora.com')
VIRTUSER_DOMAIN_FILE(`phd.wrotethebook.org')
```

This alternative works, but it is more difficult to maintain when the list of virtual domains is large or changeable.

With this recipe's sendmail configuration installed, four sendmail -bv tests show the effects of the *virtusertable*:

```
# sendmail -bv sara@support.wrotethebook.com
anna@crab.wrotethebook.com... deliverable: mailer esmtp, host crab.wrotethebook.com.,
user anna@crab.wrotethebook.com
andy@rodent.wrotethebook.com... deliverable: mailer esmtp, host rodent.wrotethebook.
com., user andy@rodent.wrotethebook.com
jane@rodent.wrotethebook.com... deliverable: mailer esmtp, host rodent.wrotethebook.
com., user jane@rodent.wrotethebook.com
# sendmail -bv sara@sales.wrotethebook.com
sara@sales.wrotethebook.com... deliverable: mailer esmtp, host orders.example.com,
user sara@orders.example.com
# sendmail -bv sales@techbooksRus.ora.com
sales@techbooksRus.ora.com... deliverable: mailer esmtp, host orders.example.com,
user jay@orders.example.com
# sendmail -bv sales@phd.wrotethebook.org
sales@phd.wrotethebook.org... Invalid address
```

The first test shows that mail addressed to any user on the virtual host *support. wrotethebook.com* is delivered to the local user *admin*. In this case, *admin* is a mailing list defined in the *aliases* file. If a *virtusertable* entry routes mail to a local user, aliasing applies.

The second test shows that mail addressed to any username on the virtual host *sales.wrotethebook.com* is delivered to that username at *orders.example.com*. This test shows how the %1 variable is used to move the username from the input address to the output address. On the other hand, the third test preserves nothing from the input address. In that case, mail addressed to *sales@techbooksRus.ora.com* is delivered to *jay@orders.example.com*.

The final `sendmail -bv` command tests the error message entry in the sample *virtusertable*. In this case, mail to any user at *phd.wrotethebook.org* returns the error message "Invalid address." This `-bv` test shows only the error message; it does not show all of the delivery triple. To see more details, you need to run more tests. Attaching to the SMTP port with *telnet* allows you to see the SMTP protocol interactions:

```
# telnet localhost smtp
Trying 127.0.0.1...
Connected to localhost.
Escape character is '^]'.
220 chef.wrotethebook.com ESMTP Sendmail 8.12.9/8.12.9; Fri, 8 Nov 2002 14:53:13 -
0500
HELO chef.wrotethebook.com
250 chef.wrotethebook.com Hello localhost.localdomain [127.0.0.1], pleased to meet
you
MAIL From:<craig@chef.wrotethebook.com>
250 2.1.0 craig@chef.wrotethebook.com... Sender ok
RCPT To:<sales@phd.wrotethebook.org>
553 5.3.0 sales@phd.wrotethebook.org... Invalid address
QUIT
221 2.0.0 chef.wrotethebook.com closing connection
Connection closed by foreign host.
```

The server's response to the *sales@phd.wrotethebook.org* recipient address shows the error codes as well as the text of the error message. The 553 SMTP response code indicates an invalid mailbox, and the DSN code of 5.3.0 indicates a permanent error with the destination mail system. Both are very appropriate codes for the nohost error keyword we put in the *virtusertable* entry for *phd.wrotethebook.org*.

Alternatives

The *aliases* file is an alternative to using the *virtusertable* for username-to-username mappings. In the sample *virtusertable* shown earlier in this section, the following address maps one specific incoming address to one specific outbound address:

```
sales@techbooksRus.ora.com          jay@orders.example.com
```

The user *sales* on *techbooksRus.ora.com* is mapped to the user *jay* on *orders.example.com*. The same result would be achieved by putting the following entry in the *aliases* database:

```
sales@techbooksRus.ora.com:         jay@orders.example.com
```

This alternative only works if the mailer that handles mail bound for *techbooksRus.ora.com* has the F=A mailer flag set. By default, only the local mailer has this flag set. The alias shown above would require reconfiguring sendmail to set the F=A flag for the esmtp mailer. Setting the F=A flag on a mailer that delivers remote mail would mean that every remote address would be looked up in the *aliases* database, which would add lots of overhead.

The *mailertable* is also an alternative to the *virtusertable*, in some cases. Three of the entries in the *virtusertable* could be covered by the *mailertable* with the following entries:

```
support.wrotethebook.com        local:admin
sales.wrotethebook.com          esmtp:orders.example.com
.wrotethebook.org               error:nohost Invalid address
```

The primary disadvantage of the *mailertable* for this application is that it cannot handle the *sales@ora.techbook.com* to *jay@orders.example.com* mapping. The *mailertable* matches only hostnames; the username is not considered in the match. For this specific application, the *virtusertable* is the best choice.

See Also

Recipe 5.7 describes additional *virtusertable* features and should be reviewed for pertinent information. The *sendmail* book covers the *virtusertable* in section 4.8.51. *Linux Sendmail Administration*, by Craig Hunt (Sybex), explains the numeric SMTP response code, error code keywords, and the DSN codes.

5.7   Routing Mail for Entire Virtual Domains

Problem

You have been asked to configure sendmail to route mail for entire virtual domains, not just individual hosts.

Solution

The domain administrator must register each virtual mail domain with an official DNS registrar. The DNS administrator must also create a minimal zone file for each virtual mail domain. In addition to the basic records required to create a zone file, the file must contain MX records that point to the mail exchanger that you are configuring. See *DNS and BIND*, by Paul Albitz and Cricket Liu (O'Reilly), for more information on DNS configuration.

On the mail server, create a */etc/mail/virtuser-domains* file that lists each virtual mail domain for which service will be provided.

Create an */etc/mail/virtusertable* text file that defines the routing for each virtual mail domain. Use *makemap* to build a hash type database from the text file.

Next, create a sendmail configuration that enables the *virtusertable* feature, loads class $={VirtHost} from the */etc/mail/virtuser-domains* file, and enables the *virtuser_entire_domain* feature. Here are examples of the lines that need to be added to the sendmail configuration:

```
dnl Use the virtusertable for mail routing
FEATURE(`virtusertable')
dnl Load $={VirtHost} from a file
VIRTUSER_DOMAIN_FILE(`/etc/mail/virtuser-domains')
dnl Interpret the values in $={VirtHost} as domain names
FEATURE(`virtuser_entire_domain')
```

As shown in Recipe 1.8, rebuild and install the *sendmail.cf* file, and restart sendmail.

Discussion

Assume that the zone files created for the *shop.wrotethebook.org*, *school.ora.com*, and *hotel.example.com* domains all contain MX records that route email to *mail.wrotethebook.com*. The *mail.wrotethebook.com* host will reject that mail unless the destination hostname is listed in class $=w or class $={VirtHost}. The configuration described in the Solution section loads the $={VirtHost} class from the */etc/mail/virtuser-domains* file specified by the VIRTUSER_DOMAIN_FILE macro. Here is a sample *virtuser-domains* file containing the names of three virtual mail domains:

```
# cat /etc/mail/virtuser-domains
shop.wrotethebook.org
school.ora.com
hotel.example.com
```

Values stored in class $={VirtHost} are replicated in class $=R, as this simple test shows:

```
# sendmail -bt
ADDRESS TEST MODE (ruleset 3 NOT automatically invoked)
Enter <ruleset> <address>
> $={VirtHost}
shop.wrotethebook.org
school.ora.com
hotel.example.com
> $=R
shop.wrotethebook.org
school.ora.com
hotel.example.com
> /quit
```

By default, values in class $=w and class $={VirtHost} are interpreted as hostnames. Values in class $=R, on the other hand, are interpreted as domain names. Use the *virtuser_entire_domain* feature to cause the values in class $={VirtHost} to also be interpreted as domain names. The *virtuser_entire_domain* feature tells sendmail to evaluate class $=R and class $={VirtHost} in an equivalent manner—every host in every domain listed in class $=R is accepted for processing by the local host, and every host in every domain in class $={VirtHost} is matched against the *virtusertable*. Here is a sample *virtusertable* we'll use to illustrate this:

```
# cat > /etc/mail/virtusertable
@mainst.shop.wrotethebook.org      logan
@mall.shop.wrotethebook.org        pat
@retro.shop.wrotethebook.org       reba
@school.ora.com                    %1@b2341.isp.wrotethebook.net
@sales.school.ora.com              jeff+sales@b2341.isp.wrotethebook.net
@info.school.ora.com               jeff+info@b2341.isp.wrotethebook.net
@motel.hotel.example.com           reservations@b0021.isp.wrotethebook.net
@lodge.hotel.example.com           reservations@b0531.isp.wrotethebook.net
@hotel.hotel.example.com           reservations@b1088.isp.wrotethebook.net
Ctrl-D
# makemap hash /etc/mail/virtusertable < /etc/mail/virtusertable
```

The first three entries route mail addressed to anyone on the three hosts in the *shop.wrotethebook.org* domain to the local user accounts where the mail addressed to these virtual hosts is read.

school.ora.com and *hotel.example.com* both run their own servers, but the servers are literally part of the *isp.wrotethebook.net* domain. *school.ora.com* has only one server. *hotel.example.com* has three servers—one at the motel, one at the lodge, and one at the hotel. Notice that *school.ora.com* uses *+detail* syntax to identify the specific mailbox in the *jeff* account where the mail should be stored. For this to work, the *jeff* account on *b2341.isp.wrotethebook.net* must have a mail filter that processes the *+detail* syntax.

A few tests of this recipe's configuration show the impact of the *virtuser_entire_domain* feature and the *virtusertable* entries:

```
# sendmail -bv info@mall.shop.wrotethebook.org
info@mall.shop.wrotethebook.org... deliverable: mailer local, user pat
# sendmail -bv cranks@sales.school.ora.com
cranks@sales.school.ora.com... deliverable: mailer esmtp, host b2341.isp.
wrotethebook.net., user jeff+sales@b2341.isp.wrotethebook.net
# sendmail -bv reservations@lodge.hotel.example.com
reservations@lodge.hotel.example.com... deliverable: mailer esmtp, host b0531.isp.
wrotethebook.net., user reservations@b0531.isp.wrotethebook.net
```

None of the hostnames in the three test addresses shown above are listed in either class $=w or $={VirtHost}. Yet all three addresses are clearly rewritten by the *virtusertable*. This is the effect of the *virtuser_entire_domain* feature—these hostnames are processed through the *virtusertable* because they belong to domains listed in the $={VirtHost} class.

Potential conflicts and solutions

However, the *virtuser_entire_domain* feature does not change the way that the keys in the *virtusertable* are interpreted. There is no domain wildcard for the *virtusertable*. Each hostname in the test above is rewritten because it exactly matches a key in the database. A common mistake is to think that an entry like *@school.ora.com* applies to every host in the *school.ora.com* domain because the *virtuser_entire_domain* feature is used. A test shows this is not the case:

```
# sendmail -bv dave@school.ora.com
dave@school.ora.com... deliverable: mailer esmtp, host b2341.isp.wrotethebook.net.,
user dave@b2341.isp.wrotethebook.net
# sendmail -bv dave@hs.school.ora.com
dave@hs.school.ora.com... deliverable: mailer esmtp, host hs.school.ora.com., user
dave@hs.school.ora.com
```

Both of the recipient addresses shown above are in a domain listed in $={VirtHost} and the *virtuser_entire_domain* feature is enabled. For these reasons, both of these addresses are matched against the *virtusertable*. But only the first address matches a key found in the database and is rerouted. The other address goes through the normal delivery process, and therein lies a possible conflict with the domain administrator.

Some domain administrators use wildcard MX records that match any hostname within a given domain. The wildcard MX makes things easy for the domain administrator but has the potential to cause problems for the sendmail administrator. The sendmail -bv test of *dave@hs.school.ora.com* shows the problem.

Mail addressed to *hs.school.ora.com* is accepted by the local host for processing because the *school.ora.com* domain is listed in class $=R, which means that the local host will relay mail for this domain. The *hs.school.ora.com* address is not modified by the *virtusertable* process, so the local host attempts to deliver the mail via the esmtp mailer directly to a host named *hs.school.ora.com*. When the local host does a DNS lookup of *hs.school.ora.com*, the lookup succeeds because this host is covered by the MX wildcard. The MX record returned by the lookup points the local host right back to the local host. Problem!

This problem can be avoided in a few different ways. All three solutions work, and all have different advantages and disadvantages. While the first solution is preferred, the solution you choose depends on your personal situation. The three solutions are:

Use individual MX records

> The MX wildcard is the root of the problem: it routes mail for a host that has no existence—real or virtual. Create a zone file customized for each virtual mail domain that explicitly defines an MX record for each host covered in the *virtusertable*. When the domain administrator and the sendmail administrator are the same person, this approach works well and it has the distinct advantage of responding to domain name errors where they should be responded to— inside the DNS. The disadvantage of this approach is that it increases the work of the domain administrator, and it reduces the ability of the sendmail administrator to solve his own problems.

Use local-host-names and list only individual hostnames

Mail addressed to *hs.school.ora.com* is accepted for relaying by the local system because the domain of which it is a part is listed in class $=R. Every entry in $={VirtHost} is replicated in class $=R, and every entry in class $=R is interpreted as a domain name. So, even if the *virtuser_entire_domain* feature is not used, listing *school.ora.com* in $={VirtHost} triggers the mail delivery problem just described. Avoid this by listing *school.ora.com* in the *local-host-names* file and using the *use_cw_file* feature to load that file into class $=w. Values in class $=w are interpreted as hostnames; thus, mail addressed to *hs.school.ora.com* is not accepted by the local system and the delivery problem is not triggered. Of course, the mail is returned to the sender as undeliverable mail. This is okay if the sender made a mistake entering the address; however, if the people at *school. ora.com* advertise this address, returning an error to the sender is a bad idea. Another disadvantage of this solution is that listing hostnames in *local-host-names* literally makes those hostnames aliases for the local host, which may cause username conflicts.

Create a catchall entry in the mailertable

A catchall entry is an entry in a database that catches all queries for which there is no specific key. Generally, a catchall entry responds to these queries with an error message. Catchall entries in the *virtusertable* handle usernames that are not specifically covered by table entries. To create a catchall entry for a hostname, use the *mailertable*. The advantages of catchall entries are that they proactively respond to error situations, and they are under the direct control of the send-mail administrator. The disadvantage of catchall entries is that they catch every-thing—even things they shouldn't. They must be fully tested and used with care.

The catchall solution

Below, we define catchall entries in the *mailertable* to avoid the possible delivery problems that would be caused if the domain administrator used wildcard MX records in our sample virtual mail domains. First, add *mailertable* support to the basic Recipe 5.7 configuration:

```
dnl Use the virtusertable for mail routing
FEATURE(`virtusertable')
dnl Load $={VirtHost} from a file
VIRTUSER_DOMAIN_FILE(`/etc/mail/virtuser-domains')
dnl Interpret the values in $={VirtHost} as domain names
FEATURE(`virtuser_entire_domain')
dnl Use the mailertable to invoke special mailers
FEATURE(`mailertable')
```

Create the *virtusertable* database and the *virtuser-domains* file as described above. Create a *mailertable* with a catchall entry for each of the virtual mail domains:

```
# cat > /etc/mail/mailertable
.school.ora.com        error:5.3.0:553 Invalid hostname
shop.wrotethebook.org  error:5.3.0:553 Invalid hostname
```

```
.shop.wrotethebook.org    error:5.3.0:553 Invalid hostname
hotel.example.com         error:5.3.0:553 Invalid hostname
.hotel.example.com        error:5.3.0:553 Invalid hostname
Ctrl-D
# makemap hash /etc/mail/mailertable < /etc/mail/mailertable
```

The first entry addresses the specific problem described in the example above. The next two entries provide similar error control for the *shop.wrotethebook.org* virtual mail domain, and the last two entries provide the protection for the *hotel.example. com* virtual mail domain. The additional entries for the *shop.wrotethebook.org* and *hotel.example.com* domains are necessary because, unlike the *school.ora.com* domain, neither of these other domains has a *virtusertable* entry that routes mail addressed to *user@domain*, as this test of this recipe's basic configuration shows:

```
# sendmail -bv jane@shop.wrotethebook.org
jane@shop.wrotethebook.org... deliverable: mailer esmtp, host shop.wrotethebook.org.,
user jane@shop.wrotethebook.org
# sendmail -bv kathy@hotel.example.com
kathy@hotel.example.com... deliverable: mailer esmtp, host hotel.example.com.,
user kathy@hotel.example.com
# sendmail -bv sara@school.ora.com
sara@school.ora.com... deliverable: mailer esmtp, host b2341.isp.wrotethebook.net.,
user sara@b2341.isp.wrotethebook.net
```

mailertable entries that begin with a dot are partial domain names that match any address that ends with the specified domain name. For example, a *mailertable* entry beginning with .wrotethebook.com would match addresses of the form *user@host. wrotethebook.com*. Full domain names (those that do not start with a dot) match mail addressed in the form of *user@domain*. Therefore, a *mailertable* entry starting with ora.com would match *craig@ora.com* but not *craig@tcp.ora.com*.

These catchall *mailertable* entries are only applicable to virtual mail domains and are only useful if the zone files for those domains use wildcard MX records. If these were real domains, the *virtusertable* entry might route mail from one host in the domain to another in the same domain. The rewritten address would then be caught by the *mailertable* catchall entry, and the "invalid hostname" error would be returned. Because these are virtual mail domains with no physical existence, the *virtusertable* never routes mail to a host in these nonexistent domains. Thus, addresses rewritten by the *virtusertable* do not match the catchall entries and are allowed to continue on their way as directed by the *virtusertable*. These catchall entries are useful, but only for the specific problem described here.

Run some tests with the new configuration to see the impact of these *mailertable* entries:

```
# sendmail -bv -C recipe5-7a.cf dave@hs.school.ora.com
dave@hs.school.ora.com... Invalid hostname
# sendmail -bv -C recipe5-7a.cf dave@school.ora.com
dave@school.ora.com... deliverable: mailer esmtp, host b2341.isp.wrotethebook.net.,
user dave@ b2341.isp.wrotethebook.net
```

```
# sendmail -bv -C recipe5-7a.cf jane@mall.shop.wrotethebook.org
jane@mall.shop.wrotethebook.org... deliverable: mailer local, user pat
# sendmail -bv -C recipe5-7a.cf jane@shop.wrotethebook.org
jane@shop.wrotethebook.org... Invalid hostname
```

These tests show that addresses that match keys in the *virtusertable* are still being properly rewritten, while addresses in the virtual mail domain that do not have entries in the *virtusertable* are now being properly identified as addressing errors. Catchall entries are useful, but they should be used with caution and be thoroughly tested to ensure that they don't catch things that they shouldn't.

All of this work could, of course, be avoided if the domain administrator did not use wildcard MX records. The best solution to this potential problem is to avoid wildcards and use individual MX records.

See Also

Recipe 5.6 defines individual virtual hosts, as opposed to virtual mail domains, and should be evaluated as an alternative before implementing this recipe. Recipes 5.1 through 5.4 and this chapter's Introduction provide additional information about the *mailertable*. The *sendmail* book covers the *virtusertable* in section 4.8.51. MX records and DNS are covered in *DNS and BIND*, by Paul Albitz and Cricket Liu (O'Reilly), and in *TCP/IP Network Administration*, by Craig Hunt (O'Reilly).

5.8   Reading the virtusertable via LDAP

Problem

You must configure sendmail to read the *virtusertable* from an LDAP server.

Solution

On the LDAP server, include the *sendmail.schema* file in the LDAP configuration and restart LDAP. Recipe 1.3 provides a detailed example of doing this on a system running OpenLDAP.

On the LDAP server, create an LDIF file containing the *virtusertable* data and use the *ldapadd* command to add it to the LDAP database. The *virtusertable* data should be entered as sendmailMTAMap object class type data. The $={VirtHost} class can also be loaded from an LDAP server. Again, the data is first entered into an LDIF file and then added to the LDAP database using *ldapadd*. The $={VirtHost} data is entered using the sendmailMTAClass object class format.

On the sendmail system, create a configuration that contains a *virtusertable* FEATURE command that tells sendmail to read the *virtusertable* via LDAP, and a VIRTUSER_ DOMAIN_FILE macro that loads class $={VirtHost} from the LDAP server. Set the confLDAP_CLUSTER define to the LDAP cluster name used in the sendmailMTACluster attribute of the *virtusertable* LDAP records. The lines that would be added to our sample sendmail configuration are:

```
dnl Define the LDAP cluster to which this host belongs
define(`confLDAP_CLUSTER', `wrotethebook.com')
dnl Read the virtusertable via LDAP
FEATURE(`virtusertable', `LDAP')
dnl Load $={VirtHost} from the LDAP server
VIRTUSER_DOMAIN_FILE(`@LDAP')
```

Using Recipe 1.8 as a guide, rebuild and install the *sendmail.cf* file, then restart sendmail.

Discussion

This recipe illustrates how the *virtusertable* data is stored in and retrieved from an LDAP server. The details of your configuration will naturally be different, but the configuration concepts will be the same. The examples in this recipe use information from an LDAP server to duplicate the configuration used in Recipe 5.6. Why and how the *virtusertable* is used, and the role of the $={VirtHost} class, is covered in that recipe.

The LDAP administrator first enters the data into an LDIF file structured in a manner compatible with the sendmail schema. This example uses three of the *virtusertable* entries from Recipe 5.6 and adds them to the LDAP database:

```
# cat > ldap-virtuser
dn: sendmailMTAMapName=virtuser, dc=wrotethebook, dc=com
objectClass: sendmailMTA
objectClass: sendmailMTAMap
sendmailMTACluster: wrotethebook.com
sendmailMTAMapName: virtuser

dn: sendmailMTAKey=@mall.shop.wrotethebook.org, sendmailMTAMapName=virtuser,
dc=wrotethebook, dc=com
objectClass: sendmailMTA
objectClass: sendmailMTAMap
objectClass: sendmailMTAMapObject
sendmailMTAMapName: virtuser
sendmailMTACluster: wrotethebook.com
sendmailMTAKey: @mall.shop.wrotethebook.org
sendmailMTAMapValue: pat

dn: sendmailMTAKey=@sales.school.ora.com, sendmailMTAMapName=virtuser,
dc=wrotethebook, dc=com
objectClass: sendmailMTA
objectClass: sendmailMTAMap
objectClass: sendmailMTAMapObject
sendmailMTAMapName: virtuser
sendmailMTACluster: wrotethebook.com
sendmailMTAKey: @sales.school.ora.com
```

```
sendmailMTAMapValue: jeff+sales@b2341.isp.wrotethebook.net

dn: sendmailMTAKey=@lodge.hotel.example.com, sendmailMTAMapName=virtuser,
dc=wrotethebook, dc=com
objectClass: sendmailMTA
objectClass: sendmailMTAMap
objectClass: sendmailMTAMapObject
sendmailMTAMapName: virtuser
sendmailMTACluster: wrotethebook.com
sendmailMTAKey: @lodge.hotel.example.com
sendmailMTAMapValue: reservations@b0531.isp.wrotethebook.net
Ctrl-D
# ldapadd -x -D "cn=Manager,dc=wrotethebook,dc=com" \
> -W -f ldap-virtuser
Enter LDAP Password: SecretLDAPpassword
adding new entry "sendmailMTAMapName=virtuser, dc=wrotethebook, dc=com"

adding new entry "sendmailMTAKey=@mall.shop.wrotethebook.org,
sendmailMTAMapName=virtuser, dc=wrotethebook, dc=com"

adding new entry "sendmailMTAKey=@sales.school.ora.com, sendmailMTAMapName=virtuser,
dc=wrotethebook, dc=com"

adding new entry "sendmailMTAKey=@lodge.hotel.example.com,
sendmailMTAMapName=virtuser, dc=wrotethebook, dc=com"
```

The *virtusertable* map name, which is virtuser, is defined in the first entry. Subsequent data entries for that map associate themselves with the map by referencing the map name using the sendmailMTAMapName attribute. *virtusertable* data are key/value pairs. The key is defined by the sendmailMTAKey attribute, and the return value is defined by the sendmailMTAMapValue attribute. Thus, the following *virtusertable* entry from Recipe 5.6:

```
@mall.shop.wrotethebook.org     pat
```

becomes the following record when entered into the LDAP database:

```
dn: sendmailMTAKey=@mall.shop.wrotethebook.org, sendmailMTAMapName=virtuser,
dc=wrotethebook, dc=com
objectClass: sendmailMTA
objectClass: sendmailMTAMap
objectClass: sendmailMTAMapObject
sendmailMTAMapName: virtuser
sendmailMTACluster: wrotethebook.com
sendmailMTAKey: @mall.shop.wrotethebook.org
sendmailMTAMapValue: pat
```

This recipe also uses LDAP to load class $={VirtHost}. The following example stores the data for the $={VirtHost} class on the LDAP server:

```
# cat > ldap-virtuser-domains
dn: sendmailMTAClassName=VirtHost, dc=wrotethebook, dc=com
objectClass: sendmailMTA
```

```
objectClass: sendmailMTAClass
sendmailMTACluster: wrotethebook.com
sendmailMTAClassName: VirtHost
sendmailMTAClassValue: shop.wrotethebook.org
sendmailMTAClassValue: school.ora.com
sendmailMTAClassValue: hotel.example.com
Ctrl-D
# ldapadd -x -D "cn=Manager,dc=wrotethebook,dc=com" \
> -W -f ldap-virtuser-domains
Enter LDAP Password: SecretLDAPpassword
adding new entry "sendmailMTAClassName=VirtHost, dc=wrotethebook, dc=com"
```

The sendmailMTAClassName attribute identifies the class as VirtHost.* The individual class values are defined by the sendmailMTAClassValue attributes in the LDAP record. This LDAP record defines the same values as did the *virtuser-domains* file used in Recipe 5.6.

ldapadd loads the data into the LDAP database. Use *ldapsearch* to check the data:

```
# ldapsearch -LLL -x '(sendmailMTAMapName=virtuser)' sendmailMTAMapValue
dn: sendmailMTAMapName=virtuser, dc=wrotethebook, dc=com

dn: sendmailMTAKey=@mall.shop.wrotethebook.org, sendmailMTAMapName=virtuser,
dc=wrotethebook, dc=com
sendmailMTAMapValue: pat

dn: sendmailMTAKey=@sales.school.ora.com, sendmailMTAMapName=virtuser,
dc=wrotethebook, dc=com
sendmailMTAMapValue: jeff+sales@b2341.isp.wrotethebook.net

dn: sendmailMTAKey=@lodge.hotel.example.com, sendmailMTAMapName=virtuser,
dc=wrotethebook, dc=com
sendmailMTAMapValue: reservations@b0531.isp.wrotethebook.net
# ldapsearch -LLL -x '(sendmailMTAClassName=VirtHost)' sendmailMTAClassValue
dn: sendmailMTAClassName=VirtHost, dc=wrotethebook, dc=com
sendmailMTAClassValue: shop.wrotethebook.org
sendmailMTAClassValue: school.ora.com
sendmailMTAClassValue: hotel.example.com
```

The *ldapsearch* test shows that the LDAP server is ready for sendmail. If the *ldapsearch* command on your sendmail system requires -h and -b arguments, those same arguments must be configured for sendmail using the confLDAP_DEFAULT_SPEC define described in Recipe 5.9.

Now, the sendmail configuration must be modified to make sendmail ready for LDAP. This recipe reimplements Recipe 5.6 in an LDAP environment. It does that by adding the string LDAP (which tells sendmail to read data from LDAP) to the *virtusertable* FEATURE command. This modification is essential to our goal of reading the *virtusertable* from an LDAP server, but it is not the only important modification.

---

* Notice that the class name is written without the enclosing curly braces ({}).

Given the specifics of the data loaded into the server, the confLDAP_CLUSTER define is also essential. The cluster name used by sendmail must match the sendmailMTACluster attribute used in the LDAP records. If a cluster name is not defined, sendmail attempts to retrieve LDAP records using the fully qualified hostname of the sendmail host, which only works if the LDAP records have that value set with a sendmailMTAHost attribute.

This recipe also uses the @LDAP string in the VIRTUSER_DOMAIN_FILE macro to load class $={VirtHost} from the LDAP server. This is not specifically required for the goal of reading *virtusertable* data from an LDAP server, but it is required in order to duplicate the Recipe 5.6 configuration, and it illustrates that classes can be loaded from an LDAP server. The point here is not really to duplicate the configuration of Recipe 5.6—the point is to demonstrate that any *virtusertable* configuration can be duplicated using an LDAP server.

After this recipe is installed on the system, a few quick tests show that the LDAP data is now available to sendmail. Here sendmail -bt is used to examine the LDAP data:

```
# sendmail -bt
ADDRESS TEST MODE (ruleset 3 NOT automatically invoked)
Enter <ruleset> <address>
> $={VirtHost}
school.ora.com
shop.wrotethebook.org
hotel.example.com
> /map virtuser @mall.shop.wrotethebook.org
map_lookup: virtuser (@mall.shop.wrotethebook.org) returns pat (0)
> /quit
```

The $={VirtHost} command displays the content of the $={VirtHost} class. It shows that the data defined for $={VirtHost} in the LDAP database has been loaded. The /map command is used to search the virtuser map using @mall.shop.wrotethebook.org as the key. The search returns the value pat. This is exactly what is expected given the records added to the LDAP database in this recipe. Clearly, LDAP data is being used for class $={VirtHost} and for the *vitrusertable*. In fact, the data for any sendmail database and for any sendmail class can be defined centrally through an LDAP server. sendmail treats the data the same, regardless of the source.

See Also

Recipe 5.6 covers the *virtusertable* and the class $={VirtHost}. The *sendmail* book covers the VIRTUSER_DOMAIN_FILE macro in section 4.8.51.2, the *virtusertable* in section 4.8.51, and the confLDAP_CLUSTER define in section 21.9.82. LDAP is covered in the *Using LDAP for Aliases, Maps, and Classes* section of the *cf/README* file.

5.9 Routing Mail with LDAP

Problem

Your enterprise wants to use the *IETF Internet Draft LDAP Schema for Intranet Mail Routing*. You have been asked to configure sendmail to use the IETF draft schema and to read internal mail routing information from the LDAP server.

Solution

This solution requires collaboration between the LDAP administrator and the sendmail administrator.

Instructions for the LDAP administrator

Locate a copy of the IETF draft schema for intranet mail routing. The schema is documented in the *draft-lachman-laser-ldap-mail-routing-02* file available from the IETF. The schema is defined as part of the *misc.schema* file provided with the OpenLDAP distribution. Include the schema file in the LDAP configuration by adding the following include command to the *slapd.conf* file:

```
include          /etc/openldap/schema/misc.schema
```

See the Discussion section for information on a possible conflict between the *misc.schema* file and other schema.

Additionally, the *sendmail.schema* file should be copied to the proper path and included in the LDAP configuration, as described in Recipe 1.3.

Restart LDAP to ensure that the IETF draft schema and the sendmail schema are available for use. Here is an example:

```
# ps -ax | grep slapd
 1426 ?        S      0:00 /usr/sbin/slapd -u ldap
# kill -TERM 1426
# /usr/sbin/slapd -u ldap
```

Create an LDIF file containing the mail routing information. Use the inetLocalMailRecipient object class from the IETF draft schema to format the mail routing data in the LDIF file. Run *ldapadd* to add the data to the LDAP database. The Discussion section shows an example of this step.

sendmail applies LDAP routing to a recipient address when the host portion of that address is listed in class $={LDAPRoute}. To store the $={LDAPRoute} class values on the LDAP server, create an LDIF file containing a sendmailMTAClass record, which is an object class defined in the *sendmail.schema* file. Set the sendmailMTAClassName attribute to LDAPRoute and define the values for that class using sendmailMTAClassValue attributes. Use *ldapadd* to convert the LDIF file and add the data to the LDAP database.

Instructions for the sendmail administrator

Direct sendmail to use LDAP intranet mail routing by adding the *ldap_routing* feature to the configuration. Add the LDAPROUTE_DOMAIN_FILE macro to load class $={LDAPRoute}, which can be loaded from the LDAP server. Lines, such as the following, should be added to the sendmail configuration:

```
dnl Stop Build from complaining
define(`confLDAP_DEFAULT_SPEC', ` -h ldserver -b dc=wrotethebook,dc=com')
dnl Identify the recipient hosts that require LDAP mail routing
LDAPROUTE_DOMAIN_FILE(`@LDAP')
dnl Enable the ldap_routing feature
FEATURE(`ldap_routing')
```

Rebuild and reinstall the *sendmail.cf* file, and restart sendmail as described in Recipe 1.8.

Discussion

This discussion covers both LDAP and sendmail configuration.

LDAP configuration

For a query to succeed, sendmail and LDAP must use and understand the same schema. The *ldap_routing* feature depends on a mail routing schema defined in a draft IETF document. That schema, which is available in the *misc.schema* file provided with the OpenLDAP distribution, must be included in the LDAP configuration in order for that LDAP to understand the mail routing queries coming from sendmail.

A problem may occur when you attempt to restart LDAP after including the *misc.schema* file in the configuration. The error might look something like the following:

```
/etc/openldap/schema/redhat/rfc822-MailMember.schema:
line 7: Duplicate attributeType: "1.3.6.1.4.1.42.2.27.2.1.15"
```

In this case, the include command for the *misc.schema* file was inserted into the *slapd.conf* file before an *rfc822-MailMember.schema* include command. When LDAP attempted to process the *rfc822-MailMember.schema* file, it found that the attribute type had already been declared—in this case, by the *misc.schema* file. If you have such a problem, you need to resolve the conflict. In this case, the resolution is straight-forward—simply remove the *rfc822-MailMember.schema* include command from the *slapd.conf* file. The include command can be safely removed because the *rfc822-MailMember.schema* file exactly duplicates the last two entries of the *misc.schema* file. This specific problem occurred on Red Hat Linux systems because the conflict is with a schema file provided by Red Hat. However, conflicts are possible any time multiple schema files are included in the LDAP configuration.

Include the *sendmail.schema* file in the LDAP configuration to provide support for the other LDAP records used by sendmail. For example, the sendmail configuration in this recipe reads LDAP records to load the $={LDAPRoute} class, which requires the sendmail schema. After the schema files are added to the *slapd.conf* file, restart *slapd* to ensure that the schema files have been read and are ready to be used.

Add the records required by the *ldap_routing* feature to the LDAP database using the draft IETF schema. This example shows three possible variations of the LDAP routing record:

```
# cat > ldap-routing
dn: uid=kathy, dc=wrotethebook, dc=com
objectClass: inetLocalMailRecipient
mailLocalAddress: kathy@rodent.wrotethebook.com
mailRoutingAddress: kathy@chef.wrotethebook.com

dn: uid=alana, dc=wrotethebook, dc=com
objectClass: inetLocalMailRecipient
mailLocalAddress: alana@wrotethebook.com
mailHost: chef.wrotethebook.com

dn: uid=craig, dc=wrotethebook, dc=com
objectClass: inetLocalMailRecipient
mailLocalAddress: craig@horseshoe.wrotethebook.com
mailHost: chef.wrotethebook.com
mailRoutingAddress: craig@crab.wrotethebook.com
Ctrl-D
# ldapadd -x -D "cn=Manager,dc=wrotethebook,dc=com" \
> -W -f ldap-routing
Enter LDAP Password: SecretLDAPpassword
adding new entry "uid=kathy, dc=wrotethebook, dc=com"

adding new entry "uid=alana, dc=wrotethebook, dc=com"

adding new entry "uid=craig, dc=wrotethebook, dc=com"
```

The object class of the records is inetLocalMailRecipient. Each record contains a mailLocalAddress attribute that sendmail uses as the database key. Records may contain one or both of the attributes mailHost and mailRoutingAddress, which are the values returned to sendmail by the LDAP database. The example shows how these values are first used to build an LDIF file that is then processed by *ldapadd* to add the records to the LDAP database. Once added to the database, the records can be viewed with *ldapsearch*:

```
# ldapsearch -LLL -x '(objectClass=inetLocalMailRecipient)' \
> mailLocalAddress mailHost mailRoutingAddress
dn: uid=kathy, dc=wrotethebook, dc=com
mailLocalAddress: kathy@rodent.wrotethebook.com
mailRoutingAddress: kathy@chef.wrotethebook.com

dn: uid=alana, dc=wrotethebook, dc=com
mailLocalAddress: alana@wrotethebook.com
```

```
mailHost: chef.wrotethebook.com

dn: uid=craig, dc=wrotethebook, dc=com
mailLocalAddress: craig@horseshoe.wrotethebook.com
mailHost: chef.wrotethebook.com
mailRoutingAddress: craig@crab.wrotethebook.com
```

sendmail only queries the LDAP server for routing information if the host portion of the recipient address is listed in the $={LDAPRoute} class. Values in this class can be individually defined using LDAPROUTE_DOMAIN macros or they can be read from a file using the LDAPROUTE_DOMAIN_FILE macro. The sendmail configuration in this recipe uses the LDAPROUTE_DOMAIN_FILE macro and reads the list of values for the $={LDAPRoute} class from the LDAP server. The following example shows how the LDAP administrator might store the $={LDAPRoute} data on the LDAP server so that sendmail can retrieve it later:

```
# cat > ldap-route-domains
dn: sendmailMTAClassName=LDAPRoute, dc=wrotethebook, dc=com
objectClass: sendmailMTA
objectClass: sendmailMTAClass
sendmailMTAHost: rodent.wrotethebook.com
sendmailMTAClassName: LDAPRoute
sendmailMTAClassValue: rodent.wrotethebook.com
sendmailMTAClassValue: wrotethebook.com
sendmailMTAClassValue: horseshoe.wrotethebook.com
Ctrl-D
# ldapadd -x -D "cn=Manager,dc=wrotethebook,dc=com" \
> -W -f ldap-route-domains
Enter LDAP Password: SecretLDAPpassword
adding new entry "sendmailMTAClassName=LDAPRoute, dc=wrotethebook, dc=com"
```

The sample LDIF file contains a sendmailMTAClass record, which is an object class defined in the *sendmail.schema* file. The record sets the sendmailMTAClassName attribute to LDAPRoute and defines the values for that class using sendmailMTAClassValue attributes. After the LDIF file is converted and added to the LDAP database using the *ldapadd* command, an *ldapsearch* command shows the content of the LDAP record:

```
# ldapsearch -LLL -x '(sendmailMTAClassName=LDAPRoute)' sendmailMTAClassValue
dn: sendmailMTAClassName=LDAPRoute, dc=wrotethebook, dc=com
sendmailMTAClassValue: rodent.wrotethebook.com
sendmailMTAClassValue: wrotethebook.com
sendmailMTAClassValue: horseshoe.wrotethebook.com
```

LDAP is ready; now sendmail needs to be configured.

sendmail configuration

Three commands in this recipe's sendmail configuration help sendmail use the LDAP records that we have just created: the confLDAP_DEFAULT_SPEC define, the LDAPROUTE_DOMAIN_FILE macro, and the *ldap_routing* feature.

The confLDAP_DEFAULT_SPEC define sets default values that sendmail uses to access the LDAP database. For many sendmail configurations that use LDAP, the confLDAP_DEFAULT_SPEC define is not required because the default values are correct. The confLDAP_DEFAULT_SPEC define is used in this recipe to prevent sendmail from displaying a warning message. When sendmail is configured with the *ldap_routing* feature, it complains every time it is run if the configuration does not also contain a confLDAP_DEFAULT_SPEC define. For example:

```
WARNING: Using default FEATURE(ldap_routing) map definition(s)
without setting confLDAP_DEFAULT_SPEC option.
```

Adding the confLDAP_DEFAULT_SPEC define to this recipe's configuration eliminates this warning, but, of course, care must be taken to set the correct values for the define. If the values in the confLDAP_DEFAULT_SPEC define are incorrect, sendmail will not be able to query the LDAP server successfully. The sample confLDAP_DEFAULT_SPEC define in the Solution section contains two values:

-h

> The -h argument defines the hostname of the LDAP server. If you have multiple servers, use the hostname of the server that stores the sendmail data. If you have a single server, the HOST value you configured in the *ldap.conf* file is probably the hostname you should use here.

-b

> The -b argument defines the LDAP default base distinguished name used for sendmail queries. The value should match the suffix of the database you wish to query, as defined in the *slapd.conf* by the suffix entry for that database. The suffix used in this recipe is the system default defined for all LDAP clients by the BASE command in the *ldap.conf* file. Because the recipe uses the system default, it is not strictly necessary to define it with the confLDAP_DEFAULT_SPEC command.

The values defined by the confLDAP_DEFAULT_SPEC define appear in the *sendmail.cf* file on the LDAPDefaultSpec option line, as this *grep* shows.

```
# grep LDAPDefaultSpec sendmail.cf
O LDAPDefaultSpec= -h ldserver -b dc=wrotethebook,dc=com
```

Use *ldapsearch* to test the -h and -b values, as in this example:

```
# ldapsearch -LLL -x -h ldserver \
> -b 'dc=wrotethebook,dc=com' \
> '(objectClass=inetLocalMailRecipient)' mailLocalAddress
dn: uid=kathy, dc=wrotethebook, dc=com
mailLocalAddress: kathy@rodent.wrotethebook.com

dn: uid=alana, dc=wrotethebook, dc=com
mailLocalAddress: alana@wrotethebook.com

dn: uid=craig, dc=wrotethebook, dc=com
mailLocalAddress: craig@horseshoe.wrotethebook.com
```

If the -h and -b arguments work with *ldapsearch*, they should work for sendmail.

The @LDAP string used in place of the file path for the `LDAPROUTE_DOMAIN_FILE` macro tells sendmail to load the `$={LDAPRoute}` class from the LDAP server. Either an `LDAPROUTE_DOMAIN_FILE` macro or some `LDAPROUTE_DOMAIN` macros must appear in the configuration file when the *ldap_routing* feature is used because sendmail only uses LDAP routing for hosts listed in the `$={LDAPRoute}` class.

Finally, the *ldap_routing* `FEATURE` macro is added to the configuration. The sendmail configuration in the Solution section uses the simplest form of this command, which contains no optional arguments; however, in this form, the *ldap_routing* feature defines two database maps using two *sendmail.cf* K commands:

- `ldapmh` accepts a recipient address as the key and returns the name of the mail host that should be used to reach that address. The mail host returned by the `ldapmh` map is used as the `$h` value for the mail delivery triple.

- `ldapmra` accepts a recipient address as the key and returns the mail routing address that should be used instead of the recipient address to deliver the mail. The value returned by `ldapmra` becomes the `$u` value for the mail delivery triple.

Testing the results

A few simple tests show the impact of this recipe. First, a `sendmail -bt` command tests that sendmail is successfully reading the LDAP data:

```
# sendmail -bt
ADDRESS TEST MODE (ruleset 3 NOT automatically invoked)
Enter <ruleset> <address>
> $={LDAPRoute}
rodent.wrotethebook.com
horseshoe.wrotethebook.com
wrotethebook.com
> /map ldapmh alana@wrotethebook.com
map_lookup: ldapmh (alana@wrotethebook.com) returns chef.wrotethebook.com (0)
> /map ldapmra kathy@rodent.wrotethebook.com
map_lookup: ldapmra (kathy@rodent.wrotethebook.com) returns kathy@chef.wrotethebook.
com (0)
> /quit
```

The `$={LDAPRoute}` command shows that sendmail successfully loaded this class from the LDAP server. The `/map` commands show that sendmail can read LDAP routing data from both the `ldapmh` and the `ldapmra` maps.

Next, `sendmail -bv` is used to show how the mail delivery triples are rewritten for recipient addresses that contain hostnames listed in `$={LDAPRoute}`:

```
# sendmail -bv kathy@rodent.wrotethebook.com
kathy@rodent.wrotethebook.com... deliverable: mailer esmtp, host chef.wrotethebook.
com., user kathy@chef.wrotethebook.com
# sendmail -bv alana@wrotethebook.com
alana@wrotethebook.com... deliverable: mailer relay, host chef.wrotethebook.com, user
alana@wrotethebook.com
```

```
# sendmail -bv craig@horseshoe.wrotethebook.com
craig@horseshoe.wrotethebook.com... deliverable: mailer relay, host chef.
wrotethebook.com, user craig@crab.wrotethebook.com
```

Refer back to the *ldapsearch* shown in an earlier example. You'll see that:

- The record for *kathy@rodent.wrotethebook.com* returns only a mail routing address.

- The record for *alana@wrotethebook.com* returns only a mail host.

- The record for *craig@horseshoe.wrotethebook.com* returns both a mail host and a mail routing address.

The `sendmail -bv` tests show how these various return values impact the mail delivery triple:

- In the first test, the mail routing address becomes the user value of the triple. The mailer and host values are necessary to deliver to that user address.

- In the second test, the mail host returned by the LDAP query becomes the host value in the delivery triple. The mailer used is the `relay` mailer because the mail will be relayed to that host for delivery. Because no mail routing address was returned by LDAP, the relay host is sent the original address, and it becomes the remote host's responsibility to deliver the mail to that address.

- The third test returns both a mail host value and a mail routing address. In that case, the `relay` mailer is again used to relay mail to the remote host specified by the mail host value, and the delivery address passed to that host is the mail routing address. It then becomes the responsibility of that remote host to deliver the mail to the mail routing address.

LDAP routing is only one step in the delivery process. The *virtusertable* and the *mailertable* are both applied after LDAP routing, and if the mailer used to deliver to the host returned by LDAP has the F=A flag set, aliasing is also applied.* If the mail is relayed to a remote host, that host also processes the address. The `sendmail -bv` test results clearly show the impact of LDAP routing, but only in part, because this recipe does not perform any subsequent processing on these addresses. On a production system with a more complex configuration, `sendmail -bv` may not provide such clear results. However, it is possible to test the impact of LDAP rulesets more directly.

The *ldap_routing* feature adds the `LDAPExpand` ruleset to query LDAP and process the return value, and it adds two rules to the `Parse1` ruleset to call the new ruleset. Use `sendmail -bt` to check whether or not LDAP routing is applied to a specific address and to see the delivery triple returned for that address. Here is an example:

```
# sendmail -bt
ADDRESS TEST MODE (ruleset 3 NOT automatically invoked)
```

---

* By default, the F=A flag is set for the local mailer.

```
Enter <ruleset> <address>
> Parse1 craig<@horseshoe.wrotethebook.com.>
Parse1            input: craig < @ horseshoe . wrotethebook . com . >
LDAPExpand        input: < craig < @ horseshoe . wrotethebook . com . > > < craig @
horseshoe . wrotethebook . com > < >
canonify          input: craig @ crab . wrotethebook . com
Canonify2         input: craig < @ crab . wrotethebook . com >
Canonify2         returns: craig < @ crab . wrotethebook . com . >
canonify          returns: craig < @ crab . wrotethebook . com . >
LDAPExpand        returns: $# relay $@ chef . wrotethebook . com $: craig < @ crab .
wrotethebook . com . >
Parse1            returns: $# relay $@ chef . wrotethebook . com $: craig < @ crab .
wrotethebook . com . >
> /quit
```

Recipe 5.10 provides another example of testing the *ldap_routing* feature by passing an address to Parse1.[*] See Recipe 5.10 for more details about this ruleset.

The ldap_routing feature

The *ldap_routing* FEATURE command used in this recipe is the simplest form of the command. The command accepts up to four optional arguments. Here is the complete syntax:

```
FEATURE(ldap_routing, mhmap, mramap, bounce, detail)
```

The four optional arguments are:

mhmap

> This is a custom mail host map definition. It replaces the default ldapmh map created by the *ldap_routing* feature. At a minimum, the map definition must include -k and -v arguments.

mramap

> This is a custom mail routing address map definition. It replaces the default ldapmra map created by the *ldap_routing* feature. At a minimum, the map definition must include -k and -v arguments.

bounce

> This argument tells sendmail what to do when a recipient address is not found in the LDAP database. Normally, delivery continues and sendmail delivers the mail to the recipient address as directed by the rest of the configuration. Two keywords can be used for this argument:

passthru

> This keyword tells sendmail to continue with the delivery, which is the default action.

---

[*] The focus characters (<>) are used in the address because Parse1, which is normally called after canonify has inserted them, expects focus characters.

bounce

> This tells sendmail to return the mail as undeliverable. Actually, any value other than passthru causes sendmail to bounce the mail; however, the sendmail developers suggest that, for the sake of clarity, you use the keyword bounce to reject the mail.

detail

> This tells sendmail how to handle recipient addresses that use the *+detail* syntax. By default, an address that contains *+detail* information is looked up as-is, with the *+detail* information intact. Two keywords can be used to change this:

strip

> This keyword directs sendmail first to lookup the address with the *+detail* information, and then, if no match is found, to lookup the address without the *+detail* information.

preserve

> Just like strip, this keyword directs sendmail first to lookup the address with the *+detail* information, and then, if no match is found, to lookup the address without the *+detail* information. In addition to modifying the lookup procedure, this keyword modifies the value returned from the LDAP database. If LDAP returns a mail routing address, sendmail appends the *+detail* information from the recipient address to the mail routing address when the preserve keyword is specified.

See Also

The *sendmail* book covers the LDAPROUTE_DOMAIN_FILE macro in section 23.7.11.18, the *ldap_routing* feature in section 23.7.11.17, and the arguments available for the confLDAP_DEFAULT_SPEC define in section 21.7.11. The *Using LDAP for Aliases, Maps, and Classes* section of the *cf/README* file also provides important information.

5.10   Using LDAP Routing with Masquerading

Problem

When the hostname part of the email address assigned to the mailLocalAddress attribute of an LDAP routing record is a masquerade value, sendmail must convert the hostname from the recipient address to the masquerade name before doing the LDAP lookup. You have been asked to configure sendmail to do this.

Solution

Recipe 5.9 provides information for the LDAP administrator on including support for the IETF draft schema for intranet mail routing and the *sendmail.schema* file in the LDAP configuration file. That recipe also explains how to add mail routing data to the LDAP database. Read Recipe 5.9 before you proceed.

On the sendmail host, create an *ldaproute-equivalents* file to load the $={LDAPRouteEquiv} class. List hostnames in the file that should be converted to the MASQUERADE_AS hostname before querying the LDAP server for routing information. Here is an example:

```
# cd /etc/mail
# cat > ldaproute-equivalents
jamis.wrotethebook.com
giant.wrotethebook.com
horseshoe.wrotethebook.com
Ctrl-D
```

Create a sendmail configuration that includes the MASQUERADE_AS macro, the confLDAP_DEFAULT_SPEC define, the *ldap_routing* feature, and the LDAPROUTE_EQUIVALENT_FILE macro, which loads class $={LDAPRouteEquiv}. Here is a sample of the lines that might be added to the sendmail configuration:

```
dnl Define the masquerade value
MASQUERADE_AS(`wrotethebook.com')
dnl Stop Build from complaining
define(`confLDAP_DEFAULT_SPEC', ` -h ldserver -b dc=wrotethebook,dc=com')
dnl Load $={LDAPRouteEquiv} from ldaproute-equivalents
LDAPROUTE_EQUIVALENT_FILE(`/etc/mail/ldaproute-equivalents')
dnl Enable the ldap_routing feature
FEATURE(`ldap_routing')
```

Following the instructions in Recipe 1.8, rebuild and reinstall *sendmail.cf*, and then restart sendmail.

Discussion

When a recipient host is a member of the $={LDAPRouteEquiv} class, sendmail converts the host's name to the MASQUERADE_AS hostname before querying the LDAP server for routing information. Hostnames can be added to $={LDAPRouteEquiv} individually using LDAPROUTE_EQUIVALENT macros, or the hostnames can be loaded into the class from a file (or an LDAP server) using the LDAPROUTE_EQUIVALENT_FILE macro. This recipe uses a local *ldaproute-equivalents* file.

The MASQUERADE_AS macro must be included in this sendmail configuration because the hostnames listed in the $={LDAPRouteEquiv} class are converted to the masquerade name. The sample configuration in the Solution section specifies *wrotethebook.com* as the MASQUERADE_AS value. Therefore, if the host portion of a recipient address matches a value in $={LDAPRouteEquiv}, the host portion is converted to *wrotethebook.com* before the LDAP server is queried.

The confLDAP_DEFAULT_SPEC define sets the LDAP server hostname and the base distinguished name that sendmail will use to query the LDAP server. Why it is needed in this configuration is covered in the Discussion section of Recipe 5.9, as is the *ldap_routing* FEATURE command and its syntax.

After this recipe is installed, use `sendmail -bt` to observe the effect of the configuration on sendmail variables and on the routing of mail to specific addresses. Here is an example:

```
# sendmail -bt
ADDRESS TEST MODE (ruleset 3 NOT automatically invoked)
Enter <ruleset> <address>
> $M
wrotethebook.com
> $={LDAPRouteEquiv}
giant.wrotethebook.com
jamis.wrotethebook.com
horseshoe.wrotethebook.com
> Parse1 alana<@jamis.wrotethebook.com.>
Parse1                input: alana < @ jamis . wrotethebook . com . >
LDAPExpand            input: < alana < @ jamis . wrotethebook . com . > > < alana @
wrotethebook . com > < >
LDAPExpand          returns: $# relay $@ chef . wrotethebook . com $: alana < @ jamis .
wrotethebook . com . >
Parse1              returns: $# relay $@ chef . wrotethebook . com $: alana < @ jamis .
wrotethebook . com . >
> /quit
```

The `$M` command shows the masquerade value, which, in this case, is *wrotethebook.com*. The `$={LDAPRouteEquiv}` command shows the list of recipient hosts that will be converted to the masquerade value before being passed to the LDAP server. The next command line calls the `Parse1` ruleset and passes it the recipient address *alana@jamis.wrotethebook.com* with the proper focus characters inserted. The *ldap_routing* feature adds two rules to the `Parse1` ruleset that call the `LDAPExpand` ruleset. One rule calls `LDAPExpand` to process hosts listed in `$={LDAPRoute}` and the other calls it to process hosts listed in `$={LDAPRouteEquiv}`. When `Parse1` calls `LDAPExpand`, it passes it three values: the original address, which is used as a pass-through value, the address used for the lookup, and any *+detail* information.

The `Parse1 alana<@jamis.wrotethebook.com.>` test shows that, when `Parse1` is passed an address containing a hostname found in `$={LDAPRouteEquiv}`, `Parse1` in turn calls the `LDAPExpand` ruleset and passes it the original address as the first parameter and a rewritten address as the second parameter. The rewritten address contains the masquerade value as the host part. The `LDAPExpand` ruleset queries the LDAP server and processes the LDAP server's response. As the test shows, `LDAPExpand` returns a mail delivery triple. Notice that the mailer in the triple is relay, and the host in the triple is chef.wrotethebook.com. The relay hostname came from the LDAP server, and it came in response to a query using the masquerade address, as these *ldapsearch* tests show:

```
# ldapsearch -LLL -x \
> '(&(objectClass=inetLocalMailRecipient) \
> (mailLocalAddress=alana@wrotethebook.com))' mailHost
dn: uid=alana, dc=wrotethebook, dc=com
```

```
mailHost: chef.wrotethebook.com
# ldapsearch -LLL -x \
> '(&(objectClass=inetLocalMailRecipient) \
> (mailLocalAddress=alana@jamis.wrotethebook.com))' mailHost
```

The first *ldapsearch* test shows that a record for *alana@wrotethebook.com* is found in the LDAP database. The second test shows that *alana@jamis.wrotethebook.com* is not in the LDAP database. Clearly, *jamis.wrotethebook.com* needs to be rewritten to *wrotethebook.com* for the lookup to succeed.

See Also

Recipe 5.9 provides detailed coverage of the *ldap_routing* FEATURE command and the confLDAP_DEFAULT_SPEC. It also provides an example of loading a sendmail class from an LDAP server. The *cf/README* file covers this topic in the *Using LDAP for Aliases, Maps, and Classes* section. The *sendmail* book covers the LDAPROUTE_EQUIVALENT_FILE macro in section 23.7.11.19, the *ldap_routing* feature in section 23.7.11.17, and the arguments available for the confLDAP_DEFAULT_SPEC define in section 21.7.11.

## CHAPTER 6

Controlling Spam

6.0 Introduction

Spam mail: you know it when you see it, and everyone has seen the ridiculous adver-
tisements for investment schemes, pornography, herbal cures, and everything else
imaginable. Many experts categorize all Unsolicited Commercial Email (UCE) as
spam, and certainly UCE clutters electronic mailboxes around the world. However,
legitimate advertisers who offer real "opt-out" schemes are not the worst problem.*
The real problems come from spammers. What distinguishes spammers from legitimate advertisers is that spammers hide their identity and abuse other people's systems. These traits can be seen by the fact that:

- Spammers hide the origin of the email so that no one knows they sent it. Legitimate advertisers proudly display their company name in the sender address. Any
  advertiser who doesn't probably has a reason to hide who they are and what
  they are doing and should be considered a spammer.

- Spammers abuse the services of other people's systems by using those systems as
  unauthorized relays.

- Spammers send information you never asked to receive. You don't join a spammers' mailing list, and when spammers provide an opt-out scheme, it does not
  opt the user out of anything. Instead, the scheme is used to collect email
  addresses to sell to other spammers.

You must do your part to reduce spam for everyone by ensuring that your system is
not misused by remote spammers and that your local users do not contribute to spam.

Spammers use open mail relays to hide their identity. See the recipes in Chapter 3 for
examples of how to configure a mail relay host. Test your relay as shown in
Chapter 3 every time the configuration is changed to ensure that it can't be abused.

---

* Purists rail against opt-out schemes, but they can work if genuinely implemented.

The first step in addressing local spammers is to create an acceptable use policy (AUP) that forbids spamming and defines the actions you will take to stop it. Make sure that the policy clearly states that email is not private and is subject to logging, scanning, and filtering. Because this is a policy, it must be approved and issued by management, and it must be reviewed and approved by the legal department. Policies are always a hassle because they are not technical solutions and because they involve management. However, it is a necessary step to give you the authority you need to analyze mail. Once the policy is in place, all users must agree to it as a condition of obtaining a user account.

In addition to ensuring that your system doesn't contribute to the spam problem, there are technical tools that you can use to actively fight spam. sendmail provides a number of tools to combat incoming junk mail:

- The *access* database blocks mail from and to specified systems.
- DNS blackhole lists block mail from suspected spammers and from open mail relays.
- Mail filtering programs, such as *procmail*, are accessible from sendmail and are capable of filtering mail based on the content of the mail.
- sendmail's header processing can detect malformed or inconsistent headers.
- sendmail automatically performs sanity checks, such as checking that the sender's domain can be resolved by DNS.

The access database

The *access* database provides fine-grained control over mail relaying and mail delivery. Use the *access_db* feature to add the *access* database to the sendmail configuration:

```
FEATURE(`access_db')
```

By default, the *access* database is a hash database, and its default pathname is */etc/mail/access.db*. Use the optional argument field with the *access_db* feature to change the default values, as in this example:

```
FEATURE(`access_db', `btree -T<TMPF> /var/mail/access')
```

This example changes the database type, specifies the -T<TMPF> option to deal with temporary lookup failures, and changes the database pathname. Only change the defaults when it is truly necessary.

Each line in the *access* database contains two fields: the key field and the return value. When the *access* database is used to control junk mail, the key to the database is an address, and the return value specifies the action that sendmail should take with regard to mail to or from the specified address. When the *access* database was used in Chapter 3, the return value was, logically enough, the keyword RELAY. To control spam, the recipes in this chapter use the *access* database to determine whether mail should be accepted from or delivered to specified addresses. For that, we need a different set of return values. The keywords that apply to controlling junk mail are listed in Table 6-1.

Table 6-1. access database keywords used for spam control

Keyword	Action
OK	Accepts messages from or to the specified address.
DISCARD	Drops any message from or to the specified address.
REJECT	Issues an error message and drops any mail from or to the specified address.
ERROR:*dsn*:*code text*	Rejects the mail with the specified response code and error message.
HATER	Adds the check_mail and check_relay rulesets for mail to the specified recipient.
FRIEND	Skips the check_mail and check_relay rulesets for mail to the specified recipient.

The OK command tells sendmail to accept mail from the source identified by the address in the key field regardless of other conditions. For example, if the hostname specified in the address field cannot be resolved by DNS, sendmail accepts mail from that host even if the *accept_unresolvable_domains* feature is not enabled. OK accepts mail for local delivery; OK does not grant relaying privileges. The RELAY keyword, described in Chapter 3, is required for that.

The REJECT keyword returns a standard error message to the source and rejects the mail. The DISCARD action drops the mail without sending an error message back to the source. Many anti-spam authorities disagree with silently discarding mail because they feel it does not discourage the spammer. For all the spammer knows, you received the mail, so he just keeps sending more junk. Other anti-spam authorities prefer to silently discard mail because they believe that responding to the mail in any form verifies the address for the spammer, which encourages the spammer to continue his assault. Both approaches protect your users from the spammer. However, using REJECT, which returns an error message to the source of the mail, helps when legitimate mail is accidentally classified as spam because it notifies the source of the mail that their mail was rejected.

The REJECT action sends a default error message. Use the ERROR keyword to reject a message with your own custom error message. For example:

```
example.com        ERROR:5.7.1:550 Relaying denied to spammers
```

In this case, the error message returned to the sender is "Relaying denied to spammers." This error message includes delivery status notification code 5.7.1 and the SMTP error code 550. Use a valid DSN code from RFC 1893 that is compatible with the RFC 821 error code and the message.[*] The format for the error message shown in

---

[*] Chapter 5 provides additional details about DSN codes and lists the SMTP code keywords. Also see RFC 2821.

Table 6-1 is ERROR:*dsn:code text*. This format is recommended, but not required. It could be specified without the keyword ERROR or the DSN code. However, that old error format has been deprecated. Use the ERROR keyword and the DSN code to ensure compatibility with future sendmail releases.

The FRIEND and HATER keywords only apply if the *delay_checks* feature is used to control when the check_mail and check_relay rulesets are applied. The FRIEND keyword in the return value allows mail that would normally be discarded by check_mail and check_relay to pass through the system to the recipient specified in the key field. When HATER is used, check_mail and check_relay are only applied to mail addressed to recipients who have the HATER keyword in their *access* database entries. FRIEND and HATER cannot appear in the same *access* database because the *delay_checks* feature must be configured to accept either FRIEND or HATER—it cannot be configured to accept both at the same time. Recipe 6.13 provides an example of how these keywords are used.

Most of the actions in Table 6-1 are described as affecting mail "from or to" an address. This is only true when tags are used or the *blacklist_recipients* feature is used. When that feature is not used, the actions only affect mail coming from a source address, unless the address field is modified by an optional To:, From:, or Connect: tag. These tags limit the address test to the envelope recipient, envelope sender, and connection address, respectively.* For example, an *access* database entry to reject connections from 10.0.187.215 might contain:

```
Connect:10.0.187.215      ERROR:5.7.1:550 UCE not accepted
```

The Connect: tag limits the match to the address of the remote system that connected to the server to deliver the mail. If that address is 10.0.187.215, the mail is rejected and the message "UCE not accepted" is returned to the sender.

The address in the key field of an *access* database entry can define a user, an individual email address, a source IP address, a network address, or the name of a domain:

- An individual is defined using either a full email address in the form *user@host. domain* or a username in the form *username@*.
- A host is identified by its hostname or its IP address.
- A domain is identified by a domain name.
- A network is identified by the network portion of an IP address.

In addition to the Connect: example shown in the access *database*, other address formats can be used to identify mail from 10.0.187.215. Here are a few:

```
10.0.187              REJECT
[10.0.187.215]        DISCARD
example.com           ERROR:5.7.1:550 Mail not accepted.
```

---

* The optional *access* database tags are covered in more detail in Chapter 3.

The first two lines in this *access* database match IP addresses. The first entry rejects mail from any computer whose IP address begins with the network number 10.0.187, which is the network from which the UCE was received. The second line defines a specific computer with the address 10.0.187.215. The square brackets surrounding the individual address indicate that this IP address doesn't resolve to a hostname.

The last entry defines an entire domain. It rejects mail from any host in the domain *example.com*. Of course, you wouldn't do this if you got only one piece of UCE from that domain, but if you consistently received junk mail from the domain, you may decide to block all mail from that domain until they improved their security. The *dnsbl* feature provides another method for blocking mail from specific hosts and domains.

Blackhole lists with dnsbl and enhdnsbl

Add the *dnsbl* feature to the sendmail configuration to use a blackhole list to block spam. A blackhole list is a DNS database that identifies spam contributors. The contributors can be the original source of the spam or open mail relays that permit spammers to relay mail. Blackhole list services are implemented through DNS. Every Unix system can issue DNS queries, so this is a very effective way to distribute information. Of course, a program can only make use of the information if it understands it, which sendmail does.

The *dnsbl* feature accepts two optional arguments. The first argument is the name of the domain that contains the blackhole list. This defaults to the Realtime Blackhole List (RBL) that is maintained by the Mail Abuse Prevention System (MAPS). There are several other groups that maintain lists and make them available to the public. Table 6-2 lists a few of these.

Table 6-2. Blackhole list services

Service name	Web site	Domain name
Spamhaus Block List	www.spamhaus.org	sbl.spamhaus.org
Relay Stop List	relays.visi.com	relays.visi.com
Distributed Server Boycott List	dsbl.org	list.dsbl.org
MAPS RBL	mail-abuse.org	None required. This is the *dnsbl* default.

To use a blackhole list specified in Table 6-2, point the first argument of the *dnsbl* feature to the domain listed in the table. For example, the following command would configure sendmail to use the Spamhaus Block List:

```
FEATURE(`dnsbl', `sbl.spamhaus.org')
```

The policies enforced by the different blackhole list services vary. Most of these services focus on blocking open relays instead of focusing on spam sources. The reason for this focus is that spam sources are constantly changing and hiding their true identities. They are aided in this, albeit unwittingly, by open relays. The open relay doesn't really want to help the spammer. Blocking the open relay's mail quickly gets the attention of the administrator of that relay, who fixes the system, and thus denies the spammer access to resources. This indirect defense against spam impacts many innocent, if naive, network users. For this reason, many consider blackhole lists to be a cure that is as bad as the disease, and they discourage the use of blackhole lists.

There are many systems listed in the public blackhole lists. Any site that relays spam—which could be your site if you don't properly configure sendmail—is likely to be blackhole listed. This is one of the reasons that it is essential to configure relaying properly. A mistake in configuring relaying could get your site added to the blackhole list. If a site stops relaying spam, it should be removed from the list after about a month. Of course, this policy varies from list to list, as does the efficiency by which sites are added to and removed from the lists. If your site gets added to a blackhole list, fix the problem and apply to have your site removed from the list by following the instructions on the list's web site. Visit the web site of each listing service to find out more about the list before you start using it.

The simplest way to block spam is to let someone else do it. However, while using a public blackhole list is simple, it isn't perfect. You can't choose which sites are added to the list, which means the list might block email from a friendly site just because the administrator at that site forgot to turn off relaying. You can, however, override entries in a blackhole list using the *access* database, as described in Recipe 6.4. For even more control, some organizations decide to build their own DNS-based blackhole list. Recipe 6.5 shows how you build and invoke your own blackhole list.

The second argument available for the *dnsbl* feature is the error message displayed when mail is rejected because of the blackhole server. The format of the default message is:

```
550 Rejected $&{client_addr} listed at dnsbl-domain
```

where $&{client_addr} is the IP address that was rejected, and *dnsbl-domain* is the DNS blackhole list that rejected the address (i.e., *dnsbl-domain* is the value from the first argument provided to the *dnsbl* feature). Use the second *dnsbl* argument only if you wish to change the standard error message. Most administrators stick with the default message.

The third argument available for the *dnsbl* feature allows you to specify how temporary DNS lookup failures should be handled. By default, sendmail does not defer the message just because the blackhole list service is not able to respond to a DNS lookup. Placing a t in the third argument field causes sendmail to return a temporary error message and defer the message. Here is an example:

```
FEATURE(`dnsbl', `sbl.spamhaus.org', ,`t')
```

An alternative to the *dnsbl* feature is the *enhdnsbl* feature. The syntax of the *enhdnsbl* feature has the same three initial arguments as the *dnsbl* feature, but it adds a fourth argument. The fourth argument is the return value that sendmail expects from the

DNS lookup. By default, any DNS lookup value returned by a blackhole list service indicates that the address being looked up is listed by the service and should therefore be rejected. The fourth argument allows you to change this so that only a value matching the fourth argument will trigger a rejection. The fourth argument does not need to be a single value: it can be a list of values or it can use the same operators as the lefthand side of a rewrite rule to match multiple values. Here is an example of the *enhdnsbl* feature:

```
FEATURE(`enhdnsbl', `sbl.spamhaus.org', , ,`127.0.0.2', `127.0.0.3')
```

This macro entry enables the *enhdnsbl* feature and uses the *sbl.spamhaus.org* blackhole list service. It tells sendmail to reject the incoming message if the blackhole list service returns either the value 127.0.0.2 or 127.0.0.3 in response to the lookup of the connection address.

The *access* database and the blackhole lists block mail from known spam sources and from open relays. But not all spam comes from known spam sources. Sometimes you don't know it is junk mail until you read it. Mail filtering tools can examine the content of the mail and decide how it should be handled based on the information found in the mail itself.

MILTER

sendmail provides direct access via the sockets interface to external mail filtering programs, called MILTERs, which are written in accordance with the *Sendmail Mail Filter API*. External mail filters are defined in the sendmail configuration using either the INPUT_MAIL_FILTER macro or the MAIL_FILTER macro. Other than the macro name, the syntax of both macros is identical. For example, here is the syntax of the INPUT_MAIL_FILTER macro:

```
INPUT_MAIL_FILTER(name, equates)
```

The *name* is an arbitrary name used by sendmail—much like an internal mailer name or an internal database name. There are up to three *equates* written in the form of *key-letter=value*, where *key-letter* is one of the following:

S

> The S equate is required because it defines the socket used to communicate with the external filter. The socket definition is written in the form S=*type*: *specification*, where *type* is the socket type and *specification* defines the socket in the manner required by the given socket type. Three socket types are supported:

S=unix:*path*

> Unix sockets are supported. *path* is the full pathname of the Unix socket. The keyword unix can be replaced by the synonym local (e.g., S=local:/ var/run/filter1.sock).

S=inet:*port@host*

> The keyword inet requests an IP socket. *port* is the network port number used by the filter. *host* is the hostname or IP address of the system on which the filter is running.

S=inet6:*port@host*

> IPv6 sockets are also supported. The keyword inet6 requests an IPv6 socket, *port* identifies the IPv6 port used by the filter, and *host* identifies the system the filter is running on. *host* can be either an IPv6 address or a hostname that maps to an IPv6 address.

F=*letter*

> Use this optional equate to define how a socket failure should be handled. By default, sendmail continues with normal mail processing if the socket fails or the filter responds in an unexpected manner. Use F=R to reject the connection with a permanent error or F=T to defer the message with a temporary error when a socket or filter problem occurs.

T=*letter*:*value*;*letter*:*value*;...

> Use this optional equate to change the default timeouts. Four letter values are available:

> C

>> Defines the connection timeout. By default, the connection times out if a successful connection has not been made in five minutes (5m).

> E

>> Defines the overall timeout. This defaults to five minutes (5m).

> R

>> Defines the timeout for reading a reply from the filter. This defaults to 10 seconds (10s).

> S

>> Defines the timeout for sending data to the filter. The default is 10 seconds (10s).

Given this syntax, an INPUT_MAIL_FILTER macro that adds support for the external *MIMEDefang* program might look like the following:

```
INPUT_MAIL_FILTER(`mimedefang',`S=unix:/var/run/mimedefang.sock, T=S:5m;R:5m')
```

This macro defines mimedefang as the internal name for this filter. sendmail will create the socket */var/run/mimedefang.sock* and communicate with the filter through this Unix socket. Because sendmail creates the socket, it should not already exist. The F equate is not used in the example, therefore, sendmail will continue to process the message in a normal manner even if the socket fails or the filter responds incorrectly. The T equate increases the send and receive timers to five minutes.

The INPUT_MAIL_FILTER macro defines only one filter. To use multiple filters, add multiple INPUT_MAIL_FILTER or MAIL_FILTER macros to the sendmail configuration. When multiple filters are used, the difference between MAIL_FILTER and INPUT_MAIL_FILTER becomes clear. Here is an example. Assume the sendmail configuration contains the following macros:

```
INPUT_MAIL_FILTER(`filter1', `S=unix:/var/run/filter1.soc')
INPUT_MAIL_FILTER(`filter2', `S=unix:/var/run/filter2.soc')
INPUT_MAIL_FILTER(`filter3', `S=unix:/var/run/filter3.soc')
```

The INPUT_MAIL_FILTER macro sets the order in which the filters are used. Given these three macros and the order in which they are listed, sendmail would send data through filter1, filter2, and filter3 in that order. To create an equivalent configuration with the MAIL_FILTER macro requires four sendmail configuration lines:

```
MAIL_FILTER(`filter1', `S=unix:/var/run/filter1.soc')
MAIL_FILTER(`filter2', `S=unix:/var/run/filter2.soc')
MAIL_FILTER(`filter3', `S=unix:/var/run/filter3.soc')
define(`confINPUT_MAIL_FILTERS', `filter1, filter2, filter3')
```

MAIL_FILTER macros do not set the order in which the filters are used; therefore, they must be accompanied by a confINPUT_MAIL_FILTERS define that specifies the order of execution. If the confINPUT_MAIL_FILTERS define is not used when MAIL_FILTER macros are used, the filters defined by the macro are ignored. Of course, when MAIL_FILTER macros and the confINPUT_MAIL_FILTERS define are used, mail filters do not need to be run in the order in which they are declared. For example, changing the confINPUT_MAIL_FILTERS define to the one shown here would run the filters in reverse order:

```
define(`confINPUT_MAIL_FILTERS', `filter3, filter2, filter1')
```

The filters used by sendmail are external programs. Any reasonably skilled programmer can write a basic filter program but creating one that is truly effective at fighting mail abuse is a challenge. Luckily, many skilled people have already created useful filters. Before you reinvent the wheel, search the Web for filters that may solve your email problems. Here are a few places to start:

http://www.milter.org/
> A clearing house for information about MILTERs in general.

http//www.mimedefang.org/
> A powerful, extensible MILTER that supports virus scanning, deletion of attachments based on name and content, and SpamAssassin processing.*

http://www.snert.com/Software/milter-sender/
> A MILTER that attempts to verify that the sending address is a valid email address. Many spammers do not use valid sender addresses.

---

* See *http://spamassassin.org/* for information on the SpamAssassin program.

http://www.amavis.org/
> A virus scanning MILTER.

http://sendmail.com/
> A variety of commercially supported MILTERs are available from Sendmail, Inc.

There are many more MILTER-related web sites and many more MILTERs available. However, MILTERs are not the only tools available for mail filtering; *procmail* is also widely used.

Filtering with procmail

Most sendmail texts, and this one is no exception, concentrate on *procmail* for mail filtering. There are a few reasons for this emphasis:

- *procmail* is tightly integrated with sendmail.
- *procmail* is a powerful tool that can be used for much more than spam filtering.
- *procmail* is the default local mail delivery program for Linux systems, and it can be used as the local mailer on any Unix system by adding the *local_procmail* feature to the sendmail configuration.
- The MAILER(procmail) command adds *procmail* to sendmail's list of mailers.

The variety of ways that *procmail* can be invoked add to the flexibility of this tool. As noted above, sendmail can be configured to use *procmail* as the local mailer. *procmail* can also be invoked from the shell command line. It can be invoked from the *mailertable*, as described in Recipe 6.8, and it can be executed from the user's *.forward* file, in the following manner:

```
$ cat > .forward
"|/usr/bin/procmail"
Ctrl-D
```

A common mistake is to think that, because system-wide mail filters affect a large number of users, the most important mail filtering takes place at the system level. User-level mail filtering is just as important as system-level filters. User-level filters:

- Provide a last line of defense against spam that makes its way through the system filters.
- Allow users to enforce their own personal email policies.
- Permit content filtering without any fear of compromising privacy.
- Deal with a much smaller volume of mail.

For these reasons, and more, it is good to encourage users to learn about and use the mail filters available to them. Many end user mail tools come with mail filtering features. These are not integrated into sendmail and thus are not discussed here.

procmail is a powerful, although complex, mail filtering system. Personal *procmail* filters are defined by the user in the user's home directory in a file named *.procmailrc*. The system administrator defines system-wide mail filters in the */etc/procmailrc* file and uses the */etc/procmailrc* file for general anti-spam filtering. The end user uses *.procmailrc* to add filtering for personal preferences. The format of both files is the same.

The *.procmailrc* file contains two types of entries: environment variable assignments and mail filtering rules, which are called *recipes* in *procmail* parlance. Environment variable assignments are straightforward and look just like these assignments would in a shell script. For example, HOME=/home/craig is a valid environment variable assignment. The *.procmailrc* manpage lists more than 30 environment variables.

The real substance of a *.procmailrc* file are the recipes. The syntax of each recipe is:

```
:0 [flags] [:[lockfile]]
[* condition]
action
```

Every recipe begins with :0, which differentiates it from an assignment statement. The :0 is optionally followed by flags that change how the filter is processed. Table 6-3 lists the flags and their uses.

Table 6-3. procmail recipe flags

Flag	Meaning
A	Execute this recipe if the preceding recipe evaluated to true.
a	This has the same meaning as the A flag, except that the preceding recipe must also have successfully completed execution.
b	Pass the body of the message on to the destination. This is the default.
B	Filter the message body.
c	Create a carbon copy of this mail.
D	Tests are case sensitive. By default, case is ignored.
e	Execute this recipe if the execution of the preceding recipe returned an error.
E	Execute this recipe if the preceding recipe was not executed.
f	Pass the data through an external filter program.
H	Filter the message headers. This is the default.
h	Pass the message header on to the destination. This is the default.
i	Ignore write errors for this recipe.
r	Write the mail out without any additional format checks.
w	Check the exit code of the external filter program.
W	This is the same meaning as the w flag, except no error message is printed.

Use the optional *lockfile* variable to specify the name of the local lock file to be used for this recipe. The lock file prevents multiple copies of *procmail* from writing to the same mailbox at the same time, which can happen on a busy system. The *lockfile* name is preceded by a colon. If the colon is used and no name is specified, a default *lockfile* name created from the mailbox name and the extension *.lock* is used. If no local lock file is specified, a default lock file will be used. However, the *procmail* documentation encourages the use of local lock files.

The conditional test is optional. If no *condition* is provided, the recipe acts as if the condition is true, which means that the action is taken. If a *condition* is specified it must begin with an asterisk (*). The *condition* is written as a regular expression. If the value defined by the regular expression is found in the mail, the condition evaluates to true and the action is taken. To take an action when mail does *not* contain the specified value, put an exclamation in front of the regular expression. Here are some examples of valid conditional tests:

```
* ^From.*simon@oreilly\.com
* !^Subject: Chapter
```

The first conditional checks to see if the mail contains a line that begins with (^) the literal string From followed by any number of characters (.*) and the literal string simon@oreilly.com. The second conditional matches all mail that does not (!) contain a line that begins with the string Subject: Chapter. If multiple conditions are defined for one recipe, each condition appears on a separate line.

While there may be multiple conditions in a *procmail* recipe, there can be only one *action*. The *action* can direct the mail to a file, forward it to another email address, or send it to a program, or the *action* can define additional recipes to process the message. If the *action* is an additional recipe, it begins with :0. If the *action* directs the mail to an email address, it begins with an exclamation (!), and if it directs the mail to a program, it begins with a vertical bar (|). If the *action* directs the mail to a file, just the name of the file is specified. The following example illustrates how mail is passed to an external program for processing:

```
:0 B
* .*pheromones
| awk -f spamscript > spam-suspects
```

The B flag applies the conditional test to the content of the message body. All messages that contain the word "pheromones" anywhere in the message body are passed to *awk* for processing. In this example, *awk* runs a program file named *spamscript* that extracts information from the mail and stores it in a file named *spam-suspects*. You can imagine that the administrator of this system created *spamscript* to extract the email addresses from suspected spam.

The example shows *procmail* filtering the message body. By default, *procmail* looks at the message headers. Message headers can also be given special attention inside of the sendmail configuration by using custom rulesets.

Custom rulesets

sendmail allows you to define custom processing for the addresses and headers from incoming mail, and it provides some hooks for this purpose. The hooks used for custom address processing are:

Local_check_relay
> This is a hook into the check_relay ruleset. The Local_check_relay ruleset is passed the hostname and the IP address of the host that initiated the email connection.

Local_check_mail
> This is a hook into the check_mail ruleset that processes the envelope sender address from the MAIL From: SMTP command. Recipe 6.10 contains a sample Local_check_mail ruleset.

Local_check_rcpt
> This is a hook into the check_rcpt ruleset that checks the envelope recipient address defined by the RCPT To: SMTP command.

These rulesets are not specially designed to detect and delete junk mail; they have a broader applicability. However, these ruleset hooks are useful for fighting spam.

In addition to these hooks that are called from standard rulesets, a ruleset can be called from a header definition to perform custom header processing. The basic syntax of the *sendmail.cf* H command defines the format of mail headers. In the basic syntax, the header definition starts with the H command followed by the name of the header and the format of that header. The syntax to call a ruleset from an H command is:

    Hname: $>ruleset

where *name* is the header name and *ruleset* is the ruleset called to process incoming headers of that name.

Use this capability to check incoming headers to detect spam mail from the header information. Recipe 6.9 provides an example of how this capability is used.

6.1   Blocking Spam with the access Database

Problem

Because the bulk of mail arriving from specific sites is junk, you have been asked to configure sendmail to block all mail from those sites.

Solution

Add the addresses you want blocked to the */etc/mail/access* text file. The key to each
entry is the spammer's address, and the return is either DISCARD, to silently drop the
mail; REJECT, to drop the mail with a standard error; or ERROR, to reject the mail with
a customer error message. Use the *makemap* script to build a hash database from the
text file.

Next, create a sendmail configuration containing the *access_db* feature. Here is the
required FEATURE macro:

```
dnl Use the access database
FEATURE(`access_db')
```

Following the example in Recipe 1.8, rebuild the *sendmail.cf* file, copy the new
sendmail.cf file to */etc/mail*, and restart sendmail.

Discussion

Use REJECT, ERROR, or DISCARD in the *access* database to block junk mail. The following sample *access* database blocks mail from three sites:

```
example.com         REJECT
wrotethebook.net    ERROR:5.7.1:550 Invalid mail source
fake.ora.com        DISCARD
```

A *telnet* test shows what the remote site sees depending on the action defined in the
database:

```
# telnet localhost smtp
Trying 127.0.0.1...
Connected to localhost.
Escape character is '^]'.
220 chef.wrotethebook.com ESMTP Sendmail 8.12.9/8.12.9; Fri, 22 Aug 2003 12:01:37 -
0400
HELO localhost
250 chef.wrotethebook.com Hello IDENT:UWSRv+Jij66J8vALUBVBECbGPVoU8OQe@localhost
[127.0.0.1], pleased to meet you
MAIL From:<crooks@example.com>
550 5.7.1 <crooks@example.com>... Access denied
MAIL From:<thieves@wrotethebook.net>
550 5.7.1 <thieves@wrotethebook.net>... Invalid mail source
MAIL From:<junk@fake.ora.com>
250 2.1.0 <junk@fake.ora.com>... Sender ok
QUIT
221 2.0.0 chef.wrotethebook.com closing connection
Connection closed by foreign host.
```

Mail from *example.com* is rejected with an "Access denied" error because the
example.com entry in the sample *access* database defines REJECT as the action taken
for mail received from that domain. Mail from *wrotethebook.net* is rejected with the
error "Invalid mail source," which was defined in the *access* database with the ERROR

command. On the other hand, from the point of view of the remote system, mail from *fake.ora.com* appears to be accepted by the server. A sendmail -bt test is needed to see the effect of the DISCARD action defined in the *access* database for mail from *fake.ora.com*:

```
# sendmail -bt
ADDRESS TEST MODE (ruleset 3 NOT automatically invoked)
Enter <ruleset> <address>
> check_mail junk@fake.ora.com
check_mail          input: junk @ fake . ora . com
Basic_check_mail    input: junk @ fake . ora . com
tls_client          input: $| MAIL
D                   input: < > < ? > < ! "TLS_Clt" > < >
D                   returns: < ? > < > < ? > < ! "TLS_Clt" > < >
A                   input: < > < ? > < ! "TLS_Clt" > < >
A                   returns: < > < ? > < ! "TLS_Clt" > < >
TLS_connection      input: $| < > < ? > < ! "TLS_Clt" > < >
TLS_connection      returns: OK
tls_client          returns: OK
CanonAddr           input: < junk @ fake . ora . com >
canonify            input: < junk @ fake . ora . com >
Canonify2           input: junk < @ fake . ora . com >
Canonify2           returns: junk < @ fake . ora . com >
canonify            returns: junk < @ fake . ora . com >
Parse0              input: junk < @ fake . ora . com >
Parse0              returns: junk < @ fake . ora . com >
CanonAddr           returns: junk < @ fake . ora . com >
SearchList          input: < + From > $| < F : junk @ fake . ora . com > < U : junk @
> < D : fake . ora . com > < >
F                   input: < junk @ fake . ora . com > < ? > < + From > < >
F                   returns: < ? > < >
SearchList          input: < + From > $| < U : junk @ > < D : fake . ora . com > < >
U                   input: < junk @ > < ? > < + From > < >
U                   returns: < ? > < >
SearchList          input: < + From > $| < D : fake . ora . com > < >
D                   input: < fake . ora . com > < ? > < ! From > < >
D                   returns: < DISCARD > < >
SearchList          returns: < DISCARD >
SearchList          returns: < DISCARD >
SearchList          returns: < DISCARD >
Basic_check_mail    returns: $# discard $: discard
check_mail          returns: $# discard $: discard
> /quit
```

In this test, the address *junk@fake.ora.com* is processed through the check_mail ruleset, which checks the MAIL From: address. The check_mail ruleset processes the address and returns "discard," meaning that mail from *fake.ora.com* will be silently discarded.

See Also

The *cf/README* file, Chapter 3, and the Introduction to this chapter provide more information about the *access* database. The *sendmail* book covers the *access* database in section 7.5.

6.2 Preventing Local Users from Replying to Spammers

Problem

Some local users encourage spam by responding to spam emails. You have been asked to configure sendmail to stop the spammers and to stop those who encourage spam.

Solution

Before creating any user accounts, create an acceptable use policy that, among many other things, gives you the power to block spam communications—both inbound and outbound. Ensure that all users agree to this policy before giving out any user accounts.

Add the spam addresses you want blocked to the */etc/mail/access* text file. Use To: and From: tags to prevent mail from being sent to spammers or from being accepted from spammers. Run *makemap* to build a hash database from the text file.

Create a sendmail configuration that enables the *access* database with the *access_db* feature. The required sendmail FEATURE command is:

```
dnl Use the access database
FEATURE(`access_db')
```

Rebuild the *sendmail.cf* file, copy the new *sendmail.cf* file to */etc/mail*, and restart sendmail, as described in Recipe 1.8.

Discussion

By default, the *access* database applies to source addresses. The action defined in the database entry is taken based on the source of the email. Given the *access* database created for Recipe 6.1, mail from *example.com*, *wrotethebook.net*, and *fake.ora.com* is rejected, as the tests in that recipe show. For example, mail from anyone at *example.com* is rejected with an "Access denied" error. However, the *access* database from Recipe 6.1 does not prevent mail from the local host being sent to someone at *example.com*.

Adding the To: tag to an *access* database entry applies the action defined in the entry to recipient addresses that match the key, while the From: tag specifically requests that the action be applied to matching source addresses. Here is the *access* database from Recipe 6.1 rewritten with To: and From: tags:

```
From:example.com           REJECT
To:example.com             ERROR:5.7.1:550 Mail to this site is not allowed
From:wrotethebook.net      ERROR:5.7.1:550 Invalid mail source
To:wrotethebook.net        ERROR:5.7.1:550 Mail to this site is not allowed
From:fake.ora.com          DISCARD
To:fake.ora.com            ERROR:5.7.1:550 Mail to this site is not allowed
```

Because the action for the From: *example.com* entry is REJECT, mail from that site is rejected as shown in Recipe 6.1. With the addition of the To: entry, mail addressed to *example.com* is also rejected, as this test shows:

```
# telnet localhost smtp
Trying 127.0.0.1...
Connected to localhost.
Escape character is '^]'.
220 chef.wrotethebook.com ESMTP Sendmail 8.12.9/8.12.9; Fri, 22 Aug 2003 12:01:37 -
0400
HELO localhost
250 chef.wrotethebook.com Hello IDENT:UWSRv+Jij66J8vALUBVBECbGPVoU8OQe@localhost
[127.0.0.1], pleased to meet you
MAIL From:<craig@chef.wrotethebook.com>
250 2.1.0 <craig@chef.wrotethebook.com>... Sender ok
RCPT To:<crook@example.com>
550 5.7.1 <crook@example.com>... Mail to this site is not allowed
QUIT
221 2.0.0 chef.wrotethebook.com closing connection
Connection closed by foreign host.
```

 Care must be taken when blocking outbound mail. Local users expect to be able to communicate with anyone, and they do not want you deciding who they can and cannot talk to. An AUP that gives you this authority is essential before you take any action. Be prepared for complaints no matter what the AUP says.

Alternatives

The *blacklist_recipients* feature is an alternative way to block outbound mail to known spammers. The *blacklist_recipients* feature applies every untagged entry in the *access* database to recipient addresses. The following lines added to the sendmail configuration enable the *access* database and apply the database to recipient addresses:

```
dnl Use the access database
FEATURE(`access_db')
dnl Also apply the access database to recipient addresses
FEATURE(`blacklist_recipients')
```

The *blacklist_recipients* feature works well, and it is very easy to use. However, because it applies to every untagged entry in the *access* database, it does not provide the level of configuration control provided by the To: tag. Additionally, tags are self-documenting. Anyone looking at the sample *access* database just shown understands that mail to *example.com* is not allowed when they see the To: tag and the error in the action field.

See Also

Chapter 3 and the Introduction to this chapter provide more information about the *access* database. The *sendmail* book covers the *access* database in section 7.5 and the *blacklist_recipients* feature in 7.5.5. The *Anti-Spam Configuration Control* section of the *cf/README* file also covers this topic.

6.3   Reading the access Database via LDAP

Problem

You have been asked to configure sendmail to read the *access* database from an LDAP server.

Solution

If necessary, recompile and reinstall sendmail to add LDAP support to the sendmail host, and add the sendmail schema to the LDAP configuration on the LDAP server. Both of these steps are shown in Recipe 1.3.

On the LDAP server, enter the *access* database records in an LDIF file using the sendmailMTAMap object class format defined by the sendmail schema. Use the *ldapadd* script to store the *access* records in the LDAP database.

On the sendmail host, add the confLDAP_CLUSTER define and the *access_db* feature to the sendmail configuration. Set the confLDAP_CLUSTER to the same value used for the sendmailMTACluster attribute in the *access* LDAP records. Add the string LDAP to the *access_db* FEATURE command to tell sendmail to read the *access* data via LDAP. Here are sample lines that could be added to the sendmail configuration:

```
dnl Define the LDAP cluster name
define(`confLDAP_CLUSTER', `wrotethebook.com')
dnl Read the access database via LDAP
FEATURE(`access_db', `LDAP')
```

Rebuild and reinstall *sendmail.cf* file, then restart sendmail. See Recipe 1.8 for an example.

Discussion

The sendmail distribution provides an LDAP schema file that defines the basic attributes needed for sendmail databases and classes. You can, of course, define your own custom schema. However, using the sendmail schema simplifies both the LDAP and sendmail configurations. Using the sendmail schema to define the *access* entries for LDAP database, the following example converts the *access* entries used in Recipe 6.1 into LDAP records:

```
# cat > ldap-access
dn: sendmailMTAMapName=access, dc=wrotethebook, dc=com
objectClass: sendmailMTA
objectClass: sendmailMTAMap
sendmailMTACluster: wrotethebook.com
sendmailMTAMapName: access

dn: sendmailMTAKey=example.com, sendmailMTAMapName=access, dc=wrotethebook, dc=com
objectClass: sendmailMTA
objectClass: sendmailMTAMap
objectClass: sendmailMTAMapObject
sendmailMTAMapName: access
sendmailMTACluster: wrotethebook.com
sendmailMTAKey: example.com
sendmailMTAMapValue: REJECT

dn: sendmailMTAKey=wrotethebook.net, sendmailMTAMapName=access, dc=wrotethebook,
dc=com
objectClass: sendmailMTA
objectClass: sendmailMTAMap
objectClass: sendmailMTAMapObject
sendmailMTAMapName: access
sendmailMTACluster: wrotethebook.com
sendmailMTAKey: wrotethebook.net
sendmailMTAMapValue: ERROR:5.7.1:550 Invalid mail source

dn: sendmailMTAKey=fake.ora.com, sendmailMTAMapName=access, dc=wrotethebook, dc=com
objectClass: sendmailMTA
objectClass: sendmailMTAMap
objectClass: sendmailMTAMapObject
sendmailMTAMapName: access
sendmailMTACluster: wrotethebook.com
sendmailMTAKey: fake.ora.com
sendmailMTAMapValue: DISCARD
Ctrl-D
# ldapadd -x -D "cn=Manager,dc=wrotethebook,dc=com" \
> -W -f ldap-access
Enter LDAP Password: SecretLDAPpassword
adding new entry "sendmailMTAMapName=access, dc=wrotethebook, dc=com"

adding new entry "sendmailMTAKey=example.com, sendmailMTAMapName=access,
dc=wrotethebook, dc=com"
```

```
adding new entry "sendmailMTAKey=wrotethebook.net, sendmailMTAMapName=access,
dc=wrotethebook, dc=com"

adding new entry "sendmailMTAKey=fake.ora.com, sendmailMTAMapName=access,
dc=wrotethebook, dc=com"
```

Four LDAP records are used to add the three *access* entries from Recipe 6.1. The first record tells LDAP the *access* database map name. Subsequent LDAP records reference that map name to add *access* records to the LDAP database.

The next three LDAP records define the three *access* entries described in Recipe 6.1. Notice that the sendmailMTAKey and the sendmailMTAMapValue attributes of each record match the key/value pairs from the original *access* entries. By varying the values stored in the sendmailMTAMapName, sendmailMTAKey, and sendmailMTAMapValue attributes, the basic LDAP record format used for the *access* database can be used for any sendmail database.

After the records are converted from the LDIF file and added to the LDAP database, they can be examined using *ldapsearch*:

```
# ldapsearch -LLL -x '(sendmailMTAMapName=access)' sendmailMTAMapValue
dn: sendmailMTAMapName=access, dc=wrotethebook, dc=com

dn: sendmailMTAKey=example.com, sendmailMTAMapName=access, dc=wrotethebook, dc=com
sendmailMTAMapValue: REJECT

dn: sendmailMTAKey=wrotethebook.net, sendmailMTAMapName=access, dc=wrotethebook,
dc=com
sendmailMTAMapValue: ERROR:5.7.1:550 Invalid mail source

dn: sendmailMTAKey=fake.ora.com, sendmailMTAMapName=access, dc=wrotethebook, dc=com
sendmailMTAMapValue: DISCARD
```

This test shows that the *access* database records are available from the LDAP server. If your sendmail system requires -h and -b values for the *ldapsearch* test, those same values will be required for the sendmail configuration. Set -h and -b using the confLDAP_DEFAULT_SPEC define, as shown in Recipe 5.9.

Now, sendmail needs to be configured to use the LDAP server. First, the confLDAP_CLUSTER command is added to the sendmail configuration to tell sendmail the LDAP cluster name. The sendmail schema allows for records that apply to a single host or to a group of hosts, called a *cluster*. If LDAP records apply to a single host, they use the sendmailMTAHost attribute. sendmail only retrieves records that use the sendmailMTAHost attribute if the value assigned to that attribute is the fully qualified name of the sendmail host. Records that apply to a group of hosts use the sendmailMTACluster attribute. To retrieve records that use that attribute, sendmail must be configured with the cluster name. That is exactly what this recipe does. It defines the LDAP *access* records using the sendmailMTACluster attribute and informs sendmail of the cluster name using the confLDAP_CLUSTER define.

Adding the LDAP argument to the *access_db* FEATURE command tells sendmail to read the access database from the LDAP server using the standard sendmail schema. If you define a custom schema, you must tell sendmail how to use it to retrieve *access* records. For example:

```
FEATURE(`access_db', `ldap: -1 -k (&(objectClass=OurAccessDB)(OurAccesDBKey=%0))
    -v OurAccessDBValue')
```

The sample attribute names should be ignored. However, the format of the FEATURE command is similar to the one you would need to define in order to retrieve *access* data using a custom LDAP schema. The -k option defines the LDAP search criteria used as a database key. The attributes used in that search criteria must match the attributes defined in your schema. The -v option specifies the LDAP attribute that contains the return value. Again, this must match the attribute from your custom schema. Using the default sendmail schema simplifies the sendmail configuration. Simply use the LDAP string in the *access_db* FEATURE command, as shown in the Solution section.

A few tests, run after this recipe is installed, show that sendmail is reading the LDAP data. First, run a sendmail -bt test and use the /map command to retrieve an *access* record from the LDAP server:

```
# sendmail -bt
ADDRESS TEST MODE (ruleset 3 NOT automatically invoked)
Enter <ruleset> <address>
> /map access fake.ora.com
map_lookup: access (fake.ora.com) returns DISCARD (0)
> /quit
```

This test shows that the *access* database functions in the same manner whether it is read from a local database or from an LDAP server. Rerunning the test used in Recipe 6.1 shows that sendmail blocks mail using LDAP exactly as it did using a local *access* database:

```
# sendmail -bs
220 rodent.wrotethebook.com ESMTP Sendmail 8.12.9/8.12.9; Thu, 27 Mar 2003 12:42:41
0500
MAIL From:<crooks@example.com>
550 5.7.1 <crooks@example.com>... Access denied
MAIL From:<thieves@wrotethebook.net>
550 5.7.1 <thieves@wrotethebook.net>... Invalid mail source
QUIT
221 2.0.0 rodent.wrotethebook.com closing connection
```

LDAP does not change the way sendmail works. The decision to use LDAP is not driven by sendmail; it is driven by LDAP. If you already use LDAP to centralize the management of information, you may choose to add sendmail configuration data to your LDAP server.

See Also

Recipes 6.1 and 6.2 explain how the *access* database is used to control spam; in particular, Recipe 6.1 explains the specific *access* database entries used for this recipe. The *cf/README* file covers this topic in the *Using LDAP for Aliases, Maps, and Classes* section. The *sendmail* book covers the *access_db* feature in section 7.5 and the confLDAP_CLUSTER define in section 21.9.82.

6.4 Using a DNS Blackhole List Service

Problem

You have been asked to configure sendmail to use a blackhole list service to stop a large amount of UCE from a wide array of sources with a minimal amount of effort.

Solution

Add the *dnsbl* feature to the sendmail configuration. Identify the specific blackhole list service you wish to use on the *dnsbl* command line. Here is an example:

```
dnl Use the DSBL blacklist service
FEATURE(`dnsbl', `list.dsbl.org')
```

Using Recipe 1.8 as a guide, rebuild the *sendmail.cf* file, copy the new *sendmail.cf* file to */etc/mail*, and restart sendmail.

Discussion

The *dnsbl* feature adds the *sendmail.cf* code needed to enable a DNS blacklist service. The *dnsbl* feature uses a K command to define the *dnsbl* database as a host type database, which means lookups in *dnsbl* are really passed to DNS for resolution.[*] The *dnsbl* feature also adds a few rules to the Basic_check_relay ruleset, which is called from the check_relay ruleset. The added rules lookup the connection address in the *dnsbl* database. If the connection address is found in the database, mail from that address is rejected with an error message. If the connection address is not found in the *dnsbl* database, the mail is passed on for further processing. A sendmail -bt test shows the impact of the added rewrite rules:

```
# sendmail -bt
ADDRESS TEST MODE (ruleset 3 NOT automatically invoked)
Enter <ruleset> <address>
> .D{client_addr}192.168.111.68
> Basic_check_relay <>
```

---

[*] This assumes the service switch file maps host lookups to DNS. See Chapter 5 for information on the service switch file.

```
Basic_check_rela    input: < >
Basic_check_rela returns: $# error $@ 5 . 7 . 1 $: "550 Rejected: " 192 . 168 . 111 .
68 " listed at list.dsbl.org"
> /quit
```

Because there is no active connection—this is just a test—the first step is to statically define a connection address for the test. Next, the Basic_check_relay ruleset is called and passed to an empty workspace. The workspace passed to the ruleset in this test is unimportant because the first rule added to the ruleset by the *dnsbl* feature unconditionally replaces the workspace with the value found in ${client_addr}. Therefore, the value looked up in the *dnsbl* database is the connection address stored in the ${client_addr} macro. In this test, the address 192.168.111.68 is found in the blackhole list maintained at *list.dsbl.org*, so mail from that address is rejected. The mail is rejected with the error message:

```
550 Rejected: 192.168.111.68 listed at list.dsbl.org
```

The error message displays the address that was rejected and the service that recommended the rejection. This information is important. The administrators at 192.168.111.68 might need to contact the blackhole service to find out why their system is blacklisted and what they can do to get it removed from the blackhole list. Often, a system is blacklisted because of a configuration error that creates an open relay. As soon as the error is fixed, the administrator wants to get the system removed from the blackhole list. Knowing which services have blacklisted the system tells the administrator which services must be contacted to get full mail service restored.

This configuration uses the blackhole server at *list.dsbl.org* because that is the service specified with the *dnsbl* feature command in this recipe, which is just an example; it is not a recommendation for the *list.dsbl.org* service. There are many blackhole services available, some of which are listed in Table 6-2. Go to each service's web site and evaluate their policy for listing hosts in the database. Select the service whose policy most closely matches the policy you want to enforce on your server.

When no service is specified on the *dnsbl* feature command line, sendmail defaults to using *blackholes.mail-abuse.org*, which is the same service that was used by the deprecated sendmail *rbl* feature.

The *enhdnsbl* feature could be used as an alternative to *dnsbl* for this recipe. However, the *enhdnsbl* feature provides no real advantage in this particular case.

See Also

Before using any blackhole service, visit its web site. Using a blackhole service places an external organization in charge of the mail that your system receives. Evaluate the policy and mission of the blackhole listing service to ensure that its goals are compatible with yours. See Recipes 6.5 and 6.6 for additional information about blackhole services before implementing this recipe. The *sendmail* book covers the *dnsbl* feature in section 7.2.1 and the *enhdnsbl* feature in 7.2.2.

6.5   Building Your Own DNS Blackhole List

Problem

You need to create your own DNS blackhole list because no external blackhole service provides exactly the listing policy and content you need.

Solution

The domain administrator must create a DNS zone file, in the proper format, that lists all of the connection addresses that are to be blacklisted. The special DNS address records in the zone file are constructed by reversing the IP address of the blacklisted system to create the DNS name field of the record and by using an address such as 127.0.0.2 in the data field of the address record. This format means that hosts are blacklisted by IP address instead of by name, which makes sense because the *dnsbl* lookup is done using the connection IP address. The DNS server must be authoritative for the domain in which the blackhole list is to be located. This is normally done by creating a special subdomain for the blackhole list within the zone of authority of the DNS server.

On the sendmail system, create a configuration containing the *dnsbl* feature.* Identify the local DNS blackhole list on the *dnsbl* command line. Here is an example:

```
dnl Point dnsbl to our local DNS blackhole list
FEATURE(`dnsbl', `dnsbl.wrotethebook.com')
```

Following Recipe 1.8, rebuild the *sendmail.cf* file, copy the new *sendmail.cf* file to */etc/mail*, and restart sendmail.

Discussion

Using a blackhole list service is simple but inflexible because you can't choose which sites are listed. This means that mail from a friendly site might be blocked just because the administrator at that site misconfigured relaying. For this reason, some organizations decide to build their own DNS-based blackhole list. Creating your own blackhole server ensures that connectivity to all of the sites you want to reach is under your direct control, but it requires both sendmail and DNS expertise.

The DNS administrator uses a zone statement in the DNS server's *named.conf* file to load the blackhole database. Assuming that the blacklisted hosts are defined in a zone file named *blacklisted.hosts*, which provides the data for a domain named *dnsbl.wrotethebook.com*, the following zone statement would be used:

```
zone "dnsbl.wrotethebook.com" IN {
        type master;
```

---

* Alternatively, the *enhdnsbl* feature can be used.

```
            file "blacklisted.hosts";
            allow-update { none; };
    };
```

Blackhole entries for addresses 10.0.187.215 and 192.168.0.3 defined in the *blacklisted.hosts* file would be the following:

```
215.187.0.10               IN A 127.0.0.2
3.0.168.192                IN A 127.0.0.2
```

The newly created DNS domain is referenced as the source for blackhole list data on the *dnsbl* feature command line in the Solution section. Mail from any site listed in the *dnsbl.wrotethebook.com* domain is rejected, as this attempt to send mail from 192.168.0.3 shows:

```
# telnet chef smtp
Trying 192.168.0.8...
Connected to 192.168.0.8.
Escape character is '^]'.
220 chef.wrotethebook.com ESMTP Sendmail 8.12.9/8.12.9; Fri, 22 Aug 2003 12:01:37 -
0400
helo rodent.wrotethebook.com
250 chef.wrotethebook.com Hello rodent.wrotethebook.com [192.168.0.3], pleased to
meet you
MAIL From:<craig@rodent.wrotethebook.com>
550 5.7.1 Rejected: 192.168.0.3 listed at dnsbl.wrotethebook.com
QUIT
221 2.0.0 chef.wrotethebook.com closing connection
Connection closed by foreign host.
```

The connection address 192.168.0.3 is found in the *dnsbl.wrotethebook.com* domain, so our server rejects the mail and returns the error message "550 5.7.1 Rejected: 192.168.0.3 listed at dnsbl.wrotethebook.com." This default error message can be changed with an additional argument on the *dnsbl* feature command line. For example, the command:

```
FEATURE(`dnsbl', `dnsbl.wrotethebook.com', `"Mail rejected. "$&{client_addr}" is a
suspected spam relay."')
```

changes the error message to "Mail rejected. 192.168.0.3 is a suspected spam relay." However, the standard message works well and provides the remote site with more information.

The small number of systems used in the blackhole list in this recipe could much more easily have been handled by the *access* database. In most cases, using the *access* database to block unwanted mail connections is much easier than creating your own blackhole list. Creating and maintaining your own blackhole list is labor intensive. The systems that should be added to and removed from the list are constantly changing. Additionally, a great deal of information is needed to initially build a list. It is possible to use a mail filtering tool, such as *procmail*, to automatically collect suspected addresses directly from mail. However, it is difficult to create a system that collects the right information and keeps it up-to-date. Most administrators prefer to create their own blackhole list based on the blackhole list provided by a blackhole list service. The services already have large lists and they constantly maintain them. Most blackhole list services provide some way to download the entire list. For example, the DSBL list can be downloaded using *rsync*:

```
# rsync rsync.dsbl.org::dsbl/bind-list.dsbl.org.
```

Periodically downloading a list and customizing it is one way to create your own blackhole list. But even if you start with a preexisting list, creating your own blackhole list is not a task that should be undertaken lightly. Creating your own blackhole list is one of the most difficult techniques for controlling unwanted junk email.

As usual, the choice between using a blackhole list service or building your own blackhole list is a choice between simplicity and flexibility. Most sites choose simplicity. If you don't have the available staff necessary to build and maintain your own blackhole list, stick with a standard blackhole list service, as described in Recipe 6.4, and use the technique described in Recipe 6.6 to make it comply with your needs.

See Also

Recipe 6.4 describes a simple method for using a blackhole list. Recipe 6.6 describes how major shortcomings of a blackhole list service can be overcome using the *access* database. Review both of these recipes before implementing this recipe. The *sendmail* book covers the *dnsbl* feature in section 7.2.1 and the *enhdnsbl* feature in section 7.2.2. For information on DNS configuration, see *DNS and BIND*, by Paul Albitz and Cricket Liu (O'Reilly), and *Linux DNS Server Administration*, by Craig Hunt (Sybex).

6.6 Whitelisting Blacklisted Sites

Problem

You use a blackhole list service that blacklists a few sites with which you must communicate. You need to configure sendmail to override the blackhole list for specific addresses.

Solution

To override the blackhole list service for a given address, add the address to the */etc/mail/access* text file, and assign the keyword OK as the return value for the address. Use *makemap* to build a hash type database from the text file.

Create a sendmail configuration that uses either the *dnsbl* feature or the *enhdnsbl* feature to select a blackhole list service and the *access_db* feature to override the blackhole list for selected sites. Here are samples lines that might be added to the sendmail configuration to enable these features:

```
dnl Use dnsbl and select a blacklist service
FEATURE(`dnsbl', `list.dsbl.org')
dnl Use the access database
FEATURE(`access_db')
```

Rebuild the *sendmail.cf* file, copy the new *sendmail.cf* file to */etc/mail*, and restart sendmail. See Recipe 1.8 for an example.

Discussion

The *dnsbl* feature adds support for a DNS blackhole list service to the *sendmail.cf* configuration, and it specifies the service that will be used. Table 6-2 provides a list of some of the available services. If no service is selected, the MAPS RBL is used by default. Choose a service carefully.

The sample blackhole list is configured to block email from 192.168.0.3, as this test, run from 192.168.0.3, shows:

```
# telnet chef smtp
Trying 192.168.0.8...
Connected to 192.168.0.8.
Escape character is '^]'.
220 chef.wrotethebook.com ESMTP Sendmail 8.12.9/8.12.9; Fri, 22 Aug 2003 12:01:37 -
0400
helo rodent.wrotethebook.com
250 chef.wrotethebook.com Hello rodent.wrotethebook.com [192.168.0.3], pleased to
meet you
MAIL From:<craig@rodent.wrotethebook.com>
550 5.7.1 Rejected: 192.168.0.3 listed at list.dsbl.org
QUIT
221 2.0.0 chef.wrotethebook.com closing connection
Connection closed by foreign host.
```

Use the *access* database to override some entries in the blackhole database. In this example, we override the blackhole list service for the following sites:

```
# cd /etc/mail
# cat > access
192.168.0.3         OK
24.199.249.90       OK
Ctrl-D
# makemap hash access < access
```

After building the *access* database, rerunning the *telnet* test from 192.168.0.3 shows the following result:

```
# telnet chef smtp
Trying 192.168.0.8...
Connected to 192.168.0.8.
Escape character is '^]'.
220 chef.wrotethebook.com ESMTP Sendmail 8.12.9/8.12.9; Fri, 22 Aug 2003 12:01:37 -
0400
helo rodent.wrotethebook.com
```

```
250 chef.wrotethebook.com Hello rodent.wrotethebook.com [192.168.0.3], pleased to
meet you
MAIL From:<craig@rodent.wrotethebook.com>
250 2.1.0 <craig@rodent.wrotethebook.com>... Sender ok
QUIT
221 2.0.0 chef.wrotethebook.com closing connection
Connection closed by foreign host.
```

Now, mail from 192.168.0.3 is accepted, even though 192.168.0.3 is still listed in the blackhole list, because the action listed for address 192.168.0.3 in the *access* database is OK.

Using the *access* database to override a blackhole list service makes creating your own DNS blackhole list unnecessary for most organization. Generally, organizations shy away from using a blackhole list service because it can block mail from a friendly site. Combining the *access* database with the blackhole service gives you the simplicity of the blackhole service and the flexibility of directly controlling which sites you communicate with. In addition, if the blackhole service does not list a site that you think should be blacklisted, you can blacklist a site using the *access* database as described in Recipe 6.1.

See Also

Recipes 6.4 and 6.5 provide further examples of using a blackhole list. Recipes 6.1 and 6.2 provide additional information about using the *access* database for spam control. For more about the *access* database in general, see Chapter 3. The *sendmail* book covers the *dnsbl* feature in section 7.2.1, *enhdnsbl* in section 7.2.2, and the *access_db* feature in 7.5. The *Anti-Spam Configuration Control* section of the *cf/ README* file covers these topics.

6.7   Filtering Local Mail with procmail

Problem

You want to filter mail with *procmail* before making deliveries to local users.

Solution

Add the *local_procmail* feature to the sendmail configuration, placing the FEATURE macro after the OSTYPE macro and before the MAILER(`local') line in the master configuration file. Values for the local mailer are usually set in the OSTYPE file. Carefully review the file for your operating system. Add the *local_procmail* feature to your master configuration file only if *local_procmail* is not already included in the OSTYPE file.

Create an */etc/procmailrc* file containing the filters you want to apply to local mail.

Build and install the new configuration, as described in Recipe 1.8.

Discussion

The *linux.m4* OSTYPE file contains the *local_procmail* feature because *procmail* is the local mailer used by default on most Linux systems. On a Linux system, just running a configuration that uses the *linux.m4* OSTYPE file is sufficient for this recipe. Other systems are not so easy. For example, assume you have a Solaris 8 system. The *solaris8.m4* OSTYPE file uses the *local_lmtp* feature to set mail.local as the local mailer. To change the local mailer to *procmail*, override the *local_lmtp* feature by placing the *local_procmail* feature in the master configuration file. Here is an example based on the *generic-solaris.mc* file:

```
VERSIONID(`Solaris with local_procmail added')
OSTYPE(solaris2)
IXIMAIN(generic)
dnl Add the local_procmail feature
FEATURE(`local_procmail')
MAILER(local)
MAILER(smtp)
```

Because the *local_procmail* feature occurs after the OSTYPE macro, it overrides the *local_lmtp* feature defined in the OSTYPE file. The *local_procmail* feature is enabled once the *sendmail.cf* file is built, copied to *sendmail.cf*, and sendmail is restarted.

When the *local_procmail* feature is used, sendmail passes local mail to *procmail* for delivery. *procmail* processes the mail, first using the commands defined in the */etc/procmailrc* file and then using the commands defined in the *.procmailrc* file in the recipient's home directory. If no *rc* file is defined, *procmail* writes the mail to the user's mailbox unaltered. Note that the user's *.procmailrc* file is applied to mail delivered by the *local_procmail* feature. When *local_procmail* is used, it is not necessary for the user to call the *procmail* program from the *.forward* file as shown in this chapter's Introduction. All the user needs to do is create a *.procmailrc* file and it will be applied to the mail. Using *procmail* as a local mailer allows both the system administrator and the user to filter inbound mail with *procmail*.

When *procmail* is used as the local mailer, sendmail runs it with three arguments: -Y, -a, and -d. The -Y argument tells *procmail* to use the standard Berkeley Unix mailbox format. The -d argument provides *procmail* with the username of the local recipient who is to receive the mail (in the mail delivery triple this is the *user* value). The -a argument passes an optional value to *procmail* that is accessible inside the *procmail* recipe as the $1 variable; in the mail delivery triple, this is the *host* value. sendmail only passes a value through -a when either the *+detail* syntax is used or mail is routed to the local mailer via the *mailertable*. In the case of the *+detail* syntax, the *detail* value is passed. In the case of the *mailertable*, the input address that was the key to the *mailertable* entry is the value passed. In all other cases, no value is passed by the -a argument and the $1 variable is unassigned.

The *local_procmail* feature has security implications for *smrsh* and for attempts to limit user mail forwarding. See Recipes 10.6 and 10.8 for more details.

See Also

Recipe 6.8 provides additional information about *procmail*. The *sendmail* book covers *.forward* in Chapter 13 and the *local_procmail* feature in section 4.8.21. See the procmail, procmailrc, procmailex, and procmailsc manpages for more information about filtering mail with *procmail*.

6.8   Filtering Outbound Mail with procmail

Problem

You want to configure sendmail to filter mail addressed to specific domains using *procmail* as the mail filtering software.

Solution

Build a *mailertable* that routes mail bound for specific domains through the procmail mailer.

Create a file in the */etc/procmailrcs* directory that defines the specific filtering needed. Multiple filters can be used.

Create a sendmail configuration that enables the *mailertable* feature and adds *procmail* to the list of available mailers. Here are the lines that should be added to the sendmail configuration:

```
dnl Enable support for the mailertable
FEATURE(`mailertable')
dnl Add procmail to the list of available mailers
MAILER(procmail)
```

Build the *sendmail.cf* file, copy it to */etc/mail/sendmail.cf*, and restart sendmail, as described in Recipe 1.8.

Discussion

The MAILER(procmail) macro adds the procmail mailer definition to the *sendmail.cf* file. The procmail mailer is not related to the *local_procmail* feature. A system can use the procmail mailer without using *procmail* as a local mailer, and *procmail* can be used as a local mailer without adding the MAILER(procmail) macro to the configuration.

The MAILER(procmail) macro does not add any code to the configuration to use the procmail mailer. You must either add custom *sendmail.cf* rules to reference the mailer, or route mail through the procmail mailer using the *mailertable*. Using the *mailertable* is the easiest and the recommended way to access the mailer. Here we add *mailertable* entries that invoke *procmail*:

```
# cd /etc/mail
# cat >> mailertable
example.com          procmail:/etc/procmailrcs/spam-filter
wrotethebook.net  procmail:/etc/procmailrcs/spam-filter
fake.ora.com       procmail:/etc/procmailrcs/uce-filter
Ctrl-D
# makemap hash mailertable < mailertable
```

The example adds three entries to the *mailertable* that route mail through the procmail mailer. The first field in a *mailertable* entry is the key against which the recipient address is matched. The second field is the *mailer* value and the *host* value that sendmail uses to build the mail delivery triple. In this example, mail with a matching recipient address is routed through the procmail mailer. A few tests of a system running this recipe show this:

```
# sendmail -bv crooks@example.com
crooks@example.com... deliverable: mailer procmail, host /etc/procmailrcs/
spam-filter, user crooks@example.com
# sendmail -bv spammers@wrotethebook.net
spammers@wrotethebook.net... deliverable: mailer procmail, host /etc/procmailrcs/
spam-filter, user spammers@wrotethebook.net
# sendmail -bv thieves@fake.ora.com
thieves@fake.ora.com... deliverable: mailer procmail, host /etc/procmailrcs/
uce-filter, user thieves@fake.ora.com
```

When mail is routed to the procmail mailer, the host value ($h) must contain the pathname of the *rc-file* that *procmail* should use to filter the mail. In the example above, two different filters, *spam-filter* and *uce-filter*, are passed to *procmail* depending on the destination of the email. sendmail calls *procmail* from the procmail mailer using the following command:

```
procmail -Y -m $h $f $u
```

The -Y flag tells *procmail* to use the Berkeley Unix mailbox format. The -m flag runs *procmail* as a general-purpose mail filter. The first argument that follows the -m flag must be the path of the *rc-file* that contains the *procmail* filter recipes. sendmail assigns the host value returned by the *mailertable* lookup to the $h macro, which it then passes to *procmail* as the first argument after the -m flag. Therefore, the *host* field of a *mailertable* entry that uses the procmail mailer must contain the full pathname of an *rc-file*.

The next two arguments passed to *procmail* are the envelope sender email address ($f) and the envelope recipient email address ($u). These values are available inside the *procmail rc-file* as variables $1 and $2, respectively.

Filtering outbound mail with *procmail* creates the potential for routing loops. Recipes that delete the mail, return it to the sender, or forward it to a third party are not a problem. However, if the mail is examined and then resent to the original recipient, it will return to sendmail, which will route it to *procmail*, which will return it to sendmail, which will.... You get the idea. If some of the outbound mail filtered by *procmail* will be resent to the original recipient, you might need to add custom *sendmail.cf* code to avoid the loop.

One common technique for avoiding a loop is to add the pseudodomain .PROCMAIL to the recipient address when mail is resent to the original recipient. The pseudodomain ensures that the recipient address no longer matches a value in the *mailertable*, which breaks the loop. The pseudodomain is added by *procmail* commands in the *rc*-file. However, a properly configured *rc*-file is not the complete solution. .PROCMAIL is not a real domain, so code must be added to the *sendmail.cf* file to ensure that the pseudodomain is properly handled. The following *m4* macros and *sendmail.cf code, added to the end of the this recipe's* master configuration file, handle the .PROCMAIL pseudodomain, if one is added by the *rc*-file:

```
LOCAL_CONFIG
# Add .PROCMAIL to the pseudo-domain list
CP.PROCMAIL
LOCAL_RULE_0
# Strip .PROCMAIL and send via esmtp
R$+ < @ $+ .PROCMAIL . >        $#esmtp $@ $2 $: $1<@$2>
```

The LOCAL_CONFIG macro marks the start of code that is to be added to the local information section of the *sendmail.cf* file. In this example, we add a comment and a C command to the local information section. The C command adds .PROCMAIL to class P. Class P lists pseudodomains that sendmail should not attempt to lookup in the DNS. Adding .PROCMAIL to class P avoids the delays and wasted resources that occur when sendmail looks up a domain name that does not exist.

The LOCAL_RULE_0 macro marks the start of *sendmail.cf* code that is added to ruleset 0—more commonly called the parse ruleset. Specifically, the code that follows the LOCAL_RULE_0 macro is added to the ParseLocal ruleset, which is a hook into the parse ruleset where locally defined rules are added.* The parse ruleset rewrites the delivery address to a mail delivery triple.

The code that follows the LOCAL_RULE_0 macro in the example is a comment and a rewrite rule. The R command matches input addresses of the form *user@domain*.PROCMAIL, and rewrites those addresses into a mail delivery triple where the mailer is esmtp, the host value is *domain*, and the user value is *user@domain*. After rebuilding the configuration with the new master configuration file, running a sendmail -bv test shows the impact of this rewrite rule:

---

* The ParseLocal ruleset is also known as ruleset 98.

```
# sendmail -bv crooks@example.com.PROCMAIL
crooks@example.com.PROCMAIL... deliverable: mailer esmtp, host example.com, user
crooks@example.com
```

See Also

Recipe 6.7 provides additional information about *procmail*. The *sendmail* book covers LOCAL_CONFIG in section 4.3.3.1 and LOCAL_RULE_0 in 4.3.3.2. See the procmail, procmailrc, procmailex, and procmailsc manpages for more information about filtering mail with *procmail*. Recipe 5.1 explains the *mailertable* and how it is used to route mail to any special purpose mailer.

6.9 Invoking Special Header Processing

Problem

You need to add customized header checks to the sendmail configuration.

Solution

Append your custom header processing to the end of the master configuration file using a LOCAL_CONFIG macro and a LOCAL_RULESETS macro. The LOCAL_CONFIG macro adds lines to the local information section of the *sendmail.cf* file, and, therefore, is used to define any macros, classes, or databases used by your customer header process. Use the LOCAL_RULESET macro to add your custom ruleset to the *sendmail.cf* file. The Discussion section provides an example of both of these macros.

Build the *sendmail.cf* file, copy it to */etc/mail/sendmail.cf*, and restart sendmail, as described in Recipe 1.8.

Discussion

The *knecht.mc* file, which comes with the sendmail distribution, contains a variety of examples that illustrate different aspects of sendmail configuration. The following sample custom header check is taken from the *knecht.mc* file:

```
LOCAL_CONFIG
#
#  Names that won't be allowed in a To: line (local-part and domains)
#
C{RejectToLocalparts}   friend you
C{RejectToDomains}      public.com

LOCAL_RULESETS
HTo: $>CheckTo
```

```
SCheckTo
R${RejectToLocalparts}@$*        $#error $: "553 Header error"
R$*@$={RejectToDomains}          $#error $: "553 Header error"
```

Custom header processing requires *sendmail.cf* code in addition to the normal *m4* configuration. The LOCAL_CONFIG macro marks the beginning of lines that are added directly to the local information section of the *sendmail.cf* file. In the example, the two C lines that follow the LOCAL_CONFIG macro define two classes and load those classes with some values.

The LOCAL_RULESET macro indicates that a locally defined ruleset follows. The first line in the example that follows LOCAL_RULESET is the header command that calls the custom ruleset:

```
HTo: $>CheckTo
```

This H command calls the ruleset CheckTo whenever a To: header arrives in a mail stream from a remote system. The $> syntax is the standard way that rulesets are called from rewrite rules and header definitions.

The ruleset itself begins with an S command that defines a ruleset name CheckTo. The ruleset contains two rewrite rules. The first rule matches any To: header containing an address with a username found in the $={RejectToLocalparts} class. In the example, that would be any mail addressed to the username *friend* or the username *you*. The mail addressed to either of these usernames is rejected with the error message "553 Header error."

The second rewrite rule matches any To: header that addresses mail to a hostname found in the $={RejectToDomains} class. In the example, the class contains only the hostname *public.com*. The mail addressed to *public.com* is rejected with the error message "553 Header error."

The CheckTo ruleset is easily tested with sendmail -bt:

```
# sendmail -bt
ADDRESS TEST MODE (ruleset 3 NOT automatically invoked)
Enter <ruleset> <address>
> CheckTo friend@wrotethebook.com
CheckTo           input: friend @ wrotethebook . com
CheckTo           returns: $# error $: "553 Header error"
> CheckTo craig@public.com
CheckTo           input: craig @ public . com
CheckTo           returns: $# error $: "553 Header error"
> CheckTo craig@wrotethebook.com
CheckTo           input: craig @ wrotethebook . com
CheckTo           returns: craig @ wrotethebook . com
> /quit
```

The ruleset is called and passed the contents of a sample To: header. Note that the ruleset is passed the contents of the header without the header name. This replicates the way that the ruleset will be called during an actual run. In all three tests, the

CheckTo ruleset works as expected—the username *friend* and the hostname *public. com* are rejected but the address *craig@wrotethebook.com* passes through the ruleset unscathed.

The CheckTo ruleset is a simplified example. Implementing a customer header processing ruleset that would be effective for fighting spam would be much more complex. However, the same H command syntax for calling a custom header ruleset, the same LOCAL_CONFIG macro, and the same LOCAL_RULESET macro used in this example would implement any custom header processing. Before you create a custom header process inside sendmail to battle spam, evaluate the alternatives, such as filtering the mail with a MILTER or *procmail*, and make sure your approach is the simplest and most effective to implement and maintain.

See Also

Recipe 6.10 also uses an example from *knecht.mc*. Recipes 6.7 and 6.8 cover *procmail* and Recipe 6.12 covers MILTER, which are alternatives for processing headers that should be evaluated before you write custom *sendmail.cf* rulesets. The *sendmail* book covers the LOCAL_RULESETS macro in section 4.3.3.5 and the LOCAL_CONFIG macro in section 4.3.3.1. See *TCP/IP Network Administration*, Third Edition, by Craig Hunt (O'Reilly), and *Linux Sendmail Administration*, by Craig Hunt (Sybex), for additional information about the *sendmail.cf* commands.

6.10   Using Regular Expressions in sendmail

Problem

Special configuration is required for sendmail to use regular expressions to search for patterns in addresses or headers.

Solution

Run the sendmail -d0.1 command. The "Compiled with:" line output by the command should contain MAP_REGEX. If it does not, recompile sendmail as described in Recipe 1.4.

Add custom code to the end of the master configuration file. Add the K command that defines the regular expression to the local information section of the *sendmail.cf* file using the LOCAL_CONFIG macro, and use a LOCAL_RULESETS macro to add a custom ruleset to access the regular expression. The Discussion section provides an example of how these commands are used.

Build the *sendmail.cf* file, copy it to */etc/mail/sendmail.cf*, and restart sendmail, as shown in Recipe 1.8.

Discussion

Regular expressions are defined using the *sendmail.cf* K command, which is the same command used to define a database. The regular expression is then accessed from within the configuration in the same manner as a normal database. The following example taken from the *knecht.mc* file, illustrates how a regular expression is defined and used:

```
LOCAL_CONFIG
#
#  Regular expression to reject:
#    * numeric-only localparts from aol.com and msn.com
#    * localparts starting with a digit from juno.com
#
Kcheckaddress regex -a@MATCH
    ^([0-9]+<@(aol|msn)\.com|[0-9][^<]*<@juno\.com)\.?>

LOCAL_RULESETS
SLocal_check_mail
# check address against various regex checks
R$*                              $: $>Parse0 $>3 $1
R$+                              $: $(checkaddress $1 $)
R@MATCH                          $#error $: "553 Header error"
```

First, the LOCAL_CONFIG macro is added to the *m4* master configuration file. The LOCAL_CONFIG macro marks the start of code that is to be added to the local information section of the *sendmail.cf* file. The K command that defines the regular expression follows this macro. The syntax of the K command is:

```
Kname type arguments
```

where K is the command, *name* is the internal name used to access the database defined by this command, *type* is the database type, and the *arguments* define the database being used. The *arguments* have the format:

```
flags description
```

where the *flags* define options used by the database and *description* identifies the database being used. The *description*, in most cases, is a path to an external database, either a local database or a map accessible through a database server. For a regular expression, however, the *description* is the definition of the regular expression against which input data is matched. The K command in the example is:

```
Kcheckaddress regex -a@MATCH
    ^([0-9]+<@(aol|msn)\.com|[0-9][^<]*<@juno\.com)\.?>
```

In this example:

- K is the command.
- checkaddress is the internal name.
- regex is the type.

- -a@MATCH is a flag that tells sendmail to return the value @MATCH when a match is found.
- ^([0-9]+<@(aol|msn)\.com|[0-9][^<]*<@juno\.com)\.?> is a regular expression. This is a basic regular expression that could be used with tools such as *egrep* and *awk*. This regular expression matches email addresses from *aol.com, msn.com,* and *juno.com* that contain numeric usernames.

The K command defines the regular expression, but a rewrite rule is needed to use it. The LOCAL_RULESETS macro is used to insert a custom ruleset into the *sendmail.cf* file. At the heart of the sample Local_check_mail ruleset are three R commands:

```
R$*                              $: $>Parse0 $>3 $1
R$+                              $: $(checkaddress $1 $)
R@MATCH                          $#error $: "553 Header error"
```

The address passed to the Local_check_mail ruleset is first processed through ruleset 3 (also called the canonify ruleset), and the result of that process is then passed through the Parse0 ruleset. Note that both of these rulesets are called by the first rewrite command. This processing puts the address into its canonical form. The address is then pattern matched against the checkaddress regular expression by the second rewrite rule. If it matches the regular expression, the address is replaced by the string @MATCH. The third rewrite rule checks to see if the workspace contains that string. If it does, a header error is returned.

A few tests show how the regular expression and the ruleset work:

```
# sendmail -bt
ADDRESS TEST MODE (ruleset 3 NOT automatically invoked)
Enter <ruleset> <address>
> Local_check_mail 123@aol.com
Local_check_mail   input: 123 @ aol . com
canonify           input: 123 @ aol . com
Canonify2          input: 123 < @ aol . com >
Canonify2        returns: 123 < @ aol . com . >
canonify         returns: 123 < @ aol . com . >
Parse0             input: 123 < @ aol . com . >
Parse0           returns: 123 < @ aol . com . >
Local_check_mail returns: $# error $: "553 Header error"
> Local_check_mail win@aol.com
Local_check_mail   input: win @ aol . com
canonify           input: win @ aol . com
Canonify2          input: win < @ aol . com >
Canonify2        returns: win < @ aol . com . >
canonify         returns: win < @ aol . com . >
Parse0             input: win < @ aol . com . >
Parse0           returns: win < @ aol . com . >
Local_check_mail returns: win < @ aol . com . >
 > /quit
```

The first test passes the address *123@aol.com* to the `Local_check_mail` ruleset. This address should match the `checkaddress` regular expression. The error returned by the `Local_check_mail` ruleset shows that it does. The second test is run to show that valid addresses from *aol.com* do not generate the error.

This example, taken from the *knecht.mc* file, is not a recommendation that you filter out numeric *aol.com* addresses. It is an example of how a regular expression is defined and used. The `LOCAL_CONFIG` macro, the `LOCAL_RULESET` macro, and the syntax of the K command are the same for the custom regular expressions and rulesets that you create as they are for this simple example.

See Also

Recipe 6.9 provides additional information that is helpful in understanding this recipe. See Chapter 1 for a description of compiling sendmail. The *sendmail* book covers the `LOCAL_CONFIG` macro in section 4.3.3.1, `LOCAL_RULESETS` in section 4.3.3.5, and the regex map type in section 23.7.20. The O'Reilly book *Mastering Regular Expressions* provides in-depth coverage of regular expressions. See *TCP/IP Network Administration*, Third Edition, by Craig Hunt (O'Reilly), and *Linux Sendmail Administration*, by Craig Hunt (Sybex), for additional information about the *sendmail.cf* commands.

6.11   Identifying Local Problem Users

Problem

Spammers hide their true identities. You want to provide as much information as possible to track down spammers that use your system.

Solution

Run the `auth` service (*identd*) to provide account information that cannot be hidden by masquerading or other email techniques.

Discussion

The IDENT protocol is defined in RFC 1413, *Identification Protocol*. The protocol provides a means for determining the identity of the user who initiated a network connection. The *identd* daemon implements the IDENT protocol on Unix systems. Run *identd* to provide additional information to remote system administrators to aid them in tracking down the cause of problems. In the context of sendmail, this information might help them track down a spammer, if one sets up shop on your system. For example, assume a user on a system running *identd* tries to perpetrate a forgery by issuing the SMTP `EHLO` command using a false hostname:

```
ehlo www.ora.com
250-rodent.wrotethebook.com Hello IDENT:r+9Gemj2wip8fAJDU8kDZlyUiReTZjYc@chef.
wrotethebook.com [192.168.0.8], pleased to meet you
```

When the remote system, in this case *rodent.wrotethebook.com*, responds to the EHLO command, it ignores the forged *www.ora.com* hostname. Instead it says "hello" to the host it finds at the connection address 192.168.0.8. It responds with the hostname associated with that address, which is *chef.wrotethebook.com*, and the identification information provided by the *identd* service running on *chef*. This information is propagated in the mail in a Received: header, as shown below:

```
Received: from www.ora.com
    (IDENT:r+9Gemj2wip8fAJDU8kDZlyUiReTZjYc@chef [192.168.0.8])
    by rodent.wrotethebook.com (8.12.9/8.12.9) with ESMTP id gB4N6T301540
    for <craig@rodent.wrotethebook.com>; Wed, 4 Dec 2002 18:06:40 -0500
```

The information provided by the *identd* service running on the host at 192.168.0.8 identifies the user who sent the mail. The string provided by *identd*, r+9Gemj2wip8fAJDU8kDZlyUiReTZjYc in the example, is not a simple username. In this case, the identd information is encrypted.

identd monitors port 113. When *identd* is running, the remote server can request information about any TCP connections from your server to the remote server by sending the source and destination port pair to the identification server. *identd* then responds by sending either the requested information associated with the connection or an error. This information allows remote mail servers to put a real username on the Received: header in incoming email. People who abuse the mail system do not like to have their real usernames known. Providing their names to their victims makes it hard for them to stay in business. Unfortunately, many firewalls block port 113 because the security people fear that too much information is given out by the *identd* service. This fear is unfounded when the *identd* information is encrypted, as it is in this example. However, many security administrators prefer to play it safe, so they block the port. If it is blocked at your firewall, you might not be able to use *identd*.

The IDENT protocol is also known by the service name auth, as this *grep* of */etc/services* shows:

```
$ grep ^auth /etc/services
auth     113/tcp     ident   # User Verification
```

Most sendmail administrators prefer to call the service *ident* or *identd* to avoid confusing it with the ESMTP AUTH keyword, which is discussed in Chapter 7. Additionally, *identd* is not an authentication tool—it is an auditing tool. Real spammers, who control their own systems, can put anything they want in an *identd* response, so the response cannot be trusted for real authentication. You, however, are not a spammer. You run *identd* to provide additional audit trail information to track down users who abuse your system.

Many Unix systems run *identd* on-demand from inetd or xinetd. The following line added to *inetd.conf* would implement Recipe 6.1 on a system using *inetd* and an on-demand *identd* service:

```
auth stream tcp nowait nobody /usr/sbin/in.identd in.identd -t120
```

This, of course, is just an example. You would need to customize the program pathname and the command-line arguments to fit your system and your needs. You should also check the *identd* manpage for options that prevent the user from disabling *identd*.

Some other Unix systems run *identd* as part of the system startup process. Our sample Red Hat Linux system is an example. A *chkconfig* command adds *identd* to the boot process, and a *service* command starts *identd* immediately:

```
# chkconfig --list identd
identd          0:off   1:off   2:off   3:off   4:off   5:off   6:off
# chkconfig --level 35 identd on
# chkconfig --list identd
identd          0:off   1:off   2:off   3:on    4:off   5:on    6:off
# service identd start
Generating ident key:                                   [ OK ]
Starting identd:                                        [ OK ]
```

The first *chkconfig* command shows that *identd* is not included in the boot process on this sample Linux system. The second *chkconfig* command adds it to the startup process for run levels 3 and 5—the run levels associated with networked, multiuser operation on most Linux systems. The final *chkconfig* command shows the effect of this change. Of course, there is no reason to reboot the system just to start *identd*, so the service command is used to run the identification service immediately.

This is the first time that *identd* has been started on this server. Notice the first line of output from the *service* command. It tells us that a key is being generated for *identd*. This key is used to encrypt the information sent to the remote system. The administrators of the remote system cannot decrypt the information because they do not have the key. If they suspect a problem, they must send you the encrypted string, which you can then decrypt using the */etc/identd.key* file and the idecrypt command. The information from the *identd* server is encrypted for security reasons. Security people dislike *identd* because it exposes information about systems and users that can be misused by spammers and intruders. Encrypting the *identd* response allows you to run the identification daemon without any significant security risks.

For example, the Received: header shown earlier in this section displays the 32 character, BASE64 encoded string r+9Gemj2wip8fAJDU8kDZlyUiReTZjYc that the remote system received from our sample system in response to the IDENT query. This does not provide any information that can be exploited by a spammer or an intruder, but it can be used by you to obtain information about the local user who sent the mail. When the remote system administrator contacts you with a problem report, obtain the 32-byte string, enclose it in square brackets, and decode it with the *idecrypt* command, as shown:

```
# idecrypt
[r+9Gemj2wip8fAJDU8kDZlyUiReTZjYc]
Wed Dec  4 17:00:24 2002 500 192.168.0.8 1029 192.168.0.3 25
Ctrl-D
```

The decoded string provides:

- The date and time the connection was made
- The UID of the user who initiated the connection (500 in this example)
- The IP address of the source of the connection (192.168.0.8)
- The source port (1029)
- The destination IP address (192.168.0.3)
- The destination port of the connection (25, which is the SMTP port)

All of this information is useful in tracking who is abusing your system. However, *identd* does have major limitations. It only returns a useful UID if the user actually logs into your system. If it is being misused in some other way, the information provided might not be useful. Additionally, running *identd* adds some processing overhead to each piece of mail. As with most things, *identd* has both pluses and minuses.

On our sample Red Hat Linux system, the identd service is preconfigured in the */etc/identd.conf* file. Additionally, the identd service can be configured from the command line using command-line options. On a Red Hat Linux system, the identd command-line options used during startup are defined as values for the IDENTDOPTS variable in the */etc/sysconfig/identd* file. See the identd manpage for specifics on the *identd.conf* configuration commands and the command-line options.

See Also

See the manpages for *identd*, *inetd.conf*, *chkconfig*, and the *service* command.

6.12   Using MILTER

Problem

You have installed an external mail filtering tool that complies with the *Sendmail Mail Filter API*. You now need to configure sendmail to make use of that external mail filter.

Solution

Run the `sendmail -d0.1` command. The "Compiled with:" line output by the command should contain MILTER. If it does not, add MILTER support by adding the following line to the *site.config.m4* file:

```
APPENDDEF(`confENVDEF', `-DMILTER')
```

Recompile sendmail as described in Chapter 1, in Recipes 1.3 through 1.7.

Add an INPUT_MAIL_FILTER macro to the sendmail configuration that identifies the external mail filter. At a minimum, the INPUT_MAIL_FILTER macro must define the internal name of the filter and the socket specification required by the filter. Refer to the documentation that comes with the MILTER to find the recommended settings. As an example, the following line could be added to the sendmail configuration to use the *vbsfilter* MILTER available from *http://aeschi.ch.eu.org/milter/*:

```
INPUT_MAIL_FILTER(`sample', `S=local:/var/run/vbsfilter.sock')
```

Rebuild the *sendmail.cf* file, copy the new *sendmail.cf* file to */etc/mail*, and restart sendmail, as described in Recipe 1.8.

Discussion

Before an external program can be used by sendmail, it must be located, downloaded, installed, and properly configured. The introduction to this chapter points to a few web sites where you can start your search for useful MILTERs. Because of the complexity of filtering for spam and scanning for viruses, and because of the constantly changing nature of the threats, configuring a MILTER can be much more challenging than configuring sendmail to use the MILTER. Read the MILTER documentation carefully so that you understand exactly what INPUT_MAIL_FILTER arguments are needed for sendmail to interface with the external filter.

The sample sendmail configuration in the Solution section uses an INPUT_MAIL_FILTER macro recommended by the documentation for the mail filter *vbsfilter*. The *vbsfilter* program identifies various dangerous executable attachments and renames them with the *.txt* extension so that they will not be automatically executed by the end user's system. The socket defined in the INPUT_MAIL_FILTER macro must match the socket used by the MILTER. For *vbsfilter*, this is accomplished by running the MILTER with a -p argument that tells *vbsfilter* which socket to use. Given the INPUT_MAIL_FILTER macro shown in the Solution section, *vbsfilter* would be started with the following command:

```
# vbsfilter -p S=local:/var/run/vbsfilter.sock
```

The *vbsfilter* is a good one to start with because it does not require much configuration. So is the sample MILTER provided in the *libmilter/README* file that comes with the sendmail distribution. The sample mail filter doesn't do any useful filtering, but it is easy to test and useful for determining that your sendmail system is properly configured and capable of interfacing with an external filter. Many filters are so complex that debugging the MILTER at the same time you are debugging sendmail can be overwhelming. Use a simple filter to debug sendmail before interfacing it to a complex filter.

See Also

The Introduction to this chapter provides more information about MILTERs. The *sendmail* book covers MILTER in section 7.6. The *libmilter/README* file also covers this topic, as do the files in *libmilter/docs*.

6.13   Bypassing Spam Checks

Problem

Your sendmail is configured to block incoming junk mail, and you have been asked to allow junk mail through when it is addressed to specific recipients.

Solution

Add an entry to the */etc/mail/access* text file for each recipient who should be allowed to receive junk mail. Use the tag Spam: and the recipient address to create the key field of the entry. Use the keyword FRIEND as the return value for each entry. Run *makemap* to build a hash type database from the text file.

Create a sendmail configuration containing the *access_db* feature and the *delay_checks* feature with the optional friend argument. Make sure that the *access_db* FEATURE macro precedes the *delay_checks* FEATURE macro in the configuration. Here are the lines that would be added to the sendmail configuration:

```
dnl Use the access database
FEATURE(`access_db')
dnl Check for spam friends before rejecting the mail
FEATURE(`delay_checks', `friend')
```

Rebuild the *sendmail.cf* file, copy the new *sendmail.cf* file to */etc/mail*, and restart sendmail, as described in Recipe 1.8.

Discussion

Someone on your system—the postmaster, a security expert, a developer writing mail filters—might need to receive junk mail that is normally blocked by sendmail. The *delay_checks* feature allows this by changing the order in which spam checks are applied. The *delay_checks* feature allows the envelope recipient address to be checked before the envelope sender address or the connection address, which, in turn, makes it possible for mail addressed to specific recipients to bypass the other two checks. To use the *delay_checks* feature in this way, it must be invoked with the friend argument, as shown in the Solution section.

The specific recipients allowed to receive junk mail are defined in the *access* database using the Spam: tag and the FRIEND return value. Here is an example *access* database:

```
Connect:example.com                   REJECT
Spam:uce@wrotethebook.com             FRIEND
Spam:clark+junk@wrotethebook.com      FRIEND
```

Given the sendmail configuration described in the Solution section, this *access* database rejects mail from *example.com* unless it is addressed to *uce@wrotethebook.com* or to *clark+junk@wrotethebook.com*.

See Also

Recipe 6.14 provides a related example. Chapter 3 and the Introduction to this chapter provide more information about the *access* database. The *sendmail* book covers the *access* database in section 7.5 and the *delay_checks* feature in section 7.5.6. The *Delay all checks* section of the *cf/README* file also covers this topic.

6.14   Enabling Spam Checks on a Per-User Basis

Problem

You have been asked to create a sendmail configuration that applies checks only when the mail is addressed to selected recipients.

Solution

Add an entry to the */etc/mail/access* text file for each recipient whose mail must pass all checks before it is delivered. Use the tag Spam: and the recipient address to create the key field of the entry. Use the keyword HATER as the return value for each entry. Run *makemap* to build a hash type database from the text file.

Create a sendmail configuration containing the *access_db* feature and the *delay_checks* feature with the optional hater argument. Make sure that the *access_db* FEATURE macro precedes the *delay_checks* FEATURE macro in the configuration. Here are the lines that would be added to the sendmail configuration:

```
dnl Use the access database
FEATURE(`access_db')
dnl Apply all checks to spam hater mail
FEATURE(`delay_checks', `hater')
```

Rebuild the *sendmail.cf* file, copy the new *sendmail.cf* file to */etc/mail*, and restart sendmail, as described in Recipe 1.8.

Discussion

The *delay_checks* feature changes the order in which checks are applied by first checking the envelope recipient address. When the *delay_checks* feature is invoked with the hater argument, as shown in the Solution section, the envelope recipient address must be found in the *access* database, and it must return the value HATER before the envelope sender address or the connection address are checked. If the envelope sender address is not found in the *access* database or does not return the value HATER, the check of the envelope sender address performed by check_mail, and the check of the connection address performed by check_relay, are bypassed.

To apply the check_mail and check_relay checks to a recipient's mail, the specific recipients must be defined in the *access* database using the Spam: tag and the HATER return value. Here are example entries:

```
Connect:example.com                REJECT
Spam:jay@wrotethebook.com          HATER
Spam:alana@wrotethebook.com        HATER
```

Using this recipe's sendmail configuration, this *access* database will reject mail from *example.com* when it is addressed to *jay@wrotethebook.com* or to *alana@wrotethebook.com*. Other users are allowed to receive mail from *example.com*.

See Also

Recipe 6.13 provides a related example. Chapter 3 and the Introduction to this chapter provide more information about the *access* database. The *sendmail* book covers the *access* database in section 7.5 and the *delay_checks* feature in section 7.5.6. The *Delay all checks* section of the *cf/README* file also covers this topic.

Authenticating with AUTH

7.0 Introduction

Strong authentication uses cryptographic techniques to verify the identity of the end points in a network exchange. For sendmail, strong authentication ensures that the connecting host and the receiving host are who they claim to be. In this chapter, we look at how AUTH can be used for authentication.

Authentication is not the same as encryption. Encryption can be used to hide the content of a piece of mail or to hide the entire SMTP protocol exchange, including the mail. (One technique for encrypting the SMTP exchange, and the mail it carries, is covered in Chapter 8.) Authentication does not hide the contents of mail; rather, it ensures that the mail comes from the correct source.

Traditional sendmail authentication systems are based on the hostname or IP address. Examples of this can be found in Chapter 3, which uses hostnames and IP addresses to grant relaying privileges. However, the current IP address of a valid client may not be known. A mobile client that obtains its address from a DHCP server may have an address that constantly changes. Mobile clients need an authentication scheme that is not dependent on a changeable IP address. Additionally, hostnames and addresses are easily spoofed and thus do not provide strong authentication. Of course, it is debatable whether a service such as mail relaying really needs strong authentication, but it is clear that mobile clients need authentication that is independent of the IP address. The AUTH protocol provides some strong authentication techniques that do not rely on the IP address or hostname.

The AUTH Protocol

AUTH is an SMTP protocol extension. It is defined in RFC 2554, *SMTP Service Extension for Authentication*. RFC 2554 outlines the negotiations that are used to select an authentication mechanism. The RFC describes three functions for the AUTH keyword:

- 250-AUTH is the response of the SMTP EHLO command. The response advertises the supported authentication mechanisms. The configuration that causes sendmail to list AUTH in the EHLO response and to accept incoming AUTH connections is covered in Recipe 7.1. That configuration applies when sendmail runs as an MTA, and it is only applicable when sendmail is run with the -bd command-line option.
- AUTH is the SMTP command used to request authentication and to select the authentication mechanism for the session. The connecting host must select one of the mechanisms advertised by the receiving host, or the authentication attempt is rejected. sendmail will request AUTH authentication when it is configured as described in Recipe 7.2. A laptop or desktop that sends SMTP mail but does not accept inbound SMTP connections could be configured using only Recipe 7.2. A system that accepts incoming AUTH connections and creates outgoing AUTH connections would combine the configurations from both Recipes 7.1 and 7.2.
- AUTH= is a parameter used on the MAIL From: line to identify the authenticated source address. The AUTH= parameter comes from the connecting host as part of the initial envelope sender address. If the receiving host trusts the AUTH= parameter, it propagates it on to the next mail relay. Recipe 7.6 provides additional information about the AUTH= parameter.

The AUTH protocol relies on SASL (the Simple Authentication and Security Layer (SASL) for the actual authentication. RFC 2222, *Simple Authentication and Security Layer (SASL)*, describes the SASL framework and defines how protocols negotiate an authentication method. RFC 2222 identifies four authentication techniques:

KERBEROS_V4
> Authentication is performed by a Kerberos 4 server.

GSSAPI
> The GSS-API is used for authentication. This type of authentication can be performed by a Kerberos 5 server.

S/KEY
> The one-time password system S/Key is used for authentication.

EXTERNAL
> Authentication depends on an external security system, such as Transport Layer Security (TLS).

Subsequently, several more authentication techniques have been added to the SASL framework. Some examples are:

ANONYMOUS
> This technique, which is defined in RFC 2245, permits unauthenticated access.

PLAIN
> Authentication is based on clear text passwords.

LOGIN

> This is an undocumented authentication technique, included for compatibility with outdated SMTP clients, that also uses clear text passwords.

CRAM-MD5

> This is a shared secret authentication method that uses Message Digest 5 (MD5) for security. Challenge Response Authentication Mode MD5 (CRAM-MD5) is an older authentication method that has been superceded by DIGEST-MD5.

DIGEST-MD5

> This is the preferred MD5 authentication method. Like CRAM-MD5, it is a shared secret authentication method that uses Message Digest 5 (MD5) for security. However, DIGEST-MD5 is more resistant to security attacks, and it supports encryption of the SMTP conversation.

sendmail does not contain implementations of the various authentication techniques. Instead, sendmail uses the techniques that are implemented and configured in SASL. For this to work, Cyrus SASL must be installed and properly configured on the sendmail system.

Cyrus SASL

Cyrus SASL is implemented as a library. The SASL library standardizes the way in which applications interface with the authentication methods. Many Unix systems come with the SASL libraries preinstalled. Our sample Red Hat Linux system is a good example. Red Hat includes SASL as one of the standard RPMs. An *rpm* command can check whether it is installed, as in this example:

```
# rpm -qa cyrus-sasl
cyrus-sasl-1.5.24-25
```

If SASL is not installed on your system, check to see if it was delivered as part of your Unix software. If it was, install the copy of SASL provided by your Unix vendor. If it is not available from your vendor, go to *http://asg.web.cmu.edu/cyrus/download/* or *ftp://ftp.andrew.cmu.edu/pub/cyrus-mail/* to download the latest version of SASL. Information on SASL is available at *http://asg.web.cmu.edu/sasl/*.

After Cyrus SASL is installed, the specific authentication techniques must be configured before they can be used. To understand SASL configuration, you must understand SASL terminology. The Cyrus SASL documentation defines four special terms:[*]

userid

> The username that determines the permissions granted to the client. The client is given the permissions normally granted to the specified user. *userid* is also called the *authorization id*.

---

[*] In addition to these four special items, SASL uses a password when one is required by the authentication technique.

authid

> The account name used to authenticate the connection. *authid* is also called the *authentication id*.

realm

> A group of users, systems, and services that share a common authentication environment. All members of a given group use the same *realm* value. It is common to use a domain name or hostname for the *realm* value.

mechanism

> Identifies the type of authentication used. For example, DIGEST-MD5 is a valid *mechanism* value.

The *userid* and *authid* values cause the most confusion. To understand how SASL uses these two values, think of an */etc/passwd* file with one entry for *craig* and another for *kathy*. In a normal login, when Kathy logs in to the *kathy* account, she is granted the permissions given to that account. With SASL, it is possible to set *authid* to *kathy* and *userid* to *craig*, which means that the *kathy* account password is required for authentication, but the permissions granted to the user are the permissions granted to the *craig* account.

Several of the strong authentication techniques available through SASL require the configuration of separate authentication services—KERBEROS_V4 and GSSAPI are good examples. This chapter focuses on the strong authentication techniques that can be implemented on a sendmail system without installing any software other than SASL. Two strong authentication techniques, DIGEST-MD5 and CRAM-MD5, are provided with the Cyrus SASL libraries. Both of these techniques can be easily configured for sendmail authentication.

DIGEST-MD5 and CRAM-MD5 are configured through the */etc/sasldb* database. This is done using the *saslpasswd* commands. Use *saslpasswd* to enter the SASL *authid* and *realm* and the password that the connecting host will use during authentication. Recipe 7.1 provides an example of how this is done.

Because these are shared-secret authentication mechanisms, the connecting host must be configured with values that match those entered in the *sasldb* file on the receiving host. On sendmail 8.12 systems, these values are defined in an AuthInfo: entry. Normally this entry is placed in the *access* database, as described in Recipe 7.2. Optionally, an *authinfo* file can be used to hold the AUTH credentials, as described in Recipe 7.3.

The SASL Sendmail.conf file

DIGEST-MD5 and CRAM-MD5 are very secure and easily configured, making them excellent choices for sendmail authentication. There are, however, other authentication techniques available through SASL that can be used with sendmail. While DIGEST-MD5 and CRAM-MD5 do not require it, some of the other mechanisms require configuration through the *Sendmail.conf* SASL application file. Three configuration commands can be used in the *Sendmail.conf* file. They are:

srvtab

> The srvtab command points to the file that contains the Kerberos 4 service key. The argument provided with this command is the full pathname of the service key file.

auto_transition

> The auto_transition command causes SASL to automatically create a *sasldb* entry for every user that authenticates using the PLAIN authentication method.

pwcheck_method

> The pwcheck_method command defines the technique that SASL should use to validate the clear text password received during PLAIN method authentication. The possible values for the pwcheck_method are:

passwd

> Tells SASL to look up passwords in the */etc/passwd* file.

shadow

> Tells SASL to look up passwords on the */etc/shadow* file. Because of the file permissions associated with the */etc/shadow* file, the application must be running as *root*.

pam

> Tells SASL to use Pluggable Authentication Modules (PAM). PAM must, of course, be properly configured to authenticate the password.

sasldb

> Tells SASL that the passwords for the PLAIN authentication method are stored in the *sasldb* file. Normally, *sasldb* is only used for DIGEST-MD5 and CRAM-MD5 authentication.

kerberos_v4

> Tells SASL to authenticate clear text passwords through the Kerberos 4 server. Kerberos 4 must be installed, configured, and running, and the Kerberos 4 server must be configured to accept clear text passwords.

sia

> Tells SASL to use Digital's Security Integration Architecture (SIA) to validate passwords.

pwcheck

> Tells SASL to pass the data to an external program for password checking.

A sendmail system that advertised the PLAIN authentication method might have a *Sendmail.conf* file similar to the one shown below:

```
# cat /usr/lib/sasl/Sendmail.conf
pwcheck_method:pam
```

The recipes in this chapter do not require the */usr/lib/sasl/Sendmail.conf* file because they each use the DIGEST-MD5 authentication mechanism, which does not require the *Sendmail.conf* file. DIGEST-MD5 is secure, easy to configure, and available as part of Cyrus SASL. If you must use another SASL authentication mechanism, see the SASL documentation for more information on how they are configured.

Passing Flags to SASL

sendmail can be configured to request optional processing from SASL for the AUTH protocol. The confAUTH_OPTIONS define can set several flags that affect the way that sendmail and SASL interact. These flag are listed in Table 7-1.

Table 7-1. SASL flags

Flag	Purpose
A	Use the AUTH= parameter only when successfully authenticated.
a	Request optional protection against active attacks during the authentication exchange.
c	Require client credentials if the authentication mechanism supports them.
d	Reject authentication techniques that are susceptible to dictionary attacks.
f	Don't use the same static shared-secret for each session.
p	Reject authentication techniques that are susceptible to simple passive attacks.
y	Don't allow the ANONYMOUS authentication mechanism.

The A option controls when the AUTH= parameter is added to the envelope sender information on the SMTP Mail From: command line. The A option is used in Recipe 7.6, which demonstrates how the confAUTH_OPTIONS flag define is used.

The a option increases the checks SASL performs to detect active authentication attacks. SASL is used in a variety of situations. In some applications, higher security is worth the cost in increased processing and authentication delays. Normally, that is not the case for email. Mail hosts are authenticating to prevent spammers from relaying through your server. Spammers do not spend the time and money to launch active authentication attacks against servers that use strong authentication. When increased security is needed for an email connection, it is probably better to use transport layer security, as described in Chapter 8.

The c flag tells SASL to require client credentials when an authentication mechanism is used that supports client credentials. (Although it is not used inside of a SASL session, the TLS protocol, described in Chapter 8, is an example of a protocol that optionally permits the use of client credentials.) Don't confuse client credentials with AUTH credentials. The AUTH credentials discussed in this chapter are the shared-secret and other AUTH values used for authentication. The DIGEST-MD5 and CRAM-MD5 authentication techniques used by sendmail require AUTH credentials without the c option.

The f option tells SASL to use *forward security* between sessions. This means that the shared-secret used for one session is not used in the next session. Some technique must be used to negotiate a new secret for each session. Of course this requires an authentication mechanism that can handle forward security. The authentication techniques commonly used by sendmail do not implement forward security; therefore, this flag is not normally used in sendmail configuration.

The three remaining options, d, p, and y, all limit the techniques that can be used for authentication. For example, specifying the p option blocks the use of the PLAIN and LOGIN techniques over an unsecured connection.

These flags pass information to SASL, changing the way that SASL serves sendmail. Values passed from SASL are also used inside sendmail.

Authentication Macros and Rulesets

sendmail uses the information provided by authentication. sendmail stores authentication data in several macros. The authentication macros are:

${auth_author}
> This macro holds the sendmail authorization id, which is the address assigned to the AUTH= parameter on the MAIL From: line.

${auth_authen}
> This macro holds the sendmail authentication id, which is either the *userid* or the *userid* and the *realm*, written as *userid@realm*.

${auth_type}
> This macro holds the name of the authentication method used to authenticate the client. For example, DIGEST-MD5 would be a possible ${auth_type} value.

${auth_ssf}
> This macro holds the number of bits used for optional SASL encryption. If no SASL link encryption is used, this macro is unassigned.

In addition to the authentication macros, the hostname and the IP address of the system at the other end of the mail transport connection are stored in macros, which can be useful information for authentication checks. The following values are stored in the macros:

${server_addr}
> The IP address of the remote server, as determined from the TCP connection. This macro is used on the client.

${server_name}
> The hostname of the remote server, as determined from a hostname lookup of the ${server_addr} value. This macro is used on the client.

${client_addr}
> The IP address of the client, as determined from the TCP connection. This macro is used on the server.

${client_name}
> The hostname of the client, as determined from a hostname lookup of the ${client_addr} value. This macro is used on the server.

sendmail also provides ruleset hooks that simplify the process of adding authentication checks. The primary hooks used with AUTH are:

Local_check_mail
> This ruleset adds checks to the check_mail ruleset, which is used to process the envelope sender address from the MAIL From: line. The check_mail ruleset is not specific to AUTH, but the overlap between the ${auth_author} value and the envelope sender address means that Local_check_mail is occasionally used for custom AUTH processing.

Local_check_rcpt
> This ruleset adds checks to the check_rcpt ruleset, which processes the envelope recipient address from the RCPT To: line. The check_rcpt ruleset is not specific to AUTH, but because it is used to authorize delivery to a recipient, Local_check_rcpt is occasionally used to modify it for AUTH processing.

Local_trust_auth
> This ruleset adds checks to the trust_auth ruleset, which is used by the server to determine whether the AUTH= parameter on the MAIL From: line should be trusted. The trust_auth ruleset is specific to the AUTH protocol because the AUTH= parameter is only used when AUTH is running on the client. Use Local_trust_auth to customize the processing of the AUTH= parameter.

Local_Relay_Auth
> This ruleset is called by the Rcpt_ok ruleset. By default, sendmail grants relaying privileges to an authenticated client only if the client authenticated is using a mechanism listed in the $={TrustAuthMech} class. Use Local_Relay_Auth to modify the process of granting relaying privileges to authenticated clients.

7.1   Offering AUTH Authentication

Problem

In order to require strong authentication before granting special privileges, such as relaying, you have been asked to configure sendmail to offer AUTH authentication.

Solution

AUTH requires the SASL library. Configure the SASL authentication technique that you wish to use. See this chapter's Introduction for information about the SASL library and where it can be obtained.

Use -d0.1 to check the sendmail compiler options. If the "Compiled with:" list displays SASL, restart sendmail to reload the freshly configured SASL libraries and you're ready to run. If SASL is not included in the "Compiled with:" list, recompile sendmail as shown in Recipe 1.5.

Discussion

There is no need to add *m4* macros to the sendmail configuration to advertise basic AUTH mechanisms. Only a properly installed and configured SASL library and a copy of sendmail that has been compiled with SASL support are needed.

The SASL configuration is driven by which SASL authentication techniques are installed on your system and by which of those techniques are selected for use. Our sample Red Hat system was delivered with SASL preinstalled. Figure 7-1 shows the *System Environment/Libraries* window from an RPM management tool.

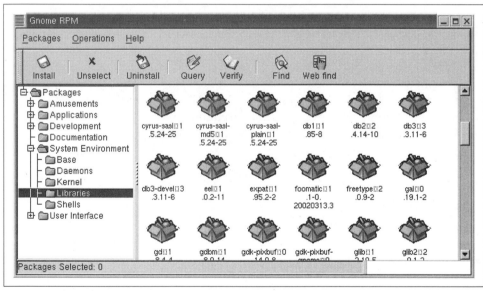

Figure 7-1. Observing the installed SASL libraries in Red Hat Linux

The figure shows the three SASL library modules that came with this Linux system. *cyrus-sasl-1.5.24-25* is the basic SASL library. *cyrus-sasl-plain-1.5.24-25* is the SASL plug-in that provides the PLAIN and LOGIN authentication techniques. *cyrus-sasl-md5-1.5.24-25* is the plug-in that provides the CRAM-MD5 and DIGEST-MD5 SASL authentication techniques. Of these, only CRAM-MD5 and DIGEST-MD5 offer any real security.

The sendmail server will not advertise the DIGEST-MD5 and CRAM-MD5 techniques unless the file */etc/sasldb* exists. *sasldb* stores the names and passwords used for MD5 authentication. The file is built by *saslpasswd* the first time it is used to create an SASL password. To authenticate a client with the *sasldb*, add the client's name and password to the database. Assume we want to authenticate *crab* using MD5 and that we assign *crab* the password: It'sasecret!. The following command would accomplish this and make both CRAM-MD5 and DIGEST-MD5 available for send-mail authentication:

```
# saslpasswd -c -u wrotethebook.com crab
Password: It'sasecret!
Again (for verification): It'sasecret!
```

The -u argument defines the SASL realm. When creating an SASL account for AUTH authentication, always explicitly define the realm with the -u argument. The realm used on both endpoints must agree in order for authentication to succeed. Take control of this important information by explicitly defining the realm that both the server and the client should use. In the example, the realm is *wrotethebook.com*, which is the same as the local domain name. The string used to name the realm is arbitrary. It can be any value you choose. While the realm does not have to be a domain name, it usually is for the sake of simplicity.

The -c argument tells *saslpasswd* to create a new account. The account name, *crab* in the example, is placed at the end of the command line. *saslpasswd* then prompts for a password for the *crab* account. This password is the shared-secret key used for DIGEST-MD5 or CRAM-MD5 authentication.

After configuring SASL, the receiving host responds to the SMTP EHLO command by listing the available AUTH authentication techniques. A *telnet* test shows this:

```
# telnet localhost smtp
Trying 127.0.0.1...
Connected to localhost.
Escape character is '^]'.
220 chef.wrotethebook.com ESMTP Sendmail 8.12.9/8.12.9; Fri, 22 Aug 2003 12:01:37 -
0400
ehlo localhost
250-chef.wrotethebook.com Hello IDENT:jlXFenYjCfmga11KxmpDxZFsKgljZB2/@localhost
[127.0.0.1], pleased to meet you
250-ENHANCEDSTATUSCODES
250-PIPELINING
250-EXPN
250-VERB
250-8BITMIME
250-SIZE
250-DSN
250-ETRN
250-AUTH DIGEST-MD5 CRAM-MD5
250-DELIVERBY
250 HELP
QUIT
221 2.0.0 chef.wrotethebook.com closing connection
Connection closed by foreign host.
```

The receiving host responds to the EHLO command with a list of the extended services that it supports. The 250-AUTH response shows that the host supports the AUTH protocol, and the response lists the specific authentication techniques that it supports. In the example, the server advertises DIGEST-MD5 and CRAM-MD5, meaning that SASL has been configured for CRAM-MD5 and DIGEST-MD5, and sendmail has been directed to advertise these authentication methods. Recipe 7.4 describes how to control which AUTH techniques are advertised by sendmail.

In the example above, the receiving system responds with 250-AUTH. If you have just configured the receiving system, and it doesn't issue the 250-AUTH response, there are several things you can do to try to discover the problem. First, check the log to see if any security problems are logged. sendmail may have been unable to open a required file.

If basic logging doesn't show the problem, increase the LogLevel to 13 and rerun the test shown above. (Recipe 1.10 provides an example of setting the sendmail LogLevel.) Examine the log again.

sendmail only advertises AUTH if some of the authentication mechanisms that it is configured to accept are available from SASL and properly configured. *grep* the log for the string *mech=*. The *available mech=* log entry lists the mechanisms that sendmail believes are offered by SASL. The *allowed mech=* entry lists the mechanisms that sendmail believes it is allowed to offer. sendmail only issues the 250-AUTH response if these lists share some common items. If the *available mech=* list identifies some mechanism, you can change the list of mechanisms that sendmail will accept using the confAUTH_MECHANISMS define described in Recipe 7.6.

If the *available mech=* list is empty, and the log contains either an error message from SASL that contains the string *listmech=0* or the sendmail error message "AUTH warning: no mechanisms," SASL is not properly installed and configured. SASL must be installed with authentication mechanisms, as noted earlier in the discussion of Figure 7-1. Make sure you download and properly install all of the required libraries.

If SASL is not complaining but sendmail is, perhaps sendmail is looking in the wrong place for SASL libraries. The path to SASL libraries can be set using the environment variable SASL_PATH by adding lines such as the following to the sendmail configuration:

```
LOCAL_CONFIG
ESASL_PATH=/usr/lib/sasl
```

Of course, this path is only an example. You would use the path value appropriate to your system.

Installing SASL, configuring the *sasldb*, and compiling sendmail with SASL support configures sendmail to accept only inbound AUTH connections. If the system must also send out mail using AUTH authentication, the configuration in Recipe 7.2 should be added to this recipe to create a complete configuration.

See Also

Recipes 7.4 and 7.5 provide related AUTH configuration examples. The *sendmail* book covers AUTH configuration in section 10.9. See the *sysadmin.html* file in the SASL documentation directory for additional information about SASL configuration.

7.2   Authenticating with AUTH

Problem

You have been asked to configure sendmail to use AUTH authentication when sending mail.

Solution

Make sure that the SASL libraries are installed and that sendmail is compiled with SASL support. See Recipe 1.5 and this chapter's Introduction if your system lacks either of these necessary components.

Add the host's authentication credentials to the *access* database using an AuthInfo: tag. Use the u: parameter to define the SASL authorization ID, the I: parameter to define the SASL authentication ID, the P: parameter to define the shared secret, the R: parameter to define the SASL realm, and the M: parameter to request an AUTH mechanism. Because the AuthInfo: entry contains a password written in clear text, it is important to make sure that the *access* database is only readable by *root*.

Create a sendmail configuration containing the *access_db* feature. Here is the required FEATURE macro:

```
dnl Use the access database for AUTH credentials
FEATURE(`access_db')
```

Following the instructions in Recipe 1.8, rebuild the *sendmail.cf* file, copy the new *sendmail.cf* file to */etc/mail*, and restart sendmail.

Discussion

To successfully authenticate, a host must be able to provide the receiving system with valid security credentials. These credentials are stored on the connecting host in the *access* database using the AuthInfo: tag. Here is an example of adding an AuthInfo: entry to the *access* database:

```
# cd /etc/mail
# cat >> access
AuthInfo:chef.wrotethebook.com "U:crab" "I:crab" "P:It'sasecret!" "R:wrotethebook.
com" "M:DIGEST-MD5"
Ctrl-D
# makemap hash access < access
# chmod 600 access access.db
```

The components of this *access* database entry are, as follows:

AuthInfo:
> This is the *access* database tag. It identifies this entry as containing information used for authentication with the AUTH protocol.

chef.wrotethebook.com
> The name of the remote system that will accept these credentials immediately follows the tag. The security credentials in this example are used by the local host to authenticate itself when it connects to *chef.wrotethebook.com*. The remote system can also be identified by IP address, although the hostname is more commonly used. If this field is empty (i.e., if no host is defined), the credentials are used for authentication when connecting to any system that advertises AUTH for which there is no specific AuthInfo: entry.

U:crab
> The U: parameter defines the SASL authorization id, which is also called the user id. The authorization id is used to grant privileges on the remote system. If no value is provided for U:, sendmail uses the value assigned to I: as the default value for U:. See the Introduction for more information about the SASL *userid*, which is also called the authorization id.

I:crab
> The I: parameter defines the authentication id. This is the account name used during the authentication process. The authentication id is the name that is associated with the password in the *sasldb* file on the receiving system. If no value is provided for I:, sendmail uses the value assigned to U: as the default value for I:. Because U: and I: reference each other for default values, at least one of these values must be included in the AuthInfo: entry. See the Introduction for more information about the SASL *authid*.

P:It'sasecret!
> The P: parameter defines the password. In the example, the password is It'sasecret!. The password assigned to the P: parameter must match the password assigned to the authentication id in the *sasldb* file on the receiving host. This value is the shared-secret used for authentication.

R:wrotethebook.com
> The R: parameter identifies the SASL realm. This value must match the SASL realm assigned to the authentication id in the *sasldb* file on the receiving host. Recipe 7.1 shows how the SASL realm is assigned to the authentication id on the receiving host using the -u argument of the saslpasswd command. If no value is provided for the R: parameter, sendmail uses the value returned by $j as the SASL realm. ($j contains the fully qualified domain name of the local host.)

M:DIGEST-MD5
> The M: parameter identifies the authentication technique that will be used. If no value is provided for M:, the AUTH protocol selects the "best" authentication technique that is available on both systems.

The authentication values defined by the AuthInfo: entry on the sending system must agree with those defined on the receiving system by *saslpasswd*. If any one of the values does not agree, authentication fails with the following error message:

```
500 5.7.0 authentication failed
```

Send mail to the remote host to test the AUTH credentials. Call sendmail with the -v option in order to watch the protocol interactions. Here is a sample test:

```
$ sendmail -Am -v -t
To: craig@chef.wrotethebook.com
From: craig@crab.wrotethebook.com
Subject: Test

Please ignore.
Ctrl-D
craig@chef.wrotethebook.com... Connecting to chef.wrotethebook.com. via esmtp...
220 chef.wrotethebook.com ESMTP Sendmail 8.12.9/8.12.9; Tue, 7 Jan 2003 13:25:58 -
0500
>>> EHLO crab.wrotethebook.com
250-chef.wrotethebook.com Hello IDENT:iE/rw7zeTz25z3Y8g3qLEbb5uGQ8RtyH@crab [192.168.
0.15], pleased to meet you
250-ENHANCEDSTATUSCODES
250-8BITMIME
250-SIZE
250-DSN
250-AUTH DIGEST-MD5 CRAM-MD5
250 HELP
>>> AUTH DIGEST-MD5 =
334 bm9uY2U9ImFZcjB6VERCSWNBYUpFTVhNWGg2THQ5VllPW1kNS1zZXNz
>>> dXNlcm5hbWU9TmNyYWlnTixyZWFsbToid3JvdGVoaGVib29ryZmU3OTI3NzEzYTg5MGJjZQ==
334 cnNwYXV0aD0zYzMyMTc5YzhiMTQwYzQzNWJiNTgwOTZmOGZjYTY4Mg==
>>>
235 2.0.0 OK Authenticated
>>> MAIL From:<craig@crab.wrotethebook.com> SIZE=97 AUTH=craig@crab.wrotethebook.com
250 2.1.0 <craig@crab.wrotethebook.com>... Sender ok
>>> RCPT To:<craig@chef.wrotethebook.com>
250 2.1.5 <craig@chef.wrotethebook.com>... Recipient ok
>>> DATA
354 Enter mail, end with "." on a line by itself
>>> .
250 2.0.0 h07IPxt01997 Message accepted for delivery
craig@chef.wrotethebook.com... Sent (h07IPxt01997 Message accepted for delivery)
Closing connection to chef.wrotethebook.com.
>>> QUIT
221 2.0.0 chef.wrotethebook.com closing connection
```

In addition to the -v option, this test invokes sendmail with -t and -Am. -t tells sendmail to obtain the recipient address from any To:, CC:, and Bcc: lines in the message. (In the example, we specified the recipient with a To: line in the message.) The first five lines after the sendmail command is our test message, which is terminated by a Ctrl-D end-of-file mark. The -Am option tells sendmail to run as an MTA, using the *sendmail.cf* configuration. If this option is not specified, sendmail runs as a message submission program (MSP), uses the *submit.cf* configuration, and displays the interaction between the user's sendmail command and the local system. Because we want to watch the MTA interaction between our system and a remote system, we need to use the -Am option.[*]

Every line after the Ctrl-D is output from sendmail. Output lines that start with >>> are SMTP commands coming from the sending system. Lines that start with a numeric response code come from the receiving system.

The local system sends an EHLO command. In response, the remote system displays the list of extended commands that it supports. One of these tells the local host that the remote system supports AUTH and that it offers two authentication techniques, DIGEST-MD5 and CRAM-MD5. The local host sends an AUTH command requesting the DIGEST-MD5 technique to authenticate the connection. The endpoints exchange MD5 challenges and responses, and the remote system displays the message:

```
235 2.0.0 OK Authenticated
```

After that message, the mail delivery proceeds normally. The only effect that the recipient might notice is the addition of the word "authenticated" to the mail's Received: header, as shown below:

```
Received: from crab.wrotethebook.com
    (IDENT:iE/rw7zeTz25z3Y8g3qLEbb5uGQ8RtyH@crab [192.168.0.15])
        (authenticated)
        by chef.wrotethebook.com (8.12.9/8.12.9) with ESMTP id
    h07IPxt01997
        for <craig@chef.wrotethebook.com>; Tue, 7 Jan 2003 13:25:59 -0500
```

The tests show that the AuthInfo: entry in the *access* database works and provides sendmail with the correct information to authenticate the local host to the remote host. However, versions of sendmail prior to sendmail 8.12 cannot store authentication information in the *access* database. On these older systems, AUTH security credentials are stored in a separate file. The file must be identified in the sendmail *m4* configuration using the confDEF_AUTH_INFO define. For example, the following line added to the sendmail configuration tells sendmail that the SASL credentials are stored in a file named */etc/mail/default_auth_info*:

```
define(`confDEF_AUTH_INFO', `/etc/mail/default_auth_info')
```

The confDEF_AUTH_INFO define is deprecated and should not be used with sendmail 8.12 or later versions of sendmail. In fact, it is ignored when added to a sendmail 8.12 configuration that also includes either the *access_db* feature or the *authinfo* feature.[†] Versions of sendmail before 8.12, however, do use the confDEF_AUTH_INFO file and do not support the AuthInfo: tag for the *access* database. If you have an older version of sendmail, upgrade to the latest version as described in Chapter 1.

---

[*] Older versions of sendmail do not use *submit.cf* configuration and do not have, or need, the -Am command-line option.

[†] It is possible to force sendmail 8.12 to use the file pointed to by confDEF_AUTH_INFO by editing the *sendmail.cf* file and deleting the authinfo ruleset. But this is not recommended.

You should only use the deprecated file if you have an old version of sendmail that you cannot upgrade. A sample */etc/mail/default_auth_info* file created for the confDEF_AUTH_INFO define shown above might contain:

```
crab
crab
It'sasecret!
wrotethebook.com
DIGEST-MD5
```

The first line defines the authorization identity, which is equivalent to the U: value in the *access* database. The second line defines the authentication identity, which is equivalent to the I: value. The third line contains the password, which is the P: value in the *access* database. The fourth line defines the SASL realm, which is the *access* database R: value. The fifth line specifies the authentication mechanism that should be used, which is equivalent to the M: value in the *access* database. (This fifth line is only useful with sendmail versions starting with 8.12; prior versions of sendmail will ignore it.) The file pointed to by confDEF_AUTH_INFO contains only one set of credentials that are used for authentication with all remote systems—the *access* database permits you to define different credentials for each remote host. The *access* database is superior and should be used if at all possible.

This recipe configures AUTH for outbound connections. Recipe 7.1 configures inbound connections. Use *saslpasswd* as described in Recipe 7.1 to configure the passwords for systems that connect to your sendmail system. Use AuthInfo: entries in the *access* database to configure the password your system uses when it connects to an external host. Combine these two recipes when your host both accepts inbound AUTH connections and makes outbound AUTH connections.

See Also

Recipe 7.3 provides an alternative way to configure AUTH credentials. Evaluate Recipe 7.3 before implementing this recipe. Recipe 1.5 covers compiling sendmail with SASL support. The *access* database is used and discussed in Chapter 3 and Chapter 6. The *sendmail* book covers the AuthInfo: tag in section 10.9.3.2 and the confDEF_AUTH_INFO define in section 24.9.27.

7.3   Storing AUTH Credentials in the authinfo File

Problem

Security requirements make it necessary for you to store AUTH authentication credentials in a file separate from the *access* database.

Solution

Create the */etc/mail/authinfo* file. Store the client's authentication credentials in that file using the same AuthInfo: tag used in the *access* database. Make sure that the *authinfo* text file and database are not readable by anyone except *root*.

Add the *authinfo* feature to the sendmail configuration. Here are the lines that should be added to the sendmail configuration:

```
dnl Use the authinfo database for AUTH credentials
FEATURE(`authinfo')
```

Following the guidance of Recipe 1.8, rebuild the *sendmail.cf* file, copy the new *sendmail.cf* file to */etc/mail*, and restart sendmail.

Discussion

An alternative to defining the AUTH credentials in the *access* database is to define the credentials in a separate file named */etc/mail/authinfo*. The primary reason for doing this is file security. AUTH passwords are stored in the *access* database and in the *authinfo* file as clear text. Because the *access* database holds a wide variety of information, there is a remote possibility that you might grant multiple users read access to that file. If, for some reason, you do grant users other than *root* read access to the *access* database, move the AuthInfo: entries from the *access* database to the *authinfo* file, and add the *authinfo* feature to the sendmail configuration. The *authinfo* feature simply tells sendmail to lookup authentication credentials in the *authinfo* database instead of in the *access* database. Here is an example of creating an *authinfo* file:

```
# cd /etc/mail
# cat > authinfo
AuthInfo:chef.wrotethebook.com "U:crab" "I:crab" "P:It'sasecret!" "R:wrotethebook.
com" "M:DIGEST-MD5"
Ctrl-D
# makemap hash authinfo < authinfo
# chmod 600 authinfo authinfo.db
```

Entries in the *authinfo* database are the standard AuthInfo: entries used in the *access* database. The entries have the same format and contain the same information. The Discussion section of Recipe 7.2 provides details of the AuthInfo: entry format.

Using this recipe's configuration, run the sendmail -Am -v -t test shown in the Discussion of Recipe 7.2. Again the message:

```
235 2.0.0 OK Authenticated
```

is displayed, indicating that sendmail successfully authenticated the local host to the remote system without using the *access* database. You can prove the *access* database was not used with a simple sendmail -bt test:

```
# sendmail -bt
ADDRESS TEST MODE (ruleset 3 NOT automatically invoked)
Enter <ruleset> <address>
> /map access AuthInfo:rodent.wrotethebook.com
```

```
Map named "access" not found
> /map authinfo AuthInfo:rodent.wrotethebook.com
map_lookup: authinfo (AuthInfo:chef.wrotethebook.com) returns "U:crab" "I:crab" "P:
It'sasecret!" "R:wrotethebook.com" "M:DIGEST-MD5" (0)
> /quit
```

This test shows that the *access* database does not exist, yet the system was success-fully authenticated. Clearly this is because the AuthInfo: entries are stored in the *authinfo* database. Of course, this is just an example. On a real system, you will have both the *access* database and the *authinfo* database. The only reasons to use the *authinfo* database are to separate the authentication data from the other data already stored in the *access* database and to secure that data so that the clear text passwords it contains cannot be easily read. In the example above, we were only able to read the *authinfo* database because we ran the sendmail -bt command as *root*.

This recipe assumes that the system has the necessary SASL support. If your system does not, see the Introduction for information on obtaining the SASL libraries, and see Recipe 1.5 for information on recompiling sendmail with SASL support before attempting to implement this recipe.

See Also

Recipe 7.2 provides an alternative way to configure AUTH credentials, which should be evaluated before implementing this recipe. Recipe 7.2 also provides information about the format and content of AuthInfo: entries. Recipe 1.5 covers compiling send-mail with SASL support, and Chapter 1 provides general information about compil-ing sendmail. The *sendmail* book covers the AuthInfo: tag in section 10.9.3.2 and the *authinfo* feature in section 10.9.3.

7.4   Limiting Advertised Authentication Mechanisms

Problem

Several different SASL authentication techniques are configured for various uses. You wish to control which authentication techniques are advertised for SMTP AUTH authentication.

Solution

Add the confAUTH_MECHANISMS define to the sendmail configuration. Use the define to list only those authentication techniques that you wish to advertise. Here is a sample confAUTH_MECHANISMS define that might be added to the sendmail configuration:

```
dnl Define the acceptable AUTH mechanisms
define(`confAUTH_MECHANISMS', `DIGEST-MD5 CRAM-MD5')
```

Build the new sendmail configuration file, copy it to *etc/mail/sendmail.cf*, and restart sendmail, as described in Recipe 1.8.

Discussion

The confAUTH_MECHANISMS define sets the values assigned to the *sendmail.cf* AuthMechanisms option. sendmail advertises any SASL authentication technique listed in the AuthMechanisms option that is configured and running on the local host. The AuthMechanisms comment in a basic *sendmail.cf* file shows the default list of authentication techniques used by sendmail:

```
$ grep AuthMechanisms generic-linux.cf
#O AuthMechanisms=EXTERNAL GSSAPI KERBEROS_V4 DIGEST-MD5 CRAM-MD5
```

By default, sendmail will advertise:

- EXTERNAL, if an external security mechanism, such as TLS, is configured and running.
- GSSAPI, if the local host is operational as a Kerberos 5 client.
- KERBEROS_V4, if the local host is operational as a Kerberos 4 client.
- DIGEST-MD5, if the *sasldb* database is configured.
- CRAM-MD5, if the *sasldb* database is configured.

The receiving host advertises the available authentication techniques, but the connecting host selects the technique that will be used. Therein lies the problem. It is possible for the connecting host to select a technique that you really don't want to use for SMTP authentication, unless you explicitly specify the advertised techniques using the confAUTH_MECHANISMS define. For example:

```
# telnet rodent smtp
Trying 192.168.0.3...
Connected to rodent.
Escape character is '^]'.
220 rodent.wrotethebook.com ESMTP Sendmail 8.12.9/8.12.9; Fri, 22 Aug 2003 12:01:37 -
0400
ehlo chef
250-rodent.wrotethebook.com Hello IDENT:/tNy4XlJuCgfwrxksOjP9e2Hm3dZuOiC@chef [192.
168.0.8], pleased to meet you
250-ENHANCEDSTATUSCODES
250-8BITMIME
250-SIZE
250-DSN
250-AUTH GSSAPI DIGEST-MD5 CRAM-MD5
250 HELP
quit
221 2.0.0 rodent.wrotethebook.com closing connection
Connection closed by foreign host.
```

This *telnet* test shows that *rodent.wrotethebook.com* advertises Kerberos 5 as a technique that can be used for SMTP authentication. If the connecting system is a Kerberos 5 client, it may choose this technique to authenticate itself, which is all well and good if the administrator of *rodent* really wants to use Kerberos 5 for SMTP authentication. If not, the confAUTH_MECHANISMS define shown in the Solution section can be used to limit the list of advertised authentication techniques. After installing that confAUTH_MECHANISMS define on *rodent*, it displays the following line in its EHLO response:

```
250-AUTH DIGEST-MD5 CRAM-MD5
```

The confAUTH_MECHANISMS define can also be used to *increase* the list of advertised authentication techniques. For example, the default SASL configuration on a Red Hat Linux system includes PLAIN and LOGIN as well as DIGEST-MD5 and CRAM-MD5. If the administrator of a Red Hat system placed the following confAUTH_MECHANISMS define in the sendmail configuration:

```
define(`confAUTH_MECHANISMS', `DIGEST-MD5 CRAM-MD5 PLAIN LOGIN')
```

the server would display the following advertisement in its EHLO response:

```
250-AUTH DIGEST-MD5 CRAM-MD5 PLAIN LOGIN
```

In most cases, this is not a good thing to do. PLAIN and LOGIN are not secure authentication techniques, and they should not be used with sendmail over an unsecured link. PLAIN sends clear text passwords over the network—where they are vulnerable to snooping. LOGIN implements nonstandard, undocumented, and unsupported authentication techniques used by older, broken SMTP clients, and it also sends clear text passwords. These techniques should *only* be used if the link itself is encrypted to prevent password snooping.

See Also

Recipes 7.1 and 7.5 provide related AUTH configuration examples. The *sendmail* book covers AUTH configuration in section 10.9 and the confAUTH_MECHANISMS define in 24.9.5.

7.5   Using AUTH to Permit Relaying

Problem

You have been asked to configure a mail relay host that cannot rely on IP addresses or hostnames to grant relaying privileges.

Solution

Compile sendmail with AUTH support as described in Recipe 1.5. Install and configure SASL as described in the chapter Introduction and in Recipe 7.1.

Add the `TRUST_AUTH_MECH` macro to the sendmail configuration to list the authentication mechanisms trusted to authorize relaying. Here is a sample `TRUST_AUTH_MECH` macro that could be added to the sendmail configuration:

```
dnl List mechanisms trusted to authorize relaying
TRUST_AUTH_MECH(`DIGEST-MD5 CRAM-MD5')
```

Build the new sendmail configuration file, copy it to */etc/mail/sendmail.cf*, and restart sendmail with the new configuration. See the example in Recipe 1.8.

Discussion

AUTH authentication sets a variety of macros that can be examined by sendmail and used inside *sendmail.cf* rulesets. (Several of these macros are discussed in the Introduction.) However, AUTH authentication does not grant special privileges. An authenticated host that is not granted relaying privileges by traditional means will have its mail rejected by sendmail if it attempts to relay mail. The following excerpt from an SMTP exchange shows this:

```
235 2.0.0 OK Authenticated
>>> MAIL From:<craig@chef.wrotethebook.com> SIZE=96 AUTH=craig@chef.wrotethebook.com
250 2.1.0 <craig@chef.wrotethebook.com>... Sender ok
>>> RCPT To:<craig@crab.wrotethebook.com>
550 5.7.1 <craig@crab.wrotethebook.com>... Relaying denied
```

The 235 response shows that the connecting host has been successfully authenticated. The 550 response shows that, regardless of authentication, the host is not granted relaying privileges.

Use the `TRUST_AUTH_MECH` macro to permit relaying by AUTH authenticated clients. The `TRUST_AUTH_MECH` macro adds the $={TrustAuthMech} class to the *sendmail.cf* file and defines the values for that class. The `TRUST_AUTH_MECH` example shown in the Solution section adds the following line to the *sendmail.cf* file:

```
C{TrustAuthMech}DIGEST-MD5 CRAM-MD5
```

The $={TrustAuthMech} class is used in the `Rcpt_ok` ruleset to authorize relaying. This test is added to the standard group of relaying tests. A host that is granted relaying privileges based on its IP address or hostname is allowed to relay even if it is not authenticated by AUTH. A host that would normally be denied relaying, however, is allowed to relay if it is authenticated by AUTH using one of the techniques listed in the $={TrustAuthMech} class.

The "Relaying denied" error shown at the start of this discussion occurred when *chef* attempted to relay mail addressed to *crab* through *rodent*. *rodent* is not configured to allow any relaying from external clients. After the `TRUST_AUTH_MECH` macro was added to the configuration on *rodent*, mail sent from *chef* to *crab* through *rodent* produced a different result, as the test below shows:

```
# sendmail -Cauth.cf -v -t
To: craig@crab.wrotethebook.com
From: craig@chef.wrotethebook.com
Subject: Relay test with auth

Please ignore.
Crtl-D
craig@crab.wrotethebook.com... Connecting to rodent.wrotethebook.com. via relay...
220 rodent.wrotethebook.com ESMTP Sendmail 8.12.9/8.12.9; Wed, 8 Jan 2003 19:14:35 -
0500
>>> EHLO chef.wrotethebook.com
250-rodent.wrotethebook.com Hello IDENT:ntwzejGL8kWjSvERN8B101kmvotCXzx9@chef [192.
168.0.8], pleased to meet you
250-ENHANCEDSTATUSCODES
250-8BITMIME
250-SIZE
250-DSN
250-AUTH GSSAPI DIGEST-MD5 CRAM-MD5
250 HELP
>>> AUTH DIGEST-MD5 =
334 bm9uY2U9ImdScXZhVjVxYkpVdjJvU3FGWnR2UXJtR2hFhtPW1kNS1zZXNz
>>> dXNlcm5hbWU9ImNoZWYiLHJlYWxtPSJ3cm9ZXRoZWJvb2YWMwZDIxM2QyYmE2MTVmZjY5
334 cnNwYXV0aD0zNzg3ZGI3N2E0OM2YyYzhhMDdkZGRiYjg5N2NjNDkx0Q==
>>>
235 2.0.0 OK Authenticated
>>> MAIL From:<craig@chef.wrotethebook.com> SIZE=96 AUTH=craig@chef.wrotethebook.com
250 2.1.0 <craig@chef.wrotethebook.com>... Sender ok
>>> RCPT To:<craig@crab.wrotethebook.com>
250 2.1.5 <craig@crab.wrotethebook.com>... Recipient ok
>>> DATA
354 Enter mail, end with "." on a line by itself
>>> .
250 2.0.0 h090EZh01410 Message accepted for delivery
craig@crab.wrotethebook.com... Sent (h090EZh01410 Message accepted for delivery)
Closing connection to rodent.wrotethebook.com.
>>> QUIT
221 2.0.0 rodent.wrotethebook.com closing connection
```

For this test, a special AUTH configuration was created on *chef* that defined *rodent* as the SMART_HOST relay. Without this special configuration, *chef* would just deliver the mail directly to *crab*—we want to test relaying through *rodent*.

In this case, *chef* is authenticated using the DIGEST-MD5 technique. This technique is listed in the $={TrustedAuthMech} class on *rodent*. Therefore, *rodent* accepts mail from *chef* for relaying.

See Also

Recipes 7.1 and 7.4 provide additional AUTH configuration examples. How relaying is controlled through the traditional means of IP address and hostname is covered in Chapter 3, and the SMART_HOST define is discussed in Recipe 3.2. The *sendmail* book covers AUTH configuration in section 10.9 and the TRUST_AUTH_MECH macro in section 10.9.3.

7.6 Controlling the AUTH= Parameter

Problem

Because some broken SMTP implementations see the AUTH= parameter as a syntax error, you have decided to configure sendmail to add the AUTH= parameter to the MAIL From: line only when authentication succeeds.

Solution

If these steps have not yet been done, compile sendmail with AUTH support as described in Recipe 1.5, and install and configure SASL as described in the chapter Introduction and in Recipe 7.1.

Next, create the AUTH credentials for outbound connections, using either the techniques described in Recipe 7.2 or 7.3.

Add a confAUTH_OPTIONS define with the A flag set to the sendmail configuration. The required define is:

```
dnl Send AUTH= only when authenticated
define(`confAUTH_OPTIONS', `A')
```

Rebuild and install the new *sendmail.cf* file, and restart sendmail, as shown in Recipe 1.8.

Discussion

Use the A option of the confAUTH_OPTIONS define to prevent sendmail from adding the AUTH= parameter to the envelope sender address when the local host has not been authenticated. sendmail does not send an AUTH= parameter to a remote system if that system does not advertise AUTH. But, by default, a sendmail system that is configured to support AUTH adds the AUTH= parameter to every mail message sent to a system that advertises AUTH, even if authentication fails, as this excerpt from an actual SMTP exchange shows:

```
500 5.7.0 authentication failed
>>> MAIL From:<craig@chef.wrotethebook.com> SIZE=111 AUTH=craig@chef.wrotethebook.com
250 2.1.0 <craig@chef.wrotethebook.com>... Sender ok
```

In fact, sendmail adds the AUTH= parameter to the MAIL From: line even if authentication is not attempted. If the remote host advertises AUTH, a sendmail host configured for AUTH always sends the AUTH= parameter. In the following test, *rodent* offers AUTH mechanisms not configured on *chef*. Therefore, *chef* does not attempt to authenticate, but because it is configured for other AUTH mechanisms, *chef* sends the AUTH= parameter:

```
# sendmail -Am -v -t
To: craig@rodent.wrotethebook.com
From: craig@chef.wrotethebook.com
Subject: Test yet again

Ctrl-D
craig@rodent.wrotethebook.com... Connecting to rodent.wrotethebook.com. via esmtp...
220 rodent.wrotethebook.com ESMTP Sendmail 8.12.9/8.12.9; Fri, 10 Jan 2003 13:52:32 -
0500
>>> EHLO chef.wrotethebook.com
250-rodent.wrotethebook.com Hello IDENT:UZFl3RUw1vRsWKcZqcKAEudx69KnFn37@chef [192.
168.0.8], pleased to meet you
250-ENHANCEDSTATUSCODES
250-8BITMIME
250-SIZE
250-DSN
250-AUTH DIGEST-MD5 CRAM-MD5
250 HELP
>>> MAIL From:<craig@chef.wrotethebook.com> SIZE=92 AUTH=craig@chef.wrotethebook.com
250 2.1.0 <craig@chef.wrotethebook.com>... Sender ok
>>> RCPT To:<craig@rodent.wrotethebook.com>
250 2.1.5 <craig@rodent.wrotethebook.com>... Recipient ok
>>> DATA
354 Enter mail, end with "." on a line by itself
>>> .
250 2.0.0 hOAIqW501445 Message accepted for delivery
craig@rodent.wrotethebook.com... Sent (hOAIqW501445 Message accepted for delivery)
Closing connection to rodent.wrotethebook.com.
>>> QUIT
221 2.0.0 rodent.wrotethebook.com closing connection
```

Setting the A option with the confAUTH_OPTIONS define changes this behavior: send-mail does not add the AUTH= parameter unless authentication succeeds. This excerpt shows that AUTH= is not added when authentication fails:

```
500 5.7.0 authentication failed
>>> MAIL From:<craig@chef.wrotethebook.com> SIZE=111
250 2.1.0 <craig@chef.wrotethebook.com>... Sender ok
```

However, if authentication succeeds, the AUTH= parameter is still added to the MAIL From: line, as this excerpt shows:

```
235 2.0.0 OK Authenticated
>>> MAIL From:<craig@chef.wrotethebook.com> SIZE=111 AUTH=craig@chef.wrotethebook.com
250 2.1.0 <craig@chef.wrotethebook.com>... Sender ok
```

The AUTH= parameter is propagated on to the next mail relay if the receiving host trusts the AUTH= parameter that it received from the connecting host. sendmail only trusts that parameter if the connecting host was authenticated. The trust_auth ruleset is passed the AUTH= parameter and determines whether this value should be trusted. You can modify the way that the server handles the AUTH= parameter by writing your own Local_trust_auth ruleset.

See Also

Recipes 7.2 and 7.3 provide additional information on configuring AUTH. The *sendmail* book covers the `AUTH=` parameter in section 21.9.6 and the `confAUTH_OPTIONS` define in section 24.9.6.

7.7 Avoiding Double Encryption

Problem

You have a system that is configured for both external encryption and SASL security. On those occasions when strong external encryption is in use, you want to avoid using AUTH encryption.

Solution

Create a sendmail configuration that sets the maximum amount of encryption with the `confAUTH_MAX_BITS` define. Set the maximum number of encryption bits to a value less than the number of bits used by the external encryption; for example, setting this define to 128 turns off AUTH encryption when the transport layer is already encrypted with TLS. The following lines added to the sendmail configuration turns off AUTH encryption when other encryption is used:

```
dnl Disable double encryption
define(`confAUTH_MAX_BITS', `128')
```

Build and install *sendmail.cf*, and then restart sendmail, as shown in Recipe 1.8.

Discussion

This recipe assumes that AUTH is configured as described in Recipes 7.1 and 7.2 and that STARTTLS is configured as described in Chapter 8.

The `confAUTH_MAX_BITS` define creates the `AuthMaxBits` option in the *sendmail.cf* file and assigns a value to that option. For example:

```
O AuthMaxBits=128
```

This option tells sendmail that SASL encryption added to any existing encryption should not exceed 128-bits of encryption. Since any existing external encryption will provide at least 128-bits of encryption, this option turns off SASL encryption when the link is already encrypted.

Chapter 8 describes how TLS is used to encrypt the mail transport. When the link is encrypted by an external mechanism, such as TLS, there is no need to add a second layer of encryption with SASL. It is also possible to specify EXTERNAL on the list of advertised authentication techniques using the `confAUTH_MECHANISMS` define. Doing this avoids adding a second layer of unneeded authentication to a link that has been authenticated by an external protocol, such as TLS.

See Also

Recipe 7.4 covers the confAUTH_MECHANISMS define. The *sendmail* book covers confAUTH_MAX_BITS in section 24.9.4.

7.8   Requiring Authentication

Problem

You have an internal mail system that is not advertised to the outside world and never provides service to the outside world. You have been asked to configure that system to always require strong authentication from connecting hosts.

Solution

Create a basic AUTH configuration as described in Recipes 7.1 and 7.2.

Add to the sendmail configuration a DAEMON_OPTIONS macro that specifies the M=a modifier to require AUTH authentication. Adding the following lines requires AUTH for any connection on the SMTP port:

```
dnl Require AUTH for all incoming SMTP connections
DAEMON_OPTIONS(`Name=MTA, M=a')
```

Build the *sendmail.cf* file, copy it to */etc/mail/sendmail.cf*, and restart sendmail. Use Recipe 1.8 as a guide.

Discussion

Use the DAEMON_OPTIONS macro on systems running sendmail 8.12. Prior to sendmail 8.12, daemon port options were set using the confDAEMON_OPTIONS define. confDAEMON_OPTIONS is no longer valid. Attempting to use it with a current release of sendmail produces the following build error:

```
WARNING: confDAEMON_OPTIONS is no longer valid.
        Use DAEMON_OPTIONS(); see cf/README.
```

If you have an older version of sendmail that uses the confDAEMON_OPTIONS define, we recommend upgrading to a newer version of sendmail. The DAEMON_OPTIONS macro provides more configuration features.

The DAEMON_OPTIONS macro adds values to a *sendmail.cf* DaemonPortOptions statement or inserts a new DaemonPortOptions statement into the *sendmail.cf* file. A basic *sendmail.cf* configuration includes two DaemonPortOptions statements—one for the message submission agent (MSA) and one for the mail transfer agent (MTA). A *grep* of the *generic-linux.cf* file shows this:

```
# grep DaemonPortOptions generic-linux.cf
O DaemonPortOptions=Name=MTA
O DaemonPortOptions=Port=587, Name=MSA, M=E
```

The DAEMON_OPTIONS macro in the Solution section adds a modifier to the message transfer agent DaemonPortOptions statement, creating the following *sendmail.cf* command:

```
O DaemonPortOptions=Name=MTA, M=a
```

The fact that the MTA is being modified is made clear by the Name=MTA parameter. However, even if that parameter was not specified, the MTA would have been modified because the Port value defaults to smtp, which is the port used by the MTA. To add the a modifier to the MSA configuration, the default MSA configuration needs to be removed with the *no_default_msa* feature, and the DAEMON_OPTIONS macro needs to explicitly refer to the MSA. For example:

```
FEATURE(`no_default_msa')
DAEMON_OPTIONS(`Port=587, Name=MSA, M=Ea')
```

The *key=value* pairs of the DaemonPortOptions statement select optional characteristics for the sendmail daemon's ports. *key* can be any of the following:

Name

> An arbitrary, internal name used to identify the daemon. Two values are predefined: MSA for the message submission agent and MTA for the message transmission agent.

Port

> The port number or the name of a well-known port defined in the */etc/services* file. This defaults to smtp, which is the name for port 25 used by the MTA. The standard port used for an MSA is 587.

Addr

> The IP address of the network interface on which the daemon should listen for email connections. This defaults to INADDR_ANY, which matches every network interface installed on the system, meaning that email is accepted on every network interface. If an interface is identified with the Addr key, mail is only accepted on that interface, which can have unintended consequences. For example, adding Addr=192.168.0.3 to the MTA DaemonPortOptions on the host 192.168.0.3 would mean that mail from the local host to itself would be rejected because the *localhost* interface is 127.0.0.1—not 192.168.0.3.

Family

> The address family, which is either inet or inet6. It defaults to inet.

Listen

> The maximum number of pending connections allowed in the listen queue. The default is operating system dependent, but, on our sample Linux system, it defaults to 10.

SndBufSize

The size of the TCP send buffer in bytes.

RcvBufSize

The size of the TCP receive buffer in bytes.

M

The modifier, which is a flag that selects optional behavior for the interface or port. The modifier flags are:

a

Causes sendmail to require authentication for every inbound connection.

b

Tells sendmail to bind to the interface through which the incoming mail was received when sending outgoing mail.

c

Enables hostname canonification.

f

Requires fully qualified hostnames on email addresses.

u

Permits unqualified sender addresses, meaning that the hostname part of the sender address is not required.

A

Disables AUTH authentication for this port.

C

Disables hostname canonification.

E

Disables the SMTP ETRN command.

O

Marks the socket as optional. Normally, sendmail listens on a new socket for every DaemonPortOptions statement defined in the *sendmail.cf* file. When O is specified, the socket is ignored if it fails to open correctly.

S

Do not allow STARTTLS on this interface. Chapter 8 covers STARTTLS.

By default, a system configured as described in Recipe 7.1 offers authentication, but it does not require it. A simple *telnet* test of a system running the basic AUTH configuration from Recipe 7.1 shows this:

```
# telnet localhost smtp
Trying 127.0.0.1...
Connected to localhost.
Escape character is '^]'.
220 chef.wrotethebook.com ESMTP Sendmail 8.12.9/8.12.9; Fri, 22 Aug 2003 12:01:37 -
0400
ehlo localhost
```

```
250-chef.wrotethebook.com Hello IDENT:QQqOd8VZzdwOiABzBr3HvETLtxcEaPg1@localhost
[127.0.0.1], pleased to meet you
250-ENHANCEDSTATUSCODES
250-PIPELINING
250-EXPN
250-VERB
250-8BITMIME
250-SIZE
250-DSN
250-ETRN
250-AUTH DIGEST-MD5 CRAM-MD5
250-DELIVERBY
250 HELP
MAIL From:<craig@chef.wrotethebook.com>
250 2.1.0 <craig@chef.wrotethebook.com>... Sender ok
RCPT TO:<craig@rodent.wrotethebook.com>
250 2.1.5 <craig@rodent.wrotethebook.com>... Recipient ok
QUIT
221 2.0.0 chef.wrotethebook.com closing connection
Connection closed by foreign host.
```

The default configuration advertises the AUTH protocol, but it allows the mail connect to continue even though the connecting host does not authenticate itself. This is not just the default, it is also a requirement of the AUTH standard. If a mail system is advertised to the outside world, it cannot require authentication. Specifically, mail exchangers are forbidden to require authentication. The reason is simple. MX records advertise the mail exchanger as available for mail delivery. It cannot then refuse the mail for which it advertises.

Only mail hosts that are not advertised to the outside world are permitted to require authentication. An example of such a system might be a corporate mail relay located behind a firewall. This recipe could be used on such a system.

Rerunning the *telnet* test, after the DaemonPortOptions modifier is installed, shows the following result:

```
# telnet localhost smtp
Trying 127.0.0.1...
Connected to localhost.
Escape character is '^]'.
220 chef.wrotethebook.com ESMTP Sendmail 8.12.9/8.12.9; Fri, 22 Aug 2003 12:01:37 -
0400
ehlo localhost
250-chef.wrotethebook.com Hello IDENT:DXXGyJYPz7FDqe1dqRJVCgvxLAaoFgWP@localhost
[127.0.0.1], pleased to meet you
250-ENHANCEDSTATUSCODES
250-PIPELINING
250-EXPN
250-VERB
250-8BITMIME
250-SIZE
250-DSN
250-ETRN
```

```
250-AUTH DIGEST-MD5 CRAM-MD5
250-DELIVERBY
250 HELP
MAIL From:<craig@chef.wrotethebook.com>
530 5.7.0 Authentication required
QUIT
221 2.0.0 chef.wrotethebook.com closing connection
Connection closed by foreign host.
```

In this case, when the connecting host attempts to start a mail dialogue without authentication, an "Authentication required" error is issued.

The limitation of the DAEMON_OPTIONS macro is that it applies to all inbound connections. If more flexibility is required by your configuration, see Recipe 7.9.

See Also

Recipes 7.1 and 7.2 cover basic AUTH configuration. The *sendmail* book covers the DAEMON_OPTIONS macro in section 24.9.24. See *TCP/IP Network Administration, Third Edition*, by Craig Hunt (O'Reilly), for information on well-known ports and the */etc/services* file.

7.9   Selectively Requiring Authentication

Problem

You have a mail host that cannot be configured to require strong authentication from every connecting host, yet you have been asked to configure that system to always require strong authentication from certain connecting hosts.

Solution

Make sure that the basic AUTH configuration requirements described in Recipe 7.1 are met.

Create Srv_Features: *access* database entries for all hosts that are required to authenticate using AUTH. The key field of each entry begins with the tag Srv_Features:, which is followed by the domain name, hostname, or IP address that identifies the system that is required to authenticate itself. The return value of each entry is the letter l.

Add the *access_db* feature to the sendmail configuration. Here is the required FEATURE macro:

```
dnl Enable the access database
FEATURE(`access_db')
```

Following the instructions in Recipe 1.8, rebuild the *sendmail.cf* file, copy the new *sendmail.cf* file to */etc/mail*, and restart sendmail.

Discussion

Srv_Features: *access* database entries allow you to control the extended features offered to the connecting host based on the domain name or IP address of the connecting host. The syntax of the Srv_Features: entry is:

```
Srv_Features:name      flags
```

Srv_Features: is the required tag. *name* is the name of the connecting host, which can be defined by a full or partial domain name or a full or partial IP address. A full domain name or IP address matches a single host. A partial domain name matches all hosts in that domain, and a partial IP address matches all hosts on the specified network. When the *name* field is blank, the entry applies to all inbound mail connections that do not have a more specific Srv_Features: match. The precedence of matches is from the longest (the most specific) to the shortest (the least specific).

The *flags* field is a list of one or more single-letter flags that indicate whether an extended service should be enabled or disabled for the specified connecting host. When the flags field contains more than one flag, the individual flags are separated by whitespace. A lowercase letter in the *flags* field enables an SMTP extension, and an uppercase letter disables the extension. All of the flags, except t, come in upper/lower case pairings. Table 7-2 lists the letters that enable and disable SMTP extensions.

Table 7-2. Srv_Features: flags

Yes	No	Description
a	A	Advertise AUTH.
b	B	Advertise the VERB command.
d	D	Advertise the DSN extension.
e	E	Advertise the ETRN command.
l	L	Require AUTH authentication from the connecting host.
p	P	Advertise PIPELINING.
s	S	Advertise STARTTLS.
t		Defer the connection with a temporary error.
v	V	Request a client certificate from the connecting host.
x	X	Advertise the EXPN command.

The a/A flag and the l/L flag are the flags that relate directly to the AUTH protocol extension. In particular, this recipe uses the l flag to selectively require authentication. For example, assume that you want to require AUTH authentication from any host connecting from the *dialin.wrotethebook.com* domain. You could do that by adding the following entry to the *access* database:

```
Srv_Features:dialin.wrotethebook.com      l
```

Now, a connection attempt from any host in the *dialin.wrotethebook.com* domain is refused if the host does not authenticate. All other hosts, however, are still allowed to connect without authenticating because there are no other Srv_Features: entries in the *access* database that relate to AUTH authentication. AUTH is still advertised to all hosts, and any host that chooses to is allowed to authenticate because that is the default sendmail behavior. In the absence of an applicable Srv_Features: entry, the default sendmail behavior applies. This is exactly what we want for this recipe, but it can be more clearly documented in the *access* database by using two entries instead of the one shown above:

```
Srv_Features:dialin.wrotethebook.com      l
Srv_Features:                             L
```

In this case, authentication is still required from the hosts in the *dialin.wrotethebook.com* domain. But this time, we explicitly show that we do not require authentication from anyone else by using a Srv_Features: entry with a blank name field and an L flag.

This configuration could be taken a step further. Using the A flag in the second Srv_Features: entry would prevent sendmail from advertising AUTH to any hosts except those in the *dialin.wrotethebook.com* domain. Here is that variation:

```
Srv_Features:dialin.wrotethebook.com      l
Srv_Features:                             L A
```

In this case, hosts outside of the *dialin.wrotethebook.com* domain are not required to authenticate and are not even given a chance to do so.

See Also

Recipe 7.1 describes the basic configuration that needs to be done before this recipe is implemented. The *sendmail* book covers the Srv_Features: entry in section 19.9.4.

CHAPTER 8
Securing the Mail Transport

8.0   Introduction

Chapter 7 contains recipes that use the AUTH SMTP extension to provide strong authentication of the end points in a mail exchange. In this chapter, the recipes use the SMTP STARTTLS extension for both strong authentication and encryption.

While encryption is one of the primary benefits of the SMTP STARTTLS extension, it is important to remember that this is not end-to-end encryption. Mail can take multiple hops before it is delivered. Some intervening hops may not use STARTTLS. Additionally, the mail message is still stored as clear text by both the sender and the recipient. STARTTLS only provides encryption for mail passing over a single hop between two sendmail systems configured for STARTTLS.

Chapter 7 explained how sendmail relied on the Simple Authentication and Security Layer (SASL) to provide the security tools necessary for AUTH authentication. STARTTLS relies on the Transport Layer Security (TLS) protocol for both authentication and encryption.

Transport Layer Security

TLS is an Internet standard protocol, defined in RFC 2246, *The TLS Protocol Version 1.0*. TLS is based on the Secure Sockets Layer (SSL) protocol that was originally developed by Netscape for web security. The manner in which TLS is used to secure mail transport is defined in RFC 2487, *SMTP Service Extension for Secure SMTP over TLS*. The SMTP extension that supports TLS is called *STARTTLS*. The receiving system advertises support for STARTTLS in its response to the client's EHLO command. The connecting system requests TLS security by issuing the STARTTLS command in response to the advertisement.

TLS uses *public key encryption*, which is also called *asymmetric encryption*. It is asymmetric because it uses two different keys. A *public key* that is made available to the world and a *private key* that is kept secret. Anything encrypted with the public key can only be decrypted with the private key, and anything encrypted with the private key can only be decrypted with the public key. Four keys are needed to authenticate both the TLS client and the TLS server: the client's public and private keys and the server's public and private keys.*

The certificate

A TLS public key is distributed in a file called a *certificate*. It is called a certificate because it is certified to contain a valid public key by a *digital signature*. There are a few different techniques used to sign the certificates used by sendmail.

First, there are commercial *certificate authorities* (CAs). For a fee, a commercial CA will sign your *certificate request* creating a signed certificate. A CA is trusted to provide reasonable assurance that the certificate is correct and represents the organization it claims to represent. Commercial CAs are well established because they have been signing certificates for web sites for a number of years. Using a commercial CA to sign sendmail certificates is easy, and it has the added benefit of supporting a global customer base—certificates signed by a commercial CA are accepted around the world. Because many web sites want access to a global customer base, they use commercial CAs. In fact, a list of trusted commercial CAs can be obtained from any web browser. Figure 8-1 shows the list of CAs displayed by Netscape.

An alternative to using a commercial CA is to create a *private CA*. Creating a private CA is more complex than using a commercial CA, and it limits the customer base to those sites that are willing to accept certificates from the private CA. While a private CA is inadequate for a web site that must support a global customer base, it is a viable solution for sendmail security because mail security is often used between a limited number of partners. Recipe 8.1 shows you how to build a private CA, and Recipe 8.3 uses that CA to create the certificates used in the other recipes.

Finally, it is possible to create a *self-signed certificate*, which is not signed by any type of CA. sendmail does not accept self-signed certificates for authentication because, without the certification of a recognized CA, there is no way to verify the certificate's information. sendmail does, however, accept self-signed certificates for encryption. In fact, if you only want encryption, the TLS client doesn't need a certificate at all. However, using a CA increases the utility of the STARTTLS protocol because it adds strong authentication to basic encryption.

If the sendmail system is also a web server, it may already have a commercially signed certificate that can be used for sendmail. If not, use *openssl* to create certificates. To have a sendmail certificate signed by a commercial CA, create a *certificate signing request* (CSR)—also called a *certificate request*—and send it to the commercial CA for signing. (See the web site of the CA you select for the exact details.) If you run a private CA, create the CSR and use the private CA to sign it. Recipes 8.2 and 8.3 show examples of creating a CSR and of signing it to produce a signed certificate.

---

* For the SMTP connection, the TLS client is the system initiating the connection, and the TLS server is the system to which the connection is being made.

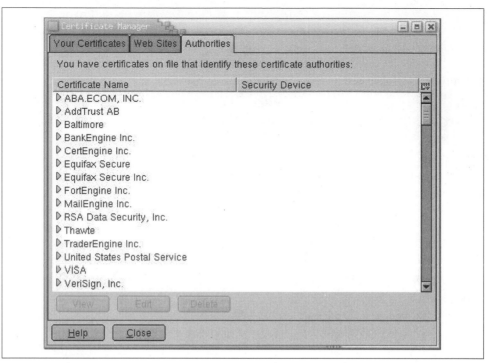

Figure 8-1. The Netscape list of recognized CAs

Certificates contain much more than just a public key. Use *openssl* to examine the contents of a certificate, as in this example:

```
# openssl x509 -noout -text -in rodent.pem
Certificate:
    Data:
        Version: 3 (0x2)
        Serial Number: 2 (0x2)
        Signature Algorithm: md5WithRSAEncryption
        Issuer: C=US, ST=Maryland, L=Gaithersburg, O=WroteTheBook,
                CN=chef.wrotethebook.com/Email=craig@chef.wrotethebook.com
        Validity
            Not Before: Jan 28 16:25:58 2003 GMT
            Not After : Jan 28 16:25:58 2004 GMT
        Subject: C=US, ST=Maryland, L=Gaithersburg, O=WroteTheBook,
                CN=rodent.wrotethebook.com/Email=alana@rodent.wrotethebook.com
        Subject Public Key Info:
            Public Key Algorithm: rsaEncryption
            RSA Public Key: (1024 bit)
                Modulus (1024 bit):
                    00:b0:91:de:51:14:19:91:61:39:ed:23:61:ef:9d:
                    e4:44:9f:ff:6a:fd:5c:cc:e8:bd:79:1f:2d:bc:eb:
                    ca:66:da:86:fb:99:17:79:07:94:dd:94:90:aa:6a:
                    44:55:ff:ec:65:e9:4e:41:b1:e9:e9:c4:09:89:81:
                    47:2b:a1:bd:a0:0b:bf:9c:c5:5e:39:de:c5:49:a3:
                    e6:5c:af:9e:32:eb:ae:63:80:7f:c6:ad:12:d0:87:
```

```
                01:db:06:a3:93:bf:41:9f:51:81:4f:09:fa:da:e3:
                ca:69:dc:35:4f:cd:43:fd:ab:6c:51:3d:24:97:60:
                bd:bf:e8:91:9c:5a:f4:b2:df
            Exponent: 65537 (0x10001)
    X509v3 extensions:
        X509v3 Basic Constraints:
            CA:FALSE
        Netscape Comment:
            OpenSSL Generated Certificate
        X509v3 Subject Key Identifier:
            76:6E:60:D0:EE:B4:62:49:84:46:04:7C:44:E6:F8:9E:CF:84:B6:DC
        X509v3 Authority Key Identifier:
            keyid:3C:D9:71:02:66:8A:D4:AD:3C:07:FD:57:2A:C5:03:C2:B8:7D:FF:D5
            DirName:/C=US/ST=Maryland/L=Gaithersburg/O=WroteTheBook/
                CN=chef.wrotethebook.com/Email=craig@chef.wrotethebook.com
            serial:00

Signature Algorithm: md5WithRSAEncryption
    c4:45:4a:e4:01:eb:0b:83:c4:26:c5:de:9e:06:8f:7a:b6:2d:
    f0:f3:63:dd:ba:1c:22:2d:f9:ac:3d:92:04:c4:4f:a8:9c:d1:
    7c:de:a7:6d:94:10:62:cb:69:c6:ba:8f:09:e7:a9:49:18:97:
    4b:aa:50:b9:0a:c9:49:59:0d:65:b6:44:1a:d6:88:6c:bd:d9:
    3e:89:e6:1c:76:c8:54:69:7f:b4:9d:7a:a7:de:92:12:cc:f5:
    43:e5:e5:da:b0:34:9d:cf:ee:b9:65:a1:a8:d7:cc:aa:96:12:
    10:7f:2b:99:94:79:f3:b4:bf:0a:58:54:65:7f:98:36:bc:a5:
    22:de
```

Several important pieces of information can be seen in this display. Foremost, of course, is the public key. It is the 1024-bit RSA public key that appears about halfway through the display. This is the key used to encrypt the session information sent to the system holding the private key—the session information includes the session key that will be used to encrypt the mail.

The system that owns this certificate is identified by the Subject field. The Subject field contains the *distinguished name* (DN) of the remote host. The DN is a formal name that can contain several fields. In this example, the DN contains a country code (C), a state code (ST), a locality (L), an organizational name (O), and a common name (CN). Inside the sendmail configuration, the DN of the subject is found in the ${cert_subject} macro, and the CN of the subject is found in the ${cn_subject} macro. In the example, the certificate belongs to the host *rodent.wrotethebook.com*.

The CA that signed the certificate is identified by the Issuer field, which contains the DN of the CA. Inside the sendmail configuration, the DN of the CA is found in the ${cert_issuer} macro, and the CN of the CA is found in the ${cn_issuer} macro. In the example, *chef.wrotethebook.com* is the private CA that is created in Recipe 8.1.

At the bottom of the display is the digital signature of the certificate created by the CA. It is an MD5 digest of the certificate, which is stored in the sendmail configuration in the macro ${cert_md5}. The digest is encrypted by the CA's private key. sendmail uses the CA's public key to decrypt the digest. If sendmail successfully decrypts and verifies the digest, it stores OK in the macro ${verify} and considers the certificate valid for authentication.

The ${verify} macro can contain any one of several different values depending on the result of the verification process. The possible values for the ${verify} macro are:

FAIL
> The certificate failed the verification process.

NONE
> STARTTLS is not being used. Thus no verification was performed.

NOT
> A certificate was not requested from the remote host. If the local system does not request a certificate from the remote system, verification is not performed.

NO
> No certificate was provided by the remote host. Therefore, there was no certificate to verify.

OK
> The certificate was successfully verified.

PROTOCOL
> A protocol error occurred.

SOFTWARE
> The STARTTLS handshake failed.

TEMP
> A temporary error occurred.

Once again, refer back to the certificate displayed by the openssl x509 command. Near the top of the output, the TLS version number is identified in the Version field of the certificate. Inside the sendmail configuration, the TLS version number is stored in the ${tls_version} macro.

As we have seen, several sendmail macros can be traced directly back to the TLS certificate. Two other important TLS related macros get their values from the session encryption used for the email connection. ${cipher} identifies the type of encryption used for the connection, and ${cipher_bits} contains the number of bits of encryption used for the connection. All of the important TLS encryption and authentication data is available for use inside the sendmail configuration.

Using the access database with TLS

The best way to control how TLS security information is applied on your system is through the *access* database. These are the *access* database records that provide control over a TLS connection:

CERTISSUER:
> Authorizes relaying based on the DN of the CA that signed the certificate. Recipes 8.5 and 8.6 provide example of using the CERTISSUER: record.

CERTSUBJECT:
> Authorizes relaying based on the DN of the host that presented the certificate. Recipe 8.6 covers the use of this record.

TLS_Srv:
> Defines the minimum security required for an outbound TLS connection. Recipes 8.7 and 8.9 show how to use the TLS_SRV: record.

TLS_Clt:
> Defines the minimum security required for an inbound TLS connection. Recipes 8.8 and 8.9 contain examples of the TLS_Clt: record.

TLS_Rcpt:
> Defines the minimum security required for mail sent to the specified recipient. Recipe 8.10 uses this record.

Try_TLS:
> Controls whether the STARTTLS command is issued to the specified remote TLS server. See Recipe 8.11 for an example of how this record is used.

Srv_Features:
> Controls whether STARTTLS is advertised to the specified remote TLS client, and whether the specified remote TLS client is required to present a certificate. See Recipes 8.12 and 8.13 for examples of this record.

sendmail provides hooks into the rulesets that process the *access* database entries related to STARTTLS:

- LOCAL_TLS_CLIENT is a hook into the tls_clt ruleset that processes TLS_Clt: database records.
- LOCAL_TLS_SERVER is a hook into the tls_srv ruleset that processes TLS_Srv: *access* database records.
- LOCAL_TLS_RCPT is a hook into the tls_rcpt ruleset that processes TLS_Rcpt: records.
- LOCAL_TRY_TLS is a hook into the try_tls ruleset that processes Try_TLS: records.

These hooks provide access to the full range of sendmail's capabilities, including all of the information that sendmail has at the time that the *access* database records are being processed. Anything that cannot be done within the confines of the standard database record formats can probably be done through a custom ruleset. The power and simplicity of using the *access* database to control delivery over a TLS connection make custom TLS rulesets largely unnecessary. However, if you have an application for a custom ruleset, sendmail provides all of the tools you need to roll your own.

OpenSSL

The sendmail implementation of STARTTLS depends on OpenSSL for authentication, encryption, and support tools. Before any of the recipes in this chapter can be used, OpenSSL must be installed.

Modern systems often include OpenSSL in order to provide web security. Our sample Red Hat Linux system includes an OpenSSL RPM file, as this simple command shows:

```
$ rpm -q openssl
openssl-0.9.6b-18
```

If your system includes OpenSSL, you can proceed. If it is not installed, install the version provided by your Unix vendor using the vendor's package management tools. If your Unix vendor does not provide OpenSSL, download the source from *http://www.openssl.org/source/* or *ftp://ftp.openssl.org/source/*. The source comes as a *gzipped* tarball. Unzip and restore the tarball. Go to the newly created directory and run *config* and then *make* to compile the source code. Then run make test and make install to install OpenSSL. If you have any problems compiling the source, see the *INSTALL* file delivered with the source code.

Additionally, sendmail must be specially compiled to support STARTTLS. If your sendmail binary was not compiled with STARTTLS support, recompile sendmail as described in Recipes 1.6 and 1.7.

8.1   Building a Private Certificate Authority

Problem

Your organization has decided not to use a commercial CA and has asked you to create a private CA to sign and manage certificates for sendmail.

Solution

Select a directory in which to place the CA directory structure (*/etc/mail/certs* is a common choice). Change to that directory and run the *CA* script provided with the OpenSSL distribution. Use the -newca command-line option of the *CA* script.* The script allows you to enter a certificate filename to work with an existing CA certificate. In this case, we are not working with an existing CA certificate, so just press the Return key to create a new CA. When prompted for a PEM passphrase, enter the password that will be required whenever the certificate authority is used to sign a certificate request. Finally, enter the distinguished name of the system that is acting as the CA. Here is an example:

```
# cd /etc/mail
# mkdir certs
# cd certs
# /usr/share/ssl/misc/CA -newca
```

---

* The *CA* script is found in the *misc* subdirectory of the OpenSSL *ssl* directory. On our sample Red Hat Linux system, the full directory path is */usr/share/ssl/misc*; on some other systems it is */usr/local/ssl/misc*.

```
CA certificate filename (or enter to create)

Making CA certificate ...
Using configuration from /usr/share/ssl/openssl.cnf
Generating a 1024 bit RSA private key
...............++++++
.............++++++
writing new private key to './demoCA/private/./cakey.pem'
Enter PEM pass phrase: SaytheSECRETword!
Verifying password - Enter PEM pass phrase: SaytheSECRETword!
-----
You are about to be asked to enter information that will be incorporated
into your certificate request.
What you are about to enter is what is called a Distinguished Name or a DN.
There are quite a few fields but you can leave some blank
For some fields there will be a default value,
If you enter '.', the field will be left blank.
-----
Country Name (2 letter code) [GB]:US
State or Province Name (full name) [Berkshire]:Maryland
Locality Name (eg, city) [Newbury]:Gaithersburg
Organization Name (eg, company) [My Company Ltd]:WroteTheBook
Organizational Unit Name (eg, section) []:
Common Name (eg, your name or your server's hostname) []:chef.wrotethebook.com
Email Address []:craig@chef.wrotethebook.com
```

The *CA* script creates a directory structure it calls *demoCA*, which contains the files needed for a private CA. Change the name *demoCA* to something that sounds less temporary, for example, to the directory name *CA*:

```
# mv demoCA CA
```

Change to the new directory structure. Tighten the security on the *private* directory, which holds the certificate authority's private key:

```
# cd CA
# chmod 0700 private
```

Copy the *openssl.cnf* file to the *CA* directory. The copy will be used by the private CA when signing sendmail certificates. To distinguish it from the original *openssl.cnf* file, the copy is renamed *sendmailssl.cnf* when it is copied to the *CA* directory:

```
# cp /usr/share/ssl/openssl.cnf sendmailssl.cnf
```

Finally, edit the *sendmailssl.cnf* file to point to the newly created *CA* directory structure. Change the line:

```
dir             = ./demoCA                # Where everything is kept
```

to read:

```
dir             = /etc/mail/certs/CA      # Where everything is kept
```

The private CA can now be used to sign certificates as described in Recipe 8.3.

Discussion

It is not absolutely necessary to build a private CA just to create the certificates needed by STARTTLS. The Introduction to this chapter describes alternative ways to obtain signed certificates. This recipe should not be taken as a recommendation for creating a private CA. It is incorporated as a recipe in this chapter because building a private CA is the most complex method of signing certificates, and thus it is the method most in need of a recipe to explain how it is done. Before you decide to build a private CA, evaluate the alternatives to make sure you choose the approach that is most suitable for your situation.

The complexity of creating a private CA is substantially reduced by the *CA* script provided with the OpenSSL distribution. The *CA* script accepts several different command-line arguments, but the one that is most useful for a sendmail system is the -newca option. -newca causes the script to create the directory structure and files needed by a CA. It also causes the script to build the private key and the certificate that will be used by the CA. An *ls* of the directory created by the CA script shows the following:

```
# ls
cacert.pem certs crl index.txt newcerts private serial
# ls private
cakey.pem
```

The directory created by the CA script contains three files:

serial
> This file contains the serial number that will be used for the next certificate signed by the CA. The *CA* script stores the serial number 01 in the initial *serial* file. The serial number is incremented every time a certificate is signed.

index.txt
> This file maps the serial number assigned to a certificate to the subject of the certificate. The serial number is identified by its numeric value, and the certificate subject is identified by its distinguished name. Initially, this file is empty. Data is added to the file each time a certificate is signed.

cacert.pem
> This file is the certificate created for the certificate authority by the *CA* script. (See the Introduction for information on the format of certificates.) This public key will be distributed to the sendmail systems that recognize this CA, and it will be referenced in their configurations. When you create a private CA to sign certificates for sendmail, it is common to make this the root CA in the sendmail configuration. See the confCACERT define in Recipe 8.4 for an example.

The private key associated with the CA certificate is stored in the *private* subdirectory and is named *cakey.pem*, as the second *ls* command in the example shows. The private key is kept safe on the CA. It is never distributed to, or used on, any other system. The *cakey.pem* file is encrypted and can only be used by someone who knows the PEM passphrase provided to the *CA* script when the *cakey.pem* file was created. In the example in the Solution section, the PEM passphrase is SaytheSECRETword!. The passphrase is required in Recipe 8.3 when the CA is used to sign certificates.

In addition to the files just described, the directory created by the *CA* script contains four subdirectories:

private
> This directory is used to hold private keys. The *CA* script places the certificate authority's private key here. In the Solution section, the permissions on this directory are changed to 0700.

newcerts
> This directory holds copies of all the certificates signed by this CA. The certificates in this directory are identified by serial numbers. This directory is empty when created by the *CA* script. Files are added to the directory by the signature process.

crl
> This directory holds certificate revocation lists. The *CA* script creates this directory to be empty. See *Network Security with OpenSSL*, by Viega, Messier, and Chandra (O'Reilly), for information on CRLs.

certs
> This directory can be used to hold certificates. However, the *CA* script does not place the CA's certificate in this directory.

This recipe recommends adding a copy of *openssl.cnf* to the files and directories created by the *CA* script. The *openssl.cnf* configuration file is read by *openssl* every time it is executed. *openssl* is used to create and sign certificates, and it will be used in subsequent recipes in this chapter. To simplify customizing the OpenSSL configuration for sendmail certificate management, and to avoid any possibility of interfering with the OpenSSL configuration used by the web site administrator, we copy *openssl.cnf* to *sendmailssl.cnf*. The new name is intended to make it clear that this configuration is used only by the sendmail CA. We then edit the *sendmailssl.cnf* file to point to */etc/mail/certs/CA* as the directory used by the default CA. This recipe assumes that the private CA is being used exclusively for sendmail certificate management. Because this CA is used exclusively for sendmail, it makes sense to create a sendmail-specific OpenSSL configuration. Recipe 8.3 uses the newly created *sendmailssl.cnf* file.

See Also

Recipes 8.2 and 8.3 are both directly related to this recipe. The Introduction to this chapter contains important information about certificates and certificate authorities. The *sendmail* book discusses certificates in section 10.10.2. The *config* manpage provides information on the *openssl.cnf* file. *Network Security with OpenSSL*, by Viega, Messier, and Chandra (O'Reilly), provides information about certificates, certificate authorities, and certificate revocation lists.

8.2   Creating a Certificate Request

Problem

You must create a certificate request before the CA can sign it, and thus provide you with a signed certificate.

Solution

On the sendmail host, create a directory to hold the certificate and private key. Here is an example:

```
# cd /etc/mail
# mkdir certs
```

Change to the new directory. Use the openssl req command to create an unsigned X.509 certificate and a private key. When prompted for the distinguished name, enter the DN of the sendmail host for which the certificate is being created. In this example we create a certificate for *crab.wrotethebook.com*:

```
# cd /etc/mail/certs
# umask 0066
# openssl req -nodes -new -x509 -keyout key.pem -out newcert.pem
Using configuration from /usr/share/ssl/openssl.cnf
Generating a 1024 bit RSA private key
.++++++
...................++++++
writing new private key to 'key.pem'
-----
You are about to be asked to enter information that will be incorporated
into your certificate request.
What you are about to enter is a Distinguished Name or a DN.
There are quite a few fields but you can leave some blank
For some fields there will be a default value,
If you enter '.', the field will be left blank.
-----
Country Name (2 letter code) [GB]:US
State or Province Name (full name) [Berkshire]:Maryland
Locality Name (eg, city) [Newbury]:Gaithersburg
Organization Name (eg, company) [My Company Ltd]:WroteTheBook
Organizational Unit Name (eg, section) []:
Common Name (eg, your name or the server's name) []:crab.wrotethebook.com
Email Address []:admin@wrotethebook.com
```

Next, use openssl x509 to generate a certificate signing request from the certificate and key pair created above. The *newcert.pem* file created above is a temporary file that can be removed after the CSR is created:

```
# openssl x509 -x509toreq -in newcert.pem -signkey key.pem -out csr.pem
Getting request Private Key
Generating certificate request
# rm -f newcert.pem
```

Send the CSR, *csr.pem* in this example, to the CA. The CA signs the sendmail host's certificate request. Recipe 8.3 shows how this is done using the private CA created in Recipe 8.1.

The CA returns a signed certificate to the sendmail host, along with a copy of the CA's certificate. On the sendmail host, place the sendmail host's signed certificate and the CA's certificate in the certificate directory created in the first step. Create a symbolic link to a hash of the CA's certificate using the following command:

```
ln -s ca_filename `openssl x509 -noout -hash < ca_filename`.0
```

In the command above, replace *ca_filename* with the filename of the CA's certificate. sendmail uses the hash created by this command for certificate verification. Run this command, replacing *ca_filename* with the name of the new CA certificate file, every time a CA certificate is added to the directory identified by the confCACERT_PATH define. Recipe 8.4 discusses the confCACERT_PATH define.

Discussion

Most of the work in this recipe is done on the sendmail host. However, it doesn't have to be. All of the files necessary to request a signed certificate for *crab. wrotethebook.com* can be generated on any system that has OpenSSL installed. The advantage of creating the CSR on the sendmail host is that the private key is created there and never has to leave the system, making it easier to maintain private key security. The disadvantage is that the administrator of *crab.wrotethebook.com* needs to use the complex *openssl* commands to build the CSR. Many sites prefer to have one CA administrator who creates the certificate and key for each sendmail host on the CA server and then distributes the signed files to the sendmail systems. The approach you use is mostly a matter of organizational style.

The only thing that *must* be created on the sendmail host is the directory that will hold the certificate and the private key. The name of this directory, the name of the certificate file, the name of the key file, and the name of the CA certificate file, are all important values used to configure sendmail for STARTTLS, as can be seen in Recipe 8.4.

The openssl req command in the Solution section creates a new, self-signed X.509 certificate (-new -x509). The certificate is written to a file named *newcert.pem* (-out newcert.pem). The private key associated with the certificate is stored in a file named *key.pem* (-keyout key.pem). The *key.pem* file is not encrypted with DES (-nodes). This is important. If the private key is accidentally placed in an encrypted file, the sendmail administrator is prompted for the password to decrypt the file every time sendmail needs to access the private key. This could cause the sendmail system to hang during the boot process until the password is entered.

The openssl x509 command processes an X.509 certificate. In this case, the command converts an X.509 certificate to a certificate request (-x509toreq). The certificate that is being converted is the *newcert.pem* file created in the first step (-in newcert.pem -signkey key.pem). The CSR is written to a file named *csr.pem* (-out csr.pem).

The CSR file is sent to the CA. The CA uses that file as input to the signature process and returns another file, which is the signed certificate. Often, one file is sent to the CA and one is returned. The Solution section, however, also mentions a second file—the CA's certificate. This certificate may not be sent from the CA as part of the signature process. There may be some other means for obtaining that file. Regardless of how the CA certificate is obtained, a hash should be made from the CA certificate as shown in the last step of the Solution. sendmail uses the hash during certificate verification.

See Also

Recipe 8.3 covers signing the certificate request created in this recipe.

8.3   Signing a Certificate Request

Problem

When you operate a private CA for sendmail, you are responsible for signing the certificate requests of the sendmail hosts.

Solution

On the CA, use the openssl ca command to sign the certificate signing request provided by the sendmail host. When prompted for the PEM passphrase, enter the password created for the private CA. Answer "yes" to the two questions, and the certificate is signed. Here is an example in which the CSR created in Recipe 8.2 is signed on the CA created in Recipe 8.1:

```
# openssl ca -config ./sendmailssl.cnf -policy policy_anything -out cert.pem -infiles
csr.pem
Using configuration from ./sendmailssl.cnf
Enter PEM pass phrase: SaytheSECRETword!
Check that the request matches the signature
Signature ok
The Subjects Distinguished Name is as follows
countryName           :PRINTABLE:'US'
stateOrProvinceName   :PRINTABLE:'Maryland'
localityName          :PRINTABLE:'Gaithersburg'
organizationName      :PRINTABLE:'WroteTheBook'
commonName            :PRINTABLE:'crab.wrotethebook.com'
emailAddress          :IA5STRING:'admin@wrotethebook.com'
```

```
Certificate is to be certified until Jan 27 19:50:16 2004 GMT (365 days)
Sign the certificate? [y/n]:y

1 out of 1 certificate requests certified, commit? [y/n]y
Write out database with 1 new entries
Data Base Updated
```

The CSR sent from the sendmail system is an intermediate file that is no longer needed. Delete the unneeded file:

```
# rm -f csr.pem
```

Send the signed certificate to the sendmail host. In this example, we send the file *cert.pem* to the sendmail host. We named the certificate file *cert.pem* because it is a neutral name well suited to textbook examples. However, the certificate filename is whatever you choose to make it, and it should be something descriptive. For example, the certificate was signed for the host *crab.wrotethebook.com* so we could have given it the name *crab.wrotethebook.com.cert.pem*.

Also, send the sendmail host a copy of the CA's certificate. Assuming that this is the CA created in Recipe 8.1, the CA certificate file sent to the sendmail host would be *cacert.pem*.

Discussion

The openssl ca command is used to sign certificates. In the Solution section, the *openssl* command signs the *csr.pem* file from Recipe 8.2 (-infiles csr.pem), producing a signed certificate in a file named *cert.pem* (-out cert.pem).

This *openssl* command references the special OpenSSL configuration file (-config ./sendmailssl.cnf) that was created in Recipe 8.1 for the private sendmail CA. If the configuration file is not identified on the command line using the -config option, the *openssl* command uses the *openssl.cnf* file. The OpenSSL file provides default values used when creating and signing certificates; it defines the pathnames of the files and directories required by a CA, and it defines the certificate signing policies. By default, the *openssl.cnf* file, and the *sendmailssl.cnf* file that Recipe 8.1 created from it, contain two signature policies:

policy_match
> Signature policies define what information must be provided by the DN of the subject before a certificate will be accepted for signing. *policy_match* requires that a common name be provided. Additionally, it requires that country, state, and organization names be provided, and that these names match the country, state, and organization names used in the certificate of the CA. It makes the organizational unit name and the email address optional. *policy_match* is the default if no -policy argument is provided on the openssl ca command line.

policy_anything
> This policy requires that a common name be provided. It makes all other DN fields optional.

This recipe uses -policy policy_anything, which is commonly used when signing sendmail certificates. After all, the administrator is shown the DN and asked whether or not the certificate should be signed. If the administrator deems that the DN does not contain enough information for email security, the administrator can refuse to sign the certificate. However, in this specific example, *policy_match* could have been used and it would have worked. Remember, this is a private CA. We know that the country, state, and organization names used in the DN of the CA match the values in the DN of the server. Yet, *policy_anything* makes a better example because it is more flexible and deals with a larger variety of configurations. Most sendmail administrators use *policy_anything* and that is why it is included in this recipe.

After signing the certificate request, the CSR (*csr.pem*) is deleted. The certificate *cert. pem* is sent to *crab.wrotethebook.com* along with the CA's certificate *cacert.pem*. The sendmail host will reference both of these certificates in the STARTTLS configuration.

See Also

Recipe 8.1 covers creating the private CA used to sign the certificate in this recipe. Recipe 8.2 creates the certificate request signed in this example. The Introduction to this chapter contains important information about certificates and certificate authorities. The *sendmail* book discusses certificates in section 10.10.2. The *config* manpage provides information on the *openssl.cnf* file. The *req* manpage documents the openssl req command. The *x509* manpage documents the openssl x509 command, and the *ca* manpage covers the openssl ca command. *TCP/IP Network Administration*, Third Edition, by Craig Hunt (O'Reilly), provides examples of using *openssl* commands in Chapter 11. *Network Security with OpenSSL*, by Viega, Messier, and Chandra (O'Reilly), provides information about certificates, certificate authorities, *openssl.cnf,* and the *openssl* command.

8.4   Configuring sendmail for STARTTLS

Problem

You have been asked to configure sendmail to offer STARTTLS service for transport layer security.

Solution

STARTTLS requires that OpenSSL is properly installed and configured. See the Introduction for information on installing OpenSSL. It also requires a copy of sendmail compiled with STARTTLS support, as described in Recipes 1.6 and 1.7. Additionally, the sendmail host needs a certificate if it will be accepting inbound STARTTLS connections. Use OpenSSL to create the certificate, as described in Recipes 8.2 and 8.3.

Create a sendmail configuration with defines pointing to the files that contain the host's certificate, the host's private key, the root CA certificate file, and the directory where CA certificates are stored. Here are examples of the defines:

```
dnl Point to the CA certificate directory
define(`confCACERT_PATH', `/etc/mail/certs')
dnl Point to the root CA's certificate
define(`confCACERT', `/etc/mail/certs/cacert.pem')
dnl Point to the certificate used for inbound connections
define(`confSERVER_CERT', `/etc/mail/certs/cert.pem')
dnl Point to the private key used for inbound connections
define(`confSERVER_KEY', `/etc/mail/certs/key.pem')
dnl Point to the certificate used for outbound connections
define(`confCLIENT_CERT', `/etc/mail/certs/cert.pem')
dnl Point to the private key used for outbound connections
define(`confCLIENT_KEY', `/etc/mail/certs/key.pem')
```

Build the *sendmail.cf* file, copy it to */etc/mail/sendmail.cf*, and then restart sendmail, as described in Recipe 1.8.

Discussion

This recipe provides a full STARTTLS configuration. A system configured with all of these defines can act as a TLS server or client and can perform both encryption and authentication. The six defines point sendmail to the files necessary for this full range of service:

confCACERT_PATH
> Sets the value for the CACERTPath option in the *sendmail.cf* file. The CACERTPath option points to the directory in which certificate authority certificates are stored. It is very common for this directory to be the same one that holds the server and client certificates.

confCACERT
> Sets the value for the CACERTFile option, which points to the certificate of the root certificate authority. The value provided to this define is the full pathname of the file that holds the CA certificate.

confSERVER_CERT
> Sets the value for the *sendmail.cf* ServerCertFile option, which holds the full pathname of the file containing the server certificate used for inbound conenctions.

confSERVER_KEY
> Sets the value for the ServerKeyFile option. The ServerKeyFile option points to the file that holds the server's private key.

confCLIENT_CERT
> Sets the value for the *sendmail.cf* ClientCertFile option, which holds the full pathname of the file containing the client certificate used for inbound connections.

confCLIENT_KEY

> Sets the value for the ClientKeyFile option. The ClientKeyFile option points to the file that holds the client's private key.

If OpenSSL is installed, sendmail is compiled with STARTTLS support, and these defines point to valid certificates, sendmail will advertise STARTTLS in response to the SMTP EHLO command. A simple *telnet* test shows that STARTTLS is ready for use:

```
# telnet localhost smtp
Trying 127.0.0.1...
Connected to localhost.
Escape character is '^]'.
220 chef.wrotethebook.com ESMTP Sendmail 8.12.9/8.12.9; Fri, 22 Aug 2003 12:01:37 -
0400
ehlo localhost
250-chef.wrotethebook.com Hello IDENT:614ZhaGP3Qczqknqm/KdTFGsrBe2SCYC@localhost
[127.0.0.1], pleased to meet you
250-ENHANCEDSTATUSCODES
250-PIPELINING
250-EXPN
250-VERB
250-8BITMIME
250-SIZE
250-DSN
250-ETRN
250-AUTH DIGEST-MD5 CRAM-MD5
250-STARTTLS
250-DELIVERBY
250 HELP
QUIT
221 2.0.0 chef.wrotethebook.com closing connection
Connection closed by foreign host.
```

If your system doesn't advertise STARTTLS in response to the EHLO command, check the logfile to make sure that all file permissions are correct. If they are, try increasing the LogLevel to 14 to log additional STARTTLS debugging information. See Recipe 1.10 for information on setting the LogLevel.

This recipe shows a system configured with both client and server certificates and keys. Many systems are configured as both clients and servers for STARTTLS because mail is often forwarded by one system to another. When the system receives inbound mail, it acts as a STARTTLS server. When it forwards that mail on to another system, it acts as a STARTTLS client. Therefore, the system needs to act as both a STARTTLS server and a STARTTLS client. Normally such a system uses the same certificate and key for both its client and server roles.

A STARTTLS client will attempt to use STARTTLS whenever the server offers it. Running the *sendmail* command with the -v option shows the STARTTLS client side of this sample configuration. An example of this is seen in the following code:

```
# sendmail -Am -v -t
To: craig@chef.wrotethebook.com
From: craig@rodent.wrotethebook.com
Subject: First STARTTLS test

Ctrl-D
craig@chef.wrotethebook.com... Connecting to chef.wrotethebook.com. via esmtp...
220 chef.wrotethebook.com ESMTP Sendmail 8.12.9/8.12.9; Fri, 22 Aug 2003 12:01:37 -
0400
>>> EHLO rodent.wrotethebook.com
250-chef.wrotethebook.com Hello rodent.wrotethebook.com [192.168.0.3], pleased to
meet you
250-ENHANCEDSTATUSCODES
250-PIPELINING
250 EXPN
250-VERB
250-8BITMIME
250-SIZE
250-DSN
250-ETRN
250-AUTH DIGEST-MD5 CRAM-MD5
250-STARTTLS
250-DELIVERBY
250 HELP
>>> STARTTLS
220 2.0.0 Ready to start TLS
>>> EHLO rodent.wrotethebook.com
250-chef.wrotethebook.com Hello rodent.wrotethebook.com [192.168.0.3], pleased to
meet you
250-ENHANCEDSTATUSCODES
250-PIPELINING
250-EXPN
250-VERB
250-8BITMIME
250-SIZE
250-DSN
250-ETRN
250-AUTH EXTERNAL DIGEST-MD5 CRAM-MD5
250-DELIVERBY
250 HELP
>>> MAIL From:<craig@rodent.wrotethebook.com> SIZE=97 AUTH=craig@rodent.wrotethebook.
com
250 2.1.0 <craig@rodent.wrotethebook.com>... Sender ok
>>> RCPT To:<craig@chef.wrotethebook.com>
>>> DATA
250 2.1.5 <craig@chef.wrotethebook.com>... Recipient ok
354 Enter mail, end with "." on a line by itself
>>> .
250 2.0.0 h0UGn9P7001230 Message accepted for delivery
craig@chef.wrotethebook.com... Sent (h0UGn9P7001230 Message accepted for delivery)
Closing connection to chef.wrotethebook.com.
>>> QUIT
221 2.0.0 chef.wrotethebook.com closing connection
```

The client (*rodent*) connects to the server (*chef*) and issues an EHLO command. In response to that command, the server advertises that STARTTLS is available. The client then issues a STARTTLS command to open the TLS connection. The server responds with the message:

```
220 2.0.0 Ready to start TLS
```

Immediately after the response, the test shows another EHLO message. Many system administrators are confused by this. Don't be. The STARTTLS negotiation takes place "outside" of the email exchange. STARTTLS creates the encrypted tunnel through which the mail travels. The first EHLO, the server's STARTTLS advertisement, the client's STARTTLS command, and the server's TLS ready response are all used to create the tunnel. The second EHLO command and all that follows it are part of the standard SMTP protocol exchange, which is sent inside the encrypted tunnel. Note that this SMTP protocol exchange is displayed by the sendmail -v command as clear text. The mail stream is only encrypted on the network. Within the end systems, the mail stream is clear text.

The effect of the STARTTLS protocol can be indirectly observed in the headers of the mail message that passed through the encrypted tunnel. The following headers are from the test message sent by the sendmail -Am -v -t command used above:

```
Return-Path: <craig@rodent.wrotethebook.com>
Received: from rodent.wrotethebook.com (rodent.wrotethebook.com
    [192.168.0.3])
        by chef.wrotethebook.com (8.12.9/8.12.9) with ESMTP id hOUGn9P7001230
        (version=TLSv1/SSLv3 cipher=EDH-RSA-DES-CBC3-SHA bits=168 verify=OK)
        for <craig@chef.wrotethebook.com>; Thu, 30 Jan 2003 11:49:10 -0500
Received: (from root@localhost)
        by rodent.wrotethebook.com (8.12.9/8.12.9) id hOUGvpSD010157;
        Thu, 30 Jan 2003 11:57:51 -0500
Date: Thu, 30 Jan 2003 11:57:51 -0500
Message-Id: <200301301657.hOUGvpSD010157@rodent.wrotethebook.com>
To: craig@chef.wrotethebook.com
From: craig@rodent.wrotethebook.com
Subject: First STARTTLS test
```

The Received: header generated by *chef.wrotethebook.com*, which is the STARTTLS server in this exchange, shows the TLS characteristics of the link over which the mail was received. The header displays the version of the TLS protocol that was used for the connection, the type of encryption used for the connection, the number of bits used for the encryption, and whether the client's certificate was verified. Because this information is only placed in the header when TLS is used for the connection, it tells us that the client is properly configured to use TLS when communicating with this server.

See Also

Recipes 8.2 and 8.3 cover how certificates and keys are created. Chapter 1 provides additional information on compiling sendmail. The *sendmail* book covers STARTTLS in section 10.10.

8.5 Relaying Based on the CA

Problem

You have been asked to configure sendmail to grant relaying privileges to START-TLS clients that present a certificate signed by a trusted certificate authority.

Solution

Make sure that OpenSSL is installed as described in the Introduction and that sendmail is compiled with STARTTLS support as shown in Recipes 1.6 and 1.7.

Identify each trusted certificate authority in the *access* database using CERTISSUER: entries. The key field of each entry begins with the CERTISSUER: tag followed by the distinguished name of the CA. The return value of the entry is the keyword RELAY, indicating that any host presenting a certificate signed by the trusted CA is granted relaying privileges.

Create a STARTTLS sendmail configuration and add the *access_db* feature. Here are samples of the defines that configure STARTTLS and the FEATURE macro that enables the *access* database:

```
dnl Point to the CA certificate directory
define(`confCACERT_PATH', `/etc/mail/certs')
dnl Point to the root CA's certificate
define(`confCACERT', `/etc/mail/certs/cacert.pem')
dnl Point to the certificate used for inbound connections
define(`confSERVER_CERT', `/etc/mail/certs/cert.pem')
dnl Point to the private key used for inbound connections
define(`confSERVER_KEY', `/etc/mail/certs/key.pem')
dnl Point to the certificate used for outbound connections
define(`confCLIENT_CERT', `/etc/mail/certs/cert.pem')
dnl Point to the private key used for outbound connections
define(`confCLIENT_KEY', `/etc/mail/certs/key.pem')
dnl Enable the access database
FEATURE(`access_db')
```

Rebuild the *sendmail.cf* file, copy the new *sendmail.cf* file to */etc/mail*, and restart sendmail. Recipe 1.8 provides an example of these steps.

Discussion

TLS can provide strong authentication of the end points and encryption of the data stream. Despite these important security features, establishing a STARTTLS connection is not, by itself, enough to grant relaying privileges. A test shows this:

```
# sendmail -Am -v -t
To: craig@crab.wrotethebook.com
From: craig@rodent.wrotethebook.com
```

Subject: Attempt to relay after successful TLS connection

Ctrl-D
```
craig@crab.wrotethebook.com... Connecting to chef.wrotethebook.com. via relay...
220 chef.wrotethebook.com ESMTP Sendmail 8.12.9/8.12.9; Fri, 22 Aug 2003 12:01:37 -
0400
>>> EHLO rodent.wrotethebook.com
250-chef.wrotethebook.com Hello rodent.wrotethebook.com [192.168.0.3], pleased to
meet you
250-ENHANCEDSTATUSCODES
250-PIPELINING
250-EXPN
250-VERB
250-8BITMIME
250-SIZE
250-DSN
250-ETRN
250-AUTH DIGEST-MD5 CRAM-MD5
250-STARTTLS
250 DELIVERBY
250 HELP
>>> STARTTLS
220 2.0.0 Ready to start TLS
>>> EHLO rodent.wrotethebook.com
250-chef.wrotethebook.com Hello rodent.wrotethebook.com [192.168.0.3], pleased to
meet you
250-ENHANCEDSTATUSCODES
250-PIPELINING
250-EXPN
250-VERB
250-8BITMIME
250-SIZE
250-DSN
250-ETRN
250-AUTH EXTERNAL DIGEST-MD5 CRAM-MD5
250-DELIVERBY
250 HELP
>>> MAIL From:<craig@rodent.wrotethebook.com> SIZE=102 AUTH=craig@rodent.
wrotethebook.com
250 2.1.0 <craig@rodent.wrotethebook.com>... Sender ok
>>> RCPT To:<craig@crab.wrotethebook.com>
>>> DATA
550 5.7.1 <craig@crab.wrotethebook.com>... Relaying denied
503 5.0.0 Need RCPT (recipient)
>>> RSET
250 2.0.0 Reset state
craig... Connecting to local...
craig... Sent
Closing connection to chef.wrotethebook.com.
>>> QUIT
221 2.0.0 chef.wrotethebook.com closing connection
```

In response to the first EHLO command, the server advertises STARTTLS. The client then issues a STARTTLS command, and the server responds that it is ready. This indicates that an encrypted session will start. The second EHLO command is the first SMTP command in the encrypted session. It is followed by a MAIL From: and a RCPT To: command. Notice the response to the RCPT To: command.* The message is rejected with a "Relaying denied" error, even though it comes in the midst of an encrypted session. Clearly, TLS does not, by itself, authorize relaying. It is up to the sendmail administrator to decide when and how TLS authentication data should be used. One way to use TLS data is through the *access* database.

The ${verify} and ${cert_issuer} macros are used in the Local_Relay_Auth ruleset to authorize relaying. ${verify} contains OK when sendmail is able to verify the CA signature on the certificate received from a remote site. sendmail takes the distinguished name of the CA that signed the certificate from the Issuer field of the certificate and stores it in the macro ${cert_issuer}. If ${verify} equals OK, sendmail searches the *access* database for a CERTISSUER: entry that matches the ${cert_issuer} value. If a match is found, the action specified by the CERTISSUER: entry is taken. If no match is found, processing continues normally. Here is an example of adding a CERTISSUER: entry to the *access* database:

```
# cd /etc/mail
# cat >> access
CERTISSUER:/C=US/ST=Maryland/L=Gaithersburg/O=WroteTheBook/CN=chef.wrotethebook.com/
Email=craig@chef.wrotethebook.com     RELAY
Ctrl-D
# makemap hash access < access
```

Given the *access* database entry just shown, a site that presents a certificate signed by */C=US/ST=Maryland/L=Gaithersburg/O=WroteTheBook/CN=chef.wrotethebook.com/ Email=craig@chef.wrotethebook.com* is granted relaying privileges. */C=US/ ST=Maryland/L=Gaithersburg/O=WroteTheBook/CN=chef.wrotethebook.com/Email= craig@chef.wrotethebook.com* is the complete DN of the private CA created in Recipe 8.1. Therefore, any host with a certificate signed by our private CA is allowed to relay mail.

A DN can contain almost any character. Several characters, however, have special meaning to sendmail and others are difficult to enter into the *access* database. For these reasons, the DN stored in the *access* database uses a special format for storing nonprintable characters, the space, the tab, <, >, (,), ", and +. These characters are stored as their hexadecimal values preceded by a plus. For example, a space becomes +20, a (becomes +25.

---

* Because of PIPELINING, which the EHLO response shows is offered on this system, some SMTP commands are sent together to save on TCP roundtrip times. For this reason, the response to the RCPT To: command follows the DATA command in this example.

After adding the CERTISSUER: entry to the *access* database, rerun the test shown earlier in this section. The RCPT To: command now produces the following result:

```
>>> RCPT To:<craig@crab.wrotethebook.com>
250 2.1.5 <craig@crab.wrotethebook.com>... Recipient ok
```

The client is now granted relaying privileges because a CA that is trusted to authorize relaying signed the client's certificate.

See Also

Recipe 8.4 covers the STARTTLS sendmail configuration used as the basis for this recipe. The private CA mentioned in the discussion of this recipe is covered in Recipe 8.1. Chapter 3 discusses the traditional techniques used to grant relaying privileges, including the *access* database. The content of a certificate, including the Issuer field, is covered in this chapter's Introduction. The *sendmail* book discusses using the *access* database for STARTTLS in section 10.10.8.

8.6 Relaying Based on the Certificate Subject

Problem

You want to grant relaying privileges to STARTTLS clients based on the client's identity, as specified by the client's certificate.

Solution

sendmail must be compiled with STARTTLS support, and OpenSSL must be installed. See Recipes 1.6 and 1.7 and the Introduction to this chapter for more information.

Create an *access* database entry using a CERTISSUER: tag followed by the DN of the trusted certificate authority to identify the CA that signed the client's certificate. The return value of the CERTISSUER: entry must be the keyword SUBJECT. Next, define each client that is to be granted relaying privileges using a CERTSUBJECT: entry in the *access* database. The key field of these entries begins with the CERTSUBJECT: tag followed by the DN of the client. The return value is the keyword RELAY.

Add the *access_db* feature to the STARTTLS sendmail configuration. Here are sample configuration lines:

```
dnl Point to the CA certificate directory
define(`confCACERT_PATH', `/etc/mail/certs')
dnl Point to the root CA's certificate
define(`confCACERT', `/etc/mail/certs/cacert.pem')
dnl Point to the certificate used for inbound connections
define(`confSERVER_CERT', `/etc/mail/certs/cert.pem')
```

```
dnl Point to the private key used for inbound connections
define(`confSERVER_KEY', `/etc/mail/certs/key.pem')
dnl Point to the certificate used for outbound connections
define(`confCLIENT_CERT', `/etc/mail/certs/cert.pem')
dnl Point to the private key used for outbound connections
define(`confCLIENT_KEY', `/etc/mail/certs/key.pem')
dnl Enable the access database
FEATURE(`access_db')
```

Following the example from Recipe 1.8, rebuild the *sendmail.cf* file. Install the new configuration, and restart sendmail.

Discussion

Successfully establishing a STARTTLS session does not, by itself, authorize relaying. (See Recipe 8.5 for a test that illustrates this.) However, the authentication data provided by STARTTLS can be used to control relaying via the *access* database. Here are *access* database entries that authorize relaying based on the value in the subject field of the client's certificate:

```
CERTISSUER:/C=US/ST=Maryland/L=Gaithersburg/O=WroteTheBook/CN=chef.wrotethebook.com/
SUBJECT
CERTSUBJECT:/C=US/ST=Maryland/L=Gaithersburg/O=WroteTheBook/CN=rodent.wrotethebook.
com/      RELAY
CERTSUBJECT:/C=US/ST=Maryland/L=Gaithersburg/O=WroteTheBook/CN=crab.wrotethebook.com/
RELAY
```

This example checks both the Issuer field and the Subject field from the certificate presented by the client. These values are matched against the *access* database by the Local_Relay_Auth ruleset, but only if the ${verify} macro contains the string OK, which indicates that the certificate was successfully verified by sendmail. Both fields are looked up because, before the subject of a certificate can be trusted, the CA that signs and verifies the certificate must be trusted.

If ${verify} returns OK, the Local_Relay_Auth ruleset looks for a CERTISSUER: entry containing the distinguished name from the Issuer field of the certificate. If a match is found and the action is RELAY, relaying is authorized for any system with a certificate signed by the specified CA, as described in Recipe 8.5. If a match is found and the action is SUBJECT, a second *access* database lookup is performed. This time, the ruleset looks for a CERTSUBJECT: entry containing the DN from the Subject field of the certificate. If it is found, and it contains the action RELAY, relaying is permitted for the specified client. If it is not found, normal processing continues. Relaying can still be granted to the client through any of the basic methods described in Chapter 3. STARTTLS provides an additional method of granting relaying privileges; it does not invalidate the other traditional methods.

A distinguished name may contain characters that require special formatting before the DN is entered in the *access* database. See the Discussion of Recipe 8.5 for information on this topic.

See Also

The *m4* configuration lines in this recipe are identical to those used in Recipe 8.5. Both use the *access* database and both are full STARTTLS configurations. See Recipe 8.5 for additional information. Chapter 3 discusses the traditional techniques used to grant relaying privileges, including the *access* database. The content of a certificate, including the Issuer and Subject fields, is covered in this chapter's Introduction. The *sendmail* book discusses using the *access* database for STARTTLS in section 10.10.8.

8.7   Requiring Outbound Encryption

Problem

To prevent mail bound for particular hosts from being sent in the clear, you have been asked to configure sendmail to only send mail to the specified hosts when the connection is satisfactorily encrypted.

Solution

OpenSSL and STARTTLS support are prerequisites. See the Introduction and Recipe 8.4 for additional details on these basic components.

Specify the level of encryption required for outbound connections using a TLS_Srv: entry in the *access* database. The key field of each entry is the tag TLS_Srv: followed by the domain name or IP address of the remote TLS server to which the local host will connect. The return value should contain the keyword ENCR: followed by the number of bits of encryption required when connecting to the specified remote host.

Create a sendmail configuration that supports STARTTLS and the *access* database. Here are sample STARTTLS defines and an *access_db* FEATURE macro:

```
dnl Point to the CA certificate directory
define(`confCACERT_PATH', `/etc/mail/certs')
dnl Point to the root CA's certificate
define(`confCACERT', `/etc/mail/certs/cacert.pem')
dnl Point to the certificate used for inbound connections
define(`confSERVER_CERT', `/etc/mail/certs/cert.pem')
dnl Point to the private key used for inbound connections
define(`confSERVER_KEY', `/etc/mail/certs/key.pem')
dnl Point to the certificate used for outbound connections
define(`confCLIENT_CERT', `/etc/mail/certs/cert.pem')
dnl Point to the private key used for outbound connections
define(`confCLIENT_KEY', `/etc/mail/certs/key.pem')
dnl Enable the access database
FEATURE(`access_db')
```

Rebuild and install the *sendmail.cf* file, then restart sendmail. See Recipe 1.8 as an example.

Discussion

Most mail is sent as clear text because the vast majority of systems do not use TLS. Even when STARTTLS is configured, a host sends outbound mail without regard to the level of encryption used. If you require encryption for mail sent to a specific site, you must tell sendmail about that requirement. The *access* database provides the means for informing sendmail of this requirement.

The TLS_Srv: entry defines the STARTTLS requirements for outbound connections. The format of the entry is:

    TLS_Srv:*name requirement*

TLS_Srv: is the required tag. *name* is the name of the remote TLS server, which can be defined by domain name or IP address. If the *name* field is blank, the entry applies to all outbound mail connections. Because most sendmail systems send mail to a wide variety of remote systems, some of which have STARTTLS and some of which do not, the name field is almost never blank. *requirement* is the keyword that tells sendmail what is required of this TLS connection.

The ENCR: keyword in the *requirement* field tells sendmail that encryption is required. The keyword is followed by the minimum number of encryption bits that must be used. Here is a sample *access* database entry:

    TLS_Srv:chef.wrotethebook.com   ENCR:168

This entry tells sendmail that when a connection is made to *chef.wrotethebook.com*, the connection must be encrypted with at least 168-bit encryption.

168-bits is the default level of encryption used on our sample STARTTLS connection. You can check the level of encryption used on your link by sending a test message and looking at the Received: header in the message. For example:

```
Received: from rodent.wrotethebook.com (rodent.wrotethebook.com
    [192.168.0.3])
        by chef.wrotethebook.com (8.12.9/8.12.9) with ESMTP id
h13GqD15001443
        (version=TLSv1/SSLv3 cipher=EDH-RSA-DES-CBC3-SHA bits=168 verify=OK)
        for <craig@chef.wrotethebook.com>; Mon, 3 Feb 2003 11:52:14 -0500
```

This header tells you that 168-bits encryption is used (bits=168). If the TLS_Srv: entry shown above was installed on *rodent*, mail would flow to *chef* because the link between the two systems has a sufficient level of encryption. However, if the link between the two systems did not meet the minimum standard of encryption, the client would abort the connection before sending the mail, as this test demonstrates:

```
# sendmail -Am -v -t
To: craig@chef.wrotethebook.com
From: craig@rodent.wrotethebook.com
Subject: Test ENCR:168 with no TLS link

Ctrl-D
```

```
craig@chef.wrotethebook.com... Connecting to chef.wrotethebook.com. via esmtp...
220 chef.wrotethebook.com ESMTP Sendmail 8.12.9/8.12.9; Fri, 22 Aug 2003 12:01:37 -
0400
>>> EHLO rodent.wrotethebook.com
250-chef.wrotethebook.com Hello rodent.wrotethebook.com [192.168.0.3], pleased to
meet you
250-ENHANCEDSTATUSCODES
250-PIPELINING
250-EXPN
250-VERB
250-8BITMIME
250-SIZE
250-DSN
250-ETRN
250-AUTH DIGEST-MD5 CRAM-MD5
250-DELIVERBY
250 HELP
>>> QUIT
221 2.0.0 chef.wrotethebook.com closing connection
craig@chef.wrotethebook.com    Deferred: 403 4.7.0 encryption too weak 0 less than
168
Closing connection to chef.wrotethebook.com.
```

In this case, the server fails to offer STARTTLS, while the client's *access* database
requires 168-bit encryption on this link. The client terminates the connection with
an "encryption too weak" error message. The message displays the number of
encryption bits used by the server (0 in this case because TLS did not start) and the
number required by the client (168 in this example). The SMTP response code of this
error message is 403, and the DSN code is 4.7.0. Each code starts with a 4, which
indicates that this is a temporary failure. The keyword "Deferred" in the message
indicates that sendmail will attempt to deliver this message again during the next
queue run.

Treating a STARTTLS failure as a temporary failure, which is the default, is generally correct. Normally, a server is identified in a TLS_Srv: entry only when the server
actually offers STARTTLS. If the server fails to successfully create a TLS connection
with the client, the failure is probably temporary. However, it is up to you to decide
whether the failure should be considered temporary. The requirement field in a TLS_
Srv: entry can be preceded by the string TEMP+ to select a temporary failure, which is
the default, or by the string PERM+ to select a permanent error. For example, assume
the *access* database on *rodent* contained the following TLS_Srv: entry:

```
TLS_Srv:chef.wrotethebook.com        PERM+ENCR:168
```

If *chef.wrotethebook.com* does not offer at least 168-bit encryption, the client terminates the session and returns the mail to the sender. No more attempts are made to
deliver the mail. The sender sees the following error in the returned message:

```
----- The following addresses had permanent fatal errors -----
craig@chef.wrotethebook.com
    (reason: 503 5.7.0 encryption too weak 0 less than 168)
```

Use the define TLS_PERM_ERR as an alternative to adding PERM+ to the requirement field. The following line added to the sendmail configuration changes the default from a temporary failure to a permanent failure:

```
define(`TLS_PERM_ERR')
```

With this setting, individual actions must be flagged as temporary failures using TEMP+.

The search for TLS_Srv: *access* database entries occurs in the tls_server ruleset, which is called by the client when the client is ready to issue the STARTTLS command. The tls_server ruleset is called with the value returned by ${verify} in its workspace. The tls_server ruleset makes three attempts to find a TLS_Srv: match. It first uses ruleset D to find a TLS_Srv: entry that matches the hostname returned by ${server_name}. If no match is found, it then uses ruleset A to find a TLS_Srv: entry that matches the value returned by ${server_addr}. If there is still no match, it looks for a TLS_Srv: entry with a blank name field. These searches process all possible matches for a given domain name and IP address. For example, for a connection to *foo.bar.example.com* with IP address 192.168.23.45, the following lookups would happen, in the order listed, until a match was found:

```
TLS_Srv:foo.bar.example.com
TLS_Srv:bar.example.com
TLS_Srv:example.com
TLS_Srv:com
TLS_Srv:192.168.23.45
TLS_Srv:192.168.23
TLS_Srv:192.168
TLS_Srv:192
TLS_Srv:
```

The ruleset TLS_connection is called and passed anything returned by the *access* database lookups. It is TLS_connection that processes the ENCR: requirement field and compares the number of bits from that field to the number of bits returned by ${cipher_bits}. If the macro ${cipher_bits} is less than the value from the requirement field, an error message is displayed and the connection ends.

The *m4* macro LOCAL_TLS_SERVER allows you to add custom *sendmail.cf* rewrite rules to the beginning of the tls_server process. Put the LOCAL_TLS_SERVER macro at the end of the master configuration file and list the custom rewrite rules after the macro.

See Also

Recipes 8.8 and 8.9 cover related *access* database entries. In particular, VERIFY: is an alternative action keyword that can be used to implement this recipe. See Recipe 8.9 for details on the VERIFY: keyword. Recipes 8.5 and 8.6 also describe how the *access* database is used with STARTTLS. The basic STARTTLS recipe upon which this recipe is built is covered in Recipe 8.4. The *sendmail* book covers the use of the *access* database with STARTTLS in section 10.10.8.

8.8   Requiring Inbound Encryption

Problem

You have been asked to configure sendmail to require that the connection is satisfactorily encrypted before accepting mail from specified hosts.

Solution

All configurations require OpenSSL, as described in the Introduction. If your system does not have a basic setup, begin there.

Specify the level of encryption required for inbound connections using a TLS_Clt: entry in the *access* database. The key field of each entry is the tag TLS_Clt: followed by the domain name or IP address of the remote TLS client that will initiate the connection. The return value should contain the keyword ENCR: followed by the number of bits of encryption required before accepting a connection from the specified remote host.

Add the STARTTLS defines and the *access_db* feature to the sendmail configuration. Here are sample additions to the configuration:

```
dnl Point to the CA certificate directory
define(`confCACERT_PATH', `/etc/mail/certs')
dnl Point to the root CA's certificate
define(`confCACERT', `/etc/mail/certs/cacert.pem')
dnl Point to the certificate used for inbound connections
define(`confSERVER_CERT', `/etc/mail/certs/cert.pem')
dnl Point to the private key used for inbound connections
define(`confSERVER_KEY', `/etc/mail/certs/key.pem')
dnl Point to the certificate used for outbound connections
define(`confCLIENT_CERT', `/etc/mail/certs/cert.pem')
dnl Point to the private key used for outbound connections
define(`confCLIENT_KEY', `/etc/mail/certs/key.pem')
dnl Enable the access database
FEATURE(`access_db')
```

Follow the example in Recipe 1.8 to build the new *sendmail.cf* file, install it, and restart sendmail.

Discussion

The TLS_Clt: *access* database entry uses the same format as the TLS_Srv: entry covered in the Discussion of Recipe 8.7. All of the fields described for the TLS_Srv: entry—*name*, *requirement*, TEMP+, and PERM+—are used in exactly the same way for the TLS_CLT: entry. The difference is that the TLS_Clt: entry is used by the server to check for any special requirements before accepting mail from the client. The *name* field of the `TLS_Clt:` entry defines the domain name or IP address of the remote TLS client. When the name or address of a client matches a `TLS_Clt:` entry, the *requirement* field of the entry is used to define the conditions imposed on the client before mail is accepted. A sample `TLS_Clt:` entry is:

```
TLS_Clt:rodent.wrotethebook.com       ENCR:168
```

This entry tells sendmail that a connection from *rodent.wrotethebook.com* must be encrypted with at least 168-bit encryption. If it isn't, mail from the client is rejected, as this test from the client *rodent* shows:

```
# sendmail -Am -v -t
To: craig@chef.wrotethebook.com
From: craig@rodent.wrotethebook.com
Subject: Test the TLS_Clt: entry

Ctrl-D
craig@chef.wrotethebook.com... Connecting to chef.wrotethebook.com. via esmtp...
220 chef.wrotethebook.com ESMTP Sendmail 8.12.9/8.12.9; Fri, 22 Aug 2003 12:01:37 -
0400
>>> EHLO rodent.wrotethebook.com
250-chef.wrotethebook.com Hello rodent.wrotethebook.com [192.168.0.3], pleased to
meet you
250-ENHANCEDSTATUSCODES
250-PIPELINING
250-EXPN
250-VERB
250-8BITMIME
250-SIZE
250-DSN
250-ETRN
250-AUTH DIGEST-MD5 CRAM-MD5
250-STARTTLS
250-DELIVERBY
250 HELP
>>> STARTTLS
220 2.0.0 Ready to start TLS
>>> EHLO rodent.wrotethebook.com
250-chef.wrotethebook.com Hello rodent.wrotethebook.com [192.168.0.3], pleased to
meet you
250 ENHANCEDSTATUSCODES
250-PIPELINING
250-EXPN
250-VERB
250-8BITMIME
250-SIZE
250-DSN
250-ETRN
250-AUTH DIGEST-MD5 CRAM-MD5
250-DELIVERBY
250 HELP
>>> MAIL From:<craig@rodent.wrotethebook.com>
```

```
403 4.7.0 encryption too weak 56 less than 168
craig@chef.wrotethebook.com... Deferred: 403 4.7.0 encryption too weak 56 less than
168
Closing connection to chef.wrotethebook.com.
>>> QUIT
221 2.0.0 chef.wrotethebook.com closing connection
```

In this test, the error message "encryption too weak" is in response to the client's MAIL From: command. The server checks the *access* database TLS_Clt: entries in the tls_client ruleset. That ruleset is called at two different points in the SMTP protocol exchange. First, it is called when the STARTTLS command is received, and it is called again when the MAIL From command is received. When the tls_client ruleset is called, it is passed the value returned by ${verify}, the literal $|, and either of the keywords STARTTLS or MAIL.

The tls_client ruleset is very similar to the tls_server ruleset described in Recipe 8.7. tls_client first uses ruleset D to look for a TLS_Clt: entry that matches the value found in ${client_name}. If no match is found, it uses ruleset A to look for a TLS_Clt: entry that matches the address in the ${client_addr} macro. If still no match is found, tls_client looks for a TLS_Clt: entry with a blank name field. tls_client would do the following lookups for a connection from a client named *foo.bar.example.com* that had the IP address 192.168.23.45, until a match was found:

```
TLS_Clt:foo.bar.example.com
TLS_Clt:bar.example.com
TLS_Clt:example.com
TLS_Clt:com
TLS_Clt:192.168.23.45
TLS_Clt:192.168.23
TLS_Clt:192.168
TLS_Clt:192
TLS_Clt:
```

tls_client then calls TLS_connection and passes that ruleset anything it has obtained from the *access* database. The TLS_connection ruleset checks to see if the connection meets the requirements defined by the TLS_Clt: record.

The *m4* macro LOCAL_TLS_CLIENT provides a hook into the tls_client ruleset. Use the macro to add custom *sendmail.cf* rewrite rules to the beginning of the tls_client process.

See Also

Recipes 8.7 and 8.9 cover related *access* database entries. In particular, VERIFY: is an alternative action keyword that can be used to implement this recipe. See Recipe 8.9 for details on the VERIFY: keyword. Recipes 8.5 and 8.6 also describe how the *access* database is used with STARTTLS. The STARTTLS recipe upon which this recipe is built is covered in Recipe 8.4. The *sendmail* book covers the use of the *access* database with STARTTLS in section 10.10.8.

8.9 Requiring a Verified Certificate

Problem

You have been asked to configure sendmail to exchange mail with a specified host only when the certificate provided by that host is verified.

Solution

The system must have OpenSSL installed and sendmail compiled with STARTTLS support before attempting to implement this recipe. See this chapter's Introduction and Chapter 1 for more information about OpenSSL and about recompiling sendmail.

Create an *access* database entry for each host that is required to provide a verified certificate. Use the TLS_Clt: tag if the remote host initiates the connection into the local host, or use the TLS_Srv: tag if the local host initiates the connection to the remote host. Use the VERIFY keyword in the return field to require a validated certificate from the remote system. Add a colon and a numeric value after the VERIFY keyword to require a level of encryption in addition to the verified certificate.

Create a STARTTLS sendmail configuration that includes the *access_db* feature. Here are sample lines that might be added to the sendmail configuration:

```
dnl Point to the CA certificate directory
define(`confCACERT_PATH', `/etc/mail/certs')
dnl Point to the root CA's certificate
define(`confCACERT', `/etc/mail/certs/cacert.pem')
dnl Point to the certificate used for inbound connections
define(`confSERVER_CERT', `/etc/mail/certs/cert.pem')
dnl Point to the private key used for inbound connections
define(`confSERVER_KEY', `/etc/mail/certs/key.pem')
dnl Point to the certificate used for outbound connections
define(`confCLIENT_CERT', `/etc/mail/certs/cert.pem')
dnl Point to the private key used for outbound connections
define(`confCLIENT_KEY', `/etc/mail/certs/key.pem')
dnl Enable the access database
FEATURE(`access_db')
```

Rebuild the *sendmail.cf* file, copy the new *sendmail.cf* file to */etc/mail*, and restart sendmail, as shown in Recipe 1.8.

Discussion

When both end points are properly configured to support STARTTLS, sendmail uses TLS to encrypt the mail transport even if the end points do not present verified certificates. In this context, a verified certificate is one signed by a CA that sendmail trusts. If sendmail can verify the signature on the certificate, sendmail sets the ${verify} macro to OK. When a certificate is received that cannot be verified,

${verify} is set to one of several possible values, all of which are covered in the Introduction of this chapter. For example, NO is one of the values indicating that the certificate was not verified. Yet TLS is still used to encrypt the link even when ${VERIFY} is set to NO, as can be seen in the Received: header shown below:

```
Return-Path: <craig@horseshoe.wrotethebook.com>
Received: from horseshoe.wrotethebook.com (horseshoe.wrotethebook.com [192.168.0.2])
        by chef.wrotethebook.com (8.12.9/8.12.9) with ESMTP id h14HeQAd001228
        (version=TLSv1/SSLv3 cipher=EDH-RSA-DES-CBC3-SHA bits=168 verify=NO)
        for <craig@chef.wrotethebook.com>; Tue, 4 Feb 2003 12:40:27 -0500
Received: (from root@localhost)
        by horseshoe.wrotethebook.com (8.12.9/8.12.9) id h14Hnn91001180;
        Tue, 4 Feb 2003 12:49:49 -0500
Date: Tue, 4 Feb 2003 12:49:49 -0500
Message-Id: <200302041749.h14Hnn91001180@horseshoe.wrotethebook.com>
To: craig@chef.wrotethebook.com
From: craig@horseshoe.wrotethebook.com
Subject: Test self-signed certificate
```

The first Received: header shows that the link was encrypted with 168-bit encryption, and that no certificate was verified for *horseshoe.wrotethebook.com*. The implications of this are two-fold:

- First, it is possible to use STARTTLS without recourse to a certificate authority if the only thing you want to do is encrypt the link.
- Second, optional configuration is required to limit STARTTLS connections to those system with verifiable certificates.

The VERIFY requirement is used with TLS_Clt: or TLS_Srv: to require a verified certificate. When VERIFY is specified, the current value stored in the ${verify} macro must be OK. Otherwise, the connection is rejected. Here are some example *access* database entries:

```
TLS_Clt:crab.wrotethebook.com          VERIFY
TLS_Srv:smtp.wrotethebook.com          VERIFY:168
TLS_Clt:horseshoe.wrotethebook.com     VERIFY:168
```

The first *access* database entry only accepts inbound mail from *crab.wrotethebook.com* if the certificate *crab* presents is verified. The TLS_Clt: entries are processed by the tls_client ruleset. See Recipe 8.8 for a description of that ruleset.

The second *access* database entry tells sendmail that an outbound connection made to the server *smtp.wrotethebook.com* must use 168-bit encryption and that the certificate presented by the server must be verified. If either of these conditions is not met, the connection is terminated. The TLS_Srv: entry is processed by the tls_server ruleset covered in Recipe 8.7.

The last entry requires 168-bit encryption and a verified certificate for the TLS client *horseshoe.wrotethebook.com*. If *chef.wrotethebook.com* had been configured with that entry, the mail that created the Received: header shown at the beginning of this discussion would not have been accepted. As the Received: header made clear, *horseshoe* used 168-bit encryption, but it did not present a verifiable certificate. A test run from *horseshoe* shows the impact of adding this TLS_Clt: entry to the configuration of the receiving host:

```
# sendmail -Am -v -t
To: craig@chef.wrotethebook.com
From: craig@horseshoe.wrotethebook.com
Subject: Test VERIFY:168

Ctrl-D
craig@chef.wrotethebook.com... Connecting to chef.wrotethebook.com. via esmtp...
220 chef.wrotethebook.com ESMTP Sendmail 8.12.9/8.12.9; Fri, 22 Aug 2003 12:01:37 -
0400
>>> EHLO horseshoe.wrotethebook.com
250 chef.wrotethebook.com Hello horseshoe.wrotethebook.com [192.168.0.2], pleased to
meet you
250-ENHANCEDSTATUSCODES
250-PIPELINING
250-EXPN
250-VERB
250-8BITMIME
250-SIZE
250-DSN
250-ETRN
250-AUTH DIGEST-MD5 CRAM-MD5
250-STARTTLS
250-DELIVERBY
250 HELP
>>> STARTTLS
220 2.0.0 Ready to start TLS
>>> EHLO horseshoe.wrotethebook.com
250-chef.wrotethebook.com Hello horseshoe.wrotethebook.com [192.168.0.2], pleased to
meet you
250 ENHANCEDSTATUSCODES
250-PIPELINING
250-EXPN
250-VERB
250-8BITMIME
250-SIZE
250-DSN
250 ETRN
250-AUTH DIGEST-MD5 CRAM-MD5
250-DELIVERBY
250 HELP
>>> MAIL From:<craig@horseshoe.wrotethebook.com>
403 4.7.0 not authenticated
craig@chef.wrotethebook.com... Deferred: 403 4.7.0 not authenticated
Closing connection to chef.wrotethebook.com.
>>> QUIT
221 2.0.0 chef.wrotethebook.com closing connection
```

The STARTTLS command is issued and accepted. The second EHLO command indicates the successful start of the encrypted session. However, the response to the MAIL From: command is the error "not authenticated" because a TLS_Clt: entry in the *access* database on *chef* required a certificate signed by a trusted certificate authority.

Notice that the response codes 403 and 4.7.0 are used on the error message. The 4 at the start of each code indicates that this is a temporary failure. In response to these temporary failures, the client will queue the message and attempt to deliver it during subsequent queue runs. By default, errors generated by a VERIFY requirement are temporary errors. Use PERM+ to make the error a permanent failure in order to prevent the remote system from resending the message at each queue run. For example:

```
TLS_Clt:horseshoe.wrotethebook.com     PERM+VERIFY:168
```

See Recipe 8.7 for more information on PERM+, TEMP+, and the define TLS_PERM_ERR, all of which control whether TLS errors are permanent or temporary.

The test shown above points out the difference between encryption and authentication. Encryption can be used even if the end points have not been authenticated. Therefore, special privileges, such as relaying, cannot be extended on the basis of the level of encryption used. Special privileges require authentication. Happily, TLS can provide both encryption and authentication when they are needed.

See Also

Recipes 8.7 and 8.8 provide additional examples of the TLS_Clt: and TLS_Srv: *access* database entries. Recipes 8.5 and 8.6 describe other ways the *access* database is used with STARTTLS. This recipe contains *m4* commands described in Recipe 8.4. The *sendmail* book covers the use of the *access* database with STARTTLS in section 10.10.8.

8.10   Requiring TLS for a Recipient

Problem

You have been asked to ensure that encryption and authentication are used for mail addressed to specific recipients.

Solution

Install OpenSSL and recompile sendmail with STARTTLS support as described in the Introduction and in Recipes 1.6 and 1.7.

Use TLS_Rcpt: *access* database entries to define those recipients that require TLS security and to specify the level of security required. The key field of each entry contains the tag TLS_Rcpt: and the full or partial address of the recipient. The return value defines the level of security required, and it can be either the keyword `ENCR:`, followed by the number of bits of encryption required, or the keyword `VERIFY`, optionally followed by a number of bits of encryption.

Add the *access_db* feature and the STARTTLS defines to the sendmail configuration. Here are sample lines that could be added to the configuration:

```
dnl Point to the CA certificate directory
define(`confCACERT_PATH', `/etc/mail/certs')
dnl Point to the root CA's certificate
define(`confCACERT', `/etc/mail/certs/cacert.pem')
dnl Point to the certificate used for inbound connections
define(`confSERVER_CERT', `/etc/mail/certs/cert.pem')
dnl Point to the private key used for inbound connections
define(`confSERVER_KEY', `/etc/mail/certs/key.pem')
dnl Point to the certificate used for outbound connections
define(`confCLIENT_CERT', `/etc/mail/certs/cert.pem')
dnl Point to the private key used for outbound connections
define(`confCLIENT_KEY', `/etc/mail/certs/key.pem')
dnl Enable the access database
FEATURE(`access_db')
```

Rebuild the *sendmail.cf* file, copy the new *sendmail.cf* file to */etc/mail*, and restart sendmail. See Recipe 1.8 for an example.

Discussion

The `TLS_Clt:` and `TLS_Srv:` *access* database entries used in Recipes 8.7, 8.8, and 8.9 enforce minimum TLS security requirements based on the name or address of the remote host. sendmail checks for ${client_name} and ${client_addr} in `TLS_CLT:` entries for inbound connections, and for ${server_name} and ${server_addr} in `TLS_Srv:` entries for outbound connections. These entries ensure that connections between the specified remote hosts and local host are secured, but these entries do not guarantee that mail addressed to a specific user will be secure. There is no guarantee because mail can reach recipients over multiple paths—some of which may be secured and others may not. Look at some sample MX records:

```
wrotethebook.com.      IN MX     10  chef.wrotethebook.com.
wrotethebook.com.      IN MX     20  rodent.wrotethebook.com.
wrotethebook.com.      IN MX     30  mail.example.com.
```

Given these three MX records, mail bound for *pat@wrotethebook.com* could go over a connection to *chef*, *rodent*, or *mail.example.com*. Assume that *chef* and *rodent* have STARTTLS support but that *mail.example.com* does not. Mail sent from our system to *pat@wrotethebook.com* would be encrypted if the delivery connection was made to *chef* or *rodent*, but the mail would be sent as clear text if the connection was made to *mail.example.com*. We don't run *mail.example.com*, so we can't change the way it is configured—what we can do is ensure that mail sent to *pat@wrotethebook.com* only goes via an adequately encrypted connection. The following `TLS_Rcpt:` entry ensures that mail is only sent to *pat@wrotethebook.com* if the remote host has presented a verified certificate and the link is using 168-bit encryption:

```
TLS_Rcpt:pat@wrotethebook.com    VERIFY:168
```

The basic format of the `TLS_Rcpt:` entry is:

```
TLS_Rcpt:recipient      requirements+suffix++suffix
```

The string `TLS_Rcpt:` is the required tag for this database record. *recipient* is the full or partial email address of the recipient. The recipient address can be:

- A full address in the format *user@host.domain*. This format matches a specific user on a specific host. `TLS_Rcpt:craig@crab.wrotethebook.com` is an example.

- A hostname in the format *host.domain*; e.g., `TLS_Rcpt:crab.wrotethebook.com`. Any user on the specified host is matched.

- A domain name to match every user on every host in the specified domain. For example, `TLS Rcpt:wrotethebook.com` would match every recipient in the *wrotethebook.com* domain.

- A username written in the form *user@*; e.g., `TLS_Rcpt:craig@`. This format matches any recipient with the specified username on any host in any domain.

- A blank field, which matches every possible recipient address. This format is used to define a default security requirement for all outbound mail.

The *requirements* field defines the minimum security requirements that must be met before mail is sent to the recipient. The keyword `ENCR` or `VERIFY` can be used in the *requirements* field to require a level of encryption or a verified certificate. For example `ENCR:168` requires a minimum of 168-bit encryption, although it does not require a verified certificate from the remote server. The `VERIFY` keyword does require a verified certificate and optionally can be combined with a numeric value to also require a level of encryption. For example, `VERIFY:168` requires a verified certificate from the remote server and 168-bit encryption on the link. Recipes 8.7, 8.8, and 8.9 provide examples of the `ENCR` and `VERIFY` keywords. The sample `TLS_Rcpt:` entry just shown uses `VERIFY:168` to require authentication and encryption.

The impact of the sample entry is seen when mail addressed to *pat@wrotethebook.com* is routed to the backup MX server *mail.example.com*:

```
# sendmail -Am -v -t
To: pat@wrotethebook.com
From: david@wrotethebook.net
Subject: Test TLS_Rcpt:

Ctrl-D
pat@wrotethebook.com... Connecting to mail.example.com. via esmtp...
220 mail.example.com ESMTP Sendmail 8.12.9/8.12.9; Wed, 5 Feb 2003 15:33:02 -0500
>>> EHLO wrotethebook.net
```

```
250-mail.example.com Hello IDENT:24znrK/hAUFBK67n3St2d8DU/5bqb70s@chef [192.168.10.
8], pleased to meet you
250-ENHANCEDSTATUSCODES
250-PIPELINING
250-EXPN
250-VERB
250-8BITMIME
250-SIZE
250-DSN
250-ETRN
250-AUTH GSSAPI DIGEST-MD5 CRAM-MD5
250-DELIVERBY
250 HELP
>>> MAIL From:<david@wrotethebook.net> SIZE=92 AUTH=david@wrotethebook.net
250 2.1.0 <david@wrotethebook.net>... Sender ok
pat@wrotethebook.com... Deferred
>>> RSET
250 2.0.0 Reset state
Closing connection to mail.example.com.
>>> QUIT
221 2.0.0 mail.example.com closing connection
```

The backup MX server *mail.example.com* does not offer the STARTTLS service in its response to the EHLO command. Therefore, the client does not issue a STARTTLS command. Instead, the client issues the MAIL From: command. The client then checks for a TLS_Rcpt: entry in the *access* database, finds it, and terminates the session with the message:

```
pat@wrotethebook.com ... Deferred
```

This message indicates that the mail has been queued and will be sent again during the next queue run, which means that sendmail is treating this delivery problem as a temporary error. By default, most TLS connection problems are treated as temporary failures. You can change by using the TLS_PERM_ERR define in the master configuration file, or you can override the default for a specific TLS_Rcpt: entry by adding PERM+ to the entry. For example, the following entry would make the failure shown above a permanent failure:

```
TLS_Rcpt:pat@wrotethebook.com      PERM+VERIFY:168
```

However, it is not a good idea to make this a permanent failure. Failures caused by TLS_Rcpt: entries should be temporary failures. The failure happened because the connection went to a backup MX server that doesn't support STARTTLS. When the mail is resent during the queue run, it will probably go to the primary MX server, which does have STARTTLS, and therefore, the mail will be successfully delivered. Making the failure permanent undermines the error recovery potential inherent in the sendmail queue process. It is more likely that you would use TEMP+ to make the failure temporary if, for some reason, the default for TLS failures had been set to permanent using the TLS_PERM_ERR define. Recipes 8.7, 8.8, and 8.9 cover TLS_PERM_ERR, PERM+, and TEMP+.

The other *access* database entries covered in this chapter also use the ENCR:, VERIFY:, PERM+, and TEMP+ keywords. However, the TLS_Rcpt: record has more options than these other *access* entries. The *requirements* field of the TLS_Rcpt: entry can be followed by one or more optional values. These options are called *suffixes* because they are added to the TLS_Rcpt: record after the ENCR or VERIFY keyword. The first suffix is added after a single plus sign (+), and subsequent suffixes are added with two plus signs (++). The possible suffixes are:

CN:*name*

> The CN option checks the common name (CN) of the subject from the certificate presented by the server. sendmail holds the CN of the subject in the macro ${cn_subject}. If *name* is provided, the value of *name* must match the value stored in the ${cn_subject} macro. If *name* is left blank, the value returned by ${cn_subject} must match the value returned by ${server_name}. The macro ${server_name} holds the hostname of the remote host to which the client is currently connected, as determined by a reverse domain lookup of the IP address used by TCP for the current connection.

CS:*name*

> The CS option compares *name* against the value returned by ${cert_subject}. The macro ${cert_subject} holds the distinguished name from the Subject field of the certificate presented by the remote server. The DN and *name* must match.

CI:*name*

> The CI option compares *name* against the value returned by ${cert_issuer}. The macro ${cert_issuer} holds the distinguished name from the Issuer field of the certificate presented by the remote server. The value in ${cert_issuer} and the value in the *name* field must match.

Here is a sample TLS_Rcpt: entry with multiple suffixes:[*]

```
TLS_Rcpt:pat@wrotethebook.com VERIFY:168+CN++CI:/C=US/ST=Maryland/L=Gaithersburg/
O=WroteTheBook/CN=chef.wrotethebook.com/
```

This TLS_Rcpt: entry requires 168-bit encryption and a verified certificate from the remote host. The common name of the subject of the certificate must be the hostname of the server at the other end of the current connection, and the certificate must be signed by the private CA created on *chef.wrotethebook.com* in Recipe 8.1.

The various options available for the TLS_Rcpt: entry make it possible to handle most potential situations. Yet, it is also possible to create a custom ruleset to do your own TLS_Rcpt: processing using the Local_tls_rcpt ruleset hook.

---

[*] This is one long line with no line breaks.

See Also

Recipes 8.7, 8.8, and 8.9 show examples of related *access* database entries, and Recipes 8.5 and 8.6 describe other ways the *access* database is used with STARTTLS. The *sendmail* book covers ${cn_subject} in section 21.9.24, ${server_name} in 21.9.84, ${cert_subject} in 21.9.15, ${cert_issuer} in 21.9.13, and TLS_Rcpt: in 10.10.8.2.

8.11   Refusing STARTTLS Service

Problem

By default, a sendmail system configured to run STARTTLS issues the STARTTLS command to any remote host that advertises STARTTLS in its response to the EHLO command. You have been asked to prevent sendmail from using the STARTTLS protocol extension when communicating with selected remote hosts.

Solution

Make sure your system meets the basic OpenSSL and STARTTLS configuration requirements described in this chapter's Introduction and in Chapter 1.

Add Try_TLS: entries to the *access* database to identify the remote sites for which STARTTLS should be disabled. The format of the Try_TLS: record is:

```
Try_TLS:name          NO
```

Try_TLS: is the required tag value. *name* is the hostname, domain name, or IP address of the remote site. NO is the required return value.

Add the *access_db* feature and the STARTTLS defines to the sendmail configuration:

```
dnl Point to the CA certificate directory
define(`confCACERT_PATH', `/etc/mail/certs')
dnl Point to the root CA's certificate
define(`confCACERT', `/etc/mail/certs/cacert.pem')
dnl Point to the certificate used for inbound connections
define(`confSERVER_CERT', `/etc/mail/certs/cert.pem')
dnl Point to the private key used for inbound connections
define(`confSERVER_KEY', `/etc/mail/certs/key.pem')
dnl Point to the certificate used for outbound connections
define(`confCLIENT_CERT', `/etc/mail/certs/cert.pem')
dnl Point to the private key used for outbound connections
define(`confCLIENT_KEY', `/etc/mail/certs/key.pem')
dnl Enable the access database
FEATURE(`access_db')
```

Using the guidance in Recipe 1.8, rebuild the *sendmail.cf* file, copy the new *sendmail.cf* file to */etc/mail*, and restart sendmail.

Discussion

Here are sample `Try_TLS:` entries that prevent STARTTLS from being used with two different remote hosts:

```
Try_TLS:example.com              NO
Try_TLS:server.wrotethebook.org  NO
```

Given these `Try_TLS:` entries, TLS is not used when connecting to the TLS server *server.wrotethebook.org* or when connecting to any STARTTLS server in the *example.com* domain.

`Try_TLS:` records are processed by the `try_tls` ruleset, which is called by the client just before the client issues the STARTTLS command. `try_tls` first uses ruleset D to look for a `Try_TLS:` record that contains the hostname or the domain name returned by `${server_name}`. If no match is found, it uses the A ruleset to look for a `Try_TLS:` record that contains the IP address returned by `${server_addr}`. If still no match is found, the STARTTLS command is issued. If a match is found that returns the value NO, the connection is terminated with a permanent failure.

The `LOCAL_TRY_TLS` macro provides a hook into the `try_tls` ruleset for your own custom rewrite rules.

`Try_TLS:` entries only apply to outbound connections, which are a client function. See Recipe 8.12 for an example of using the `SRV_Features:` entry to control the TLS server functions offered on inbound connections.

See Also

Recipe 8.4 explains the STARTTLS defines used in this configuration. Recipes 8.5 to 8.10 show examples of using the *access* database with STARTTLS. The *sendmail* book covers `${server_addr}` in section 21.9.83, `${server_name}` in 21.9.84, and `Try_TLS:` records in 10.10.8.4.

8.12 Selectively Advertising STARTTLS

Problem

You have configured STARTTLS but do not want to encrypt the link for every remote host that is also configured for STARTTLS. You want to configure sendmail to only offer STARTTLS to selected hosts.

Solution

Make sure the system meets the basic OpenSSL and STARTTLS configuration requirements described in the Introduction and in Chapter 1.

Create Srv_Features: *access* database entries for all hosts to which STARTTLS should be advertised. The key field of each entry begins with the tag Srv_Features:, which is followed by the domain name, hostname, or IP address that identifies the connecting host. The return value of each entry is the letter s.

Add the *access_db* feature to the STARTTLS sendmail configuration. Here is the required FEATURE macro and sample defines:

```
dnl Point to the CA certificate directory
define(`confCACERT_PATH', `/etc/mail/certs')
dnl Point to the root CA's certificate
define(`confCACERT', `/etc/mail/certs/cacert.pem')
dnl Point to the certificate used for inbound connections
define(`confSERVER_CERT', `/etc/mail/certs/cert.pem')
dnl Point to the private key used for inbound connections
define(`confSERVER_KEY', `/etc/mail/certs/key.pem')
dnl Point to the certificate used for outbound connections
define(`confCLIENT_CERT', `/etc/mail/certs/cert.pem')
dnl Point to the private key used for outbound connections
define(`confCLIENT_KEY', `/etc/mail/certs/key.pem')
dnl Enable the access database
FEATURE(`access_db')
```

Following the instructions in Recipe 1.8, rebuild the *sendmail.cf* file, copy the new *sendmail.cf* file to */etc/mail*, and restart sendmail.

Discussion

Use the Srv_Features: *access* database entry to control the extended SMTP features offered to connecting hosts. The return value of a Srv_Features: entry is one or more single character flags, some of which indicate whether an extended service should be advertised. (When more than one flag is used, the individual flags are separated by whitespace.) Lowercase flags enable SMTP extensions and uppercase flags disable extensions. The s flag selectively advertises STARTTLS, and the S flag selectively blocks advertising STARTTLS. These are the flags of particular interest for this recipe.[*]

Assume that you want to limit advertising STARTTLS to only those hosts in the *wrotethebook.com* domain. You could do that by adding the following two entries to the *access* database:

```
Srv_Features:wrotethebook.com          s
Srv_Features:                          S
```

In this case, STARTTLS is advertised to the hosts in the *wrotethebook.com* domain as directed by the s flag. The S flag in the second entry prevents STARTTLS from being advertised to any other host. A blank name field in a Srv_Features: entry indicates that the entry applies to every host for which there is not a more specific Srv_Features: entry. In effect, the second entry creates a default policy for advertising

[*] All of the flags are described in Table 7-2, which is shown in the Discussion section of Recipe 7.9.

STARTTLS. This second entry is necessary because the normal default is for sendmail to advertise STARTTLS when STARTTLS is configured. In the absence of an applicable Srv_Features: entry, the default sendmail behavior applies.

Alternatives

Changing the default sendmail behavior with a DAEMON_OPTIONS macro is an alternative to using the second Srv_Features: entry described above. You could add a DAEMON_OPTIONS macro that specifies the M=S modifier to the sendmail configuration. For example, adding the following lines to the configuration prevents sendmail from advertising STARTTLS to any connecting host:

```
dnl Do not advertise STARTTLS
DAEMON_OPTIONS(`Name=MTA, M=S')
```

After changing the default, you could then override the default for the hosts in the *wrotethebook.com* using a single Srv_Features: entry:

```
Srv_Features:wrotethebook.com          s
```

This alternative approach works, but I prefer the first approach of putting both policies in the *access* database. I think that putting both policies in one place makes it easier for others to understand exactly what the configuration is doing.

The examples in this section assume that you want to limit advertising to selected hosts. The opposite may be true. You may wish to advertise STARTTLS to most hosts and only block advertising to specific hosts with which you are having trouble. In that case, the specific Srv_Features: entries would use the S flag. No default Srv_Features: entry would be required because the normal sendmail default is to advertise STARTTLS.

See Also

Recipe 8.4 describes the basic STARTTLS configuration that needs to be done before this recipe is implemented. Recipe 7.9 and Recipe 8.13 provide other examples of using the Srv_Features: record. Recipes 8.5 through 8.13 show how the *access* database is used with STARTTLS. The *sendmail* book covers the Srv_Features: entry in section 19.9.4.

8.13 Requesting Client Certificates

Problem

By default, STARTTLS does not require a TLS client to present a certificate. You want to configure sendmail to request certificates from selected TLS clients.

Solution

Make sure the system meets the basic OpenSSL and STARTTLS configuration requirements described in the Introduction and in Chapter 1.

Create Srv_Features: *access* database entries for all clients that will be required to present a certificate. The key field of each entry is the tag Srv_Features: followed by the domain name, hostname, or IP address of the selected client. The return value of each entry is the letter v.

Add the *access_db* feature to the STARTTLS sendmail configuration. Here is the required FEATURE macro and sample defines:

```
dnl Point to the CA certificate directory
define(`confCACERT_PATH', `/etc/mail/certs')
dnl Point to the root CA's certificate
define(`confCACERT', `/etc/mail/certs/cacert.pem')
dnl Point to the certificate used for inbound connections
define(`confSERVER_CERT', `/etc/mail/certs/cert.pem')
dnl Point to the private key used for inbound connections
define(`confSERVER_KEY', `/etc/mail/certs/key.pem')
dnl Point to the certificate used for outbound connections
define(`confCLIENT_CERT', `/etc/mail/certs/cert.pem')
dnl Point to the private key used for outbound connections
define(`confCLIENT_KEY', `/etc/mail/certs/key.pem')
dnl Enable the access database
FEATURE(`access_db')
```

Following the instructions in Recipe 1.8, rebuild the *sendmail.cf* file, copy the new *sendmail.cf* file to */etc/mail*, and restart sendmail.

Discussion

Srv_Features: entries control the way in which a server interacts with its clients. See Recipe 8.12 and Recipe 7.9 for more general information about the Srv_Features: entry.

Use the v return value on a Srv_Features: entry to request the TLS client's certificate. Use the V return value to specifically prevent sendmail from asking for the client's certificate.

Adding the following entry to the *access* database requires a certificate from all hosts connecting to the local host from the *dialin.wrotethebook.com* domain:

```
Srv_Features:dialin.wrotethebook.com        v
```

By itself, the Srv_Features: entry does not do anything with the client certificate. It merely requests that the client present a certificate, which can then be used for special purposes such as authorizing relaying. Using the certificate for a special purpose requires additional configuration as shown in other recipes in this chapter.

See Also

Recipe 8.4 describes the STARTTLS defines used in this configuration. Recipe 7.9 provides other examples of using the Srv_Features: record. Recipes 8.5, 8.6, and 8.9 use client certificates to grant relaying privileges. The *sendmail* book covers the Srv_ Features: entry in section 19.9.4.

## CHAPTER 9

Managing the Queue

9.0   Introduction

The *queue* is where mail is held until it can be successfully delivered. The queue holds mail for later delivery when a temporary error is encountered during the delivery process. Most sendmail administrators have seen "Deferred" appear in an error message and know that it means the mail will be held in the queue until the next queue run. Mail is also placed in the queue when the system load exceeds the load average defined by the *sendmail.cf* QueueLA option, and when certain delivery modes are used. Queuing is an important component of creating a robust, reliable mail delivery system.

Each mail message in the queue can be represented by up to four queue files:

- The *df* file contains the message body.
- The *qf* file contains the message headers and the queue control information needed to deliver the message.
- The *xf* file is a temporary file that contains a transcript of any error messages sendmail receives when attempting to deliver the message. Any error messages collected in the *xf* file are returned to the sender, and the *xf* file is deleted after the delivery attempt.
- The *tf* file is a temporary work file that sendmail uses to produce the updated *qf* file. The queue control information in the *qf* file is updated each time a message is requeued. Any changes to that information take place in the *tf* file to safeguard the *qf* file. After the *tf* file is successfully updated, it is renamed as a *qf* file.

Of the four file types, only the *df* and *qf* files are long-term residents of the queue. The content of these files, even of the *qf* files that contain queue control information, have no impact on the recipes in this chapter, and therefore, we won't describe the content of these files in any more detail. If you're curious about the internals of the *qf* file, see section 11.11 of the *sendmail* book.

df, *qf*, *xf*, and *tf* are filename prefixes that identify the type of queue file. The full name of a queue file is composed of one of these prefixes followed by the unique queue identifier associated with an individual message. For example, this *ls* command lists all of the *df* files in the queue:

```
# ls df*
dfg7KEK4W9001253   dfg8Q82lkj002190   dfg8RDYB6v001254
```

While this *ls* command lists all of the files associated with a specific mail message:

```
# ls *g8Q82lkj002190
dfg8Q82lkj002190   qfg8Q82lkj002190
```

These *ls* commands are used to illustrate the structure of a queue filename. *ls* is not normally used to examine the queue. Use the *mailq* command to see what messages are queued.

By default, the *sendmail.cf* configuration uses the */var/spool/mqueue* directory for the queue files. The *submit.cf* configuration uses */var/spool/clientmqueue* as the default. However, several of the recipes in this book contain commands that change the default queue and create a more complex and flexible queue directory structure for the *sendmail.cf* configuration, and those same commands can be used in the *submit.cf* configuration.

The queue can be processed immediately by running sendmail with the -q command line option. More typically, however, the -q option is provided with a time interval argument, which causes sendmail to process the queue periodically. For example, -q15m would process the queue every 15 minutes.

Timing, and not just the timing of how often the queue is processed, is part of the nature of a queue. After all, a queue is created to store undelivered messages for a specified amount of time. A sendmail queue also has timers for how often the sender is warned that the message is still undelivered and waiting in the queue. These timers can be configured for normal, urgent, and non-urgent messages. The timer options in the *sendmail.cf* file that relate to how long messages are held in the queue are:

Timeout.queuereturn

> The Timeout.queuereturn option defines the amount of time a message is kept in the queue before it is returned to the sender as undeliverable. This option is configured by the confTO_QUEUERETURN define. This timer, which defaults to five days (5d), applies to most mail messages.

Timeout.queuereturn.normal

> This option defines the amount of time a message containing a Precedence: normal header is kept in the queue before it is returned to the sender as undeliverable. This option is configured by the confTO_QUEUERETURN_NORMAL define. The default is five days (5d).

`Timeout.queuereturn.urgent`

> This option defines the amount of time a message containing a `Precedence:` urgent header is kept in the queue before it is returned to the sender as undeliverable. This option is configured by the `confTO_QUEUERETURN_URGENT` define. The default is two days (`2d`).

`Timeout.queuereturn.non-urgent`

> This option defines the amount of time a message containing a `Precedence:` non-urgent header is kept in the queue before it is returned to the sender as undeliverable. This option is configured by the `confTO_QUEUERETURN_NONURGENT` define. The default is seven days (`7d`).

`Timeout.queuewarn`

> The `Timeout.queuewarn` option defines the amount of time sendmail waits before sending a warning message telling the sender that a message is still undelivered. This option is configured by the `confTO_QUEUEWARN` define. This timer, which defaults to four hours (`4h`), applies to most mail messages.

`Timeout.queuewarn.normal`

> This option defines the amount of time sendmail waits before sending a warning message telling the sender that a message containing a `Precedence:` normal header is still undelivered. This option is configured by the `confTO_QUEUEWARN_NORMAL` define. The default is four hours (`4h`).

`Timeout.queuewarn.urgent`

> This option defines the amount of time sendmail waits before sending a warning message telling the sender that a message containing a `Precedence:` urgent header is still undelivered. This option is configured by the `confTO_QUEUEWARN_URGENT` define. The default is one hour (`1h`).

`Timeout.queuewarn.non-urgent`

> This option defines the amount of time sendmail waits before sending a warning message telling the sender that a message containing a `Precedence:` non-urgent header is still undelivered. This option is configured by the `confTO_QUEUEWARN_NONURGENT` define. The default is 12 hours (`12h`).

As an example, adding the following `confTO_QUEUERETURN` define to the sendmail configuration would reduce to three days the amount of time a normal message is allowed to remain in the queue before it is returned to the sender as undeliverable:

```
dnl Return normal messages after three days in the queue
define(`confTO_QUEUERETURN', `3d')
```

Timing might be changed on any system. The recipes in this chapter, however, are primarily of interest to large sites that have large queues. On most systems, the queue is so small that the amount of time spent processing the queue is negligible. However, when the queue grows to tens of thousands of messages, significant time can be used on each queue run. If your system normally has a small queue of a few hundred or a few thousand queued messages, the default sendmail configuration is probably adequate. If your queue often grows to tens of thousands of messages, read on.

9.1   Creating Multiple Queues

Problem

You have been asked to create multiple mail queues spread over multiple physical devices in order to efficiently handle a large amount of mail.

Solution

Prepare the physical devices that will hold the mail queues. Each device must be formatted according to the requirements of your system and must contain a filesystem that is compatible with your operating system. Formatting devices and building Unix filesystems is beyond the scope of this book. See *Essential System Administration*, Third Edition, by Æleen Frisch (O'Reilly).

Create the directories needed for the various mail queues:

```
# cd /var/spool/mqueue
# mkdir queue.1 queue.2 queue.3
# chmod 700 queue.?
```

Mount the physical devices on the newly created directories. This example uses Linux device names:

```
# mount /dev/hda1 /var/spool/mqueue/queue.1
# mount /dev/hdb2 /var/spool/mqueue/queue.2
# mount /dev/hdd1 /var/spool/mqueue/queue.3
```

Edit the */etc/fstab* or */etc/vfstab* file to mount the devices during every boot. Here are the sample mounts defined in an */etc/fstab* file on a Red Hat Linux system:

```
/dev/hda1    /var/spool/mqueue/queue.1    ext3    defaults  1 2
/dev/hdb2    /var/spool/mqueue/queue.2    ext3    defaults  1 2
/dev/hdd1    /var/spool/mqueue/queue.3    ext3    defaults  1 2
```

 Note that the lines above are *added* to the current */etc/fstab* file. Overwriting or deleting the existing entries in the *fstab* file could severely impact the system—rendering it incapable of rebooting. Use care when adding lines to the *fstab* file.

Add the QUEUE_DIR define to the sendmail configuration to use the new queue directories. Here is an example of the define:

```
dnl Declare the queue directory path
define(`QUEUE_DIR', `/var/spool/mqueue/queue.*')
```

Build *sendmail.cf*. Copy it to */etc/mail/sendmail.cf*, and restart sendmail, as shown in Recipe 1.8.

Discussion

By default, sendmail uses a single queue directory, which is usually named */var/spool/ mqueue* in the *sendmail.cf* file. The queue directory pathname is defined by the QueueDirectory option. A *grep* of a basic sendmail configuration shows the default:

```
$ grep QueueDirectory generic-linux.cf
O QueueDirectory=/var/spool/mqueue
```

Use the *m4* QUEUE_DIR define to set the value of the QueueDirectory option. After reconfiguring sendmail with the QUEUE_DIR define shown in the Solution section, another *grep* shows the change:

```
$ grep QueueDirectory sendmail.cf
O QueueDirectory=/var/spool/mqueue/queue.*
```

This recipe uses a special pathname format. The asterisk at the end of the pathname indicates that there are multiple queue directories. Only an asterisk can be used to indicate multiple queues, and it must appear at the end of the pathname. Given the QueueDirectory option shown above, sendmail looks for queues with names that begin with /var/spool/mqueue.queue. followed by any other string of characters.

This recipe mounts a separate physical device on each queue directory. While this is not absolutely necessary, it illustrates a common use of multiple directories. Placing multiple directories on a single device provides performance gains, but using multiple devices can provide even larger performance gains. *sendmail Performance Tuning*, by Nick Christenson (Addison Wesley), provides insight into these performance gains.

Multiple queues, as implemented in this recipe, speed the processing of large queues. If your server sometimes has more than 10,000 messages waiting in the queue, Recipe 9.1 may help improve your server performance and reliability.

Note that it is not necessary to use QUEUE_DIR to create multiple queues simply to organize mail into specific queues. *qf*, *df*, and *xf* subdirectories organize the queue by queue file types, as described in Recipe 9.2. *Queue groups*, which are discussed in Recipe 9.3, organize mail in separate queues. The separate queues used for queue groups can be subdirectories of a single default queue. Although *qf*, *df*, and *xf* subdirectories and queue groups can be used with multiple queues defined by a QUEUE_DIR command, they do not require that command.

See Also

Recipe 9.2 describes another technique for creating multiple queues that can be combined with this recipe. The *sendmail* book covers multiple queues in section 11.3. The QueueDirectory option is explained in the *Sendmail Installation and Operations Guide* found in the *doc/op* directory of the sendmail distribution.

9.2 Using qf, df, and xf Subdirectories

Problem

Special configuration is required to use multiple mail queues for the different queue file types.

Solution

Create a new queue directory structure with separate directories for *df*, *qf*, and *xf* queue files. Here is an example:

```
# umask 077
# mkdir /var/spool/mqueue.new
# cd /var/spool/mqueue.new
# mkdir df qf xf
```

Move the old queue directory out of the way so that the new queue directory structure can be given the pathname defined by the QueueDirectory option in the *sendmail.cf* file. Here is an example:

```
# mv /var/spool/mqueue /var/spool/mqueue.old
# mv /var/spool/mqueue.new /var/spool/mqueue
```

Start another copy of sendmail as a queue runner to drain the old queue. Use the -O argument on the *sendmail* command line to point the queue runner to the old queue. Here is an example:

```
# sendmail -L sm-oldq -q15m -O QueueDirectory=/var/spool/mqueue.old
```

Discussion

sendmail stores *df*, *qf*, and *xf* files in separate directories when the default queue directory contains subdirectories named *df*, *qf*, and *xf*. As with the multiple queues described in Recipe 9.1, *df*, *qf*, and *xf* subdirectories reduce the size of any individual queue directory, and they allow the subdirectories to be placed on separate devices to overcome the I/O limitations of a single device. These benefits aid in the processing of a very large mail queue. Additionally, using separate subdirectories for the different queue files allows you to select a device that is optimized for the type of queue file that it will handle. These are the file characteristics to consider when selecting a device:

df

A *df* file contains the body of the mail message. Usually, it is the largest of the three files. A *df* file is written to the queue once and read once for each delivery attempt, so it is usually handled less than the other files. Storage capacity is the primary consideration when selecting a device for *df* files.

qf

A *qf* file contains the delivery and queuing instructions for the message, as well as the message headers. A *qf* file is small, but it is rewritten each time a delivery is attempted. When a message has many recipients or is requeued several times, sendmail handles the *qf* file many times. Performance is an important consideration when selecting a device to handle *qf* files.

xf

An *xf* file is created for each delivery attempt and is valid only for that attempt. *xf* files are small and they have a short life. Performance is the primary consideration when selecting a device for *xf* files.

These subdirectories can be created in any combination. You could, for example, create just an *xf* directory—sendmail would place *xf* files in that directory and place *df* and *qf* files in the base directory. This recipe creates a temporary directory, */var/spool/mqueue.new*, as the base directory. All three subdirectories, *df*, *qf*, and *xf*, are then created within that directory. The old queue directory is moved out of the way and the new directory is renamed to the value defined by the *sendmail.cf* QueueDirectory option, which, in the example, is */var/spool/mqueue*. sendmail will begin to use the new directory structure as soon as it is renamed.

As Nick Christenson explains in his book, *sendmail Performance Tuning* (Addison Wesley), the apparent race condition caused by renaming sendmail's queue directory while sendmail is running is minimal. Mail sent by the MSP uses the queue directory defined in *submit.cf*, which is usually */var/spool/clientmqueue*, so it is unaffected when *mqueue* is renamed.[*] A process that is running when the directory is renamed is unaffected because it uses the inode of the queue directory not the logical name. Therefore, if the process started with the old queue, it will continue with the old queue even after the queue directory is renamed. After the master sendmail process is restarted, all subsequent sendmail processes will use the new queue.

Of course, mail queued in the old directory will remain there after the directory is renamed unless a process is started to drain the old queue. Use the -O argument on the command line to point the queue runner to the old queue, as shown in the Solution section. Periodically check the old queue to see if it has drained using a command such as the following:

```
# sendmail -bp -O QueueDirectory=/var/spool/mqueue.old
```

When the old queue is empty, kill the special queue runner and remove the unneeded directory.

The *df*, *qf*, and *xf* subdirectories can be placed on separate physical devices. For example, on a Linux system, the *xf* subdirectory could be placed on */dev/shm*, which is a shared memory device using the Linux tmpfs filesystem format. Placing the *xf*

[*] sendmail prior to Version 8.12 did not use the *submit.cf* file.

subdirectory on a volatile, memory-based filesystem that provides very high performance at the cost of long-term storage works because *xf* files do not need to be preserved between queue runs or reboots.

Multiple queues, such as those created in Recipe 9.1, can be combined with *df*, *qf*, and *xf* subdirectories to gain the advantages of both multiple queues and subqueues for a system that handles a very large mail queue. Recipe 9.1 created three queue directories. Within each of those, we could create *df*, *qf*, and *xf* subdirectories for a total of nine different directories, which could then be allocated to physical devices in any manner you wished.

See Also

Recipe 9.1 also creates multiple queues that can be combined with this recipe. The *sendmail* book covers the *df*, *qf*, and *xf* subdirectories in section 11.3.2 and in section 6.5. *sendmail Performance Tuning*, by Nick Christenson (Addison Wesley), covers this topic in section 3.4.4.

9.3   Defining Queue Groups

Problem

Special configuration is required to define different mail queues with unique characteristics.

Solution

Create the directories for the queue groups. The queue group directories must be subdirectories under the default queue directory. In this example, four queue group directories are created:

```
# cd /var/spool/mqueue
# mkdir slowq fastq.1 fastq.2 fastq.3
# chmod 700 slowq fastq.?
```

Add QUEUE_GROUP macros to the sendmail configuration to use the queue group directories created in the first step. Here are sample QUEUE_GROUP macros:

```
dnl Define a queue group
QUEUE_GROUP(`slowq', `Path=/var/spool/mqueue/slowq')
dnl Define a queue group
QUEUE_GROUP(`fastq', `Path=/var/spool/mqueue/fastq.*, I=10m, F=f, R=3')
```

Build *sendmail.cf*. Copy it to */etc/mail/sendmail.cf*, and restart sendmail. See Recipe 1.8.

Discussion

The first step in the Solution section creates four queues in the */var/spool/mqueue* directory: *slowq*, *fastq.1*, *fastq.2*, and *fastq.3*. These queues are then referenced by the QUEUE_GROUP macros as the *slowq* and *fastq* queue groups. The directories for queue groups are created in the base path of the default queue. When a single directory is used for the default queue, the base path is the path specified by the QueueDirectory option. When QUEUE_DIR is used to define multiple queue directories, as it was in Recipe 9.1, the default queue pathname specified by the QueueDirectory option and the base pathname are not exactly the same. For example:

```
define(`QUEUE_DIR', `/var/spool/mqueue/queue.*')
```

This QUEUE_DIR define sets the default queue to */var/spool/mqueue/queue.**. The base pathname in this case is */var/spool/mqueue*, not */var/spool/mqueue/queue.**. The directory that contains the subdirectories used for multiple queues is the base path in which the queues used for other queue groups should be placed.

Use the QUEUE_GROUP *m4* macro to declare queue groups. The syntax of the QUEUE_GROUP command is:

```
QUEUE_GROUP(`groupname', `equates')
```

The *groupname* is an arbitrary name assigned to a queue. The *groupname* is used to reference the queue from within the sendmail configuration and in QGRP: records in the *access* database. The default queue is named *mqueue*, and it can be referenced by that name.

The *equates* are a comma separated list of queue attributes written in the form *keyword=value*. The *equates* field must be present, although it can be explicitly empty. The QUEUE_GROUP commands in the Solution section have values in the *equates* field. Here is an example with an empty *equates* field:

```
QUEUE_GROUP(`normalq', `')
```

Notice the single quotes enclosing the empty *equates* field in the example above. When the *equates* field is empty, the queue group inherits all of the attributes of the default queue, *mqueue*. Given the QUEUE_GROUP command shown above, *normalq* would use the same queue directory and all of the same attributes as the *mqueue* queue group.

All queue groups inherit the attributes of the default queue. The *keyword=value* equates defined in the *equates* field are used to override the default values for specific queue attributes. Table 9-1 lists the available keywords and describes the queue attribute associated with each keyword.

Table 9-1. Queue group attributes

Keyword	Function
Flags=	Sets optional runtime flags.
Interval=	Specifies the time interval between queue runs.
Jobs=	Limits the number of envelopes processed during a single queue run.
Nice=	Defines the nice value used for the queue run.
Path=	The full pathname of the queue directory used for this queue group.
Recipient=	Sets the maximum number of recipients allowed for one envelope.
Runners=	Defines the maximum number of queue processors that can be used in any one queue run.

The effect of the equates listed in Table 9-1 can be altered by other configuration options.

confFAST_SPLIT

> The number assigned to this option sets the maximum number of envelopes that can be delivered during the initial delivery, without regard to the value set by Jobs. Additionally, assigning a positive number to this option prevents MX lookups of recipient addresses when the envelope is being split. Skipping the MX lookup can speed up envelope processing, and limiting the number of delivery processes can enhance performance on a heavily loaded system. By default, sendmail performs MX lookups when splitting envelopes, and it runs as many delivery processes as needed to deliver all of the envelopes in parallel.

confMAX_QUEUE_CHILDREN

> The number assigned to this option is the maximum number of queue processes allowed across all queue groups. The upper limit set by this option is not affected by the values set for Runners or Flags. If confMAX_QUEUE_CHILDREN is set to 10 and the total number of Runners is set to 15, sendmail limits the number of queue processes to 10. By default, confMAX_QUEUE_CHILDREN is set to 0, which means that sendmail allows an unlimited number of queue processes (up to the limit set by Runners).

confMAX_RUNNERS_PER_QUEUE

> This option sets the default maximum number of queue runners allowed per queue group. The value set by Runners in a QUEUE_GROUP macro overrides this default value for a specific queue group.

confMIN_QUEUE_AGE

> This option sets the minimum amount of time that a queued message must wait in the queue before a delivery attempt is made. This value is not affected by how frequently the queue is processed. If the Interval is set to 10 minutes (10m) and confMIN_QUEUE_AGE is set to 1 hour (1h), it is possible for a message to sit in the queue for 6 queue runs before sendmail attempts to deliver it. This option is

used to reduce the load on systems that have very large queues, yet use a short queue interval. By default, sendmail attempts to deliver all of the mail in the queue (up to the limit set by Jobs) every time the queue is processed.

confNICE_QUEUE_RUN

This option sets the default nice value used for queue runs. It can be overridden for a specific queue group by using Nice in a QUEUE_GROUP macro.

confMAX_QUEUE_RUN_SIZE

This option sets the maximum number of queue messages that will be processed during a queue run across all queue groups. By default, sendmail attempts to deliver all of the mail in the queue. This option sets an upper limit on the number of messages sendmail will attempt to process, much like Jobs does for a single queue group.

The sendmail configuration in this recipe contains two QUEUE_GROUP commands:

```
QUEUE_GROUP(`slowq', `Path=/var/spool/mqueue/slowq')
QUEUE_GROUP(`fastq', `Path=/var/spool/mqueue/fastq.*, I=10m, F=f, R=3')
```

The first QUEUE_GROUP command defines a queue group and assigns it the name *slowq*. The path to the *slowq* group's queue directory is defined as */var/spool/mqueue/slowq*. All of the other attributes used by *slowq* are the default queue attributes.

The second QUEUE_GROUP command defines the *fastq* queue group. The *fastq* group uses multiple queues, as indicated by the asterisk suffix on the queue directory's pathname. The asterisk is used to define multiple queues for any queue group in exactly the same way that it is used to define multiple queues for the default queue group. See Recipe 9.1 for more about multiple queues and the asterisk suffix.

In addition to the Path attribute, the second QUEUE_GROUP command defines three other attributes: Interval, Flags, and Runners. Notice that the keyword in each equate does not need to be spelled out; only the first character of the keyword is significant. Thus I=10m is equivalent to Interval=10m, and the Path attribute could have been set with P=/var/spool/mqueue/fastq.*. Also, notice that each item in the equate list is separated by a comma. The whitespace used in the example enhances readability, but it is not required.

Setting the attribute I=10m means that sendmail will process the queues in this queue group every 10 minutes. Setting the f flag, F=f, tells sendmail to fork queue runners for each queue, up to the limit of queue processes defined with the Runners keyword. f is the only value currently valid for Flags. Always use F=f when you use the Runners keyword.

Setting R=3 means that sendmail can use up to three separate processes to process the queues in this queue group. This recipe created three queues (*fastq.1*, *fastq.2*, and *fastq.3*) for the *fastq* group. Setting R=3 means that each queue will have a single queue processor for each queue run. Setting R=15 would have dedicated five processes to each queue during each queue run. However, a large number of queue runners is not always a good thing. To find out why, see Recipe 9.5.

The QUEUE_GROUP macros create Q commands inside the *sendmail.cf* file. The Q commands created by this recipe are:

```
# grep '^Q' recipe9-3.cf
Qslowq, Path=/var/spool/mqueue/slowq
Qfastq, Path=/var/spool/mqueue/fastq.*, I=10m, R=3
```

Queue groups are used by queue management features. For example, you can configure a sendmail mailer to use a particular queue group as its default mail queue. The Q parameter of the mailer definition tells the mailer which queue group it should use. All mailers have an *m4* define for the Q parameter; all of these defines are used in exactly the same way; and most have names in the form of *NAME*_MAILER_QGRP, where *NAME* is the mailer's internal name. For example, use PROCMAIL_MAILER_QGRP to set Q if the name of the mailer is procmail.

Additionally, queue groups can be used in the *access* database. Recipe 9.4 shows an example of this.

See Also

Recipe 9.1 covers the QUEUE_DIR command and discusses multiple queues. Recipe 9.2 covers the *df*, *qf*, and *xf* subdirectories, which can be created in the queue directory of any queue group. The *sendmail* book covers queue groups in section 11.4, confQUEUE_FILE_MODE in 29.9.84, confFAST_SPLIT in 29.9.32, confMAX_QUEUE_CHILDREN in 29.9.65, confMIN_QUEUE_AGE in 24.9.72, confMAX_QUEUE_RUN_SIZE in 24.9.66, confNICE_QUEUE_RUN in 24.9.74, and confMAX_RCPTS_PER_MESSAGE in 24.9.67.

9.4   Assigning Recipients to Specific Queues

Problem

To use queues optimized for the characteristics of the destination host, you must route mail bound for recipient addresses on those hosts to the optimized mail queues.

Solution

Create the directories for the queue groups and, if necessary, the physical devices the queue group directories will use. See Recipes 9.1 and 9.3 for details.

Add QGRP: records to the *access* database to specify the queue groups used for specific recipients. The key of each entry is the tag QGRP: followed by a full or partial recipient address. The return value of the entry is the name of the queue group that should be used for the specified recipient.

Create a sendmail configuration that defines the queue groups, enables the *access* database, and uses the *queuegroup* feature. Here are sample lines that might be added to the sendmail configuration:

```
dnl Define a queue group
QUEUE_GROUP(`slowq', `Path=/var/spool/mqueue/slowq, I=2h')
dnl Define a queue group
QUEUE_GROUP(`fastq', `Path=/var/spool/mqueue/fastq.*, I=10m, R=10')
dnl Enable the access database
FEATURE(`access_db')
dnl Enable the queue group feature
FEATURE(`queuegroup')
```

Build and install */etc/mail/sendmail.cf*, then restart sendmail, as shown in Recipe 1.8.

Discussion

The *access* database provides the most flexible means to utilize queue groups. QGRP: records in the *access* database allow you to assign individual domains, and even individual users, to specific queue groups. This makes it possible to create queue groups that have characteristics that are compatible with the characteristics of a recipient site. For example, the queue for a site that has repeated, long-duration outages might have a large Interval value, or multiple queues might be dedicated to a few domains that constitute the bulk of your outbound traffic.

Here is a sample QGRP: entry:

```
QGRP:example.com          slowq
```

The QGRP: record tells sendmail to use the *slowq* queue group to queue mail for every user on all hosts in the *example.com* domain. The recipient address in a queue group entry can identify an individual user or a group of hosts. The possible recipient address formats are:

- A full address in the format *user@host.domain*. This format matches a specific user on a specific host. QGRP:craig@crab.wrotethebook.com is an example.
- A hostname in the format *host.domain*; e.g., QGRP:crab.wrotethebook.com. Any user on the specified host is matched.
- A domain name to match every user on every host in the specified domain. For example, QGRP:wrotethebook.com would match every recipient in the *wrotethebook.com* domain.
- A username written in the form *user@*; e.g., QGRP:craig@. This format matches any recipient with the specified username on any host in any domain.
- A blank field, which matches every possible recipient address.

Mail addressed to recipients not covered by a QGRP: entry is queued in the default queue.

See Also

Recipe 9.3 covers the QUEUE_GROUP macro. The *access* database is used extensively in recipes throughout this book, with particularly detailed coverage in Chapter 3 and Chapter 6. The *sendmail* book covers the QGRP: record in section 11.4.4.

9.5   Using Persistent Queue Runners

Problem

Queues can become so large that queue runners interfere with each other.

Solution

In the system startup files, locate the command that starts sendmail with the -bd flag. Look for a line that is something like the following:

```
/usr/sbin/sendmail -bd -q15m
```

Change the -q argument to a -qp argument. For example:

```
/usr/sbin/sendmail -bd -qp
```

Terminate the currently running sendmail daemon queue processor:

```
# kill -TERM `head -1 /var/run/sendmail.pid`
```

Start a new daemon process using the new command-line arguments:

```
# /usr/sbin/sendmail -bd -qp
```

Discussion

The first step in this recipe modifies the startup script so that sendmail starts with the correct command-line arguments every time the system reboots. On some systems, finding and changing the line that starts sendmail at boot time is simple; on some other systems it is more complicated. Different Unix versions use different techniques to start sendmail at boot time, but all have some technique.

Most versions of Unix use a command similar to the following one to start the sendmail daemon:

```
/usr/sbin/sendmail -bd -q15m
```

This line contains two options: -bd and -q. Use -bd to accept inbound mail. The -bd argument causes sendmail to listen for inbound mail on the configured TCP ports, which, by default, are ports 25 and 587. Without a daemon running with -bd set, a properly configured system can still send outbound mail, but it will not collect inbound mail.* The -q option causes the daemon to periodically start queue processors. In this particular example, the daemon is told to start queue processors every 15 minutes (15m).

This recipe changes the -q flag to -qp. Changing the -q flag to -qp runs this daemon as a persistent queue processor. The difference between forking a queue runner every 15 minutes with -q15m and requesting a persistent queue runner with -qp is significant. In the first case, a new queue runner is launched every 15 minutes without regard to the status of the previous queue run. In the second case, a new queue runner is launched one second after the previous queue run completes. One second is the default interval timer for the -qp option. It can be changed on the command line by defining a different interval value; for example, sendmail -qp15s would set the interval to 15 seconds. However, one second is a good value. It provides essentially continuous queue processing without any interference between queue runners because the interval timer for the next queue runner doesn't start until the current queue run finishes.

At the start of every queue run, the queue runner reads all of the *qf* files, extracts certain control information, sorts it, and uses it to control the order in which queued messages are delivered. A persistent queue runner can be beneficial when an individual queue is so large that this first step takes longer than the selected queue interval. For example, using -q15m sets the queue interval to 15 minutes. If the initial step took 30 minutes, sendmail would start another queue runner at the 15-minute point and a third at the 30-minute point. Each runner would repeat the initial step only to be succeeded by additional runners doing the same job. Unfortunately, additional queue runners do not always speed up this first step. In fact, they sometimes interfere with each other so much that they slow things down. Using persistent queue runners avoids this problem.

When a persistent queue runner is used, it is allowed to finish its job without the interference of other queue runners. The persistent queue runner finishes the first step, forks multiple processes to deliver the mail it has sorted, and sleeps the queue interval before awaking to do it again. Because the queue interval does not start until after the persistent queue runner has finished the sort, no other queue runners are started while it is running. This completely avoids the problems associated with multiple runners sorting the same queue.

In addition to modifying the boot script, the Solution section closes out the current sendmail process with a SIGTERM and reruns sendmail from the command line using the new options. After restarting sendmail, a *cat* of the *sendmail.pid* file would show the command line /usr/sbin/sendmail -bd -qp. Subsequent restarts of the daemon can be done with the HUP signal because HUP uses the command found in *sendmail.pid* to restart sendmail.

---

* Recipe 10.1 configures sendmail to send outbound mail without running a daemon with the -bd option.

Emergency queue clearance

Because this recipe permanently changes the system's default configuration, it is intended for systems where processing a very large queue is a chronic system problem. Manually running sendmail with settings that skip the time-consuming initial step is an alternative solution that can be used when the queue grows extremely large because of some unusual circumstance. In that case, kill all of the currently running sendmail processes and then enter the following command:

```
# /usr/sbin/sendmail -OQueueSortOrder=filename -q15m
```

This QueueSortOrder option tells sendmail to deliver the mail in filename order. Alternatives are to deliver the queued mail in random order by using -OQueueSortOrder=random or in order of modification time from the oldest to the newest by using -OQueueSortOrder=modtime. In all of these cases, the *qf* files are not opened and read. Therefore the delivery order is not optimized. However, an enormous amount of time is saved at the start of the queue process, which is just what is needed to clear out an overstuffed queue. Once the queue is clear, kill this special copy of sendmail and restart the normal configuration.

Use Recipe 9.5 when chronic system performance problems are routinely caused by the overhead of processing very large mail queues. Use the QueueSortOrder option as a quick fix for an unusual queue processing problem.

See Also

The *sendmail* book describes persistent queue runners in section 6.1 and the QueueSortOrder option in section 6.1.1. The *sendmail* book provides interesting statistics about the queue processing time based on queue size and on the performance gains using these alternate solutions. Chapter 3 of *sendmail Performance Tuning*, by Nick Christenson (Addison Wesley), covers queue contention and recommends solutions for this problem.

9.6   Using a Queue Server

Problem

Special configuration is required to route mail to a queue server instead of queuing it locally.

Solution

Configure a system with a large amount of storage to act as a queue server. Configure the server to:

- Have abundant queue storage. See Recipe 9.1 for information on creating multiple queues that span multiple physical devices.

- Use a long queue interval. It should be at least one hour; e.g., -q1h.
- Act as a relay server for its queue clients. See Chapter 3 for information on granting relaying privileges to clients.

Configure clients to use the queue server using the confFALLBACK_MX define in the client's sendmail configuration. Assume that the queue server created in the first step is *jamis.wrotethebook.com*. Here is a sample define that could be added to the client's sendmail configuration to use that server:

```
dnl Use jamis as the fallback mail exchanger
define(`confFALLBACK_MX', `jamis.wrotethebook.com')
```

Rebuild and install */etc/mail/sendmail.cf*, then restart sendmail (see Recipe 1.8).

Discussion

MX records tell sendmail where to deliver mail. sendmail looks up the MX records for a recipient address. If there are no MX records for the recipient host, sendmail attempts to deliver to the recipient host itself using the host's address record or CNAME record. If DNS returns MX records for the recipient host, sendmail attempts to deliver mail to each mail exchanger in order. If none of these delivery attempts is successful, sendmail queues the mail. For example, imagine sendmail needs to deliver mail to *wrotethebook.org* and that the MX records provided are:

```
wrotethebook.org.    IN    MX    10 mail.example.com.
wrotethebook.org.    IN    MX    20 oreilly.com.
```

sendmail first tries delivering the message to *mail.example.com*. If it works, sendmail is done. If delivery fails, it tries delivering to *oreilly.com*.* If that delivery fails, the mail is queued. confFALLBACK_MX changes this last step.

The host defined by confFALLBACK_MX is treated as the mail-exchanger-of-last-resort for all deliveries. When mail cannot be successfully delivered to any of the mail exchangers listed on the MX records provided by DNS, sendmail sends the mail to the host specified by the confFALLBACK_MX define. If there are no MX records for the recipient host, sendmail attempts to send the mail using the host's A or CNAME record, and if that attempt fails, the mail is sent to the confFALLBACK_MX host. Additionally, if DNS does not respond to any of sendmail's queries for the recipient host's MX, A, or CNAME records, the mail is sent to the host defined by confFALLBACK_MX. All of this prevents the mail from being queued on the client.

When the fallback mail exchanger receives the mail, it treats it as mail being relayed to the recipient. This means that it will only accept the mail if the client has been granted relaying privileges. If the fallback mail exchanger accepts the mail, it retrieves the recipient's MX records from DNS and attempts delivery. If it is unable to deliver the mail, it queues it.

---

* MX records are looked up for every system in the MX list, except for the system added by the confFALLBACK_MX define.

The advantage of this approach is that the bulk of systems (i.e., the clients) can be optimized to handle the average case, and the queue server can be optimized to handle queue processing. Recipe 9.7 describes one case of optimizing clients to operate in this environment. The disadvantage of using a queue server is that there are two failed delivery attempts before the mail is queued, although this does not result in any delay in delivering the mail.

A sendmail -bt test shows the effect of this recipe:

```
# sendmail -bt
ADDRESS TEST MODE (ruleset 3 NOT automatically invoked)
Enter <ruleset> <address>
> /mx aol.com
getmxrr(aol.com) returns 5 value(s):
        mailin-02.mx.aol.com.
        mailin-04.mx.aol.com.
        mailin-03.mx.aol.com.
        mailin-01.mx.aol.com.
        jamis.wrotethebook.com.
> /mx sendmail.org
getmxrr(sendmail.org) returns 5 value(s):
        smtp.neophilic.net.
        services.sendmail.org.
        smtp.gshapiro.net.
        playground.sun.com.
        jamis.wrotethebook.com.
> /quit
```

The /mx command returns the MX list sendmail will use to deliver to the specified recipient host. No matter what recipient host is entered with the /mx command, the last system in the list is the host defined by confFALLBACK_MX.

See Also

Important background information for configuring a queue server is found in Chapter 3 and earlier in this chapter. The *sendmail* book covers confFALLBACK_MX in section 24.9.45, and it provides an excellent discussion of using a queue server in section 6.2.2. Section 6.3.1 of *sendmail Performance Tuning*, by Nick Christenson (Addison Wesley), provides additional information on using queue servers.

9.7   Setting Protocol Timers

Problem

Clients require special configuration to quickly move problem mail to the queue server.

Solution

Create a queue server as described in Recipe 9.6.

On the clients of that server, add defines to the sendmail configuration to quickly timeout bad connections and to quickly timeout remote systems that fail to respond to or provide SMTP commands in a timely manner. Here are sample protocol timer defines that could be used with the confFALLBACK_MX define:

```
dnl Use jamis as the fallback mail exchanger
define(`confFALLBACK_MX', `jamis.wrotethebook.com')
dnl Set the protocol timers to low levels
define(`confTO_CONNECT',         `15s')
define(`confTO_COMMAND',         `5m')
define(`confTO_DATABLOCK',       `5m')
define(`confTO_DATAFINAL',       `5m')
define(`confTO_DATAINIT',        `15s')
define(`confTO_HELO',            `15s')
define(`confTO_HOSTSTATUS',      `15s')
define(`confTO_ICONNECT',        `15s')
define(`confTO_INITIAL',         `15s')
define(`confTO_MAIL',            `15s')
define(`confTO_QUIT',            `15s')
define(`confTO_RCPT',            `15s')
define(`confTO_RSET',            `15s')
```

Build *sendmail.cf*, copy it to */etc/mail/sendmail.cf*, and restart sendmail, as described in Recipe 1.8.

Discussion

The confFALLBACK_MX define sets the value of the FallbackMXhost option in the *sendmail.cf* file. Mail is sent to the server defined by FallbackMXhost when the client cannot successfully deliver the mail.

This recipe sets various protocol timers low so that mail to slow or unresponsive hosts is also passed to the queue server for delivery. This recipe also optimizes the client for the average case—quick, successful mail deliveries—and sends all problematic mail to the queue server for delivery.

By default, sendmail has very generous SMTP protocol timers. These generous timers mean that sendmail will not give up delivery until it is sure the remote end is dead. This is great for ensuring delivery, but it ties up the sending system waiting for the remote system to respond. Setting short timeouts, such as those in this recipe, means that more deliveries fail, but it also means that the client is not tied up by slow deliveries. Because the queue server uses the default timeouts, much of the undelivered mail that timed out on the client is successfully delivered by the queue server on the first attempt.

Table 9-2 lists each timeout define used in this recipe, its purpose, and the default that is normally used.

Table 9-2. The SMTP protocol timers used in this recipe

The define command	Sets timeout for	Default
confTO_CONNECT	The connect system call to finish	5m
confTO_COMMAND	Waiting for the next command	1h
confTO_DATABLOCK	A read to complete	1h
confTO_DATAFINAL	Acknowledgment of the . at the end of the DATA block	1h
confTO_DATAINIT	Acknowledgment of the DATA command	5m
confTO_HELO	Acknowledgment of the HELO/EHLO command	5m
confTO_HOSTSTATUS	How long host status information is saved	30m
confTO_ICONNECT	Completion of the initial connection attempt	5m
confTO_INITIAL	Receipt of the greetings message	5m
confTO_MAIL	Acknowledgment of the MAIL From: command	10m
confTO_QUIT	Acknowledgment of the QUIT command	2m
confTO_RCPT	Acknowledgment of the RCPT To: command	1h
confTO_RSET	Acknowledgment of the RSET command	5m

This recipe reduces the timeout for most of these protocol timers to 15 seconds (15s), which is enough time for most computers to respond. Some exceptions are the timeout values set for confTO_DATAFINAL, confTO_DATABLOCK, and confTO_COMMAND, which are given a more generous five minute timeout.

The values set in this recipe are based on the fast daemon example in section 6.2.1 of the *sendmail* book. The values used here are more generous than those used in the *sendmail* book, but these values are more appropriate for our sample network. You need to create your own values based on the performance of your system and your network. The *sendmail Performance Tuning* book discusses protocol timers in section 6.1.1.

See Also

Recipe 9.6 provides related material that should be reviewed before implementing this recipe. The *sendmail* book covers the use of these timers in section 6.2, and, in particular, covers an alternate solution that uses the quick timers and the default timers on a system that does not use a queue server. The *sendmail* book also covers the timers in section 24.9.109. *sendmail Performance Tuning*, by Nick Christenson (Addison Wesley), covers fallback MX hosts in section 6.3.1.

CHAPTER 10
Securing sendmail

10.0 Introduction

Security is essential. Security is so important that it is touched upon many times in this book. In fact, several earlier chapters are really about security, such as Chapter 7 and Chapter 8. But even the chapters on relaying and spam control are really chapters about security because theft of service is just as big of a security problem for sendmail as system and data integrity.

A sendmail server requires all of the security precautions used on any networked system, and then some. By its very nature, a sendmail server must accept connections and data from unknown remote hosts, while many other network servers offer their services to a limited set of clients. The system running sendmail must be secured against attack, and the sendmail service must be secured against exploitation. General system security is beyond the scope of this book. For that, use a good security reference, such as *Practical UNIX and Internet Security*, by Simson Garfinkel and Gene Spafford (O'Reilly), or *Computer Security Basics*, by Debbie Russell and G.T. Gangemi (O'Reilly). This book focuses on only those things that are specific to sendmail security.

sendmail's file and directory permissions are one area of general system security that is specific to sendmail. All of the directories used for sendmail's administrative files should only be writable by the TrustedUser (usually *root*), and all of the parents of those directories back to the root should only be writable by *root*—none of those directories should have group or world write permissions. The file permissions used by sendmail are defined by confTEMP_FILE_MODE and confQUEUE_FILE_MODE. Don't change these permissions. sendmail comes with these permission set as tight as possible.

Despite a spotty security reputation, out-of-the-box sendmail uses tight security settings. Take care not to compromise security when configuring sendmail. Some configuration changes reduce security, as explained in the Introduction to Chapter 3. For example, the confDONT_BLAME_SENDMAIL define accepts more than 40 arguments that relax sendmail's normally strict security.

On occasion, a sendmail administrator is forced to relax security in order to gain flexibility. Many of the recipes in this chapter take the opposite tack—increasing security even at the cost of flexibility. You won't see any `DontBlameSendmail` options used. You will see restrictions of the files sendmail can write and the SMTP commands the server will support—all done to increase security.

Don't undertake these security recipes lightly. Increasing security at the cost of utility and flexibility should be done only after careful study. Be sure that the cure is not worse than the disease. All sites can benefit from keeping sendmail software updated as described in Recipes 10.3 and 10.4. Most sites can benefit from limiting the number of systems that accept inbound mail from the network, as described in Recipes 10.1 and 10.2. Many may benefit from using *smrsh*, as covered in Recipe 10.6. But some of the recipes in this chapter provide more security than the average site needs, particularly when you consider that the enhanced security comes at the cost of utility. These recipes are *not* suggesting that you should do such things as disable delivery to files or disable the `VRFY` command; they *are* telling you how to do these things if you decide that it is necessary for your system. For most sites, sendmail's standard security is more than adequate.

10.1 Limiting the Number of sendmail Servers

Problem

Because every network service that accepts inbound connections is a potential target of security attacks, you want to limit the number of systems running a sendmail listener to reduce security vulnerability and maintenance.

Solution

Select a limited number of hosts to act as mail exchangers and mail relay hosts for your enterprise. Configure the selected systems as described in Chapter 2 and in Chapter 3. The other sendmail systems should be configured as described here.

Make a backup copy of the *submit.mc* file:

```
# cd /usr/local/src/sendmail-8.12.9/cf/cf
# cp submit.mc submit.mc.original
```

Edit the *submit.mc* file. Add the `MASQUERADE_AS` macro to the configuration so that replies to mail sent by the local host will go to a server that has an active SMTP port, and add the name of the mail relay host to the *msp* `FEATURE` command. Here are the active lines in the *submit.mc* file from the sendmail 8.12.9 distribution after the changes have been made:

```
VERSIONID(`submit.mc modified for recipe 10.1')
define(`confCF_VERSION', `Submit')
define(`__OSTYPE__',`')dnl dirty hack to keep proto.m4 from complaining
```

```
define(`_USE_DECNET_SYNTAX_', `1')dnl support DECnet
define(`confTIME_ZONE', `USE_TZ')
define(`confDONT_INIT_GROUPS', `True')dnl
MASQUERADE_AS(`chef.wrotethebook.com')
FEATURE(`msp', `chef.wrotethebook.com')
```

Rebuild the *submit.cf* file and restart the MSP daemon. Here is an example from our sample Linux system:

```
# ./Build submit.cf
Using M4=/usr/bin/m4
rm -f submit.cf
/usr/bin/m4 ../m4/cf.m4 submit.mc > submit.cf || ( rm -f submit.cf && exit 1 )
chmod 444 submit.cf
# cp submit.cf /etc/mail/submit.cf
# kill -HUP `head -1 /var/spool/clientmqueue/sm-client.pid`
```

Edit the system startup script. Change the command that starts the sendmail daemon by removing the -bd flag. For example, change this:

```
/usr/sbin/sendmail -bd -q15m
```

to this:

```
/usr/sbin/sendmail -q15m
```

Terminate the currently running daemon and rerun sendmail without the -bd flag:

```
# kill -TERM `head -1 /var/run/sendmail.pid`
# /usr/sbin/sendmail -q15m
```

Discussion

Most Unix startup configurations start the sendmail daemon as both an SMTP listener and a queue processor. The listener function, which is requested by the -bd command-line flag, binds sendmail to TCP ports where it listens for inbound mail.* The -bd option is only needed if the system collects inbound mail. Most Unix workstations do not need to collect inbound mail. A central server can collect and hold the mail for a large number of workstations, and users on the workstations can retrieve the mail using tools such as POP and IMAP.

Limiting the SMTP listener to servers provides some security advantages. As the Introduction points out, SMTP servers are targets for attack because they accept connections and data from unknown hosts via the SMTP port. Intruders scan networks looking for systems that respond to SMTP connections and target their attacks against those systems. Running an SMTP listener on a system means that the system becomes a possible target. Mail servers must run the SMTP listener, but on other systems, the listener is an unnecessary risk. Controlling the SMTP ports at the firewall and limiting the number of systems listening to those ports provides *defense in depth*.

---

* The ports used by sendmail can be changed in the configuration, but the default ports are 25 and 587.

If an administrator fails to disable the ports on a host, the firewall should stop an attack. If the firewall fails, limiting the number of systems listening to the SMTP ports limits the number of targets.

Limiting the number of systems that run the SMTP listener not only reduces risk, it also reduces the security administrator's workload. Recipes 10.3 and 10.4 are good examples of this. They discuss applying fixes to sendmail to thwart an attack that comes through the SMTP port. Every system that accepts inbound SMTP connections is vulnerable to this attack. If only servers listen on that port, only servers are critically in need of the security maintenance necessary to fix this vulnerability. A site with thousands of desktop workstations might have only a handful of valid sendmail servers. Fixing a few servers is much easier than fixing thousands of desktops. Not only that, the skill level of the server administrators is generally high. Most of those administrators can handle the fix by themselves. Desktop users, on the other hand, require much more support. If anyone fails to correctly apply a critical security fix, the entire network remains in danger. Reducing the number of systems that require a critical fix is clearly a security and maintenance win.

This recipe describes changes to the *submit.cf* configuration. *submit.cf* is a special configuration used by sendmail when it acts as a mail submission program (MSP). The MSP configuration is an option available for systems running sendmail Version 8.12 and higher. When the *submit.mc* change is made and sendmail is restarted without the -bd flag, it is not necessary to update the *sendmail.cf* configuration. Recipe 10.2 shows an alternative to this recipe that changes the *sendmail.cf* configuration instead of the *submit.cf* configuration.

When a recipient replies to a message received from a system configured with this recipe, the reply must go to the server because replies sent directly to the workstation fail when the workstation does not have a listener on an SMTP port. Replies can be routed to the server with MX records, with masquerading on the workstation, or with masquerading on the server when all outbound mail is relayed through the server, as it is in this recipe's *submit.mc* configuration. Masquerading on the workstation is used here because it makes a simpler example and all configuration changes can be made in one file.

The *msp* feature in the *submit.mc* file configures sendmail as a mail submission program. By default, the MSP sends mail to the MTA by connecting to an SMTP port at 127.0.0.1—the local host address. In that case, the local host must be running an SMTP listener in order to send outbound mail. Adding a hostname to the *msp* FEATURE command causes the MSP to connect to the SMTP port on the specified host. This means that the client does *not* need a listener to send outbound mail because outbound mail goes directly from the MSP to the MTA on the specified host. In this recipe, the hostname *chef.wrotethebook.com* is added to the FEATURE(`msp') command. Therefore, all outbound mail is sent to *chef.wrotethebook.com* for delivery. *chef* must be configured to accept this mail, as described in Chapter 2 and Chapter 3.

After creating the new configuration, edit the system startup files to ensure that they do not start an SMTP listener when the system reboots. The currently running version of sendmail must be terminated to end the current listener. Finally, run sendmail from the command line with the -q flag but without the -bd flag to start a queue runner that will drain the queue.

See Also

Recipe 10.10 provides an additional example of the *submit.mc* configuration. Chapter 1 describes how the MSP configuration is initially created during the installation of the sendmail source code distribution. Recipe 10.2 discusses an alternative solution that does not require changes to the *submit.mc* configuration; evaluate Recipe 10.2 before implementing this recipe. Chapters 2, 3, and 4 provide related recipes for clients sending outbound mail through servers and for configuring those servers to accept that mail. The *sendmail* book covers the *msp* feature in section 4.8.27 and the MASQUERADE AS macro in section 4.4.2.

10.2   Limiting the Number of Network Accessible Servers

Problem

Accepting SMTP connections from the network makes a system a potential target of network-based security attacks. Special configuration is required to prevent the sendmail daemon from accepting inbound email connections from the network.

Solution

Select a limited number of hosts to act as mail exchangers and mail relay hosts for your enterprise. Configure the selected systems as described in Chapters 2 and 3. The other sendmail systems should be configured as described here.

Add the *no_default_msa* feature to the sendmail configuration to prevent sendmail from creating a default MSA configuration. Then add DAEMON_OPTIONS macros to create your own configuration that limits inbound mail connections to the loopback address. Finally, add the MASQUERADE_AS macro to the configuration so that replies to mail sent by the local host will go to a server that has an active SMTP port. Here are sample lines that could be added to the sendmail configuration:

```
dnl Don't create a default MSA configuration
FEATURE(`no_default_msa')
dnl Limit the MSA to the loopback address
DAEMON_OPTIONS(`Name=MSA, Port=587, Addr=127.0.0.1, M=E')
dnl Limit the MTA to the 127.0.0.1 interface
```

```
DAEMON_OPTIONS(`Name=MTA, Addr=127.0.0.1')
dnl Make sure replies go to the mail host
MASQUERADE_AS(`chef.wrotethebook.com')
```

Following the example in Recipe 1.8, rebuild and reinstall *sendmail.cf*, then restart sendmail.

Discussion

The DAEMON_OPTIONS macro sets values for the *sendmail.cf* DaemonPortOptions statements. A basic sendmail configuration has two DaemonPortOptions statements—one for the MTA mode of the sendmail daemon and one for the MSA mode. A *grep* shows this:

```
# grep 'DaemonPortOptions' generic-linux.cf
O DaemonPortOptions=Name=MTA
O DaemonPortOptions=Port=587, Name=MSA, M=E
```

Both port 25, used by the MTA, and port 587, used by the MSA, are accessible from the network, and thus are potentially vulnerable to network attacks. This book contains many examples of connecting to port 25. Here is one to illustrate the network accessibility of port 587:

```
$ telnet chef 587
Trying 192.168.0.8...
Connected to chef.
Escape character is '^]'.
220 chef.wrotethebook.com ESMTP Sendmail 8.12.9/8.12.4; Mon, 29 Sep 2003 10:45:59 -
0400
HELO rodent
250 chef.wrotethebook.com Hello rodent.wrotethebook.com [192.168.0.3], pleased to
meet you
MAIL From:<craig@rodent.wrotethebook.com>
250 2.1.0 <craig@rodent.wrotethebook.com>... Sender ok
RCPT To:<craig@chef.wrotethebook.com>
250 2.1.5 <craig@chef.wrotethebook.com>... Recipient ok
DATA
354 Enter mail, end with "." on a line by itself
Subject: 587 test

.
250 2.0.0 h8TEjxrm001514 Message accepted for delivery
QUIT
221 2.0.0 chef.wrotethebook.com closing connection
Connection closed by foreign host.
```

The default Addr value used by DaemonPortOptions is INADDR_ANY, which means that the daemon accepts connections from any address. Identifying a specific address with the Addr value limits incoming connection to that specific address. Thus, setting Addr=127.0.0.1 means that only connections from the local host that come through the loopback interface will be accepted, which eliminates any inbound connections from the network. Rerunning the previous *telnet* test after completing this recipe shows that network connections are no longer allowed:

```
$ telnet chef 587
Trying 192.168.0.8...
telnet: connect to address 192.168.0.8: Connection refused
$ telnet chef 25
Trying 192.168.0.8...
telnet: connect to address 192.168.0.8: Connection refused
```

These tests show that network connections are not accepted on either port 25 or port 587. However, mail can still be sent from the local host.

Note that the *no_default_msa* feature must be used before you can change the DaemonPortOptions settings of the MSA. The FEATURE macro must precede the DAEMON_OPTIONS macro in the configuration. This feature is not required when you are changing only MTA values.

Recipe 10.1 is an alternative to this recipe; it prevents sendmail from accepting SMTP connections from the network. In fact, that recipe prevents sendmail from accepting any SMTP connections—even from the local host. Recipe 10.1 provides slightly more security than this recipe because even someone with login access to the local host cannot attack sendmail through the SMTP ports. However, Recipe 10.1 is more complex and difficult to implement than this recipe. Here, all changes take place in the sendmail configuration file; Recipe 10.1 requires changes to the sendmail configuration and to the system startup files. Thus, the increased security of Recipe 10.1 comes at the cost of increased complexity.

See Also

Recipe 7.8 covers the syntax of the DAEMON_OPTIONS macro and provides another example of its use. Recipe 10.1 discusses an alternative solution that changes the *submit.mc* configuration to accomplish a similar goal. Recipe 10.1 should be evaluated before implementing this recipe. Chapter 4 covers the MASQUERADE_AS macro. The *sendmail* book covers the DAEMON_OPTIONS macro in section 24.9.24, the *no_default_msa* feature in section 4.8.30, and the MASQUERADE_AS macro in section 4.4.2.

10.3   Updating to Close Security Holes

Problem

You must close known sendmail security holes that intruders are exploiting.

Solution

Subscribe to the *sendmail-announce* mailing list to receive notification of important security updates by sending mail to *majordomo@lists.sendmail.org* that contains the following line:

```
subscribe sendmail-announce
```

Download the sendmail source code distribution to fix any known security problems. Detailed instructions for downloading the sendmail distribution are found in Recipe 1.1.

Restore, recompile, and reinstall sendmail as described in Recipe 1.2.

Discussion

Failure to fix known security problems is the single biggest security threat to all systems. Intruders frequently exploit known security holes to crash systems or gain access—even *root* access. Subscribing to *sendmail-announce* lets you know if there are sendmail security fixes that affect your system. Downloading, compiling, and installing the new version of sendmail is a security priority.

See Also

Recipes 1.1 and 1.2 cover downloading, compiling, and installing sendmail. Recipes 1.3 to 1.7 provide additional examples of recompiling sendmail. Chapter 2 of the *sendmail* book provides extensive details on installing an updated version of sendmail.

10.4   Patching to Close Security Holes

Problem

You need to apply patches to close known sendmail security holes.

Solution

Subscribe to the *sendmail-announce* mailing list to receive notification of important security patches by sending mail to *majordomo@lists.sendmail.org* that contains the following line:

```
subscribe sendmail-announce
```

Download the patch from *ftp.sendmail.org* or from *www.sendmail.org*. Use the *patch* command to apply a security patch to the sendmail source code.

Recompile and reinstall sendmail, as described in Recipe 1.2, using the patched source code.

Restart sendmail. For example:

```
# kill -HUP `head -1 /var/run/sendmail.pid`
```

Discussion

Fixing a problem with a source code patch is very similar to installing a completely new sendmail source code distribution. In both cases:

- You download source code from *sendmail.org*. In one case, it is a large *tar* file, and in the other, it is a small patch file, but in both cases the download is essentially the same.
- You download a signature file to verify the source code.
- You use *gpg* or *pgp* to verify the downloaded source file.
- You recompile, reinstall, and restart sendmail.

The biggest differences between the two approaches to closing a security hole are:

- In one case, you use *tar* to create a completely new source tree.
- In the other case, you use *patch* to change files in an existing source tree.

The approach you use depends on your personal preferences and the nature of the sendmail currently installed on your system. If you use a version of sendmail provided by a vendor that has some special features, patching may be a way to fix a security problem while retaining those features. Of course there is no guarantee. If the vendor has extensively modified the sendmail source, the patch may not work.

If you really are dependent on a vendor supplied version of sendmail, the best approach is to go directly to the vendor for the security fix. For example, for a Red Hat Linux system, you can obtain critical security fixes directly from the Red Hat web site. Figure 10-1 shows a web page at *redhat.com* that points to the RPM files containing a sendmail security fix.

This chapter, like the rest of this book, uses the sendmail source code distribution instead of a vendor's copy of sendmail. In particular, sendmail 8.12.9 is used throughout this book because it was the latest version of sendmail available when the bulk of this book was written. The following example shows sendmail 8.12.9 being patched to fix a critical security problem.

Fixes for the sendmail source code distribution can be obtained directly from *sendmail.org*. This example begins by downloading the patch from the *pub/sendmail* directory on *ftp.sendmail.org*. The source code patch file is *parse8.359.2.8* and the signature file for the patch file is *parse8.359.2.8.sig*:

```
# ftp ftp.sendmail.org
Connected to ftp.sendmail.org (209.246.26.22).
```

Figure 10-1. sendmail fixes available from Red Hat

```
220 services.sendmail.org FTP server (Version 6.00LS) ready.
Name (ftp.sendmail.org:WIN): anonymous
331 Guest login ok, send your email address as password.
Password: win@wrotethebook.com
230 Guest login ok, access restrictions apply.
Remote system type is UNIX.
Using binary mode to transfer files.
ftp> cd pub/sendmail
250 CWD command successful.
ftp> get parse8.359.2.8
local: parse8.359.2.8 remote: parse8.359.2.8
227 Entering Passive Mode (209,246,26,22,196,166)
150 Opening BINARY mode data connection for 'parse8.359.2.8' (346 bytes).
226 Transfer complete.
346 bytes received in 0.000351 secs (9.6e+02 Kbytes/sec)
ftp> get parse8.359.2.8.sig
local: parse8.359.2.8.sig remote: parse8.359.2.8.sig
227 Entering Passive Mode (209,246,26,22,196,171)
150 Opening BINARY mode data connection for 'parse8.359.2.8.sig' (152 bytes).
226 Transfer complete.
152 bytes received in 0.000672 secs (2.2e+02 Kbytes/sec)
ftp> quit
221 Goodbye.
```

Verify the patch using the signature file downloaded from *sendmail.org*:

```
# gpg --verify parse8.359.2.8.sig parse8.359.2.8
gpg: Signature made Thu 18 Sep 2003 10:17:20 AM EDT using RSA key ID 396F0789
gpg: Good signature from "Sendmail Signing Key/2003 <sendmail@Sendmail.ORG>"
gpg: checking the trustdb
gpg: checking at depth 0 signed=1 ot(-/q/n/m/f/u)=0/0/0/0/0/1
gpg: checking at depth 1 signed=0 ot(-/q/n/m/f/u)=1/0/0/0/0/
```

To verify the signature, you must have previously downloaded the PGP keys from *sendmail.org* and added those keys to your key ring. Downloading the PGP keys and adding them to the key ring is shown in Recipe 1.1.

Apply the source code patch:[*]

```
# cd /usr/local/src/sendmail-8.12.9/sendmail
# patch < /usr/local/src/patches/parse8.359.2.8
patching file parseaddr.c
```

After the source code is patched, it must be recompiled and reinstalled, as described in Recipe 1.2. Then the sendmail daemon must be restarted to ensure that it is using the patched software.

Installing a completely new sendmail distribution is an alternative to patching the old one. The same fix installed by patching sendmail 8.12.9 could have been made by installing sendmail 8.12.10.

See Also

Recipe 10.3 provides an alternative way to fix a security hole.

10.5 Disabling Delivery to Programs

Problem

By default, sendmail allows mail to be addressed to programs. Special configuration is required if you wish to disable this feature.

Solution

Check the flags set for the mailers used in the *sendmail.cf* configuration file. Here is an example of using *grep* and *awk* to display the mailer flags:

```
# grep '^M' sendmail.cf | awk '{ print $1 $3 }'
Mlocal,F=lsDFMAw5:/|@qSPfhn9,
Mprog,F=lsDFMoqeu9,
Msmtp,F=mDFMuX,
```

---

[*] The pathnames used here are just examples. You should use the paths that are correct for your system.

```
Mesmtp,F=mDFMuXa,
Msmtp8,F=mDFMuX8,
Mdsmtp,F=mDFMuXa%,
Mrelay,F=mDFMuXa8,
Mcyrus,F=lsDFMnPqAh5@/:|,
Mcyrusbb,F=lsDFMnPu,
```

Add a MODIFY_MAILER_FLAGS macro to the sendmail configuration to remove the | flag for each mailer that has that flag set. Given the listing of flags shown above, this system has the | flag set for both the local mailer and the cyrus mailer. To remove the | flag from these two mailers, add the following lines to the sendmail configuration:

```
dnl Remove the | flag with the cyrus mailer
MODIFY_MAILER_FLAGS(`CYRUS', `-|')
dnl Remove the | flag from the local mailer
MODIFY_MAILER_FLAGS(`LOCAL', `-|')
```

As described in Recipe 1.8, rebuild and reinstall *sendmail.cf*, and then restart sendmail.

Discussion

In certain circumstances, sendmail will deliver mail to a program when the email address begins with a vertical bar. sendmail only delivers to a program when the mailer used for that delivery has a | in the flags defined by the mailer's F parameter. Disable delivery to programs by removing the | flag from all *sendmail.cf* mailer definitions.

Flags can be added to or removed from a mailer definition using the MODIFY_MAILER_FLAGS macro. To add a flag to a mailer specify the flag with a plus sign (+). To remove a flag use a minus sign (-) with the flag. The MODIFY_MAILER_FLAGS macros used in the Solution section remove the | flag from the local and the cyrus mailers because the flag on the macro command line is preceded by a minus sign. To replace the flags of a mailer, list the new flags without plus or minus signs. For example:

```
dnl Define new flags for the local mailer
MODIFY_MAILER_FLAGS(`LOCAL', `lsDFMAw5:/@qSPfhn9')
```

Note that this MODIFY_MAILER_FLAGS line has the same impact as the second one used in the Solution section because the new set of flags contains all of the flags from the default configuration except the | flag. -| was used in the Solution section because it shows more clearly exactly what is being modified, and it is less prone to a typographical error than is the full list of flags.

Most commonly, mail is sent to programs from the *aliases* database or the user's *.forward* file. If your intention is to prevent users from forwarding mail to programs, eliminating the | flag from sendmail mailers may not be enough. sendmail is often not the most powerful tool at a user's disposal. If users can login to the system providing mail service, they have the full power of a shell at their disposal. If the system uses *procmail* as the local mailer, as Linux does, users have full access to the power of *procmail* simply by creating a

.procmailrc file. (Recipe 10.8 shows how to override the *local_procmail* feature on a Linux system.) Before you eliminate a sendmail feature or reset a mailer flag that may make sendmail less flexible and less powerful, evaluate the true security impact of the change.

See Also

Recipe 10.7 shows another example of using MODIFY_MAILER_FLAGS to disable a sendmail feature. Recipe 10.6 shows an alternative to completely eliminating delivery to programs. The *sendmail* book covers MODIFY_MAILER_FLAGS in section 20.5.6.1.

10.6   Controlling Delivery to Programs

Problem

Special configuration is needed to control which programs are started by the prog mailer.

Solution

Check the *smrsh* manpage for the location of the *smrsh* execution directory, which is usually either */etc/smrsh* or */usr/adm/sm.bin*. (The Discussion section shows how the *smrsh* program can be checked for the execution directory path.) If the *smrsh* program directory does not already exist, create the appropriate directory, making sure that it is owned by *root* and only writable by *root*. Here is an example:

```
# mkdir /usr/adm/sm.bin
# chmod 751 /usr/adm/sm.bin
```

To make a program accessible via the prog mailer, create a symbolic link for the program in the *smrsh* execution directory. Here is an example of creating links to the *vacation* and *slocal* programs:

```
# cd /usr/adm/sm.bin
# ln -s /usr/local/bin/vacation
# ln -s /usr/lib/nmh/slocal
```

Add the *smrsh* feature to the sendmail configuration to use *smrsh*, the Sendmail Restricted Shell, as the binary for the prog mailer. Here is an example of the required FEATURE macro:

```
dnl Use smrsh as the prog mailer
FEATURE(`smrsh')
```

Build the *sendmail.cf* configuration file, copy it to */etc/mail/sendmail.cf*, and restart sendmail, as described in Recipe 1.8.

Discussion

sendmail uses the prog mailer to deliver mail to a recipient address that begins with the pipe character. The P parameter of the prog mailer definition defines the path to the prog mailer program and the A parameter defines the command used to run the mailer. With the default sendmail configuration, the P parameter is P=/bin/sh and the A parameter is A=sh -c $u. $u is a sendmail macro that contains the email address of the user to which the mail is being delivered. For example, given the following *.forward* file:

```
"|/usr/lib/nmh/slocal -user reba"
```

the command executed for the prog mailer would be:

```
/bin/sh -c "/usr/lib/nmh/slocal -user reba"
```

When the -c option is used with */bin/sh*, shell commands are read from the string that follows -c. In this case, sendmail causes the shell to execute a program named *slocal*. sendmail attaches its output to the standard input of the shell and prints out the mail message, which, in the example, sends the mail message to the *slocal* program. sendmail also attaches the standard output and standard error of the shell to its input.

The shell will execute any command passed to it. The potential security risks of executing any command that follows the pipe character in a recipient address are obvious. Using the Sendmail Restricted Shell (*smrsh*) for the prog mailer instead of */bin/sh* limits the commands that can be executed, thus enhancing security. *smrsh* enforces the following restrictions:

- Only a few built-in shell commands—exec, exit, and echo—work; most do not.
- Standard I/O redirection is not allowed.
- Most of the special characters used by the shell—carriage return, newline, <, >, ;, $, (, and)—are not allowed.
- Most importantly, only those programs that you choose to make available to *smrsh* through its special program directory are available to the user. On a system running *smrsh*, mail addressed to programs not listed in the *smrsh* execution directory is rejected with the error "unavailable for sendmail programs."

The default path for the *smrsh* program directory is */usr/adm/sm.bin*. Vendors often change the path. For example, the Red Hat sendmail RPM distribution defines the path as */etc/smrsh*. To find out where your version of sendmail puts the *smrsh* program directory, check the manpage or look inside the *smrsh* program, using the following commands:

```
# grep '^Mprog' /etc/mail/sendmail.cf
Mprog,          P=/usr/sbin/smrsh, F=lsDFMoqeu9, S=EnvFromL/HdrFromL,
                R=EnvToL/HdrToL, D=$z:/,
# strings /usr/bin/smrsh | grep '^/'
/lib/ld-linux.so.2
```

```
/usr/adm/sm.bin
/bin:/usr/bin:/usr/ucb
/bin/sh
```

The first *grep* command prints out the first line of the prog mailer definition from the *sendmail.cf* file. The P parameter of the prog mailer definition tells us where sendmail expects to find the *smrsh* program. We use the value from the P parameter to point the *strings* command to the correct program. The *strings* command displays all of the literal strings found in the *smrsh* executable. We pass its output through *grep* to select only those strings that are pathnames. Because we know that the default path for the *smrsh* program directory is */usr/adm/sm.bin*, it is easy to pick the program directory path out of this list.

To force *smrsh* to use some other directory as its program directory, recompile *smrsh*. The # define CMDDIR line in the *smrsh.c* source file points to the program directory. Compile *smrsh* with the -DSMRSH_CMDDIR compile option to specify a different directory path. This can be done by adding a command, such as the following, to the *devtools/Site/site.config.m4* file:

```
APPENDDEF(`conf_smrsh_ENVDEF', `-DSMRSH_CMDDIR=\"/etc/smrsh/\"')
```

Most administrators decide to create the program directory where *smrsh* expects to find it instead of recompiling *smrsh* to change the default path. When working with the sendmail tarball, creating your own */usr/adm/sm.bin* directory is both easier and better than recompiling *smrsh* with compile options or modified source code; this is true for three reasons. First, most system administrators find the *mkdir* command easier to work with than the *cc* command or C source code. Second, this is the standard directory where most Unix administrators expect to find the *smrsh* programs. Third, the *smrsh* manpage that comes with the sendmail tarball tells readers that the programs are located in the */usr/adm/sm.bin* directory. (If you change the directory, you should also change the manpage.) When using the sendmail distribution provided by a vendor, use the vendor's default directory. When using the sendmail tarball, use */usr/adm/sm.bin*.

Populate the directory with the programs that are trusted to be accessible through the prog mailer. Programs are added to the *smrsh* program directory in two ways:

1. The program is moved to the directory.
2. A symbolic link is placed in the directory pointing to the program.

The Solution section uses symbolic links. This is the most popular way to add programs to the *smrsh* program directory. It is slightly less secure than actually moving programs to the directory because both the *smrsh* program directory and the other directories in which the programs actually reside must be secured against unauthorized changes. The more things there are to secure, the more likely a security mistake will be made. However, the risk is small, so most administrators prefer using symbolic links.

Take care when adding programs to the *smrsh* execution directory. Poorly written programs are popular targets for attackers. Additionally, do not add programs that can be used to launch other programs. Shells, such as */bin/sh*, and programs, such as *procmail*, which can be directed by the user to start other programs, defeat the purpose of *smrsh* and thus do not belong in the *smrsh* execution directory.* Every program is a potential hole for an intruder to exploit. Choose them carefully.

In the Solution section two symbolic links are added to the *smrsh* program directory. On our sample system, these links allow access to:

- The *vacation* program—a program that automatically responds to mail when the user is out of the office for an extended period.
- The *slocal* program—a mail filtering program.

Users can then create *.forward* files that use these programs. For example, Kathy could define the following *.forward* file when she goes on vacation:

```
\kathy, "|/usr/local/bin/vacation kathy"
```

smrsh strips the initial pathname off of the program to which mail is being forwarded. Thus, when */usr/local/bin/vacation* is the program name in the recipient address, *smrsh* strips the program name down to *vacation* and looks for a file of that name in the *smrsh* program directory.

See Also

Recipe 10.5 describes how to completely disable delivery to programs. The *sendmail* book covers the *smrsh* program in section 5.8.

10.7   Disabling Delivery to Files

Problem

Special configuration is required to block delivery directly to a file or device.

Solution

Check the flags set for the mailers used in the *sendmail.cf* configuration file. Here is an example of using *grep* and *awk* to display the mailer flags:

```
# grep '^M' sendmail.cf | awk '{ print $1 $3 }'
Mlocal,F=lsDFMAw5:/|@qSPfhn9,
Mprog,F=lsDFMoqeu9,
Msmtp,F=mDFMuX,
```

---

* Using *procmail* as the local mailer also defeats the purpose of *smrsh*.

```
Mesmtp,F=mDFMuXa,
Msmtp8,F=mDFMuX8,
Mdsmtp,F=mDFMuXa%,
Mrelay,F=mDFMuXa8,
Mcyrus,F=lsDFMnPqAh5@/:|,
Mcyrusbb,F=lsDFMnPu,
```

Add a MODIFY_MAILER_FLAGS macro to the sendmail configuration to remove the / flag for each mailer that has that flag set. Given the listing of flags just shown, this system has the / flag set for both the local mailer and the cyrus mailer. To remove the / flag from these two mailers, add the following lines to the sendmail configuration:

```
dnl Remove the / flag with the cyrus mailer
MODIFY_MAILER_FLAGS(`CYRUS', `-/')
dnl Remove the / flag from the local mailer
MODIFY_MAILER_FLAGS(`LOCAL', `-/')
```

Rebuild and reinstall *sendmail.cf*, and then restart sendmail. See Recipe 1.8 for an example of these steps.

Discussion

Every user who has a valid login shell is allowed to send mail to files or programs. This makes sense because anyone who has a login shell on the mail host already has greater access to the system than that which is granted via the prog mailer, particularly if *smrsh* is used for the prog mailer. Care should be taken to ensure that no user ID is given a login shell unless it is really needed. Controlling login access is clearly more important for security than anything that can be done in the sendmail configuration.

Additionally, as the Discussion of Recipe 10.5 points out, other sendmail features can give users the ability to run programs or write to files independent of which mailer flags are set. For example, using *procmail* as the local mailer gives the user access to all of the power of *procmail*, including the ability to write files.[*] Before you implement this recipe, make sure it is necessary, and make sure it will work in your environment. That said, removing the / flag from all *sendmail.cf* mailer definitions will disable delivery to files because sendmail only delivers to files and devices when the mailer used for that delivery has the / flag set.

At this writing, only the local mailer and the cyrus mailer have this flag set by default, and most configurations don't use the cyrus mailer. Therefore, for most configurations, only the local mailer can deliver to files, and removing the / from the flags for the local mailer definition would completely disable this feature.

Use the MODIFY_MAILER_FLAGS macro to remove, add, or change mailer flags. Recipe 10.5 covers the syntax of the MODIFY_MAILER_FLAGS macro in some detail.

---

[*] Recipe 10.8 shows how to avoid using *procmail* as the local mailer on a Linux system.

See Also

Recipe 10.5 shows another example of using `MODIFY_MAILER_FLAGS` to disable a send-mail feature. The *sendmail* book covers `MODIFY_MAILER_FLAGS` in section 20.5.6.1.

10.8 Bypassing User .forward Files

Problem

You want to control which users are allowed to define their own *.forward* files.

Solution

Create a directory that will list all users who are allowed to use their own *.forward* files:

```
# cd /etc/mail
# mkdir forward
# chmod 751 forward
```

Grant users the right to use their own *.forward* files by adding symbolic links to the */etc/mail/forward* directory that point to the users' *.forward* files. For example, assume that the sendmail administrator trusts *craig*, *alana*, and *david* to build safe *.forward* files. The administrator can "activate" their files with the following commands:

```
# cd /etc/mail/forward
# ln -s /home/craig/.forward craig
# ln -s /home/alana/.forward alana
# ln -s /home/david/.forward david
```

Add a `confFORWARD_PATH` define to the sendmail configuration that points to the directory created above. Here is an example:

```
dnl Use a special ForwardPath
define(`confFORWARD_PATH', `/etc/mail/forward/$u')
```

Build the new configuration file, copy it to */etc/mail/sendmail.cf*, and restart sendmail, as described in Recipe 1.8.

Discussion

Security is improved when users are given only those privileges that they can use effectively. Many users have no interest in using the *.forward* file. A few lack the skill to create a safe and effective file. Only a subset of users want, need, and know how to use the *.forward* file. This recipe takes the approach of blocking access to every user's *.forward* file and then, on an exception basis, granting access to the *.forward* file to individual users who can effectively use it.

The first step is to build a directory that is only writable by *root*, and to populate that directory with links to the *.forward* files of users who are allowed to use *.forward* files. In the example, the directory is named */etc/mail/forward*. Each symbolic link is given the username of a user allowed to use a *.forward* file.

The sendmail configuration is modified so that sendmail looks for the *.forward* file in the */etc/mail/forward* directory. In this recipe, the path defined for the ForwardPath option is /etc/mail/forward/$u, where $u returns the local recipient's username. Therefore, if $u returns *craig*, sendmail looks for a file named */etc/mail/forward/craig*. If it finds a file with that name, sendmail uses that file as the *.forward* file.

Any user can create a *.forward* file, but the file they create is ignored unless the system administrator adds a symbolic link for the user to the */etc/mail/forward* directory. The Solution section shows the administrator adding symbolic links for *craig*, *alana*, and *david*. In this example, only those three users are allowed to use a *.forward* file.

Overriding the local_procmail feature

Most of the examples in this book were created on a Red Hat Linux system. Linux systems use *procmail* as the local mailer. When *procmail* is the local mailer, a user can forward to any address they wish without creating a *.forward* file. All they need to do is create a *.procmailrc* file to forward the mail. There is no point in implementing this recipe on a system that uses *procmail* as the local mailer.

If you're positive that you want to use this recipe on a Linux system, you need to make additional configuration changes. Linux uses *procmail* as the local mailer because the *local_procmail* feature is specified in the *linux.m4* file loaded by the OSTYPE macro. Override the configuration changes made by the FEATURE(local_procmail) command by adding the following three lines to your sendmail configuration after the OSTYPE macro and before the MAILER(local) line:

```
undefine(`LOCAL_MAILER_PATH')
undefine(`LOCAL_MAILER_FLAGS')
undefine(`LOCAL_MAILER_ARGS')
```

These three lines undefine the local mailer path, flags, and arguments defined by the *local_procmail* feature. These lines cause sendmail to use */bin/mail* as the local mailer, and they set the correct flags and arguments for */bin/mail*. This recipe can be implemented on a system using */bin/mail* with no problems.

See Also

Aliasing and the role of the *.forward* file are covered in Chapter 2. The *sendmail* book covers the confFORWARD_PATH macro in section 24.9.48, the LOCAL_MAILER_PATH define in section 20.5.11.1, the LOCAL_MAILER_FLAGS define in section 20.5.6.2, the LOCAL_MAILER_ARGS define in section 20.5.2.1, and the *local_procmail* feature in section 4.8.21.

10.9 Controlling Delivery to Files

Problem

You want to limit the files and devices to which sendmail writes mail messages.

Solution

Create a directory to contain all of the files to which users can deliver mail. In this example, we create a directory for this purpose that we name */var/mail/archives*:

```
# cd /var/mail
# mkdir archives
# chmod 700 archives
```

Add a confSAFE_FILE_ENV define to the sendmail configuration to point the SafeFileEnvironment option to the newly created directory. The following provides an example of the confSAFE_FILE_ENV define:

```
dnl Limit delivery to files to the /var/mail/archives directory
define(`confSAFE_FILE_ENV', `/var/mail/archives')
```

Build the configuration, copy it to */etc/mail/sendmail.cf*, and restart sendmail, as described in Recipe 1.8.

Discussion

Recipe 2.11 shows examples of users writing to files via their *.forward* files. When the delivery address for a piece of mail contains a / and no @*host* part, sendmail assumes that the address is the name of a file and appends the mail message to that file. By default, sendmail will append the mail to any device or file that does not have execute permissions set.

Specify the SafeFileEnvironment option to tell sendmail that it should only append to ordinary files or */dev/null*. To limit the ordinary files sendmail may write, add a path to the confSAFE_FILE_ENV define. When a path is used, sendmail only writes to files located in that path. This recipe limits this form of mail delivery to either */dev/null* or to nonexecutable, ordinary files located in the */var/mail/archives* path.

See Also

Recipe 10.8 shows how delivery to files can be completely disabled. Delivery to files normally takes place through aliases defined in the *aliases* database or the user's *.forward* file. For more information on the *aliases* database and the *.forward* file, see Chapter 2. The *sendmail* book covers delivery to files in sections 10.8.2.8, 12.2.2, and 24.9.95.

10.10 Running sendmail Non-Set-User-ID root

Problem

You wish to reduce the amount of time that sendmail runs as a *root* process.

Solution

Upgrade to the latest release of sendmail 8.12. Create an entry for the user *smmsp* in the */etc/passwd* file and an entry for the group *smmsp* in the */etc/group* file. Install and compile the new sendmail distribution as described in Recipe 1.2.

Discussion

sendmail runs as a daemon or an interactive process. As a daemon, sendmail is used to listen on network ports or to periodically check the mail queue. sendmail can also be launched as an interactive process by a user's mail program or by the user from the command line to submit a message to the message transmission agent (MTA). A daemon that binds a listener to a privileged network port must run as *root*, but many of sendmail's other duties can be done without *root* privileges. In particular, when sendmail is used as a message submission program (MSP) launched by a user to send mail to the MTA, it does not need *root* privilege. Recipe 1.2 describes a configuration that ensures that sendmail has *root* privilege only when necessary.

The decision to run the *sendmail* program as set-user-ID *root* must be taken early in the installation process. Beginning with sendmail 8.12, the default is to run the *sendmail* program as set-group-ID *smmsp*, as a simple *ls* command shows:

```
$ ls -l /usr/sbin/sendmail
-r-xr-sr-x   1 root     smmsp      615263 Jan 24 16:13 /usr/sbin/sendmail
```

To force sendmail to install the *sendmail* program as set-user-ID *root*, which would *reduce* security, run Build install-set-user-id instead of Build install during the initial installation of the sendmail distribution. Of course, we don't recommend this.

The set-group-ID *smmsp* configuration is a definite security improvement over earlier versions of sendmail because users no longer use a set-user-ID *root* program to send mail. Instead, the sendmail process launched by the user from the command line retains the user's UID. The GID of the process is set to *smmsp* in order to allow the process to queue mail in the case of a delivery failure.

In earlier versions of sendmail, the program always ran set-user-ID *root*. However, sendmail must run as *root* only when it is run as a daemon listening for inbound mail. *root* privilege is not necessary for sending outbound mail.

It is necessary, however, to create a separate mail queue that is owned by the user *smmsp* for those times when sendmail is running as a non-*root* process. That queue, named */var/spool/clientmqueue*, is created by the Build install command during the installation of the sendmail distribution, as this snippet of messages from an installation shows:

```
You must have setup a new user smmsp and a new group smmsp
as explained in sendmail/SECURITY.
mkdir -p /var/spool/clientmqueue
chown smmsp /var/spool/clientmqueue
chgrp smmsp /var/spool/clientmqueue
chmod 0770 /var/spool/clientmqueue
install -c -o root -g smmsp -m 2555 sendmail /usr/sbin
```

In addition to its own queue, MSP sendmail has its own configuration file. That file is always called *submit.cf* and is built from the *submit.mc* file. The *submit.mc* file delivered with the sendmail 8.12.9 distribution contains the following lines:

```
VERSIONID(`$Id: ch10,v 1.20 2003/12/03 15:09:32 marlowe Exp jhawks $')
define(`confCF_VERSION', `Submit')
define(`_OSTYPE_',`')dnl dirty hack to keep proto.m4 from complaining
define(`_USE_DECNET_SYNTAX_', `1')dnl support DECnet
define(`confTIME_ZONE', `USE_TZ')
define(`confDONT_INIT_GROUPS', `True')
dnl
dnl If you use IPv6 only, change [127.0.0.1] to [IPv6:::1]
FEATURE(`msp', `[127.0.0.1]')
```

The VERSIONID macro defines version information for the *.mc* file. The confCF_VERSION define specifies version information for the *.cf* file. By default, the *.cf* file version information, which is stored in the $Z macro, matches the sendmail version number. In this example, that would be 8.12.9. The confCF_VERSION define adds the string "Submit" to that information, as this *grep* shows:

```
# grep '^DZ' submit.cf
DZ8.12.9/Submit
```

The next two lines define internal *proto.m4* variables in ways that are designed to trick the system into doing something a little out of the ordinary. The first defines the _OSTYPE_ variable. Normally this variable is defined by the OSTYPE macro. If this variable does not exist, the error "No system type defined (use OSTYPE macro)" is displayed and the *m4* process terminates. Setting the variable directly tricks the system into continuing on without an OSTYPE macro.

The _USE_DECNET_SYNTAX_ define allows DECnet style *node::user* addressing. Normally, this variable is set to 1 by the DECNET_RELAY macro when a DECnet relay host is defined. The *submit.cf* file does not define a DECnet relay host. All mail is sent by the relay mailer to the host defined in the ${MTAHost} macro. The _USE_DECNET_SYNTAX_ define is required in order to support DECnet syntax without a DECnet relay host.

confTIME_ZONE defines the way in which sendmail should determine the local time zone. Because the MSP configuration does not run as *root*, it can safely determine the local time zone from the TZ environment variable. Thus, the confTIME_ZONE define is set to USE_TZ in the *submit.mc* file used for the MSP configuration.

The last define is confDONT_INIT_GROUPS. In the *submit.cf* file it sets the DontInitGroups option to True. This setting prevents sendmail from changing its UID and GID when performing certain tasks, such as running a mail delivery agent. Because the MSP configuration is supposed to run as user *smmsp* and not supposed to use any special privileges, it makes sense to include this define in the configuration.

After two comment lines, the last command in the configuration enables the *msp* feature, which is the heart of the configuration. The *msp* feature creates the configuration that makes this a message submission program. The argument passed to the *msp* feature is the hostname or IP address of the MTA to which the MSP should send the mail. The argument is stored in the *submit.cf* macro ${MTAHost}.

In the *submit.mc* file delivered with sendmail 8.12.9, the *msp* argument is [127.0.0.1], which is the loopback address for the local host on all IPv4 systems. Square brackets are always placed around a numeric address; when placed around a hostname, they prevent sendmail from looking up the MX records for that hostname. [127.0.0.1] is the default value for ${MTAHost}, so this argument is not really needed on the *msp* command line. The reason it is used in the *submit.mc* file provided with 8.12.9 is as an example for administrators who might need to change the ${MTAHost} value. Recipe 10.1 provides an example of changing the ${MTAHost} value to enhance system security.

Only minimal edits should be made to the *submit.mc* file. Good examples of appropriate edits are the changes made by Red Hat and those shown in Recipe 10.1. Red Hat modifies the *submit.mc* file to put the *sm-client.pid* file into the */var/run* directory instead of into the */var/spool/clientmqueue* directory, where it is placed by default. Recipe 10.1 shows an example of how the *submit.mc* file is modified on a system that does not run an SMTP listener. It is the only recipe in this text that modifies *submit.cf*; every other recipe applies to *sendmail.cf*.

The default *submit.cf* file sets the RunAsUser option to *smmsp*. It is the RunAsUser option that tells sendmail to run as something other than *root*. This option predates the *submit.cf* configuration and was originally created for use on some firewall bastion hosts that run sendmail as a non-*root* process. However, the *submit.cf* configuration is the most effective use of this option that I have seen. Don't confuse the RunAsUser option with the DefaultUser option—they are incompatible. RunAsUser defines the user ID used instead of *root*. DefaultUser defines the user ID used in addition to *root* when a copy of sendmail that has *root* privileges gives up those privileges. DefaultUser is covered in Recipe 10.11.

See Also

Chapter 1 covers the installation of sendmail, including the creation of the *smmsp* user and group IDs. Recipe 10.1 provides a realistic example of editing the *submit.mc* configuration. The *sendmail* book covers the MSP configuration in section 2.6.2, the *msp* feature in section 4.8.27, confCF_VERSION in 21.9.100, confTIME_ZONE in 24.9.110, confDONT_INIT_GROUPS in 24.9.38, ${MTAHost} in 21.9.67, RunAsUser in 24.9.94, and DefaultUser in 24.9.29.

10.11 Setting a Safe Default User ID

Problem

sendmail requires its own user ID for when it is not running as *root*.

Solution

Check the */etc/passwd*, */etc/shadow*, and */etc/group* files to see if your system has entries for the user *mailnull* and the group *mailnull*.* If you find *mailnull* entries in these files, you're done. Otherwise, add *mailnull* to */etc/passwd* using UID and GID values that are available on your system. On our sample system, we used the following entry:

```
mailnull:x:65533:65533:Sendmail DefaultUser:/var/spool/mqueue:/bin/false
```

Next, add *mailnull* to the */etc/group* file, as in this example:

```
mailnull:x:65533:
```

And, if you use the */etc/shadow* file, add a *mailnull* entry to that file. Here is an example that is compatible with the *shadow* file used on Red Hat Linux systems:

```
mailnull:!!:11530:0:99999:7:::
```

Discussion

When sendmail is running with *root* privileges, the DefaultUser option identifies the user ID and group ID that sendmail uses when it gives up *root* privileges. This is the UID and GID used to do such things as run mailers and other external commands. When DefaultUser is not explicitly defined in the configuration, four possible default values are available. The order in which these defaults are used is:

1. If the user *mailnull* is defined in the */etc/passwd* file, the user ID and group ID assigned to *mailnull* are used.

---

* This example assumes that these are local files. If your system uses NIS or some other server for this information, make sure you check the correct source.

2. If *mailnull* is not defined and the user *sendmail* is defined in the */etc/passwd* file, the user ID and group ID assigned to the user *sendmail* are used.

3. If neither *mailnull* nor *sendmail* is defined in */etc/passwd* and the user *daemon* is defined, the user ID and group ID assigned to *daemon* are used.

4. If neither *mailnull*, nor *sendmail*, nor *daemon* is defined in the */etc/passwd* file, 1 is used as the user ID and 1 is used as the group ID.

Use `confDEF_USER_ID` in the *m4* master configuration file to override these default values. The master configuration file delivered with Red Hat Linux 8.0 provides an example of how the `confDEF_USER_ID` command is used. It contains the following:

```
define(`confDEF_USER_ID',`8:12')
```

This `define` command sets the user ID to 8 and the group ID to 12 for the `DefaultUser` option. These values are associated with the username *mail* and the groupname *mail* found in the */etc/passwd* and */etc/group* files delivered with the Red Hat Linux 8.0 system. The Red Hat configuration uses numeric UID and GID values for the `confDEF_USER_ID` define. However, string values are also acceptable. The following command sets exactly the same values for the Red Hat system:

```
define(`confDEF_USER_ID',`mail:mail')
```

This would also work:

```
define(`confDEF_USER_ID',`mail')
```

This works because, when the GID field is empty and the UID is a string value, the GID value defined in the */etc/passwd* entry for the specified username is used. It is also possible to define the GID value separately using `confDEF_GROUP_ID`. However, `confDEF_GROUP_ID` has been deprecated and should not be used.

Given all of these options for setting the `DefaultUser` value, it is interesting to note that not one of them is used here. Instead, we opted to use the default *mailnull* user ID. There are two advantages to doing so:

- First, using the default *mailnull* user ID can be done without any sendmail configuration changes.

- Second, *mailnull* is the default value that most sendmail administrators expect to find.

In fact, many Unix systems come with an entry for the user *mailnull* already in the */etc/passwd* file. If that is the case on your system, there is no need to implement this recipe because your system is already using the `DefaultUser` option. A simple *grep* shows the *mailnull* entries from the */etc/passwd* file and the */etc/shadow* file, if they exist:

```
# grep mailnull /etc/passwd
mailnull:x:47:47::/var/spool/mqueue:/dev/null
# grep mailnull /etc/shadow
mailnull:!!:11267:0:99999:7:::
```

Some Unix systems don't provide */etc/passwd* and */etc/group* entries for the DefaultUser option, so you will need to add them yourself. If you do add a *mailnull* user account, there are three characteristics of that account that you need to be aware of:

- *mailnull* must not have an associated password. The *mailnull* user created in this recipe does not have a valid password in either the */etc/passwd* file or the */etc/shadow* file.

- *mailnull* must not have a valid login shell. In this recipe, *mailnull* is given */bin/false* as its login shell in the */etc/passwd* file.

- *mailnull* must not own any files.

These three requirements help prevent the account from being exploited to gain unauthorized access.

See Also

Recipe 10.10 covers the RunAsUser option—an incompatible option that is sometimes confused with the DefaultUser option. For information on the */etc/passwd*, */etc/shadow*, and */etc/group* files see a good system administration text, such as *Essential System Administration*, Third Edition, by Æleen Frisch (O'Reilly). The *sendmail* book covers the DefaultUser option in sections 10.8.2.1 and 24.9.29.

10.12 Defining Trusted Users

Problem

System changes, such as installing a new mail delivery program, may require adding names to the list of users who can override the sender address.

Solution

Carefully determine if there is really a need for additional trusted users. Only when absolutely necessary, add a confTRUSTED_USERS define to the sendmail configuration, such as the one shown below:

```
dnl Add a user to the list of trusted users
define(`confTRUSTED_USERS', `bin')
```

Rebuild the configuration, copy it to */etc/mail/sendmail.cf*, and restart sendmail. See Recipe 1.8.

Discussion

The users identified in the *sendmail.cf* file by T commands are allowed to override the sender address, and they are allowed to rebuild the *aliases* database. Limit the users identified by T commands to only those UIDs needed for important mail delivery programs that actually use the *sendmail* command with the -f switch to deliver mail. The *rmail* program is a good example. It runs using *uucp* as its UID. Mail delivered by *rmail* would appear to come from the user *uucp* if it did not use the -f switch to change the sender address to the address of the person who really sent the mail. For this reason, *uucp* is included in the default sendmail configuration as one of the trusted users, as this *grep* shows:

```
# grep '^T' generic-linux.cf
Troot
Tdaemon
Tuucp
```

The confTRUSTED USERS define does not override the trusted users list found in the default configuration—it adds to it. A *grep* of this recipe's configuration file shows this:

```
# grep '^T' sendmail.cf
Troot
Tdaemon
Tuucp
Tbin
```

The confTRUSTED_USERS define identifies those users that are allowed:

- To use sendmail's -f command-line switch to override the sender address.
- To use the -bi option to rebuild the *aliases* file.
- To use an alternative queue directory without an X-Authentication-Warning.
- To change the syslog label without generating a warning.

Using confTRUSTED_USERS reduces security by adding to the list of users granted a special privilege. Avoid using it except when it is required to get a mail delivery program running. We do not recommend adding *bin* to the trusted users list—exactly the opposite is true.

Use care when entering the confTRUSTED_USERS define. confTRUSTED_USER, without an "S" on the end, is a different security setting; see Recipe 10.13 for information about confTRUSTED_USER.

See Also

The *sendmail* book discusses trusted users in section 10.8.1.1.

10.13 Identifying the sendmail Administrator

Problem

You want to avoid having administrators login as *root* to manage sendmail files.

Solution

Select or create a user account, other than *root*, that will be used to manage sendmail. Change file and directory ownership in order to give the selected account ownership of and access to all of the files necessary to maintain sendmail, without providing access to unneeded files. This can be simplified by keeping the sendmail configuration files in a limited number of directories. For example, on the sample system, operational files are kept in */etc/mail* and development files are kept in */usr/local/src/sendmail-8.12.9*.

Add a confTRUSTED_USER define to the sendmail configuration to identify the sendmail administrator. Here is an example using *mailman* as the user account name:

```
dnl The mail administration account is mailman
define(`confTRUSTED_USER', `mailman')
```

Build and install *sendmail.cf*, and then restart sendmail as shown in Recipe 1.8.

Discussion

The TrustedUser option identifies the user that owns sendmail's administrative files, such as the database files. TrustedUser defaults to *root*. Override the default value with the confTRUSTED_USER define. For example, the confTRUSTED_USER define in the Solution section sets TrustedUser to *mailman*.

Once a TrustedUser is defined, the TrustedUser is given ownership of files that might be maintained by the sendmail administrator. On most systems, this means changing the ownership of the sendmail development directory, the */etc/mail* directory, and the files inside these directories to the TrustedUser.*

The file permissions in the development directory are properly set by the sendmail source code *tar* file. The */etc/mail* file permissions are more sensitive, but they should already be properly set by the vendor on any system running sendmail. If you're not sure about the permissions set for your */etc/mail* directory, see Table 10-1.

---

* Changing the ownership of the development directory does *not* change the fact that the Build install phase of installing sendmail must still be run as *root*.

Table 10-1. Permissions for selected /etc/mail files

File	Mode
aliases	0640
aliases.db	0640
aliases.dir	0640
aliases.pag	0640
helpfile	0444
sendmail.cf	0640
statistics	0600

The permissions for the */etc/mail* directory are set to 755. Database source file permissions are set to 640.[*] Database permissions are set to 640, as are permissions on the *.cf* files. Permission on the *helpfile* are set to 444. Execute permissions are not granted to anyone, on any file. sendmail files that fall outside of the */etc/mail* directory—on some systems this might be */etc/sendmail.cf* and */etc/aliases*—should also be owned by the TrustedUser and assigned permissions similar to those used for files in the */etc/mail* directory. If the *m4* master configuration file contains the confCONTROL_SOCKET_NAME define, the socket file must be owned by the TrustedUser and set to mode 600. The directory containing the socket file should be owned by *root* or the TrustedUser and set to mode 700. The TrustedUser does not own the mail queue or the mail spool directories—those are still owned by the *root* user.

The *root* user, which is the default value for TrustedUser, is at least as secure as any other user ID. Changing the TrustedUser does not improve file security. It does, however, make it possible to maintain sendmail databases without using *root* privileges.

Recipe 10.11 covers the DefaultUser option. The DefaultUser executes commands, such as mailers, but does not own files. The TrustedUser owns files but does not execute commands from within sendmail. This division of labor improves security.

See Also

See Recipe 10.12 for information on confTRUSTED_USERS, with an "S", which is a define that is sometimes confused with confTRUSTED_USER. The *sendmail* book covers confTRUSTED_USER in sections 10.8.2.3 and 24.9.112, recommended file permissions in section 10.5.4, and the confCONTROL_SOCKET_NAME define in section 24.9.23.

---

[*] The *access* database requires more restrictive permission if it contains AuthInfo: entries. See Recipe 7.2.

10.14 Limiting the SMTP Command Set

Problem

You want to disable certain SMTP commands.

Solution

Add the `confPRIVACY_FLAGS` define to the sendmail configuration to set `PrivacyOptions` that disable unwanted, optional SMTP commands. This sample define disables the EXPN, VRFY, VERB, and ETRN commands:

```
dnl Disable EXPN, VRFY, VERB and ETRN
define(`confPRIVACY_FLAGS', `noexpn,novrfy,noverb,noetrn')
```

Build the *sendmail.cf* file, copy it to */etc/mail/sendmail.cf*, and restart sendmail, as described in Recipe 1.8.

Discussion

The `confPRIVACY_FLAGS` define sets `PrivacyOptions` flags in the *sendmail.cf* file. One of the things that these flags can do is disable unwanted, optional SMTP commands. By default, sendmail supports the full array of SMTP commands, as this simple test shows:

```
# sendmail -bs -Cgeneric-linux.cf
220 chef.wrotethebook.com ESMTP Sendmail 8.12.9/8.12.9; Mon, 10 Mar 2003 14:39:47 -
0500
EHLO localhost
250-chef.wrotethebook.com Hello root@localhost, pleased to meet you
250-ENHANCEDSTATUSCODES
250-PIPELINING
250-EXPN
250-VERB
250-8BITMIME
250-SIZE
250-DSN
250-ETRN
250-AUTH DIGEST-MD5 CRAM-MD5
250-DELIVERBY
250 HELP
EXPN <admin>
250-2.1.5 <anna@crab.wrotethebook.com>
250-2.1.5 <andy@rodent.wrotethebook.com>
250 2.1.5 <jane@rodent.wrotethebook.com>
VRFY <alana>
250 2.1.5 Alana Henson <alana@chef.wrotethebook.com>
QUIT
221 2.0.0 chef.wrotethebook.com closing connection
```

In response to the EHLO command, the SMTP server lists the SMTP extensions it supports, including optional commands. Some of these commands, VRFY, EXPN, and VERB, provide information that a security-conscious site might not wish to provide:

- The VERB command places the SMTP protocol exchange into verbose mode, which provides debugging help but might also reveal information about your site that you would rather not advertise.

- The VRFY command verifies an email address and provides additional information about the user at that address. In the example just shown, the system provides the user's real name and the user's full email address.

- The EXPN command expands a mailing list and displays the email address of each member of the list, as the test above shows. Intruders and spammers might collect this information and use it against your system.

After reconfiguring sendmail with the confPRIVACY_FLAGS define shown in the Solution section, rerunning the test produces very different results:

```
# sendmail -bs
220 chef.wrotethebook.com ESMTP Sendmail 8.12.9/8.12.9; Mon, 10 Mar 2003 14:47:35 -
0500
EHLO localhost
250-chef.wrotethebook.com Hello root@localhost, pleased to meet you
250-ENHANCEDSTATUSCODES
250-PIPELINING
250-8BITMIME
250-SIZE
250-DSN
250-AUTH DIGEST-MD5 CRAM-MD5
250-DELIVERBY
250 HELP
EXPN <admin>
502 5.7.0 Sorry, we do not allow this operation
VRFY <alana>
252 2.5.2 Cannot VRFY user; try RCPT to attempt delivery (or try finger)
QUIT
221 2.0.0 chef.wrotethebook.com closing connection
```

Now the server advertises a smaller set of features, and returns errors when the EXPN and VRFY commands are entered.

In addition to the *noexpn*, *novrfy*, and *noverb* flags, the sample define in the Solution section uses the *noetrn* flag. In the first test, the system advertised the ETRN command. After this recipe is applied, the server no longer advertises or supports that command. ETRN is used by remote systems to cause the server to run the queue. ETRN is an important command for supporting dial-in clients that need to have the queue run while they are online. Our sample system does not support dial-in SMTP clients, so we have disabled the ETRN command to prevent remote sites from forcing the server to run the queue.

The *noexpn*, *novrfy*, and *noverb* flags could all have been set using the *goaway* flag. The *goaway* flag sets several flags at once. In addition to the *noexpn*, *novrfy*, and *noverb* flags, the *goaway* flag sets:

authwarnings
> *authwarnings* tells sendmail to insert X-Authentication-Warnings: headers into the mail whenever it suspects that the message is not authentic. *authwarnings* is the default PrivacyOptions flag used when the *sendmail.cf* file is built by *m4*. If the system administrator directly edits the *sendmail.cf* file and inserts a PrivacyOptions statement that has no flags set, *public* becomes the default. *public* tells sendmail that it should not do any special security checks or SMTP syntax checks.

nobodyreturn
> The *nobodyreturn* flag tells sendmail not to return the original message body when it bounces a message, even if the return is specifically requested with the RET=FULL DSN extension on the MAIL From: SMTP command. *noreceipts* is a related flag that is not used by *goaway*. *noreceipts* causes sendmail to ignore the NOTIFY=SUCCESS DSN extension of the RCPT To: command and to ignore Return-Receipt-To: headers. When *noreceipts* is used, sendmail does not advertise or support DSN. For this reason, *goaway* does not set *noreceipts*, and it is not recommended that you use it either. *nobodyreturn* only affects the RET=FULL DSN extension; the other DSN features are still available.

needmailhelo, needvrfyhelo, and needexpnhelo
> These three flags cause sendmail to require a valid HELO/EHLO command from the client before accepting certain other commands. *needmailhelo*, *needvrfyhelo*, and *needexpnhelo* are used and discussed in Recipe 10.15.

The *goaway* flag does not set the *noetrn* flag used in this recipe, nor does it set the *public* and *noreceipts* flags described above. Additionally, it does not set the *restrictexpand*, *restrictmailq*, and *restrictqrun* flags. *noetrn* and *noreceipts* are not used because they disable features that are, in certain circumstances, very useful. The *goaway* flag does not use *public* because it lessens security. *restrictexpand*, *restrictmailq*, and *restrictqrun* are not used because those flags affect who can use certain options on the *sendmail* command line; they do not affect the SMTP protocol or security interactions with remote systems that are the target of the *goaway* flag.* *goaway* is a good choice for enhanced sendmail security. However, this recipe shows that individual flags can also be selected to create a custom security configuration.

Even more custom control is available through creating custom rulesets. The rulesets check_vrfy, check_expn, and check_etrn can be used to define custom controls for the VRFY, EXPN, and ETRN commands, respectively. This recipe disables these commands completely.

---

* Recipe 10.16 covers the *restrictexpand*, *restrictmailq*, and *restrictqrun* flags.

See Also

Recipes 10.15 and 10.16 provide related material. The *sendmail* book covers the PrivacyOptions in section 24.9.80.

10.15 Requiring a Valid HELO

Problem

You do not want to accept mail from a host that does not first provide a HELO/EHLO command.

Solution

Require the HELO command by adding a confPRIVACY_FLAGS define to the sendmail configuration. Here is an example of the define:

```
dnl Don't accept mail without a HELO
define(`confPRIVACY_FLAGS', `needmailhelo')
```

Rebuild the configuration, copy it to */etc/mail/sendmail.cf*, and restart sendmail, as shown in Recipe 1.8.

Discussion

By default, sendmail accepts incoming mail even if the remote host does not identify itself with an SMTP HELO or EHLO command, as the following test shows:

```
# sendmail -bs -Cgeneric-linux.cf
220 chef.wrotethebook.com ESMTP Sendmail 8.12.9/8.12.9; Mon, 10 Mar 2003 13:16:30 -
0500
MAIL From:<craig@wrotethebook.com>
250 2.1.0 <craig@wrotethebook.com>... Sender ok
RCPT To:<kathy@chef.wrotethebook.com>
250 2.1.5 <kathy@chef.wrotethebook.com>... Recipient ok
QUIT
221 2.0.0 chef.wrotethebook.com closing connection
```

Adding the *needmailhelo* flag to the PrivacyOptions requires sendmail to receive a HELO or EHLO command before it will accept inbound mail. Rerunning the test with the configuration created by this recipe shows the effect of this flag:

```
# sendmail -bs
220 chef.wrotethebook.com ESMTP Sendmail 8.12.9/8.12.9; Mon, 10 Mar 2003 13:17:45 -
0500
MAIL From:<craig@wrotethebook.com>
503 5.0.0 Polite people say HELO first
QUIT
221 2.0.0 chef.wrotethebook.com closing connection
```

Attempting to start the mail transfer without first issuing a HELO/EHLO command causes an error.

Two related PrivacyOptions flags are *needvrfyhelo* and *needexpnhelo*. With these flags the VRFY and EXPN commands, respectively, are rejected unless sendmail has received a HELO/EHLO command. *needvrfyhelo* and *needexpnhelo* provide very limited security benefits. From a security perspective, it is best just to disable EXPN and VRFY as described in Recipe 10.14.

See Also

Recipe 10.14 provides another example of using PrivacyOptions. The *sendmail* book covers the *needmailhelo* flag in section 24.9.80.6, the *needvrfyhelo* flag in section 24.9.80.7, and the *needexpnhelo* in section 24.9.80.5.

10.16 Restricting Command-Line Options

Problem

You want to limit which users can run the sendmail program with the -q, -bp, -v, and -bv options.

Solution

Add the confPRIVACY_FLAGS define to the sendmail configuration. Set the *restrictexpand*, *restrictmailq* and *restrictqrun* flags, as in this example:

```
dnl Limit use of expand, mailq and qrun flags
define(`confPRIVACY_FLAGS', `restrictexpand,restrictmailq,restrictqrun')
```

Rebuild and install *sendmail.cf*, then restart sendmail as shown in Recipe 1.8.

Discussion

The PrivacyOptions flags *restrictexpand*, *restrictmailq*, and *restrictqrun* add to the restrictions on who can use certain sendmail command-line options. The flags and the options they affect are:

restrictexpand

The *restrictexpand* flag limits the -bv and -v command-line options to *root* and the TrustedUser. The -bv option verifies an email address. In the process, it performs aliasing on the address and displays the result. The -v option puts the sendmail program into verbose mode, which displays additional information about the delivery process. Use *restrictexpand* to prevent nonprivileged users from discovering information about how mail is delivered to other users on the system.

restrictmailq

When the *restrictmailq* flag is set, only members of the group that owns the queue directory can examine the contents of the queue by running *sendmail* with the -bp option or by running *mailq*. *mailq* and sendmail -bp are synonymous. Both of these commands print the contents of the queue.

restrictqrun

The queue is processed whenever the *sendmail* program is executed with the -q option. The *restrictqrun* flag tells sendmail that it should only process the queue if the sendmail -q command was run by the *root* user or the queue directory owner.

Most of the PrivacyOptions flags—those discussed in Recipes 10.14 and 10.15—impact how sendmail interacts with remote systems. Those flags are used by sendmail when it is run as a daemon. The three flags used in this recipe affect sendmail when it is run from the command line. Because the default for sendmail 8.12 is to no longer run sendmail as set-user-ID *root*, these flags are most useful with earlier versions of sendmail.

See Also

Recipes 10.14 and 10.15 provide other examples of using PrivacyOptions. The *sendmail* book covers *restrictexpand* in section 24.9.80.13, the *restrictmailq* flag in section 24.9.80.14, and *restrictqrun* in section 24.9.80.15.

10.17 Denying DoS Attacks

Problem

You want to limit the possibility that a denial-of-service (DoS) attack aimed at sendmail will cripple other services offered by the sendmail server.

Solution

Add confCONNECTION_RATE_THROTTLE and confMAX_DAEMON_CHILDREN defines to the sendmail configuration to set limits on how fast sendmail accepts mail connections and how many concurrent connections are accepted. Here are examples:

```
dnl Accept up to 10 connections per second
define(`confCONNECTION_RATE_THROTTLE', `10')
dnl Allow no more than 200 concurrent connections
define(`confMAX_DAEMON_CHILDREN', `200')
```

Following the guidance in Recipe 1.8, build the *sendmail.cf* file, copy it to */etc/mail/ sendmail.cf*, and restart sendmail.

Discussion

A denial-of-service (DoS) attack can overwhelm a server and effectively block useful inbound and outbound mail. For example, a mail-bombing attack delivers so much mail so rapidly to a single target that the target system is unable to keep up with the workload. Worse yet, sendmail can becomes so busy handling the attack, it takes all of the system's resources and thus prevents other useful services from running. This recipe uses two configuration commands that lessen the impact that a DoS attack aimed at sendmail has on its other services.

The confMAX_DAEMON_CHILDREN define sets the maximum number of sendmail processes that this sendmail daemon can run simultaneously. Every system has an upper limit on the number of processes it can effectively handle. A variety of DoS attacks are designed to overwhelm a system by launching so many mail processes that the system is no longer able to do any productive work. The confMAX_DAEMON_CHILDREN define protects the operating system from this type of attack.

By default, sendmail sets no upper limit on the number of child processes that can be launched to process mail. This recipe limits sendmail to 200 children so that sendmail accepts mail only when fewer than 200 children are running. This is not a recommended value; it is just an example. Study the actual usage patterns of your system before you select a value, and then set the value at least 50 percent above the observed value to allow for usage spikes.

confMAX_DAEMON_CHILDREN is most useful for systems that do more than just provide sendmail service. A good example is a general purpose server that has a relatively light email workload and that provides many other important user services. The confMAX_DAEMON_CHILDREN define protects the other services from runaway sendmail daemons. It makes sure that the user can still open an X window or start an editor even if the sendmail server is under attack. confMAX_DAEMON_CHILDREN provides this protection for the other services at the cost of making it simple for the attacker to shut down mail service. Simply sending enough mail to exceed the maximum number of children shuts down the SMTP port. Use this define carefully.

The confCONNECTION_RATE_THROTTLE define sets the maximum number of SMTP connections that are permitted for any one-second period. Like confMAX_DAEMON_CHILDREN, the confCONNECTION_RATE_THROTTLE command protects the server from being overwhelmed by email. Neither of these defines protects sendmail from attack; they both protect the system when sendmail is under attack.

By default, no limit is set on the rate at which new SMTP connections are accepted. sendmail handles connections as fast as they arrive. This recipe limits sendmail to 10 new connections per second so that sendmail rejects any network connections after the first 10 in any 1-second period. As before, this is not a recommended value; it is just an example. Study the actual usage patterns of your system before you select a value, and then set the value at least 50 percent above the observed value to allow for usage spikes.

Often, confCONNECTION_RATE_THROTTLE and confMAX_DAEMON_CHILDREN are used together. confMAX_DAEMON_CHILDREN sets an upper limit on the number of simultaneous email connections and confCONNECTION_RATE_THROTTLE sets the rate at which the system climbs to that maximum. An attacker can easily overrun the connection rate you set in order to deny mail access. However, setting the rate protects the other services on the system so that the system remains operational to help you deal with the attack.

It is impossible to completely protect sendmail from denial-of-service attacks. Limiting the amount of damage done by the attack is the real purpose of the defines used in this recipe, which is really meant to protect the system as a whole.

See Also

The *sendmail* book covers the confCONNECTION_RATE_THROTTLE define in section 24.9.21 and the confMAX_DAEMON_CHILDREN define in section 24.9.60.

Index

A

-Ac option, launching sendmail, 28
access database
 AuthInfo: entry, 253
 CAs, identifying trusted, 293
 Connect: tag, 200
 encryption levels
  TLS_Clt: entry, 302
  TLS_Srv: entry, 298
 encryption requirements and, 299
 From: tag, 212
 key field, spam and, 198
 keywords, spam and, 199
 LDAP server, reading from, 214–218
 queue groups and, 330
 return value, spam and, 198
 spam and, 198, 209, 212
 Srv_Features: entry, 272
 STARTTLS, ruleset hooks, 279
 suffixes, encryption and, 312
 support, adding, 100
 TLS and, 278
 To: tag, 212, 213
access_db feature, 100
addresses
 delivery, displaying processing of, 30
 envelope sender, masquerading, 129–132
 masquerading, 104
 migrating users to new, 62–64
 recipient, masquerading, 116–118
 sender
  adding hostnames, 105–107
  mail relay host and
   masquerading, 118–120

masquerading all, 114–116
masquerading hostname, 110–113
reformatting all in local domain with
  genericstable, 137–141
reformatting with
  genericstable, 132–137
administrator, identifying, 365
alias database, 349
 creating, 44–47
 delivery address processing, 37
 forward loops, fixing, 69
 location, 45
 Red Hat 7.3, NIS and, 52–55
 Solaris 8, NIS and, 56–57
Alias0 missing map file error,
  correcting, 44–47
aliases
 forwarding messages to programs, 65
 LDAP, reading from, 48–52
 local hostnames, limiting
  masquerading, 120–123
 mailing lists, creating for, 58–62
 recursion, setting number, 46
 testing handling, 45
aliases file
 adding aliases, 57
 alternative to virtusertable, 173
 delivery and forwarding, 37
ALIAS_FILE define, 45
 aliases database, 45
 LDAP, reading aliases, 48, 50
 NIS, reading Red Hat 7.3 alias
  database, 55
aliasing, delivery address processing, 37

We'd like to hear your suggestions for improving our indexes. Send email to *index@oreilly.com*.

D

About the Author

Craig Hunt has worked with computer systems for the last 25 years. His first computer job was as a programmer and systems programmer for the federal government. He left the government to work on the global WWMCCS network for Honeywell. After Honeywell, Craig went to work for the National Institute of Standards and Technology (NIST), where he built their first enterprise network, administered the central servers on that network, and eventually moved into network research. Craig left NIST to consult, write, and teach about Linux, Unix, and networking. In addition to *sendmail Cookbook*, Craig has written six other books, coauthored two books, and edited five. He is available to consult with companies about system and network issues. To find out more about what Craig is doing, visit his web site at *http://www.wrotethebook.com*.

Craig lives with his wife and youngest daughter in Gaithersburg, Maryland. He loves the outdoors and has a passion for exploring it on his mountain bike.

Colophon

Our look is the result of reader comments, our own experimentation, and feedback from distribution channels. Distinctive covers complement our distinctive approach to technical topics, breathing personality and life into potentially dry subjects.

The animal on the cover of *sendmail Cookbook* is a common European bat (*Pipistrellus pipistrellus*). Pipistrelles are the most common bat in Britain and are abundant throughout Europe and Asia, although they are reportedly endangered in Germany and Austria. Among the world's smallest bats, Pipistrelles have a body length of 35 to 45 millimeters (about 1.5 inches) and a wingspan of 190 to 250 millimeters (about 9 inches). These tiny mammals have a voracious appetite, consuming up to 3,000 insects a night when the weather is warm. Averse to the cold, their behavior during winter months is mostly unknown. There has been a marked decline in the number of pipistrelles due to modern agricultural practices, including the use of insecticides and the illegal disturbance of their habitats by builders.

Marlowe Shaeffer was the production editor and proofreader for *sendmail Cookbook*. Derek Di Matteo was the copyeditor. Reg Aubry, Claire Cloutier, and Emily Quill provided quality control. Jamie Peppard provided production assistance. Tom Dinse wrote the index.

Ellie Volckhausen designed the cover of this book, based on a series design by Edie Freedman. The cover image is a 19th-century engraving from the Dover Pictorial Archive. Emma Colby produced the cover layout with QuarkXPress 4.1 using Adobe's ITC Garamond font.

David Futato designed the interior layout. This book was converted to FrameMaker 5.5.6 by Julie Hawks with a format conversion tool created by Erik Ray, Jason McIntosh, Neil Walls, and Mike Sierra that uses Perl and XML technologies. The text font is Linotype Birka; the heading font is Adobe Myriad Condensed; and the code font is LucasFont's TheSans Mono Condensed. The illustrations that appear in the book were produced by Robert Romano and Jessamyn Read using Macromedia FreeHand 9 and Adobe Photoshop 6. The tip and warning icons were drawn by Christopher Bing. This colophon was written by Marlowe Shaeffer.